Exit *with* HONOR

THE RIGHT WING IN AMERICA

Glen Jeansonne, Series Editor

Exit *with* HONOR

The Life and Presidency
of Ronald Reagan

William E. Pemberton

M.E. Sharpe

Armonk, New York
London, England

Library of Congress Cataloging-in-Publication Data

Pemberton, William E., 1940–
Exit with honor: the life and presidency of Ronald Reagan /
William E. Pemberton
p. cm. — (The right wing in America)
Includes bibliographical references and index.
ISBN 0-7656-0095-1 (alk. paper)
1. Reagan, Ronald. 2. Presidents—United States—Biography.
3. United States—Politics and government—1981–1989.
I. Title. II. Series.
E877.P46 1997
973.927′092—dc21
[B]
97-7269
CIP

Printed in the United States of America

The paper used in this publication meets the minimum requirements of
American National Standard for Information Sciences—
Permanence of Paper for Printed Library Materials,
ANSI Z 39.48-1984.

BM (c)   10   9   8   7   6   5   4   3   2   1

To my wife Marty, and in memory of our friend Sage Tsou

Reagan . . . had that dream distance; the powerful thing about him as President was that you never knew how much he knew, nothing or everything, he was like God that way, you had to do a lot of it yourself.

—John Updike, *Rabbit at Rest*

Contents

Series Editor's Foreword

The Right has appalled and consumed historians, who have barely begun to describe and analyze it. Some of them have argued that the Right has no tradition in the United States, or that it is fueled by paranoia or a religious fervor inappropriate to politics. Others have seen it as linked closely to corporate capitalism, to a wealthy elite, to Western romantics longing for nineteenth-century rugged individualism. But the Right has always been a part of American society, whether in the mainstream, on the margins, or misunderstood. For good or ill, it has affected the course of history and warrants a rich historiography (although works on the Right sometimes are confined to obscure corners of academic bookshelves).

The M.E. Sharpe series The Right Wing in American History is an attempt to resurrect the Right from the substratum of serious scholarship. By publishing biographies, studies of movements, institutions, and political, cultural, and religious developments from colonial times to the present, the series will present the Right in its variety and complexity and reveal its deep roots. Books in the series are reasonably succinct, thoroughly documented, analytical, and meant to appeal to a general audience as well as scholars and students.

William E. Pemberton's provocative biography of Ronald Reagan is the story of a major conservative politician. If Reagan has been an enigma to historians, he is no more of an enigma than some liberal idols such as Franklin D. Roosevelt, who like Reagan was accused of being detached from details in his administration and whose important contribution was inspiration. Reagan rose from a humble background and ascended through the media of radio, motion pictures, and television before entering politics. He married and divorced actress Jane Wyman, then wed another actress, Nancy Davis, with whom he had an idyllic relationship. Shielding himself from the pain of childhood poverty, his alcoholic father, his divorce, and his difficult relationships with his children, Reagan rarely revealed his thoughts to anyone but Nancy. Gregarious, an excellent communicator, he maintained an optimism that often reflected a Hollywood vision of reality rather than reality itself.

Twice elected governor of California, the nation's most populous state, Reagan ran unsuccessfully for the Republican presidential nomination in 1968 and 1976 before winning it in 1980 and handily defeating the Democratic incumbent, Jimmy Carter. Having won with promises to cut taxes, increase military spending, and balance the budget, he accomplished the first two at the price of ballooning the budget deficit and the trade deficit. Yet he remained popular regardless of his administration's failures, including the scandal that dogged his second term, the Iran-contra affair, and survived an assassination attempt, showing bravery after he was seriously wounded. In perhaps his greatest achievement, he helped end the Cold War. Like Soviet president Mikhail Gorbachev, he was one of the central figures of his time on the world stage and was instrumental in facilitating arms reductions and the collapse of communism in Eastern Europe.

Pemberton's centrist interpretation concludes that despite his flaws, Reagan defended American values and provided spirited leadership. Even in the sunset of Reagan's life, it was always morning.

Glen Jeansonne

Preface

Ronald Wilson Reagan rose from the obscurity of small-town life in the American heartland to a spectacular career that took him to film stardom in Hollywood, leadership of the American conservative movement, eight years as governor of California, and the first successful two-term presidency since Dwight D. Eisenhower. He had a powerful impact on national life during his years in office, and he had a continuing influence on history because he built the fiscal and political framework within which his successors operated.

Despite the decades he spent in the public eye, he remained a mystery to his friends and admirers. There were many contradictions in his life, career, and personality. While he was an unfailingly gentle and charming man, he distanced himself emotionally from others, erecting a barrier impenetrable even by his closest friends and family members. His unvarying public persona was that of an average American, a citizen-politician, yet from the time he entered the Hollywood film colony in 1937 through his years in Sacramento and Washington he led a cloistered existence, interacting with his countrymen only through the media. He led the American conservative movement to power, but he had started his political career as an outspoken advocate of such notable liberals as Franklin D. Roosevelt, Harry S. Truman, and Hubert H. Humphrey. He spent his career as conservative spokesman attacking big government and federal spending, yet government grew in size during his presidency and deficit spending ballooned to levels never before imagined by American political leaders. His patriotic rhetoric and fervent anticommunist stance caused many citizens to fear that he would be quick to use American military power, but he was restrained in his use of force and, with Soviet premier Mikhail S. Gorbachev, helped bring the half-century-long cold war to an end. He conducted one of the largest military buildups in American history, but concluded the first treaty that reduced nuclear weapons stockpiles. His many admirers—he left office after eight years with a 70 percent approval rating—saw him as a forceful and confident leader, yet he was a disengaged manager who relied on his staff to carry out many of the responsibilities of his office. Liberal critics labeled him an "empty suit," and historians ranked him as a below-average president, but he had a major impact on the history of his time. He moved the entire political spectrum to the right and imposed harsh political and fiscal constraints on his successors. Reagan, known as the Great Communicator, lived in a world of sunrises; it was morning again in God's chosen land, he said. He left his conservative followers with a forward-looking, optimistic promise of a future without limits, a sunny vision that proved popular with voters.

This Reagan biography was the most difficult writing project I have ever undertaken, and I have many debts of gratitude. The staff at the Ronald Reagan Library in Simi Valley, California, made my work there pleasant and productive. Archivist Greg Cumming helped guide me through the records and other staff members, especially Kate Sewell, answered countless questions. I owe thanks to many fine archivists at the Hoover Institution, Lyndon Baines Johnson Library, Richard Nixon Library, the Pacific Southwest region of the National Archives, Gerald R. Ford Library, and the Jimmy Carter Library.

Members of the staff of the Murphy Library at the University of Wisconsin at La Crosse and of the La Crosse public library tracked down material and answered many questions. The University of Wisconsin at La Crosse provided me with research grants and with a timely sabbatical leave. My history department colleagues have been generous in their encouragement and willingness to take up the slack when I have been occupied by this project. I wish to thank Professor Glen Jeansonne, general editor of this series of books on the American right wing, and Professors Thomas C. Reeves and Lewis L. Gould for their comments on the manuscript. I deeply appreciate the work and encouragement of Peter Coveney and the fine editorial staff of M.E. Sharpe.

I owe thanks to many individuals. Michael Welch and S. S. "Bud"

Jenkins oriented me to conservative thinking and thinkers. Robert and Judith Green helped me locate medical studies of Alzheimer's disease. Many friends spent hours patiently listening to me struggle with the mystery of Ronald Reagan: Richard and Susan Snyder, Ruth and Jim Harritt, Noel Richards, Jim Parker, Phil McColgin, Emilio and Monica De Grazia, Ken and Janie Maly, and Carol Gundersen. Greg and Lety Pemberton provided wonderful company during my research trips to California. Richard Snyder read the entire manuscript and as chair of the history department helped me balance my teaching responsibilities with my research and writing demands. Only he understands how central he was to this work.

I was able to complete the book because of the hard work and emotional support of my wife, Martha Wallace Pemberton. My debt to her can never fully be repaid. My little friend Fia provided her own special encouragement and affection.

Exit *with* HONOR

1

Growing Up in the Heartland, 1911–1937

From 1937 when Ronald Wilson Reagan starred in his first film in Hollywood until 1989 when he finished his second term as president, he remained a mystery even to his closest friends and associates. Historian Edmund Morris, Reagan's official biographer, once told the president that after years of studying, observing, and talking to him, he remained an enigma. Reagan, in his best "aw shucks" manner, said, "But, I'm an open book." "Yes, Mr. President," Morris replied, "but all your pages are blank."[1]

Reagan's friends found that this most charming and seemingly open of men carefully guarded a private core that no one could penetrate. He struck most observers as rather passive, even lazy, and he never openly displayed any hunger for money, fame, or power. Yet he emerged from the poverty and obscurity of small-town Illinois to become a major world leader. He acquired a college education during the Great Depression, won regional fame in radio during the 1930s, and went on to become a movie and television star. He led Hollywood actors during the postwar Red Scare, established himself as the undisputed leader of the American conservative movement in the 1960s, served as governor of California for two terms, and won two terms as president of the United States, leaving office as one of the most popular chief executives in recent history. Reagan was a successful president, measured by his popularity and by his effect on history, yet even his strongest defenders admitted that he was dependent on his staff and that he knew little about the activities of the White House. Opponents and supporters alike puzzled over how a chief executive who was so disengaged from the work of his own administration achieved so much of what he set out to accomplish.

There were other puzzles. Observers noted the irony of Reagan, a long-time leader of the anticommunist movement in the United States, joining with Soviet premier Mikhail S. Gorbachev to bring the cold war to an end. Reagan completed the largest defense buildup in American history, yet he joined with Gorbachev to begin the process of removing whole categories of nuclear weapons from superpower arsenals. Reagan chroniclers often referred to him as the Great Communicator and searched for the sources of his seemingly effortless ability to touch deep chords in the hearts of Americans. Others struggled with the question of how a man who continuously reshaped himself to fit changing circumstances appealed to millions because he symbolized to them unchanging aspects of traditional American character.

The source of many of the mysteries surrounding Ronald Reagan appeared in his youth, when he was growing up in the Midwest. His paternal ancestors, the O'Regans, lived in county Tipperary in Ireland, where they and their peasant neighbors struggled to survive by working in fields owned by absentee landlords. They lived in a village, Doolis, whose filth and poverty horrified a member of the English Parliament who described it after he visited there in 1829. The family survived when the potato famine hit in 1845, but life remained hard. In 1852, twenty-three-year-old Michael O'Regan ran off to London with a local woman, Catherine Mulcahy. When they married in October 1852, Michael signed himself Reagan. In 1856 Michael and Catherine, Ronald's great-grandparents, moved to the United States and homesteaded land in Carroll County, Illinois. Their son, John Michael Reagan, married Jenny Cusick and settled near Fulton, Illinois, where in 1883 John Edward "Jack" Reagan, Ronald's father, was born. When he was six, Jack's parents died from tuberculosis, and he was raised by his relatives.

Nelle Clyde Wilson, Ronald's mother, was born near Fulton on 24 July 1883. Her father's family came from Scotland, first settling in Canada and then moving on to the United States. On her mother's side she was descended from an English immigrant who came to the United States at age sixteen and, after her parents died, worked as a domestic servant.[2]

Ronald Reagan's parents shaped his values and taught him many of the skills that turned him into the Great Communicator. Jack received only a few years of elementary school education, but he was a street-smart, ambitious man, attuned to the commercial bustle of midwestern main streets. He was a superb shoe salesman, who dreamed of owning the largest shoe store in Illinois. Tall and handsome, he had a flair for the dramatic, a presence that turned heads, a gift with words, a genius for telling stories. He was a talented salesman, as his son would be, whose words could create an optimistic aura for his customers, a bright future that would be made even better by a shiny pair of new shoes, whose price faded into insignificance as Jack talked.

Jack Reagan was a "sentimental Democrat," an Irish Catholic who during the Great Depression became an avid supporter of President Franklin D. Roosevelt. Jack detested the Ku Klux Klan and hated racism and bigotry. He supported working men and women and was suspicious of the power structure, especially when it was in the hands of Republicans. He held that all people were created equal, but he also believed that each individual shaped his or her own destiny and that success came through hard work and ambition.[3]

Jack was a restless man, moving from town to town pursuing success as a salesman. He met Nelle Wilson when they both worked at the same dry goods store in Fulton, Illinois. In November 1904 they married and in 1906 moved to the small town of Tampico, Illinois. There two children were born, John Neil on 16 September 1908 and Ronald Wilson on 6 February 1911. Neil and Ronald, "Moon" and "Dutch" to their family, knew little stability as they grew up. In 1914 Jack and Nelle moved to Chicago and then to a succession of small Illinois towns: Galesburg, Monmouth, back to Tampico, and finally in 1920 to Dixon, which Ronald would regard as his hometown.[4]

Ronald Reagan recalled his childhood as similar to "rare Huck Finn–Tom Sawyer idylls." A later associate said that Reagan had the ability to create "little worlds" that existed only in his imagination. The Great Communicator could use these scenes to touch the hearts of listeners who responded to his sunny vision of a way of life that no longer survived and, indeed, probably never had existed in the fashion that Reagan and his listeners remembered. Huck Finn did not describe his life in the idyllic terms that Reagan remembered. Huck's mother was dead and his "pap" had abandoned him, returning only to abuse him and to steal his money. He fled down the Mississippi on a raft to escape his father, who had tried to kill Huck. His journey, usually taking place at night, exposed him to examples of child abuse, racial oppression, religious hypocrisy and superstition, and murderous psychopaths. After his friend Buck was hunted down and executed in front of him, Huck wrote: "I ain't agoing to tell *all* that happened—it would make me sick again if I was to do that. I wished I hadn't ever come ashore that night, to see such things. I ain't ever going to get shut of them—lots of times I dream about them."[5]

Reagan's powerful imagination allowed him to transform reality, even Huck's reality, into a vision that had a powerful appeal to himself and to millions of other Americans. Reagan rewrote his own life, as he rewrote Huck's, to make it fit his image of small-town boyhood in the early twentieth century, and he turned his memory of the few dark sides of his childhood into positive experiences that taught him valuable lessons.

Despite Jack's hard work and ambition, he never succeeded in achieving his dream of becoming an independent businessman. The small midwestern farming communities he lived in suffered from hard times in the decade after World War I, followed in the 1930s by the Great Depression. But Jack failed also because he was an alcoholic, a binge drinker who would go on drunken sprees that lasted for days. Jack was not known as the town drunk, but his drinking hurt his family and undermined his dream of owning a big shoe emporium.

Jack's drinking provoked a crucial event in his son's psychological development. One snowy evening Ronald, at age eleven, came home to find his father passed out in the front yard. He confronted the choice of either ignoring Jack and rushing inside to hide in bed, as he had done before in similar episodes with his drunken father, or of facing the humiliation of dragging Jack into the house. Ronald's story of encountering his drunken father passed out in a snowstorm and confronting himself in a searing moment of character-defining crisis sounded suspiciously like a Hollywood movie scene. Still, in Ronald's mind it became a critical moment in his psychological history. Always before he had let Nelle and Neil deal with Jack's alcoholism; this time he dragged Jack inside their home and felt that he had taken a turn toward responsibility and maturity.[6]

While Jack pursued his elusive dreams, Nelle held the family together. A small, pretty woman with auburn hair and blue eyes, she was as intelligent and ambitious as Jack, but she focused her dreams for the future on her boys. She stretched her limited budget to keep the family fed and well clothed, drilled into her sons the value of education, read to them at night, and took the boys to church several times a week. She was a missionary in her community for the Disciples of Christ Church and had a reputation in Dixon for healing through prayer. Nelle had a flair for the theatrical, giving dramatic readings to church groups and acting in religious plays that she wrote herself from the material of everyday life.

She prayed often for Jack, but her prayers and her hatred for alcohol had little effect. While Nelle sometimes seemed to be a morally judgmental person who believed that people brought their troubles on themselves, she described Jack's alcoholism as a disease and told her boys that they must not hold it against him. She taught Ronald that God had a plan for everyone and that everything happened according to God's plan. This belief became a fundamental part of his makeup. Nelle was an optimistic and trusting woman who looked for the good in people. Ronald said she taught him to dream and to expect those dreams to come true.[7]

Ronald learned other things as well. Jack and Nelle were loving parents but not physically demonstrative, seldom kissing and hugging their children. There were mysteries in the Reagan household that Ronald did not understand until later: angry voices and cursing from Jack, hushed conversations or silences sometimes when Ronald entered the room, unexpected extended visits to his aunt's home. Jack did not get deeply involved in his sons' lives. He never attended Neil's ball games or Ronald's high school plays, and while Ronald felt secure in being loved, he developed a protective barrier between himself and other people. Children of alcoholics sometimes escape into "little worlds" of fantasy and become adept at role playing. Jack's alcoholism and the tension it produced in his home was an additional force shaping young Ronald Reagan, and his own children would later feel this same distancing from their father.[8]

Looking back on the "Huck Finn" days of his youth, Reagan said, "Those were the happiest times of my life." Nelle and Jack were poor. "Our family didn't exactly come from the wrong side of the tracks, but we were certainly always within sound of the train whistles," Ronald wrote. It was the kind of poverty that people of Reagan's generation often idealized in looking back at their youths, of not being aware that they were poor, of being part of a community that provided help and support for its own members, without, in Reagan's memory, intervention by government. Reagan's life in Dixon seemed secure and wholesome as he looked back at it from the perspective of adulthood. His wife, Nancy Reagan, wrote, "To this day, Ronnie thinks that's the way it should be, and it's one reason he bristles at the idea of a large, impersonal government that takes care of the things neighbors once did for each other."[9]

Reagan's feeling of security was of a peculiar sort, dependent on selective memory. The Reagans were vulnerable to every change in the business cycle and to the long decline in midwestern family farming. They depended on the economic health of the small farming communities in the increasingly urban, industrial state of Illinois, and the family relied on Jack's ability to make judicious career decisions and to control his alcoholism. It was an uncertain existence, seeming secure to the adult Ronald Reagan because he remembered only the portions that sustained his optimistic out-look on life.

Dixon was a self-contained farming town of just over eight thousand people, surrounded by rich, fertile land. A beautiful stretch of Rock River ran through the town, which was known for its parks, including Lowell Park where Ronald would win fame as a lifeguard. The house at 816 South Hennepin Avenue, later designated as the Reagan family home, was located in a pleasant middle-class neighborhood. It was a fairly large seven-room home, although when Ronald visited it in 1984 he asked, "Tell me, what did you do to shrink it?" The public library, Ronald's school, and Nelle's church were nearby. Life in Dixon "was as sweet and idyllic as it could be," Reagan later wrote. But there was also a boring, stifling side to life in small midwestern communities. Reagan once remarked to a White House associ-ate, "There was nothing in those towns. . . . Lord, that's why I left."[10]

As Jack moved his family from town to town, his sons attended four different schools in four years. They lived in five different homes after they settled in Dixon. Nancy Reagan believed that her husband's "inwardness," the distance that he maintained from everyone, including herself, was partly due to his lack of roots and stable friendships when he was a child. Reagan himself revealed a darker side to his youth: "Although I always had lots of playmates, during those first years in Dixon I was a little introverted and probably a little slow in making really close friends. In some ways I think this reluctance to get close to people never left me completely. I've never had trouble making friends, but I've been inclined to hold back a little of myself, reserving it for myself." Later observers often assumed that this "inwardness" came from his need to maintain privacy after he became a movie star, but its roots went far back in his life.[11]

Ronald was a quiet child who would spend hours alone. He described himself as a loner, living in a "world of pretend," where he "was allowed to dream." The previous tenant of one of the family's rented houses left be-hind a collection of bird eggs and butterflies, and young Ronald spent hours dreaming over the collections, as he did later with a prized array of lead soldiers. The hours he spent playing along the streams and in the forests and fields around Dixon left Reagan with a lasting love of the outdoors. When he learned to read at age five, he found access to a new world of imagina-tion in Bible stories and later in the pretend worlds of Horatio Alger, the Tom Swift books, and the books of Edgar Rice Burroughs.[12]

One day when he was about thirteen, Ronald tried on his mother's eye-glasses and shouted with delight and surprise at seeing a world that he had not known existed. Jack and Nelle quickly addressed his acute shortsighted-ness by buying him glasses, and Ronald found he could then play baseball and football. By his junior year in high school, he was nearly five feet, eleven inches tall and weighed 160 pounds. He won his greatest local recognition, however, not as a sports hero but as a lifeguard at Lowell Park, where the Rock River swept along the forested bluffs, creating dangerous currents. At age fifteen Reagan started working there as a lifeguard and in seven summers saved seventy-seven people, a number verified by contemporary newspaper accounts.[13]

He found additional avenues of success. He was football captain, drum major, class president, and a decent (low-B average) student. His mother had included him in her productions of dramatic "readings" and plays, which won him applause and approval. His high school English teacher, B. J. Fraser, introduced him to serious acting and taught him the basic lessons that carried him through Hollywood. He also fell in love with Margaret Cleaver, the intelligent and pretty daughter of Christian Church minister Ben H. Cleaver. "For almost six years of my life I was sure she was going to be my wife," he wrote. "I was very much in love." Life was good for him during his high school years and laid the foundation for him to become a secure adult, entirely comfortable with himself. He wrote the caption for his yearbook picture: "Life is just one grand, sweet song, so start the music."[14]

Nelle Reagan's church had a deep and lasting effect on Ronald. Many of the themes in Reagan's famous speeches in the 1980s had been heard for one hundred and fifty years in the Christian Church (often interchangeably called the Disciples of Christ). It emerged in the early 1800s, growing from the ministries of liberal frontier Presbyterian reformers, such as Barton Warren Stone and Thomas and Alexander Campbell. Disciples believed that the Bible contained all truths necessary for a successful and moral life and that God's message could be understood through rational study and discussion. They preached an optimistic theology that placed humanity's destiny in human hands and that promoted a belief in progress and desire for reform. They opposed slavery, supported temperance, and assumed that capitalism and the middle-class work ethic were fundamental parts of Christ's message. Success came to those who worked hard, were frugal, moral, and disciplined. The subtext was that the unsuccessful brought failure on themselves.

Alexander Campbell spoke movingly of the City on a Hill, the belief that God had chosen the American people to fulfill a special mission on earth. That vision of the City on a Hill became the foundation of Ronald Reagan's political philosophy. Campbell believed that God had raised the United States to bring such light to the world that it would penetrate the "dungeons of European despots," a message that Reagan would update for the late twentieth century. Ben Cleaver taught young Ronald Reagan additional messages. Cleaver talked to him about the beauty of a color-blind society and described to him Mohandas Gandhi's vision of a nonviolent society. Cleaver stressed individual responsibility for the quality of one's life, respect for human dignity, distrust of governmental experimentation, and faith that God had a special mission for the Judeo-Christian West.[15]

Ronald was baptized into the Dixon Christian Church. He taught Sunday school there and led prayer sessions. The older parishioners said that the young boy could make the Bible come alive with his voice. He had never "been a great one for introspection," he wrote, holding his religious beliefs so deeply that he did not have occasion to think much about them. Later in life, when he was a member of the Presbyterian Church in Bel Air, California, his sporadic attendance caused some people to question the depth of his convictions. In fact, his faith was deep, secure, and part of his daily life, rather than a Sunday ritual. He prayed often during the day, as Nelle had taught him to do; and in 1973 he told Reverend Cleaver that he would be "lost and helpless" without her religious legacy. He so unquestionably believed that God had a plan for him that he struck some of his associates as a fatalist. In the 1970s, he told ministers that he was a "born-again" Christian—although that was not a phrase his childhood church used—who knew Christ as his personal savior.[16]

Nelle encouraged her sons to work for a better life than Jack had provided. Ronald was one of the only 8 percent of his high school class that went on to college. He entered Eureka College in 1928, and Neil followed him there. Eureka, Illinois, about eighty miles south of Dixon, was a small town of eighteen hundred, an oasis of trees and hills surrounded by flat farmland. The college was a Christian Church liberal arts school established in 1855. It had just under two hundred students and employed twenty faculty members teaching courses in twenty-eight departments. Reagan fell in love with the campus the first time he saw it, and he wanted in so badly, he recalled, that he hurt when he thought about it—partly, no doubt, because Margaret Cleaver intended to go there. They became engaged during their years together at Eureka. Ronald had been saving for college for years, and despite the Great Depression he paid for his education by working at campus jobs and getting small scholarships.[17]

The small faculty included dedicated teachers who taught a full array of liberal studies courses. During his freshman year, Reagan studied rhetoric, French, history, English literature, mathematics, and physical education, and he went out for football and swimming. He majored in economics and social science. Margaret Cleaver described him as an "indifferent student," and Ronald later noted that he had kept his grades just high enough to allow him to participate in what he valued most: football, dramatics, and campus politics. Reagan relied on his excellent memory to reduce the time he spent studying. A friend recalled that Reagan hated to study, and his 1932 year-book picture caption read, "The time never lies heavily upon him; it is impossible for him to be alone."

Reagan became a big man on campus. He was not an especially talented football player, but his coach valued him because he loved the game and never gave up. He went out for track and became captain and coach of the swim team. He juggled work, classes, and sports, while serving two years on the student senate, three years as basketball cheerleader, three years as president of the Eureka Booster Club, and two years as the yearbook features editor. He served as student body president his senior year.[18]

As a freshman, Reagan got an introduction to campus politics that he regarded as a formative event in his life. He participated in a student strike that brought widespread media attention to Eureka and led to the resignation of college president Bert Wilson, who struggled with growing problems as depression hit the nation's farming sector. Enrollment dropped and church and alumni contributions declined. The college could not pay its faculty, and it used produce grown on a college-owned farm to settle some of its bills. Wilson, believing that Eureka had to undergo a drastic reorganization, outraged the faculty with a plan to consolidate departments and drop some programs. He angered the community and alumni by suggesting that the school might even have to be moved to an area that had a heavier Christian Church population. Students, already irritated with Wilson because of earlier conflicts over a strict student behavior code that banned dancing, feared that the cutbacks would affect their graduation and damage the college's academic standing. Faculty members, motivated by personal pique and political conflicts with the president, manipulated the students to an extent. Although Wilson lacked the ability to unify the college community, he was trying to cope with real problems, and on 16 November 1928 the college board of directors approved his plan.

On 20 November 1928, the students demanded that Wilson resign. He agreed to do so because he wanted to focus debate on the reorganization plan rather than on himself. The students continued their agitation because they feared that the board would not accept Wilson's departure. The board met early on 27 November and, as the students had anticipated, rejected Wilson's resignation. The chapel bell began to ring, calling the students to action. Reagan served as freshman representative on a strike committee. As a gesture of unity with the juniors and seniors, who felt most threatened by Wilson's reorganization plan, protest leaders asked freshman Reagan to offer a motion calling on students to return from Thanksgiving vacation on strike. Late that night the students accepted the motion. "I discovered that night that an audience has a feel to it and, in the parlance of the theater, that audience and I were together," Reagan recalled. "When I came to actually presenting the motion there was no need for parliamentary procedure: they came to their feet with a roar—even the faculty members present voted by acclamation. It was heady wine."

Reagan often rearranged events to make them fit what should have been. In his memory, the students returned from the holiday on strike and the faculty supported them by not counting them absent; the strike committee assigned homework and enforced study hours; Wilson resigned, and the students' stalwart action preserved Eureka's academic standards. In fact, when the board met on 4 December, it was in the mood to fire some faculty members and to ask student strike leaders to leave the college. To end the confrontation, the parties formulated a grand compromise. The students retracted their demand for Wilson's resignation and Wilson voluntarily resigned; the board placed the leader of the faculty malcontents on probation; Wilson's reorganization plan took effect.[19]

The strike was a defining moment for Reagan. He experienced for the first time the thrill of moving an audience by words. Years later when Reagan was governor of California, his critics savored the irony of the Eureka rebel confronting the Berkeley student rebellion. Historian Garry Wills, who closely analyzed the Eureka strike to show the selective nature of Reagan's memory, found that at both Eureka and Berkeley Reagan acted in conformity with the majority against an unpopular minority. At Eureka, he joined with students, faculty, and the local community in opposition to the beleaguered Wilson. In the 1960s he won the applause of the huge middle-class electorate by ridiculing the student rebels as foolish, pampered young people manipulated by hard-core communists. He had always been Nelle's good boy, never Huck Finn, not even for a moment. Ronnie hung out with a bunch of sissies and probably had never even been in a pool hall, his brother Neil sneered. During the Eureka strike, Reagan was a rebel of a particular sort, a "dissenting conformist," wrote Garry Wills: "He could attack authorities by the community's authority, a wonderful combination of traditionalism and innovation. He had been a leading follower in a conformist rebellion, the kind he would always prefer."[20]

During the tension-filled Thanksgiving holiday in 1928, Ben Cleaver took Margaret and Ronald to see a London-based touring company present *Journey's End,* a play set in World War I. Reagan was transfixed and responded both as an actor and as an audience member. He experienced the peculiar sensation of being in a trench on the Western front and, at the same time, being on stage, facing the audience. He later recalled that he already knew that he wanted to be an actor, but acting was not considered a realistic career choice in small-town Illinois.

Back at Eureka, he and Margaret joined the Dramatics Club, which Reagan dismissed to friends as a way to walk his girlfriend home at night: "Secretly I really thought I was communing with the Arts." He found an English teacher, Ellen Marie Johnson, who took acting as seriously as had his high school teacher, B. J. Fraser. Reagan played the lead roles in various student productions, and in his junior year participated in a national competition of one-act plays held at Northwestern University. Eureka placed second, and Reagan received a special acting award. In her study of Reagan's early life, Anne Edwards, analyzing photographs from these years, found that he was becoming aware of his "presence," that he had become studied in presenting himself and aware of the dramatic effect of his appearance on others.[21]

Ronald Reagan's deep-dyed optimism received a severe test after he graduated from Eureka in June 1932. The nation plunged deeper into the depression, and the Reagans were hit hard. Jack had devised a plan that would allow him to take ownership of a shoe store but that opportunity collapsed, and in late 1932 he lost his position as salesman. Ronald later described to a young admirer his mood when he graduated from Eureka: "I wish I could tell you that I had noble thoughts about what to do with my life, but at that time, my only ambition was to get any job that would support me." His new college degree won him back his old job as lifeguard.

The future looked bleak for both him and his family. To many people confronting the depression a secure job teaching in a small high school would have seemed like a godsend. Reagan often struck observers as passive and conformist in his thinking and in his behavior. His friends and associates seldom sensed burning ambition or obsessive drive in him. He seemed to fear his own passivity. He later claimed that he deliberately chose not to do better academically in college because he was afraid that he might be trapped in a career as a football coach in some small school. Yet, while he seemed to fear his inclination toward passivity, he was bold enough to avoid the conventional paths most easily available to him. Ronald Reagan was ambitious, but he could never express that ambition in personal terms, could never reveal, even to himself, hunger for wealth, power, or fame. Yet ambition drove him forward. His life's path was marked by unconventional career decisions: a small-town midwestern young man finding success in Hollywood, a movie star winning the governorship of California in 1966 and immediately trying for the 1968 Republican presidential nomination, a loyal Republican challenging an incumbent president of his own party, Gerald R. Ford, for the nomination.

In the summer of 1932, Sid Altschuler, a wealthy Kansas City businessman with ties to Dixon, befriended Reagan, and they discussed the young man's future. Altschuler told Reagan not to base his career decisions on the promise of a big income, which was most people's first priority in 1932. Someday the depression would end, and Reagan should concentrate on what he wanted to spend his life doing. Reagan passed sleepless nights struggling with that question. He knew that he wanted to be an actor but that seemed outrageous in the context of his time and place. Instead, he confessed to Altschuler that he would like to get into radio. Altschuler told his young friend to get started in the business immediately, even as a janitor.[22]

In the late summer or fall of 1932, Reagan canvassed the big radio stations in Chicago, but met refusal everywhere. Tired, overwhelmed by the big city and by rejection—it was the lowest point in his life, he recalled—he hitchhiked home in the rain.

A sympathetic woman at one of the Chicago firms had advised the discouraged young man to go out into the "sticks" and get some experience at small stations. So Reagan borrowed Jack's car and toured smaller towns. At Davenport, Iowa, seventy-five miles away, WOC station manager Peter MacArthur gave Reagan a tryout, letting him broadcast a University of Iowa football game the following Saturday. A local newspaper said that Reagan's debut broadcast "sounded like a carefully written story." MacArthur hired him to do three other home games (at ten dollars a game), and in early 1933 found a place for him as a staff announcer at one hundred dollars a month, a good wage for a young person in 1933. He ate at a cafeteria for $3.63 a week and paid $18 a month rent. He sent money home to Jack and Nelle and helped Neil complete his education at Eureka.[23]

Life took a better turn for Jack and Nelle. Reagan would later say that the Great Depression was the single most important event of his life. It made Jack and Ronald passionate Roosevelt admirers. New Deal relief agencies opened in Dixon and put unemployed people to work. A government job allowed Jack to get back on his feet. He became a local supervisor in one of the agencies, and, after having failed to achieve his dream of owning a small business, he found a new purpose in life.[24]

Ronald had found his place in the world as well. Peter MacArthur replaced Altschuler as a father figure and adviser, coaching Reagan to use his expressive voice in a fluid, unstilted delivery and to learn how to control his natural ability to convey vocal intimacy. With that skill in hand, the young sportscaster moved on to learn other things. B. J. Palmer, one of the greatest promoters in the Midwest, owned WOC, as well as a chiropractic college, printing firm, restaurant, dance hall, and roller rink. He was a genius at self-promotion and a master in using advertising media, which taught additional lessons to the young man from Dixon. In 1933 Palmer merged his

Davenport station with WHO in Des Moines, whose fifty-thousand-watt power gave it one of the strongest signals in the nation. In May 1933, MacArthur and Reagan moved to Des Moines, and they flourished in the bigger market. Reagan started at about seventy-five dollars a week, and he added to his income by writing newspaper columns, speaking on the banquet circuit, and announcing local sports events. He made Nelle and Jack financially secure, and he helped his brother get a job with Palmer, which provided the foundation for Neil Reagan's successful career in public relations.[25]

In later life Reagan became known for having his briefest statements, even those made in small private meetings, meticulously written out on index cards. That practice left the impression that he was totally dependent on staff to write his scripts. The portrayal of Reagan as a mindless salesman of other people's ideas distressed friends who had seen evidence of his mental agility. As a sports announcer, Reagan entered a special field of journalism, one that did not make objectivity its founding principle. Sportswriters and announcers often promoted specific teams, and they were not as interested in the bare facts of an event as in using it to teach moral lessons and to entertain the audience.

Reagan's success was based on his ability to use his fertile imagination and glib tongue to create word portraits that made partly fictionalized contests come alive for his audience. Sitting in an enclosed, antiseptic Des Moines studio, he broadcast hundreds of baseball games as if he were on the scene in the stadium. He followed the action by telegraph, with a bare-boned bulletin handed to him after each pitch. For example, the message might say "Out 4 to 3," with 4 representing second base and 3 first base. Reagan immediately had to translate that laconic code into a visual image: The batter hit a sharp grounder to the second baseman who threw the runner out at first. Between pitches Reagan used his imagination to fill in details, describing changing weather conditions, shadows moving across the field, the pitcher picking up the resin bag, the batter tapping the plate with his bat, action starting in the bullpen. His years in radio provided excellent training for the future Great Communicator. Critics who were astounded later at Reagan's ability to describe vividly and with absolute sincerity "little worlds" that did not exist were witnessing the skill that first brought him success, and it long predated his use of index cards.[26]

Reagan was a celebrity in the Midwest. He was well-off financially while millions of people were still suffering from the depression. He made new friends, many at the local Christian Church college, Drake, interviewed such national celebrities as actors Leslie Howard and James Cagney and the charismatic religious figure Aimee Semple McPherson, joined a dance club, swam daily, and enlisted in the cavalry reserve so that he could regularly indulge a favorite hobby, horseback riding.

One disappointment came when Margaret Cleaver broke their engagement. Neil said that Ronald had been so intent in getting his career started that he had neglected Margaret, and on a trip to Europe she met and fell in love with a foreign service officer. Reagan was emotionally shattered when she returned his engagement ring, and although he dated many women in Des Moines, he did not establish a committed relationship with any of them. One woman recalled that he never seemed to be truly present with her; he was always looking over her shoulder, scanning the crowd for important people. It did not surprise her that he became a politician.[27]

Indeed, Reagan was a politician in the making. Older residents in Dixon recalled that even as a teenager Reagan had been fascinated by politics. Some of his political values were emerging, such as distaste for religious bigotry and racism. His father taught him to detest the Ku Klux Klan, and his parents gave him practical lessons in tolerance. In college, when his team passed though Dixon, two of his black teammates were denied hotel lodgings. Reagan took them to his home, where Jack and Nelle welcomed them. Ronald shared Jack's fear of big unions, his detestation of dole payments rather than work relief, and his belief that abortion was wrong. As Ronald matured during his years in Des Moines, his admiration for Franklin Roosevelt deepened, especially for his ability to take bold, dramatic action in a crisis and for his gift in using his voice to bring comfort to millions of Americans gathered around their radios. Reagan followed current events closely and spent hours debating H. R. Gross, WHO's news director and later one of the most anti–New Deal members of the House of Representatives in the post–World War II era. Most of all, Reagan prepared for politics by honing the speaking skills he would later use so effectively.[28]

Many personality traits that puzzled people during Reagan's political career were in evidence early in his life. His contradictory nature confused many observers. One is tempted to see him as an example of Robert Jay Lifton's "protean" personality or Kenneth Gergen's "saturated self." Lifton and Gergen believed that rapid, unceasing change in the twentieth century—including wars, revolutions, and technological innovations, especially the emergence of modern electronic media that flooded individuals with many, often contradictory, ways of being—had produced a new personality type, the protean or saturated self. The saturated self lacked a stable center; it reinvented itself or changed shape on an ad hoc basis as it confronted changing people and circumstances. It was a personality type that created itself as it went along through life, a self under "continuous construction and reconstruction," in Gergen's words. One could view Reagan as a man who reinvented himself as he moved from Dixon to regional celebrity and Roosevelt defender in Des Moines to stardom in Hollywood to the leadership of the American conservative movement and on to political office. Yet one of the qualities that many of his admirers found most appealing in Reagan was that in a rootless and unstable world filled with people constantly reinventing themselves, he seemed to represent unchanging American values and beliefs. He seemed to provide a solid foundation of ancient verities for people disturbed by their society's rootlessness.[29]

One of Reagan's personality traits that everyone recognized as basic to him was his optimism. Perhaps the major source of his popular appeal was his ability to translate his personal optimism into a vision of confidence in America and its future. In his speeches, he would typically sketch the glory of the American past and the mission set for the United States by God, discuss the dire threats that the nation currently faced, and then express his confidence that Americans could successfully deal with any threats, his faith that it was always morning again in God's chosen land. Reagan could make that theme sing in the hearts of his admirers because it was the most deeply ingrained part of his self. His daughter Maureen Reagan sometimes fumed at his unfailingly upbeat approach to life: "It's enough to drive you nuts," she said. Michael K. Deaver, the Reagan adviser who best understood him, said one thing that had never changed since their first meeting was Reagan's optimism and trust, a trust so deep that he survived politically only by having people around him protecting him from himself. Optimism remained his outstanding characteristic throughout his life. In his 1994 letter to the American people revealing that he had Alzheimer's disease, he wrote, "I now begin the journey that will lead me into the sunset of my life. I know that for America there will always be a bright dawn ahead."[30]

While all friends and observers agreed on Reagan's deep-dyed optimism, they often found contradictory aspects to many of his personality traits. He was a masterly image manager, as children of alcoholics often are, a trait enhanced by his interest in acting and his sense of his "presence," his effect on other people. He learned from Jack, a wonderful storyteller, and from Nelle, with her plays and dramatic readings, how to convey feeling, mood, and story line. Radio taught him how to use words to create those "little worlds" that he conveyed so skillfully.

Reagan invariably struck people as a man of unfailing charm. Yet those closest to him were often left feeling mystified and puzzled. Nancy Reagan said that he was an affable and gregarious man, unfailingly nice to everyone, but with no deep connection with anyone, even family members. He enjoyed people but did not need them for companionship or approval. "There's a wall around him," she said. "He lets me come closer than anyone else, but there are times when even I feel that barrier." Some later associates believed that he built a protective boundary when he became a movie star, but Reagan biographer Edmund Morris, who had access to Reagan's writings from the late 1920s and early 1930s, found him already to be a dreamy, detached young man. Reagan never openly manipulated and used his friends and associates, as did, for example, Franklin Roosevelt, but those who believed that the unfailingly charming Reagan offered them friendship in return for their service and devotion to him were often disappointed to find that, finally, he had no friends. He was the easiest of men to work for, one aide recalled, but those who turned to him for emotional support were in trouble, because they would encounter surface affability and an inner void.[31]

Optimism, self-confidence, and personal distance were all traits found early in Reagan's life. To this list Reagan's friends and associates added passivity. His father's drinking problem was beyond Ronald's control, he told Lou Cannon, so he could only passively stand by and love him. Margaret Cleaver found his presence attractive and found herself drawn to him, yet she felt he would not accomplish much: "He lacked ambition, a sense of adventure, a cultural curiosity." Later in his life aides who briefed him were disconcerted as he sat quietly, not reacting even by body language. He typically made no response to what was presented, asked no questions, demanded no further information. His aides learned to protect him because they realized that he accepted all reports at face value. Reagan's Central Intelligence Agency director, William Casey, a close and puzzled observer of his boss, said that Reagan was passive about his job and about life. He left it to his staff to call meetings and set the agenda. He never told Casey "let's do this" or "get me that," unless in response to the actions of others or to events.[32]

A few of his associates concluded that the mystery of Reagan's personality lay in the minds of the observers rather than in Reagan himself. Most people tended to assume that Reagan, an actor and politician, would present the world with a mask, that the real Reagan was hidden. Some of his closest friends concluded, to the contrary, that there was no mystery. They often said about Reagan: What you see is what you get. Nancy Reagan summed it up: "The secret to Ronald Reagan is that there really is no secret. He is exactly the man he appears to be. The Ronald Reagan you see in public is the same Ronald Reagan I live with."[33]

Michael Deaver found him to be the least introspective of men, because, he believed, Reagan had long before figured out who he was and wrestled with no insecurities. Speechwriter Peggy Noonan quoted a Reagan friend: "He lived life on the surface where the small waves are, not deep down where the heavy currents tug." He never revealed any angst or existential despair. His deep belief that God had a plan for everyone and his optimistic trust in the future led to a degree of naïveté, but it created in him a simplicity that appealed to many people as they confronted an increasingly confusing world.[34]

Reagan loved to read while he was growing up. He listened to Jack's stories, read the great Bible stories with Nelle. Storytellers have always been revered, and Reagan became the great storyteller of his generation, a powerful political tool that he used in communicating with his public. Reagan's mind seemed to work in terms of such stories, and he learned how to make them live for his audience during his years as a public speaker. He transformed complex political problems or policies into anecdotes always involving concrete, easily visualized individuals or situations, whether the subject was "welfare queens" abusing a social support system or young American and Soviet citizens discussing their dreams of a better world.

His stories usually involved people triumphing over evil or adversity. When he became a public figure reporters began to realize that some of the stories that Reagan told were untrue. Most of his associates, who often fought losing battles to get him to drop such stories from his repertoire, concluded that Reagan was not lying in the usual sense. The stories he learned in his youth might not have been literally true, but they taught a deeper truth. His career as a radio announcer and actor reinforced his talent for enhancing reality. His associates realized that the first victim of his ability to reinvent or enhance reality was Reagan himself, for his ability to convince others rested on his unshakable belief in his own stories. He was a romantic, said Michael Deaver, not an impostor.[35]

Among Reagan's contemporaries, there was sharp disagreement over his intelligence. Many who knew him and worked closely with him were astounded at his ability to absorb information quickly and to retain it. They often described his memory as photographic. On the other hand, many others agreed with Democratic Party maven Clark Clifford, who referred to Reagan as an "amiable dunce." His detractors pointed to countless mistakes he made in press conferences as examples of his lack of intelligence; his admirers said that the very nature of his excellent memory led to his mistakes, because he remembered whatever he read or heard, accurate or inaccurate. Yet during the 1980 presidential campaign, William Casey warned an aide to present material to Reagan in one paragraph, because "He doesn't absorb a hell of a lot." Speechwriter Peggy Noonan, a perceptive admirer of Reagan, believed that many of his closest aides did not think he was very bright, and she found that there was a theory in the White House that Nancy Reagan's fierce protective watch over her husband stemmed from her belief that he was "innocent and dumb."

Some explained the dichotomy in perceptions of Reagan's intelligence as stemming from the selectivity of his interests. If he was interested in something, he remembered everything about it. On the other hand, the range of his interests was narrow, and he did not remember things that did not appeal to him. A friend said, "Behind those warm eyes is a lack of curiosity that is, somehow, disorienting."[36]

Journalist Lou Cannon, who observed Reagan closely for decades and wrote three books about him, had long been puzzled by the question of Reagan's intelligence. Cannon knew that Reagan was intelligent, but he also knew that he had little analytical ability. Harvard psychologist Howard Gardner offered Cannon an explanation. Gardner rejected the conventional idea that intelligence was a single attribute that could be measured by a number on an IQ test and instead described seven categories of intelligence. He suggested that Reagan was low in logical-mathematical intelligence, in which lawyers and politicians normally excelled. Reagan, on the other hand, would probably score highly in bodily-kinesthetic intelligence, which involves the capacity to observe and mimic motion and emotion as actors do, in linguistic intelligence, which includes the ability to use language and to remember words and phrases that have power, and in interpersonal intelligence, which allows one to read moods, emotions, motivations, and intentions of others and to move people in a desired way. Cannon concluded that Reagan was smart but that he confused people because he did not display the forms of intelligence that they expected in politicians.[37]

In 1937, Reagan left the Midwest for Hollywood because, he said, there was nothing for him in those small towns. He never returned for any extended time, but he took much with him. Many enduring aspects of his personality were already fully formed. He used the values and stories and images that he took away from Dixon and other small towns to build his movie star role as the fresh-faced boy-next-door and later to build his political persona as a citizen-politician, coming from the American heartland to renew and restore an endangered nation.

2

Finding Fame and Fortune in Hollywood, 1937–1966

It seemed easy in Ronald Reagan's retelling, without any hint of ambition for fame or wealth. In 1937 he persuaded his radio station to send him to the Chicago Cubs' spring training camp, held on Catalina Island, near Los Angeles. He had dinner with Joy Hodges, who had worked at WHO and was trying to break into the movies. He told her about his dream of becoming an actor, and she introduced him to her agent, George Ward of the Meiklejohn Agency. Ward, who represented actors Robert Taylor and Betty Grable, called the Warner Bros. casting director, Max Arnow, and claimed that he had a future star sitting in his office. Arnow heard similar hype several times a day, but he agreed to meet Reagan and then offered him a screen test. Despite the indignity of being told that his head looked too small, Reagan tested well, and studio boss Jack L. Warner liked the result.[1]

On Monday, 22 March, Reagan returned to work in Des Moines and laughingly told his WHO colleagues about his screen test. That day George Ward telegraphed, telling him that Warner Bros. Pictures had offered a seven-year contract, starting at two hundred dollars a week. Ward asked Reagan what he wanted to do. Reagan answered, SIGN BEFORE THEY CHANGE THEIR MINDS. The beaming Reagan, in a scene repeated many times in the next half century, regaled his friends with his already developing repertoire of Hollywood stories.[2]

Late on Monday evening, 31 May, Reagan arrived in Hollywood ready to begin his new career. Incredibly, on 7 June, a week later, he began work as the lead character in *Love Is on the Air,* the first of his fifty-three feature films.[3]

When Reagan came to Hollywood, an oligopoly of seven major studios dominated the movie industry. They made 75 percent of American films and owned the national theater chains that showed the movies. Harry Warner ran the business end of Warner Bros. from New York and Jack Warner managed the production studio in Hollywood. The studio operated in assembly-line style, often releasing one or more films a week. It retained under contract directors, screenwriters, actors, and specialists in costumes, special effects, photography, sound, and editing. When Reagan joined Warner Bros. Pictures, its actors included James Cagney, Edward G. Robinson, Humphrey Bogart, Bette Davis, Paul Muni, Errol Flynn, Olivia de Havilland, and many other major stars. Although Warner Bros. was known for its intense work schedule, comparatively low salaries, and tight control over its actors' lives and careers, Reagan looked back on the studio system with nostalgia. The studio provided stability for those under contract, and there was a family feeling on the lot, although it was sometimes a rambunctious family with rivalry and conflict.[4]

The studio's B-film production was handled by Bryan Foy, who turned out twenty-six films a year on a five-million-dollar budget. B films played on double bills with more prestigious A films, which had bigger stars. *Love Is on the Air* was a typical B film. It took three weeks to complete and had a budget of $119,000. "The studio didn't want good," Reagan said, "it wanted them Thursday."[5]

Love Is on the Air did well what a B film was supposed to do: It provided an hour's solid entertainment. Reagan played the leading character, Andy McLeod, an idealistic young crusading journalist fighting on the public's behalf against government corruption. It was the first of Reagan's many roles as citizen-crusader, and it presented the prototype of the character he later played throughout his political career. He seemed a little stiff on the screen, but critics concluded that he had a bright future, and one even said that he gave the best first performance seen in years.[6]

Reagan was exhausted after his first film, shot while he was still trying to absorb the fact that he was part of the Hollywood dream factory. He hoped for a rest, but a few days after he finished his first movie, he was cast as the leading man in *Sergeant Murphy,* a film based on a true story about an army horse, Sergeant Murphy, who won the British Grand National steeplechase.

Reagan again performed well. A review in the *New York Daily News* said that the film showed Ronald Reagan in "palpitating proximity" and that his "looks and personality scoop out toeholds for a plot that can barely make the grade."[7]

From a later perspective, the most interesting scene in *Sergeant Murphy* came in a brief exchange between Reagan and black actor Sam McDaniels. McDaniels, while the two were at the steeplechase in England, pointed to an Indian wearing a turban and asked who those "darkies" were. Reagan replied, "They're not darkies." McDaniels quickly answered, "If dey ain't, I ain't." Reagan explained that in England they were considered Caucasians and were "taken up" by society. McDaniels asked, what was the difference between them and him? Reagan answered, "None. Only the turban." McDaniels responded, "If dat's all it takes, I'll get me one of them dem" and chuckled at that fantasy.[8]

Reagan wrote about these busy months in seventeen articles published in the *Des Moines Sunday Register*. He described his work on his first few films, told about the film stars he met, and related his adventures in eating at the Brown Derby, dancing at the Palomar ballroom, and attending a film premiere. The articles projected the image that Reagan maintained from his first days in Hollywood through the rest of his film and political careers. He presented himself as Mr. Average, thrust into an extraordinary situation, and he laughed at himself for being part of a publicity operation so effective that he started receiving fan mail before his first film was released. In his last article, on 3 October 1937, he announced to his friends back home that Warner Bros. had renewed his contract, with a salary increase. He began hunting for a house so he could bring Jack and Nelle to live in Los Angeles.[9]

Reagan asked Bryan Foy to keep the pictures coming, and he appeared in eight films during his first eleven months in Hollywood, eight more in 1939, and thirty before he entered the army in April 1942. "I was the Errol Flynn of the B's," he wrote. In *Accidents Will Happen* (1937) and *Girls on Probation* (1938), he played idealistic young men, exposing a corrupt insurance ring in one and defending a young woman caught up in the criminal justice system in the other. In *Brother Rat* (1938) he appeared in a substantial film with two other newcomers, Wayne Morris and Eddie Albert, along with his future wife, Jane Wyman. This film, about a trio of rowdy upperclassmen at the Virginia Military Institute, stretched Reagan as an actor and placed him in a light comedy role that many critics believed best suited him.[10]

Was Reagan a good actor? "He was a director's delight—always on time, always totally prepared and extremely cooperative," recalled director Frederick de Cordova. Reagan's good memory made him a quick study, and his pleasant nature pleased directors and producers who often engaged in ferocious battles with Bette Davis, Humphrey Bogart, and other Warner. Bros. stars. Reagan worked hard and followed actor Pat O'Brien's advice to him to play "those 'B's as if they were 'A's." Reagan acted with many major stars, including Dick Powell, Humphrey Bogart, Pat O'Brien, James Cagney, Bette Davis, Ann Sheridan, Jane Wyman, Errol Flynn, Olivia de Havilland, Claude Rains, Shirley Temple, Eleanor Parker, Patricia Neal, Doris Day, Ginger Rogers, and Barbara Stanwyck.

Reagan never embarrassed himself or his fellow actors. He was well suited to the characters he usually played, as idealistic heroes in action films or as the-boy-next-door types in light comedy roles. Critics found that he did not have the indefinable quality that allowed stars like Bette Davis or Clark Gable to dominate the screen. He did not get inside the characters he played as did his future wife Jane Wyman, who to the dismay of her friends and family took the role of a deaf-mute woman and stopped talking for six months. Fellow actors approved his steadiness but found that he lacked dramatic flair. Reagan wanted to be a star rather than a great actor; he seldom fought for good roles and usually accepted what the studio offered.[11]

He had a comfortable life in the film colony. He enjoyed having Nelle, Jack, and Neil nearby. He rode horseback at every opportunity and bought a ranch as soon as he could afford it. He dated many actresses, although his romances were often arranged by the studio publicity department and a photographer followed the couple around Hollywood glamour spots. In 1939 he was briefly engaged to actress Ila Rhodes, but he started dating Jane Wyman when they worked together on *Brother Rat and a Baby,* an uninspired sequel to *Brother Rat.*

Jane Wyman always refused to discuss her early, unhappy life, which left her hurt and distrustful. When she was a young girl, her mother moved the family to Los Angeles, and Jane took dancing lessons and began to get small movie parts. She was pretty, graceful, and smart, although when she got a Warner Bros. contract in 1939 the studio quickly typecast her as a dumb blonde.[12]

Wyman liked Ronald Reagan and found his optimism and trust in people infectious. She had been part of the Hollywood nightclub scene, but she began attending church with Nelle and became a tomboy to fit in with Reagan's sports-loving crowd. When Jane Wyman and Ronald Reagan married on 26 January 1940, the Warner Bros. publicity department went into high gear, exploiting the fact that it was one of the few marriages at that time between a team of relatively important actors. Hundreds of fan magazine articles portrayed them as the film colony's "perfect couple." Hollywood was on a campaign to clean up its moral image, and Ronald

Reagan and Jane Wyman fit the role perfectly, especially after their daughter, Maureen, was born in January 1941.[13]

Wyman and Reagan established as traditional a marriage as possible, despite the publicity machine that ground ceaselessly. Wyman regarded her husband as more mature and wise than she was. She deferred to him on big matters, while he left the "feminine-frivolous" household matters for her to handle within the strict budget he set for her. Friends noticed an undercurrent in their relationship. Wyman was quicker and tougher than Reagan, possessing "street smarts" he did not have. Reagan treated her as cute and flighty, which she resented. Actress June Allyson, married to Dick Powell, a committed Republican, said that she and Jane spent hours listening to their husbands argue over politics. Jane told her, "Don't ask Ronnie what time it is because he will tell you how a watch is made."[14]

Jane Wyman fought for her career, a fight that would eventually take her from bit parts into the top rank of film actors. In 1940, she prodded Reagan into fighting for something he wanted. He learned that Warner Bros. intended to film the life of Knute Rockne, the famous Notre Dame football coach, with Pat O'Brien playing Rockne. Reagan wanted the part of George Gipp, a legendary football player, who had died two weeks after his final game. Reagan fought hard to get the role, and he used it to break from the pack of the studio's huge stable of young actors. He played Gipp as a loner with a rebellious edge, as something of a mystery. In Gipp's death scene Reagan murmured a line that would be associated with him every time he faced an election or a tough vote in Congress. Sometime when Notre Dame faced defeat, the dying Gipp told Rockne, "Ask 'em to go in there with all they've got; win just one for the Gipper."[15]

Reagan knew that Gipp probably did not say those words. Rockne, like Reagan, was an expert communicator who could use words to create a "little world" that never existed. Reagan dismissed Rockne's invention of the Gipp statement as unimportant, since it served bigger purposes, which was Reagan's attitude toward factual truth throughout his career.[16]

Reagan received marvelous publicity and reviews for *Knute Rockne—All American* and established himself in A films. He had called himself the "poor man's Errol Flynn," and he soon got a chance to try to hold his own against Flynn, famous for scene stealing. They were cast in *Santa Fe Trail,* which provided good entertainment and laughable history. Flynn played General Jeb Stuart, with Olivia de Havilland as Kit Carson Halliday, Raymond Massey as John Brown, and Reagan as George A. Custer.[17]

In 1941, *Knute Rockne—All American* and *Santa Fe Trail* won Reagan official studio designation as a star. The Music Corporation of America (MCA) had bought out the Meiklejohn Agency, and Lew Wasserman represented both Reagan and Wyman. In August 1941, Reagan got a new three-year contract at $1,650 a week. In 1942, the Gallup polling organization estimated that Reagan was making $52,000 a film (compared with $210,000 by Clark Gable, the biggest box-office draw). In mid-1941, a Gallup poll ranked Reagan in eighty-second place as a box-office draw, and in January 1942 he tied with Laurence Olivier in seventy-fourth place.[18]

In 1941 Reagan was cast with Robert Cummings and Ann Sheridan in *Kings Row.* This stylish soap opera, based on a best-selling novel by Henry Bellamann, had been considered too controversial to film because it dealt with the seamy side of turn-of-the-century life in a small town. To keep the censors happy the final script eliminated the novel's themes of incest, euthanasia, and homosexuality. The movie provided high melodrama, with good acting by Reagan and Sheridan and great supporting work by Claude Rains, Charles Coburn, and Judith Anderson.[19]

Reagan believed that *Kings Row,* released in 1942, would have propelled him into the top rank of stars if World War II had not prevented him from capitalizing on opportunities the film opened for him. Warner Bros. delayed Reagan's draft as long as possible, but after several deferments his draft board ordered him in April 1942 to report to Fort Mason, California, near San Francisco, as a second lieutenant in the United States Army Cavalry Reserve. After a short period, the army assigned him to the First Motion Picture Unit at the Hal Roach Studio in Culver City, which allowed him to return to his nearby home each weekend. Reagan joined about thirteen hundred other actors, writers, directors, and film technicians at "Fort Roach," turning out war propaganda films.[20]

Reagan and Wyman became propaganda commodities themselves. Warner Bros. had been depicting them as examples of hardworking, clean-cut young members of the film colony. Now Hollywood's "perfect couple" became part of the war effort, with Reagan portrayed as patriotically giving up his career to serve his country, while Wyman bravely faced life alone and stoically endured her fear that her loved one was in danger. During the war Reagan's and Wyman's fan magazine coverage, by writers loyally overlooking the fact that Reagan was working a few miles from home, was virtually unmatched in film history.[21]

After his discharge in July 1945, Reagan turned to the problem of renewing his film career. He made twenty-two films after he returned from the service (he made *This Is the Army* during the war). There were some failures among them, but they were generally better than his prewar films. Financially he seemed secure. His 1946 tax return showed that he earned $169,750, compared with Errol Flynn's $199,999, while Humphrey Bogart earned $432,000 and Bette Davis, $328,000. Lou Cannon estimated that

Reagan's 1946 salary would be worth about one million in 1990 dollars and was enough to put him in the highest income tax bracket.[22]

Warner Bros. assumed Reagan had a bright future, but film production slowed after the war, and the industry had a glut of established stars returning from wartime service, while a new generation crowded in, all hungry for roles. Months passed as the studio searched for the right film to reestablish Reagan. Finally, in 1947, he began work on *Stallion Road*. He played a horse rancher–veterinarian, trying to win the love of leading lady Alexis Smith and fighting a desperate, life-threatening battle against anthrax. *Stallion Road,* a good film, failed as a vehicle to restart Reagan's career. The studio had intended it for Humphrey Bogart and Lauren Bacall, big box-office draws who would have helped Reagan reestablish himself, but they backed out at the last moment.

Stallion Road was followed by Reagan's least-favorite movie, *That Hagen Girl,* which represented Shirley Temple's attempt to break through as an adult actor. He played a light comedy role in *The Voice of the Turtle,* with Eleanor Parker and Eve Arden. It was a good film but did not give him access to the quality parts he thought he had earned with *Kings Row.*[23]

As Reagan's movie career stalled, his marriage went into a depressing tailspin. Studio executives took note after Jane Wyman, determined to break from the dumb-blonde roles usually assigned her, got a small but rich part in director Billy Wilder's *The Lost Weekend* (1945). She fought for and landed a role in *The Yearling* (1946), which brought her the first of four Academy Award nominations. In 1948 she won the Oscar for her performance in *Johnny Belinda,* and a fan magazine asked if Ronald was slated to become "Mr. Wyman." She immersed herself emotionally in her roles in ways that Reagan never attempted. Their daughter, Maureen, learned sign language because Wyman stopped talking when she played a mute woman in *Johnny Belinda.* "It's a strange character I'm married to," Reagan said, "but I love her."[24]

The strain on their marriage increased. In June 1947 Wyman gave birth to a premature baby that died the next day. Reagan could not be with her because he was in the hospital battling life-threatening viral pneumonia. His illness lingered for months, and he was out of action as he fretted over his film career and became preoccupied by his increasingly important role in the Screen Actors Guild. Wyman turned to actor Lew Ayres for friendship. Ayres, a wise and gentle friend, treated Wyman as a serious adult. She denied that she had an affair with him, but their emotional involvement made her rethink her relationship with Reagan. In late 1947 she told Reagan she wanted to leave him, and after separating and reconciling several times, Wyman filed for divorce in June 1948. It was all her fault, she told a friend.[25]

Divorce devastated Reagan. "Ronnie is not a sophisticated fellow. It was very hard," Nancy Reagan said. In his autobiography, Reagan revealed the innocent side to his nature that often struck observers: "I suppose there had been warning signs, if only I hadn't been so busy, but small-town boys grow up thinking only other people get divorced. The plain truth was that such a thing was so far from even being imagined by me that I had no resources to call upon." From the few comments Wyman made, she seemed to have resented Reagan's growing obsession with politics, his incessant talk about national and international affairs, and his inattention to her views and needs. "Perhaps I should have let someone else save the world and have saved my own home," Reagan said.[26]

Reagan was also distracted from his career and marriage by his work with the Screen Actors Guild (SAG), a labor union organized in response to the exploitative situation that actors faced in the 1920s and 1930s. There were a few rich stars in Hollywood, but most actors scraped by financially and worked under poor conditions in studios bossed by tough entrepreneurs. In July 1933 actors formed SAG to fight producers' attempts to cut salaries and to tighten their oligopolistic control over the industry. The actors fought back and in 1937 won a closed-shop contract with the studios.[27]

Reagan resented joining the union until actress Helen Broderick told him about working conditions before he arrived in Hollywood: "After that I turned really eager and I have considered myself a rabid union man ever since. My education was completed when I walked into the [SAG] board room. I saw it crammed with the famous men of the business." Reagan twisted SAG's history to make it an altruistic organization created and maintained by a few stars to benefit other actors, rather than a labor union composed mainly of financially hard-pressed and hardworking actors battling a powerful oligopoly.[28]

In 1941 SAG executive secretary John Dales recruited Reagan to the union's board of directors. In 1947 Reagan, articulate and hardworking, replaced Robert Montgomery as SAG president, and he was reelected each year until he stepped down in 1952. He continued to serve on the SAG board and returned to the presidency in 1959.[29]

Reagan helped lead SAG during several bitter postwar strikes. The conflicts pitted the International Alliance of Theatrical Stage Employees (IATSE) against the Conference of Studio Unions (CSU). IATSE, one of the oldest unions within the American Federation of Labor (AFL), represented movie technicians, including carpenters, painters, plumbers, and other skilled employees. In the 1930s a corrupt element took over IATSE, but by the end of the war Roy Brewer, IATSE's international representative, claimed that the gangsters had been defeated. Brewer said, however, that Hollywood faced a new danger, that communists intended to take over the movie industry as a first step toward subverting the nation.

The threat came from the CSU, Brewer argued, which Herbert K. Sorrell, a leftist, had organized as an alternative to IATSE corruption. IATSE and CSU battled for control, and in 1945 and 1946 they engaged in bitter disputes that led to strikes. Officially SAG was neutral, but John Dales later admitted that the actors' guild was a conservative body led by a wealthy elite whose members did not think like labor leaders. During the 1946 conflict Reagan, as a board member, led the fight to have SAG declare that the strike was a jurisdictional dispute, which by AFL rules would allow actors to cross picket lines. Reagan had become convinced that Sorrell was a communist, as Roy Brewer argued, trying to take control of Hollywood. On 20 October 1946, after a sharp conflict, SAG membership supported Reagan's position. The strike collapsed, and the weakened CSU soon folded.

Rather than being the Moscow-directed attempt at subversion Reagan imagined, the strikes resulted from the producers and IATSE ganging up to destroy, with SAG's help, an independent, aggressive union. Sorrell's opponents used the postwar Red Scare to destroy his organization. Father George H. Dunne, asked by *Commonweal* to report on the strike, concluded: "The record is clear. It is a shameful record of collaboration between the producers and the leadership of IATSE ... to destroy the opposition of democratic trade unionism represented by the Conference of Studio Organizations." Reagan, the "victim of a snow job" said Father Dunne, came on the scene like a "Rover Boy" and did not understand what was happening.[30]

Reagan's work with SAG brought him directly into the political world. His Hollywood friends were not surprised later when he entered elective politics. They noticed that he had little interest in discussing acting or indulging in film colony gossip; he brightened when he could turn conversations to national and international affairs. While most actors read trade papers like *Variety,* actress Jane Bryan remembered Reagan carrying around the *Congressional Record.*[31]

Reagan later wrote that he emerged from the war as a bleeding-heart liberal intent on making the world a better place. He assumed leadership positions in the Hollywood Independent Citizens Committee of the Arts, Sciences, and Professions (HICCASP), the American Veterans Committee (AVC), and the Americans for Democratic Action (ADA). In December 1945 he impressed liberal leaders when he spoke at a mass anti-nuclear-weapons rally. In an article he charged that individuals were using "Fascist ideas" to destroy American faith in their government and in the United

States–Soviet alliance. He spoke out against racism and hatemongering. He actively supported Minnesota liberal Democrat Hubert H. Humphrey for the Senate in 1948 and introduced Harry S. Truman at a Los Angeles rally in the 1948 presidential campaign. He worked for the liberal activist Helen Gahagan Douglas in her 1950 Senate campaign against Richard M. Nixon.[32]

Nonetheless, soon after the end of the war, Reagan began to move to the right. In 1946 he resigned from HICCASP on the grounds that it was a communist-front organization, and he reduced his role in AVC and ADA. He became more cautious in a fight that he had been leading against racial stereotyping in films, and although he had supported Helen Gahagan Douglas for the Senate in 1950, two years later he supported Nixon in his 1952 quest for the vice presidency. Although many people believed that in the 1950s Nancy Reagan and her father, outspoken right-winger Dr. Loyal Davis, converted Reagan to conservatism, his commitment to liberalism began to recede in the immediate postwar period, before he met Nancy.[33]

Reagan was never as liberal as he remembered, nor would he become as conservative as his later supporters believed he was. He admired Franklin Roosevelt and his quick response to people's needs during the Great Depression. Reagan responded emotionally to Roosevelt's bold leadership and to his magnificent speaking ability but not particularly to his institutional reforms. After World War II, Reagan found himself in the 90 percent income tax bracket, and big government began to take on a new meaning for him. Soon after World War II ended, he began to speak out on the threats of communism and high taxes, two of the major themes he used when he emerged as a conservative leader in the 1960s.

Reagan had been exposed to the ideas of many articulate conservatives, including H. R. Gross in Des Moines, his brother Neil, who had long before become a conservative Republican, and his conservative actor friends, including Dick Powell (who always claimed credit for converting Reagan) and George Murphy (who himself had switched from the Democratic Party and would later be elected to the United States Senate). One of Reagan's former leading ladies, Jane Bryan, had married Justin Dart, an immensely wealthy businessman who became friends with Reagan and worked hard to convince him of the evils of big government. Dart was one of Reagan's earliest backers for the governorship of California. Through Dart, Reagan met such important Republicans as Goodwin Knight, a future governor of California, and other rich, conservative southern Californians. Reagan was wealthy himself, and by the late 1940s most of his friends were wealthy actors and businessmen.[34]

The postwar Red Scare, called McCarthyism after Senator Joe McCarthy

(Rep., Wis.), also shaped Reagan's political views. On 12 March 1947 President Truman divided the world into communist and "free world" blocs and pledged that the United States would aid any freedom-loving people resisting a communist takeover. A few days after his Truman Doctrine speech aimed at the Soviet Union, the president mounted a war on internal subversives. By executive order he initiated a loyalty program designed to weed subversives from federal government employment and at his direction the attorney general compiled a list of alleged subversive organizations. Democratic debate eroded as criticism of American foreign and domestic policy became suspect, and Red hunters examined books and films for evidence of attempted subversion.[35]

The Red Scare served the interests of many people. Their enemies purged leftists from unions, business firms, and universities. Republicans used the Red Scare to bludgeon the Democrats for being soft on communism, individual members of both parties used it against opponents. Business used the Red Scare to discredit radical labor leaders and unions, as Roy Brewer and Ronald Reagan used it against the CSU. Many in Hollywood had their careers destroyed; many others joined Reagan in a trek to the right, toward safer terrain. He later wrote: "Light was dawning in some obscure region in my head. I was beginning to see the seamy side of liberalism." Reagan led SAG in an anticommunist crusade. "We stopped the Communists cold in Hollywood," he claimed.[36]

On 20 October 1947 the House Un-American Activities Committee (HUAC), looking for high-profile opportunities to expose threats to the republic, opened hearings on the communist menace in Hollywood. On 23 October Reagan testified. He did not name any names, but he confirmed that there had been a "small clique" operating in SAG that had generally followed the communist party line. The film community had confronted the problem and had turned back the threat, he said. He angered HUAC chair J. Parnell Thomas (Rep., N.J.) by saying, "In opposing those people, the best thing to do is make democracy work. . . . I believe that, as Thomas Jefferson put it, if all the American people know all of the facts they will never make a mistake." He said it was up to Congress to decide whether to outlaw the Communist Party: "As a citizen, I would hesitate to see any political party outlawed on the basis of its political ideology." He said that while he abhorred the communist philosophy, he hoped fear would never push the United States into compromising its democratic principles: "I still think that democracy can do it."[37]

Liberals admired Reagan's lecture to HUAC on Jeffersonian principles. They did not know that Reagan was a Federal Bureau of Investigation (FBI) informant who had secretly already named names and had suggested that

Congress outlaw the Communist Party. On 10 April 1947 Reagan and Wyman were interviewed by FBI agents, and Reagan gave them names of SAG members he thought were following the communist party line. The FBI gave him an informant's code name, T-10. The agents reported: "T-10 stated it is his firm conviction that Congress should declare, first of all, by statute, that the Communist Party is not a legal party, but is a foreign-inspired conspiracy. Secondly, Congress should define what organizations are communist-controlled so that membership therein could be construed as an indication of disloyalty. He felt that lacking a definitive stand on the part of the government it would be very difficult for any committee of motion picture people to conduct any type of cleansing of their own household." Actress Karen Morley, her career ruined by the film industry blacklist of suspected subversives, said of Reagan: "It isn't that he's a bad guy really. What's so terrible about Ronnie is his ambition to go where the power is. . . . I really don't even think he realizes how dangerous the things he does really are."[38]

Reagan and other "friendly witnesses" had been followed before HUAC by a number of individuals who had been accused publicly of being subversives, including scriptwriters Alvah Bessie and Dalton Trumbo and actor Larry Park. In contentious, highly publicized testimony they refused to cooperate or to reveal their political affiliations. Congress cited them for contempt and, known as the Hollywood Ten, they were convicted and sentenced to prison.

On 24–25 November 1947 Hollywood producers met to discuss the threat that the industry faced: media hostility, local boycotts of theaters, an American Legion threat to shun all Hollywood films. The producers announced that they would fire the Hollywood Ten and would not knowingly employ communists. They encouraged SAG and the other Hollywood unions to cooperate in eliminating subversives. While the SAG board publicly criticized the producers' blacklist, it privately decided to cooperate.[39]

Reagan proclaimed publicly that SAG "will not be a party to a blacklist," but the guild banned from membership communists and witnesses who refused to cooperate with legislative investigations. Academy Award–winning actress Anne Revere, who was the SAG treasurer, told the board that HUAC intended to call her as a witness. She asked what she should do, and Reagan told her to give the committee some names already made public. Revere refused to save herself by hurting someone else, and the industry blacklisted her for eighteen years.[40]

On 13 March 1951 Academy Award–winning actress Gale Sondergaard, whose husband was one of the Hollywood Ten, wrote the SAG board an open letter published in *Variety*. She described her love for acting and her loyalty to the United States but said she had been subpoenaed by HUAC and intended to take the Fifth Amendment. She urged the board to resist the blacklist. On 20 March the board answered in a public letter drafted by a small group that included Reagan. The letter crossed the line into outright McCarthyism. It opened by referring to Sondergaard's criticism of HUAC and said that communists had also attacked HUAC, as part of a "typical Communist Party line" to create disrespect for the government. The times were too dangerous for "dialectic fencing," the board said: "Like the over-whelming majority of the American people, we believe that a 'clear and present danger' to our nation exists. The Guild Board believes that all participants in the international Communist Party conspiracy against our nation should be exposed for what they are—enemies of our country and of our form of government." SAG would fight any blacklist, but, "on the other hand, if any actor by his own actions outside of union activities has so offended American public opinion that he has made himself unsalable at the box office, the Guild cannot and would not want to force any employer to hire him. That is the individual actor's personal responsibility and it cannot be shifted to this union."[41]

Reagan became a full-fledged anticommunist leader after the HUAC hearings. He was in constant demand as a speaker and writer, always stress-ing the film colony's commitment to traditional American values, to hard work, family, and church. He never became an angry, obsessed Red hunter as did many McCarthyites. He viewed himself as a citizen-crusader—his favorite role—mobilizing decent people to defeat a threat, then he and the others returning to their real work.[42]

Reagan led Hollywood actors in confronting other challenges that di-rectly affected more of them than did the Red Scare. In 1948 the Supreme Court, verifying that the major studios had engaged in monopolistic prac-tices, forced the studios to divest themselves of their theater chains. Since the studios could no longer deny independent film producers access to theaters, small companies had new opportunities. In 1949, the major studios made 80 percent of all films; that figure had dropped to 35 percent by 1958. The big studios cut production and reduced their stables of contract actors, directors, and writers. The studio system's breakdown allowed top stars to negotiate lucrative contracts, but it increased insecurity by turning the actors loose in an individualistic marketplace.[43]

Even while Hollywood struggled with the collapse of the studio system, film actors confronted a scary new challenge from television. Reagan's attempts to deal with the fall of the studio system and television's challenge for control of the entertainment industry led him into a relationship with the Music Corporation of America (MCA) that later proved embarrassing to him personally and threatening to his political career. Investigative reporter Dan E. Moldea opened his book, *Dark Victory: Ronald Reagan, MCA, and the Mob,* with the epigraph, "Organized crime will put a man in the White House someday—and he won't know it until they hand him the bill."

In 1924 Jules Stein founded MCA, and by the 1930s it represented over half the country's big bands, including those of Harry James, Tommy Dorsey, and Artie Shaw. Moldea said that Stein's relationship with organized crime was unclear but that he surely arrived at some accommodation with the mob, which controlled many night clubs. In 1937, Stein decided to expand and sent Taft B. Schreiber to open an MCA office in Hollywood. Lew Wasserman soon joined MCA, bringing with him Ronald Reagan, who became Wasserman's first "million-dollar client." In 1947 Stein became chair of the board, and Wasserman took over as MCA president. The brilliant, hard-driving Wasserman led the firm into a new era of expansion, and by 1950 MCA represented half of Hollywood's major stars.

Wasserman quickly recognized that the collapsing studio system had left a vacuum. The studios could no longer maintain their stables of actors, directors, and writers, and they, "the talent," could now negotiate their own individual contracts, film by film, under MCA guidance. Producers, who had to put together a company of actors for each movie, depended on MCA for access to the talent.[44]

Meanwhile, television had panicked Hollywood, which feared that New York–based live television was going to destroy the film industry. From 1947 to 1951, SAG membership declined 19 percent and film actors' total annual salaries dropped from $38 million to $32 million. Many in the film colony believed those figures were the first warning of a grim future. MCA offered a solution: It promised to move television production to Los Angeles. Reagan's response to MCA, wrote historian Garry Wills, shaped the future of Hollywood more than anything else he did as an actor or labor leader.[45]

MCA wanted to move into television production. However, since 1939 SAG had prohibited talent agencies from producing movies, and industry leaders assumed that SAG would apply that same rule to television production. SAG wanted to prevent conflicts of interest that could occur if a talent agency combined its role as employer (when it produced shows) with its role as a representative of an employee, the actor. In 1952 MCA formed Revue Productions to produce television programs, and it hired many of its own clients as actors. MCA asked SAG for a "blanket waiver" that would let MCA/Revue produce shows. Although SAG was suspicious of MCA's proposal, Wasserman convinced Reagan and the board that bringing television production to Hollywood meant jobs for actors.

In the meantime SAG had been involved in a bitter fight with producers over "residuals," which were payments to actors for television rebroadcast of their performances. SAG's highest priority was to obtain for its members the right to residuals, but the producers fought back in a solid front against such payments. As producers and actors began to understand television's capability for unlimited reuse of movies and other productions, they knew that they were battling over immense sums. Older actors especially, seeing their movies fed into the television gristmill, wanted some benefits.

On 14 July 1952 Reagan signed a blanket waiver for MCA, allowing it to act as talent agency and producer. MCA simultaneously broke the producers' united front and accepted a contract giving SAG members television residuals. In 1954 SAG extended MCA's blanket waiver. In a 1962 federal grand jury investigation, Justice Department attorney John Fricano asked Reagan if he had ever heard it said that SAG had granted MCA its waiver in return for an agreement on residuals. Reagan said no. Fricano then read a letter to Wasserman from the lawyer who negotiated the contract. The lawyer wrote that "the letter of July 23, 1952 [which granted the MCA waiver], was executed under a specific set of circumstances where Revue was willing to sign a contract giving the guild members reuse fees when no one else was willing to do so." Reagan said he did not recall that.[46]

Other agencies found it difficult to compete against a firm that could promise actors jobs in television if they signed up with MCA. An MCA competitor said that "MCA and we are playing in the same ball game, but there is one set of rules for them and quite a different set of rules for everyone else." On the other hand, an MCA agent said, "Every writer, actor and director in this town ought to get down and kiss Ronald Reagan's feet . . . because the man got television residuals. That has paid for most of the houses in the [San Fernando] Valley."[47]

After MCA got its waiver, it became the dominant force in television. In 1958 it bought Paramount studio's vault of films, and in 1962 bought Decca Records and Universal Studio. By the early 1960s, MCA controlled 60 percent of the entertainment industry. Some insiders traced this empire back to the SAG blanket waivers in 1952 and 1954.[48]

Was there a secret agreement between Reagan and MCA? It is almost inconceivable that Reagan could have made an explicit "sweetheart" deal. He was incorruptible in that sense. If MCA representatives had offered him an outright bribe, Nelle Reagan's son would have walked from the room in a huff. On the other hand, Reagan helped his friends and assumed his friends would help him when he needed it. Throughout his life his "aw shucks" kind of naïveté served him well when he made decisions that benefited him personally. His decision was made easier because MCA argued that the blanket waiver would bring jobs to Hollywood generally.[49]

Clearly, Reagan's involvement with MCA produced important opportunities for him. In 1954, MCA/Revue revived Reagan's flagging acting career by choosing him to host its "General Electric Theater." When that show folded in 1962, MCA stepped in again, offering him "Death Valley Days," and in 1964 Revue production company got him his final movie, *The Killers*. MCA executive Taft Schreiber was one of those who helped bring Reagan into the Republican Party. Schreiber, Wasserman, and Jules Stein were among his major backers in his 1966 governor's race. Schreiber and Stein also helped arrange real estate transactions that made Reagan wealthy. They negotiated the sale of a 236-acre ranch he owned in the Santa Monica Mountains. He had bought the ranch for $293 an acre fifteen years before, and Schreiber and Stein sold it to Twentieth Century–Fox, owned by another friend of Reagan's, for $8,000 an acre. Fox then resold it to the state of California, when Reagan was governor, for $1,800 an acre. Reagan's investment increased from $69,000 to nearly $2 million.[50]

In November 1959 SAG elected Reagan president once again, bringing him back to handle a crisis provoked by MCA. MCA had bought a back list of seven hundred Paramount films for television release, which raised the question of what residuals actors in those films would receive. John Dales wanted Reagan to return to conduct the negotiations. Reagan was reluctant, and he called Lew Wasserman, a party to the dispute, to ask his advice. Wasserman said do it, and Reagan agreed to serve again as SAG president. In 1960, SAG struck, and after intense negotiations signed a contract in which actors forfeited all claims to residual payments for films made prior to 1960, while receiving residuals for movies made in 1960 and afterward. The studios agreed to create a pension and welfare fund for actors, with a one-time contribution of $2.65 million. Dales said SAG got 90 percent of what it wanted, but many within SAG thought the contract sold out older actors. After the settlement Reagan resigned as a SAG board member to become a partner in a joint production venture with MCA/Revue.[51]

The Justice Department had long been suspicious of MCA's hold on the entertainment industry. In 1961, Attorney General Robert F. Kennedy initiated a grand jury investigation of alleged MCA violations of antitrust criminal laws. It was a serious matter that could have led to Reagan's indictment and the destruction of any future political career. On 5 February 1962 Reagan testified, questioned by John Fricano of the Justice Department. Despite Reagan's reputation for having a photographic memory, he recalled little about the relevant negotiations between SAG and MCA. "I don't want to appear as though I am trying deliberately to be vague," Reagan told

Fricano, "but, as I say, I would like you to realize in my history of holding an office with the Guild, my memory is like a kaleidoscope of meetings." He said that SAG granted the MCA waiver because he saw no harm in it and thought it might help produce jobs. He admitted that since he had felt "self-conscious" about his relationship with MCA, he "kind of ran for cover" and did not play a leading role in the waiver decision. Actually he had told John Dales that he had decided not to run for SAG president again in 1952 because he had too much influence with the board and could get it to do whatever he wanted.

Fricano asked Reagan about the 1954 waiver extension and wondered if Reagan, who had remained on the SAG board, remembered the negotiations. Reagan answered, "No. It's like saying what I was doing on October 25, the night of the murder." Fricano, frustrated with Reagan's vagueness, said, "I don't care what you were doing October 25." He told Reagan to take his time. Reagan said it sounded right that the negotiations took place in 1954: "To tell you of my own memory, in my mind I can tell you whether we did or not, no, I can't. Serving with Screen Actors Guild long years of negotiating on meetings for a long time, just retaining things that happened, the lawyers' reports and then so forth, and then you find yourself in a battle like we had with the communists or with the strikes." Fricano interrupted, saying that he could not understand what Reagan meant, and asked if he was saying that he did not remember whether he was aware of the 1954 SAG-MCA negotiations. Reagan replied, "That's right." Fricano sarcastically responded that Reagan's answers had been a surprise. Reagan responded, "Well, yes, you are asking me thing[s] I haven't thought about for a long time, as a matter of fact, I [didn't] think about [them] too much then." Fricano said his question was whether Reagan was aware of the 1954 negotiations. Reagan told the attorney that if they took place he must have been aware of them.

Fortunately for MCA, and possibly Reagan, the Justice Department did not bring criminal indictments. It brought a civil suit against MCA for conspiracy in restraint of trade, with SAG named as a coconspirator. MCA avoided trial by divesting itself of its talent agency, which by that time was a minor part of its operation.[52]

The years from 1945 to 1952 were busy and frustrating years for Reagan. He struggled to revive his acting career, dealt with the emotional aftermath of his divorce from Wyman, suffered a life-threatening bout with pneumonia, and later shattered his leg in an accident while playing softball. It was a rewarding period as well. He emerged as a leader of the acting community and served as one of its most prominent spokesmen during the postwar strikes and the Red Scare. He helped Hollywood meet the challenges stemming from the breakdown of the studio system, the coming of television, and the changes that MCA brought to the industry.

The brightest spot in his life came when he met Nancy Davis. She became the love of his life, his best friend, and his chief adviser, as well as one of the most powerful and controversial women of her time. She was born on 6 July 1921 (her Hollywood biography said 6 July 1923) in New York City. Her mother was Edith Luckett, a stage actress who worked with George M. Cohan, Spencer Tracy, Walter Huston, and other major entertainment figures. In 1916 Edith married Kenneth Seymour Robbins, but her marriage failed soon after Nancy was born.

In 1929 Edith married a wealthy and socially prominent Chicago surgeon, Dr. Loyal Davis. He was a conservative, old-fashioned man who stressed proper behavior and polite manners for ladies. Nancy broke through his reserve, and in her mind he became her true father. Nancy loved her mother and worshiped Dr. Davis, who sent her to the Girls' Latin School in Chicago and then to Smith College, where she graduated in 1943.[53]

At Smith, Nancy acted in several plays and worked as an apprentice in summer stock theater in New England. After World War II her mother's good friend, actress ZaSu Pitts, got her a small part in a touring stage play, and she later was cast in a Broadway play, *Lute Song*, with Mary Martin and Yul Brynner. Her mother's friends looked out for her; her protectors included such major figures in the entertainment world as Walter Huston, Katharine Hepburn, Lillian Gish, and Spencer Tracy. She dated Clark Gable and powerful Metro-Goldwyn-Mayer (MGM) executive Benjamin Thau. In March 1949 Tracy and Thau arranged for her to go to Hollywood for a screen test. MGM offered her a seven-year contract at $250 a week.[54]

Nancy Davis appeared in nine films and a number of television productions. Despite her hard work, good connections, beautiful expressive eyes, and ability to project purity and wholesomeness on screen, her career never clicked. She was trying to break into Hollywood just as it was adjusting to the studio system's decline and television's challenge, and in September 1951 MGM dropped her contract.[55]

At that time Ronald Reagan was in emotional turmoil. After his divorce from Jane Wyman he dated many actresses, but despite his lively social life he was miserable. "You know," he later remarked, "if Nancy Davis hadn't come along when she did, I would have lost my soul."[56]

The often-repeated story is that Nancy found herself on a list of communist sympathizers because she had been confused with another Nancy Davis. She called a friend, director Mervyn LeRoy, and he sent her to Reagan, who took her to the dinner that began their romance. Author Anne

Edwards's research convinced her that the confusion over names came several years after Ronald and Nancy first met. Their first meeting was in September 1949 at producer Dore Schary's home. Nancy found Reagan to be an attractive, interesting man who talked to her about history, politics, and his love for his ranch. After they began dating regularly, Nancy realized that Reagan's divorce had left him emotionally scarred. "I could see that Jane [Wyman] knew how to play on Ronnie's good nature," Nancy wrote. "She had convinced him that he shouldn't get married again until she did. It took me a little time, but I managed to unconvince him."

They married on 4 March 1952. Nancy, conservative and socially proper, for years tried to deny what the calendar revealed. In her autobiography she finally admitted, "During that year we had our first child, Patti, who was born—go ahead and count—a bit precipitously but very joyfully, on October 22, 1952."[57]

The Reagan marriage became one of the great romances in modern political life. Their critics sometimes suggested that it was too perfect, a show put on for public consumption. If so, it was a better performance than either ever gave on film, and in fact there is little creditable evidence to suggest that their private life differed from their public presentation of it. "We have always been each other's first priority," Reagan told an admirer. Years later he wrote, "Sometimes, I think my life really began when I met Nancy."[58]

After the Reagans married, they lived for a time in Nancy's apartment in Pacific Palisades and struggled with finances as Ronald found it harder to get films. They settled into a stereotypically 1950s married life, a little square by Hollywood standards. Friends remembered Ronald delivering little homilies on family life. They were probably similar to the one that he wrote to his newlywed son Michael Reagan: "There are more men griping about marriage who kicked the whole thing away themselves than there can ever be wives deserving of blame. There is an old law of physics that you can only get out of a thing as much as you put in. The man who puts into the marriage only half of what he owns will get that much out. Sure, there will be moments ... when you will be challenged to see if you can still make the grade, but let me tell you how really great is the challenge of proving your masculinity and charm with one woman for the rest of your life."[59]

Ronald did not want Nancy to pursue her career, but he did not discuss it with her. "I shouldn't have worried," he wrote. "She was her mother's daughter and it was ingrained in her to simply say, 'If you try to make two careers work, one of them has to suffer.' " Although she proved to be a strong woman who helped shape Reagan's career throughout their marriage, she also accepted the subordinate role of dutiful wife. "I've always believed that if Ronnie feels strongly about something," she wrote, "I'd be foolish to go against him."[60]

When Ronald Reagan became one of the country's foremost spokesmen for "family values," his critics enjoyed pointing out that his own family hardly served as an exemplary model for the nation. "What I wanted most in all the world was to be a good wife and mother," Nancy wrote. "As things turned out, I guess I've been more successful at the first than at the second." As their children grew up they admitted that the intensity of the devotion between Ronald and Nancy made them feel left out. Nancy often received blame for the Reagan family problems, faulted both by the public and by her children. She was a "difficult" person, self-centered, high-strung, and edgy. It was easy to blame her and to overlook the responsibility of her charming, relaxed husband.[61]

Yet Reagan's role cannot be ignored. He was father to four children and each suffered to some degree from his neglect. Maureen was born in January 1941, and Reagan and Jane Wyman adopted Michael in March 1945, several days after his birth. Maureen suffered the emotional turmoil of being caught between a remote father she adored and a mother obsessed with her career and drained emotionally by each movie character she played. Michael believed that his parents adopted him to shore up their troubled marriage. They placed him in a boarding school at age six, and he was sexually molested in a summer camp when he was seven. He found it so difficult to cope with the mercurial Jane Wyman that at age fourteen he moved in with Ronald and Nancy. "Like everyone else in the house, including Dad, I was a little intimidated by Nancy," Michael wrote. "She, like Mom, seemed to go through maids and cooks every month, and I was always worried that with one wrong move I might be the next to go." His father seemed so perfect that Michael could not tell him about his troubles, not even the sexual molestation. Michael could not approach his remote, perfect father for a hug: "Dad has a hard time doing that even today. He can give his heart to the country but he just finds it difficult to hug his own children."[62]

Patti was born in October 1952. She did not find out until she was seven who Maureen and Michael were. When Maureen asked Ronald why Patti had not been told that she had a stepbrother and stepsister, he replied, "Well, we just haven't gotten around to that yet." Patti, like Michael, found Ronald to be a perfect, if remote, father, and she directed her anger at Nancy. Patti vented her rage in a most public fashion, through an autobiography and autobiographical novels. She portrayed Nancy as obsessed with control, as a woman who misused tranquilizers and sleeping pills and who physically abused Patti. She did not ask her father for help: "My parents' love for each other was territory circled by fences and border patrols." Ronald Jr., born in May 1958, was the only one of the children who did not engage in public exchanges with his parents. Like his father he seemed to have the ability to project a sunny and open countenance while maintaining a private core.[63]

In addition to his family responsibilities, Reagan had his own crises to deal with, as his movie career came to an end. "They [the studio bosses] thought I was the hottest thing around and didn't realize that the sixteen-year-olds didn't know who I was," he wrote. He had been almost always cast in roles that used his boyish, all-American qualities, and as he approached middle age, he did not have either the star appeal or the acting ability to carry his career forward.[64]

The extent of his frustration became evident when the usually tractable Reagan began a public feud with Jack Warner. On 6 January 1950 Reagan told a reporter that he was going to start producing his own films: "I have come to the conclusion that I could do as good a job of picking as the studio has done. At least I could do no worse." He added, "With the parts I've had I could telephone my lines in and it wouldn't make any difference." The hot-tempered Jack Warner dashed off a letter suggesting that Reagan cancel his contract, but rather than mailing it, he sent the studio attorney to talk to Reagan. Reagan was friendly but complained of the films he had been offered. He especially felt misused because after he himself had located a script for a western film, *Ghost Mountain,* that he wanted to star in, the studio planned to give it to Errol Flynn.

The feud continued. In May 1950 Reagan wrote Warner about rumors that the studio was going to cast someone else in *Ghost Mountain.* "Naturally I put no stock in these rumors—I know you too well to ever think you'd break your word," he wrote sarcastically. Warner again dispatched his attorney, who reported back: "I . . . told him that with respect to 'Ghost Mountain' that the company's attitude had changed considerably since his article about phoning in his lines to the studio and did not want to risk assigning him to a picture of heavy costs when he had such an attitude and frame of mind about his work." The lawyer, speaking for Warner, suggested that it might be in the interest of both parties to cancel his contract.[65]

Reagan was not temperamentally suited to conducting a feud. He decided he was being foolish, and he apologized to Jack Warner, who responded warmly. In the meantime Wasserman had negotiated Reagan a new three-year contract with Warner Bros. for one movie a year at half his former salary, but with the right to do outside films. With Reagan now a free agent, Wasserman then signed a five-picture contract with Universal.[66]

Despite Reagan's unhappiness most of his postwar films were good, if not of the first rank. *The Hasty Heart,* filmed in 1949, cast Richard Todd as a dour Scottish soldier confined in a military hospital in Burma with Reagan and several other injured soldiers. Todd's character, who rejected all offers of friendship and help, was dying but had not been told. Patricia Neal played a nurse and Reagan a fiery Yank who forced Todd to accept him and the others as his family as he faced death. Todd dominated the film, and received an Academy Award nomination, but Reagan provided much of the impetus for the plot development.[67]

Reagan also performed well in his final film with Warner Bros., *The Winning Team,* one of his personal favorites. In it he played the great baseball pitcher Grover Cleveland Alexander, whose epilepsy (not mentioned on-screen) and drinking destroyed his career until he staged a remarkable comeback in the 1926 World Series. Reagan displayed a maturity and vulnerability in that role that he had seldom achieved before.[68]

Like many actors who had longed to be free agents, Reagan found the 1950s to be a difficult time to lose the security of a studio. He made several more films: *Tropic Zone* (Paramount), *Law and Order* (Universal), *Prisoner of War* (MGM), *Cattle Queen of Montana* (RKO), *Tennessee's Partner* (RKO), *Hellcats of the Navy* (Columbia), and finally, in 1964, *The Killers* (NBC-TV). These films paid his bills but did not help his career. A young actor, Robert Horton, was surprised to find himself acting with Reagan in a third-rate film, *Prisoner of War* (1954), and asked him why he was doing it. "I know it's a dog," Reagan answered, "but I'm not in a position *not* to do it." Reagan did not want to do *The Killers* but Wasserman's advice was, "take it and be grateful."[69]

Reagan was drained financially by taxes and mortgage payments on his ranch. The low point of his life, he recalled, came in February 1954 when he agreed to a well-paid but humiliating stint in a Las Vegas nightclub show. It was then that Taft Schreiber and MCA came through for him with "General Electric Theater." The deal gave Reagan $125,000 a year, increasing to $169,000. He introduced the television play each week and acted in several shows each year. He also contracted to spend a number of weeks each year touring General Electric plants and working with its community relations program. When the General Electric offer came along, Reagan did not have any bargaining power left in Hollywood: "They weren't beating a path to my door offering me parts and this television show came riding along, the cavalry to the rescue." When "General Electric Theater" ended in 1962, brother Neil Reagan, an advertising executive, repaid Ronald for his past help by lining him up as host of the television series "Death Valley Days."[70]

In a sense, Reagan chose to end his film career. After World War II he became more interested in political matters and film industry problems than in acting. Director Irving Rapper, who made *The Voice of the Turtle* with him, said that even after he shouted "Action!" Reagan was still discussing politics. During his years with General Electric, Reagan clarified his political ideology and learned to move audiences with his conservative message. By the early 1960s he had become one of the leading conservative speakers in the United States.[71]

3

The Turn toward Conservatism, 1947–1980

Conservatism poses a special problem for American historians. Many scholars cannot find an important conservative tradition in the American past; they believe, rather, that the major political parties represent variations of liberal thought and programs. If scholars recognize a conservative movement, they often regard it as the product of maladjusted and pessimistic reactionary groups that want to escape from the confusing present and to return to some lost golden age. Sometimes, in this view, right-wing demagogues spark explosions among lower-class, poorly educated people that lead to nativistic movements or to such irrational crusades as McCarthyism. More commonly scholars believe that conservative activity is a hidden force, expressing the elitist needs and quiet power of wealthy people and big business interests.[1]

Yet conservative hero and spokesman Ronald Reagan was the most optimistic of men. He did not speak the dour language of limits and decline but of a bright and sunny future. He looked backward only to define God's mission for the United States, but he energized his supporters by sketching a resplendent future of change and progress. He presented himself as the spokesman for the average American, not for a wealthy elite. If he criticized specific groups, he regarded their behavior as correctable by ordinary democratic and constitutional processes.

The conservative movement that Reagan led had deep roots in the American past. Its emergence as a powerful force in the last half of the twentieth century puzzled many scholars because they had relegated conservatism to the periphery of American history. However, conservatism had always offered a stable core of American ideas and values, and it remained a major force when it was presumably at its weakest, during the New Deal. Even while unemployment was running at 20 percent, 60 percent of Americans thought that Franklin Roosevelt's relief programs were too costly. Roosevelt, whose largest peacetime federal budget was $9 billion, was able to build a weak welfare state system only by carefully justifying it in the language of the family, religion, and local control.

After the modest liberal reforms of the New Deal era, there was a distinct rightward shift in the United States, first under Roosevelt during World War II and then in a more pronounced fashion with cold war presidents Harry S. Truman, Dwight D. Eisenhower, and their successors. Republicans won seven of the thirteen elections from Roosevelt's death through William J. "Bill" Clinton's election in 1996. In that period, conservative Republicans decimated the liberal wing of their party and helped shift the entire political spectrum to the right. Reagan and other conservative leaders exploited successive new issues: communism in the 1950s, racial problems and controversial extensions of federal power in the 1960s, gender and sexuality issues in the 1970s, national security and taxes in the 1980s.[2]

Reagan was not an original thinker who added to the body of conservative thought that he articulated so powerfully. Indeed, his unsystematic use of conservative ideas helped him to hold together the diverse groups that he led for over two decades. Virtually all conservatives, including Reagan, held two core beliefs: that flawed human nature was an unchanging mixture of both good and evil, and that an objective moral order existed, independent of humanity. Those two principles provided a common set of ideas for otherwise distinct conservative groups, and they explained the tension in conservative thought, a tension so important that some regarded it as part of the very definition of conservatism. Conservatives believed that authority was required to impose order on flawed human beings for their own and the collective well-being. Yet individuals needed freedom to bring themselves and their society into conformity with the objective moral order. The need for both authority and freedom created the continuing tension in conservative thought.[3]

After World War II, libertarian, traditional, and anticommunist conservatives, sharing the same two core beliefs, cooperated in an uneasy alliance.

They believed that they confronted a common enemy, and they struggled to assess the meaning for the twentieth century of the collectivism of V. I. Lenin's and Joseph Stalin's communism, of Benito Mussolini's and Adolf Hitler's fascism, and of Franklin and Eleanor Roosevelt's New Dealism. To libertarians, the 1930s represented the rise of big government, to traditional conservatives it was the decade of nihilism and mass society, and to the anticommunists it was, simply, the Red Decade.

While most conservatives could easily distinguish Roosevelt's America from the totalitarianism of fascist Germany and the communist Soviet Union, they believed that the New Deal had started the United States down a path toward collectivism. To conservatives, Roosevelt's New Deal was based on relativistic moral values and a misguided belief in humankind's perfectibility. They protested the redistribution of political power and economic wealth that came with the welfare state and the progressive tax structure. They opposed the regulatory state's interference with the capitalist marketplace. They criticized Keynesian economic planning and Roosevelt's cavalier attitude toward what seemed at the time to be an enormous federal budget deficit. Many conservatives, formerly isolationists, had difficulty accepting Roosevelt's and Truman's internationalism. They believed that Truman threatened local authority when he added civil rights for black Americans to the liberal agenda, and they opposed Lyndon B. Johnson's Great Society programs that extended new social and health benefits to poor, elderly, and minority people.[4]

Libertarian conservatives resisted what seemed an inexorable movement toward collectivism. Economists Friedrich A. von Hayek and Ludwig von Mises influenced the postwar generation with their arguments that individual freedom depended on limited government and a largely unfettered capitalist marketplace. Journalists and essayists founded such publications as *Human Events* and *The Freeman* and formed societies to exchange ideas and promote conservative programs. By the mid-1950s, libertarian conservatives had produced a body of literature extolling individualism and the free marketplace and assaulting mass society and New Deal statism.[5]

A group of young university scholars energized traditional conservatism. One of the most influential was University of Chicago English professor Richard M. Weaver, who in *Ideas Have Consequences* (1948) traced the horrors of twentieth-century war, revolution, and mass society to the dissolution of Western civilization that began before 1500. The West had abandoned its belief in absolute and eternal truths and had placed its faith in relativism, rationalism, and human perfectibility. Secularism and pragmatism, Weaver found, had eroded the moral foundations required for free, democratic societies. Eric Voegelin, Leo Strauss, Russell Kirk, and other scholars explored Western history for the sources of its decadence. They searched for the "Great Tradition," the moral foundation of Western civilization, as a way to escape the madness and deadly relativism of the twentieth century. Most of these thinkers turned to Christianity as the necessary foundation for an orderly society.

Traditional conservatives accepted the authority of tradition and the existence of eternal truths. Libertarians fretted under any restraints on the free individual. Both groups were antistatist, but traditionalists found more room for government to regulate behavior than did libertarians, with their emphasis on individual freedom and a self-governing marketplace. While traditional conservatives spoke of absolute values, spiritual life, and family and community, libertarians stressed material needs and viewed capitalism as society's essential foundation. Traditionalists wanted to conserve, while capitalism was an engine for unceasing change.[6]

Reagan appealed to both groups, seeing the need for both order and freedom: "My political philosophy has been called conservative. I don't know if that is the proper word or not. I believe our system was created to give the ultimate in individual freedom consistent with an orderly society. Government exists to protect us from each other—not from ourselves."[7]

The tension between libertarians and traditionalists was partly resolved by a third strain of postwar conservative thought, anticommunism. All conservatives abhorred communism, which threatened capitalism and rejected belief in God, tradition, and absolute values. Most conservatives valued free speculation, but they also believed that society had the right and duty to protect itself by suppressing communism within the United States. Many agreed with William F. Buckley Jr., who in 1952 said that the battle against communism temporarily required high taxes, big government, and a powerful military establishment. Anticommunism helped conservative politicians shed their prewar isolationism, and most conservatives supported Senator Joe McCarthy's anticommunist crusade, although some deplored his tactics.

Communism provided conservatives with a common enemy, and it provided an issue that mainstream politicians—usually Republicans—could use to recruit such individuals as SAG leader Ronald Reagan. Anticommunism also had a populist edge to it that Senator Barry M. Goldwater (Rep., Ariz.) and Ronald Reagan drew on to broaden conservatism's appeal and to erode its identification with big business. The huge American middle class provided the essential barrier against communism, and postwar conservatives began to cast their message toward that "silent majority."[8]

In the early 1950s, conservative intellectuals and political activists seemed to confront a hopeless situation. The liberal Democratic Party, based on the powerful Roosevelt coalition of urban labor, small farmers, new immigrants, much of the middle class, and most journalists and university intellectuals, controlled the political center. The Republican Party seemed to offer conservatives the best path to power, but Eisenhower's moderate and liberal followers, the hated "Eastern establishment," dominated it. Eisenhower Republicans accepted Roosevelt's welfare state and Truman's containment policy, which conservatives criticized as not being aggressive enough in fighting Soviet communism.

Yet as the decade passed power began to shift within the Republican Party, a change that continued at a faster pace in the 1960s. Population and wealth grew rapidly in the West, Southwest, and South, expanding the Republican Party's conservative base. Sunbelt conservative Republicans innovated techniques of "bottom-up" campaigning, with grassroots organizing and fund-raising. Intellectuals like Buckley and politicians like Goldwater cooperated in devising programs and policies true to conservative principles and popular enough to win elections. Conservative Republicans stressed individual initiative rather than welfare state programs, free enterprise instead of government regulation, and local control over such matters as taxes, education, and race relations. They advocated a more aggressive anti-Soviet foreign policy than Truman's containment program. They began to clean up their own house by rejecting anti-Semitism, overt racism, and the extreme McCarthyism that had led such groups as the John Birch Society to name Eisenhower and other popular figures as communist sympathizers.[9]

Reagan did not contribute to the formulation of postwar conservative thought, but he was a powerful spokesman for those ideas. He also was one of the first to sense that change was coming. On 27 June 1959 he described to Richard Nixon the positive reaction to his, Reagan's, speeches: "I am convinced there is a ground swell of economic conservatism building up which could reverse the entire tide of present day 'statism.' As a matter of fact we seem to be in one of those rare moments when the American people with that wisdom which is the strength of Democracy are ready to say 'enough!'"[10]

While conservative intellectuals and activists were sorting out their similarities and differences in the 1950s, Reagan was making his trek to the right. The journey was not as long or as difficult as it seemed in Reagan folklore. Ronald Reagan was never as deeply liberal as he believed he was. He loved Franklin Roosevelt for his style and rhetoric and bold leadership rather than for his welfare and regulatory state programs. He regarded Roosevelt as a heroic figure who failed to understand that the emergency programs and bureaucracies he built would take on a life of their own. He believed that the Democratic Party had been taken over by "tax-and-spend" liberals who had forgotten the warnings of Thomas Jefferson and Woodrow Wilson that government was a threat to liberty.

In the immediate postwar era he had become a fervent anticommunist and had helped destroy the most militant labor union in Hollywood. He had become an FBI informer and a cold warrior who found Truman's foreign policy too accommodating to the Soviet Union. He had developed an absolute hatred for taxes required by the welfare state programs. As SAG president, he had lobbied against government economic regulations that had forced studios to divest their theater chains, thereby destroying the studio system that had given him economic security. He campaigned for Truman in 1948, but he never supported another Democratic presidential candidate.[11]

Reagan's conservative thought was founded on his absolute belief in American exceptionalism, the idea that he would develop movingly in his verbal portraits of America as God's shining "City on a Hill." In June 1952 Reagan delivered the commencement address at William Woods College in Fulton, Missouri. He did not use the phrase "City on a Hill," but the idea was there. America is less a place than an idea "that has been deep in the souls of man ever since man started his long trail from the swamps," he told his audience. "It is nothing but the inherent love of freedom. . . . It is simply the idea, the basis of this country and of our religion, the idea of the dignity of man, the idea that deep within the heart of each one of us is something so God-like and precious that no individual or group has a right to impose his or its will upon the people, that no group can decide for the people what is good for the people so well as they can decide for themselves." Summing up, Reagan said, "I, in my own mind, have thought of America as a place in the divine scheme of things that was set aside as a promised land."[12]

During the 1950s Reagan honed his message into what his admirers called "the Speech," and he became one of the nation's most popular conservative orators. He sharpened his antitax, anticommunist, City on a Hill themes during his eight years as spokesman for General Electric. The company was so right-wing, said one of its employees, "that it was not unlike the John Birch Society." Ralph J. Cordiner, General Electric's president, wanted to decentralize management of the company's 139 plants scattered over thirty-nine states. He had Reagan tour the plants to keep the employees linked in a corporate community. When Reagan arrived at a plant, he usually met the managers, then spoke to an assembly of workers, followed that night by an address to a local civic or veterans' group.[13]

Edward Langley, a General Electric public relations man who traveled with Reagan, estimated that Reagan spoke nine thousand times on his tours. "Reagan was steeped in, saturated with and overpowered by Middle America," he said. Reagan's appearances before the 250,000 company employees and the various Rotary Clubs, Chambers of Commerce, and other civic bodies shaped him into the public figure the nation saw when he entered politics in the 1960s, Langley believed: "It would have changed Jane Fonda into Margaret Thatcher." Reagan believed that his years with General Electric helped him direct his evolving populist brand of conservatism toward working- and middle-class people. He added to his antitax, patriotic, and anticommunist themes a probusiness, antigovernment, essentially anti–New Deal message.[14]

His 1961 talk entitled "Encroaching Control" was a typical version of the Speech. He opened by describing the attempted communist takeover of Hollywood. Reagan said that the United States was losing its struggle with the Soviet Union because Americans did not understand communism and did not know that they were at war. Karl Marx had said that communism and capitalism could not coexist and that the American way of life must be destroyed so communism could be built on its ruins, according to Reagan. Since the United States was too strong to be overcome militarily, the Kremlin intended to subvert it step by step, socialist measure by socialist measure. Reagan typically laced his speeches with quotations, in this case from Soviet premier Nikita Khrushchev: "We can't expect the American people to jump from Capitalism to Communism, but we can assist their elected leaders in giving them small doses of Socialism, until they awaken one day to find they have Communism."

"Encroaching control" was embodied in measures sponsored by liberal Democrats, Reagan continued. The communists used the American people's humanitarian nature, their urge to help the less fortunate, to subvert the United States, he charged. The next major step toward "statism" would be government-financed medical care. It had started already in the Veterans Administration, where 75 percent of its hospital beds were filled with people hospitalized from illnesses not related to their military service. With a flood of statistics that he typically laced through the Speech, Reagan claimed that 70 percent of all citizens had private medical insurance and that coverage would rise to 90 percent by 1970. Helping the 10 percent who did not have insurance did not require a government takeover of the entire medical system, he argued.

He discussed other examples of "encroaching control" and said that tax revenues fueled the whole statist structure: "We have received this progressive tax direct from Karl Marx who designed it as the prime essential of a socialist state. . . . There can be no moral justification of the progressive tax." Taxation was a primary tool of subversion: "No nation in history has ever survived a tax burden of one-third of its national income. Today, 31 percent out of every dollar earned is tax."[15]

Reagan was not an original thinker and did not bring an intellectually rigorous analysis to his speeches. He fit his anticommunist, traditional, and libertarian conservative message into a package that made emotional sense to his listeners. Richard Nixon told his speechwriters that he wished he could aim for the people's hearts the way Reagan did.[16]

By the late 1950s Reagan was increasingly identified as a conservative spokesman. In 1960 he gave two hundred campaign speeches for Nixon. In 1961 the AFL-CIO tagged him as an extremist, and the Federation of Teachers in St. Paul, Minnesota, objected to Reagan's appearance at a local high school. Some associates on "General Electric Theater" believed that his anticommunism had gotten out of hand. Two of them recalled an argument with him about a plot involving religion and communism. One said that Reagan told them, "Any atheist is a Communist and any American family that doesn't teach its children to pray is a Communist family."[17]

As Reagan became more politically controversial, General Electric tried to get him to drop the Speech and concentrate on promoting company goodwill. Reagan refused. In 1962 "General Electric Theater" ratings began to slip, and the company canceled the show. Reagan never knew if General Electric killed the program because of the lower ratings or the controversy surrounding him.[18]

In the 1960s Reagan and the conservatives faced what appeared to be overpowering liberal domination of politics. Many analysts regarded conservatism as a spent force, irrelevant except in some southern backwaters. Yet even as conservatives suffered defeat at the ballot boxes, a new vitality made itself felt. After John F. Kennedy defeated Richard Nixon in 1960, conservative intellectuals and politicians found ways to work together, and they began a drive to take over the Republican Party.

The relationship between Reagan and the pragmatic but conservative-oriented Richard Nixon typified these new alliances. In 1950, Reagan had campaigned against Nixon when he ran against Helen Gahagan Douglas, but afterward Reagan began to revise his opinion of the vice president. The politically astute Nixon, who quickly recognized Reagan's potential importance on the national scene, became a perceptive Reagan watcher. On 18 June 1959 Nixon complimented Reagan on the Speech and said that it expressed "solid thinking" about the dangers of tax-and-spend politicians. Three weeks later he again wrote and encouraged Reagan to continue speaking: "You have the ability of putting complicated technical ideas into words everyone can understand. Those of us who have spent a number of years in Washington too often lack the ability to express ourselves in this way."[19]

As Nixon prepared to run for the presidency in 1960, Reagan offered him some advice. He said that based on the reaction to his speeches he believed that Americans were economically conservative and might respond to a Republican who refused to try to outbid the Democrats on spending programs. He derided the platitudes that he had heard from the Democratic convention but said, "I do not include Kennedy's acceptance speech because beneath the generalities I heard a frightening call to arms. Unfortunately he is a powerful speaker with an appeal to the emotions." He added: "One last thought—shouldn't someone tag Mr. Kennedy's *bold new imaginative* program with its proper name. Under the tousled boyish hair cut it is still old Karl Marx—first launched a century ago. There is nothing new in the idea of a Gov't being Big Brother to us all. Hitler called his 'State Socialism' and way before him it was 'benevolent monarchy.' "[20]

Reagan, for all his advice to Nixon, was ideologically closer to Barry Goldwater. Goldwater was sometimes referred to as Reagan's John the Baptist. Their ideas were similar (although Goldwater would later prove more libertarian on social issues), and they both were supreme marketers of conservative ideas. Goldwater spoke of religion, family, and community, of the value of hard work, and of freedom balanced with order. He sensed that the middle class was uneasy with the direction the nation was taking. The bold and blunt-spoken Arizona senator captured national attention in the late 1950s as he gently but firmly separated himself from the moderate wing of the Republican Party led by Eisenhower. At the 1960 Republican convention he called on conservatives to organize: "If we want to take this party back—and I think we can some day—let's get to work." F. Clifton White, William A. Rusher, and other young conservatives took him at his word and organized to capture the 1964 Republican nomination.

In the 1964 campaign Democrats easily turned Goldwater's western style and blunt speech into the image of a gunslinger itching to get his finger on the nuclear button; his call for rededication to freedom ("Extremism in the defense of liberty is no vice and . . . moderation in the pursuit of justice is no virtue") was interpreted as an endorsement of McCarthyism; his belief in local control of schools was seen as approving racial segregation; his free-market economic policies were portrayed as throwbacks to nineteenth-century social Darwinism.[21]

Despite Lyndon Johnson's landslide victory over Goldwater, young conservatives found a sense of solidarity during the campaign and developed new political and organizational skills, especially in working at the grassroots level. They noted that Goldwater had received twenty-seven million votes and had found widespread support in the South. Of the 507 southern counties Goldwater carried, 233 had never before voted Republican. Johnson won a clear majority of white voters only in Texas. Goldwater also showed such notable strength in northern Irish, German, and Italian Catholic neighborhoods that Republican political analyst Kevin Phillips predicted a realignment among northeastern Catholics away from the party of Roosevelt to that of Goldwater and Reagan.[22]

There was another bright spot for the conservatives amid the ruins of the Goldwater campaign. Reagan's nationally televised speech for Goldwater on 27 October 1964 lightened the gloom of impending defeat. Several wealthy Republicans (including the core of Reagan's early political backers, A. C. "Cy" Rubel, Holmes P. Tuttle, and Henry Salvatori) heard Reagan speak for Goldwater and were so impressed that they bought time for Reagan to deliver "A Time for Choosing" on NBC television.

In the speech Reagan said that the issues the nation confronted were so great that Democrats should cross party lines and vote for Goldwater. It had been stated in the campaign that Americans have never had it so good, Reagan said

> but I have an uncomfortable feeling that this prosperity isn't something on which we can base our hopes for the future. No nation in history has ever survived a tax burden that reached a third of its national income. Today thirty-seven cents out of every dollar earned in this country is the tax collector's share, and yet our government continues to spend $17 million a day more than the government takes in. We haven't balanced our budget twenty-eight out of the last thirty-four years. We've raised our debt limit three times in the last twelve months, and now our national debt is one and one-half times bigger than all the combined debts of all the nations of the world. We have $15 billion in gold in our treasury; we don't own an ounce. Foreign dollars claims are $27.3 billion, and we've just had announced that the dollar of 1939 will now purchase forty-five cents in its total value. As for the peace that we would preserve, I wonder who among us would like to approach the wife or mother whose husband or son has died in South Vietnam and ask them if they think this is a peace that should be maintained indefinitely.

Behind the Vietnam War, he noted, was the Soviet Union, the most dangerous enemy humanity had faced on its climb from the swamp on its way to the stars.

He said this in the first two minutes of the broadcast, and he continued with a flood of facts and statistics for nearly thirty more minutes. He spoke rapidly, with a sense of urgency. Viewers who knew Reagan only from his films must have been startled by the transformation and made uneasy about the state of the nation by his fact-laden presentation. He portrayed the United States as humanity's last hope and argued that the election would determine if we would maintain our heritage of freedom. It is not a choice of left and right, he said, but of up and down; up toward individual freedom or down to the "ant heap of totalitarianism." "You and I have a rendezvous with destiny. We'll preserve for our children this, the last best hope of man on earth, or we'll sentence them to take the last step into a thousand years of darkness," he said in his closing.[23]

"A Time for Choosing," seen in 4,260,000 homes, brought money pouring into the Goldwater campaign. Journalist David S. Broder estimated that Reagan's speech brought in $600,000, a large amount in 1964, and Reagan later claimed it garnered $8 million after the Republican National Committee rebroadcast it twice and local Goldwater groups used it hundreds of times.[24]

After the election Reagan issued a call to arms to his conservative comrades, angry at Republicans who had not supported Goldwater: "I don't think we should turn the high command [of the Republican Party] over to leaders who were traitors during the battle just ended. The conservative philosophy was not repudiated." On the day after the election, a group of Michigan Republicans formed a Reagan for president club, and early in 1965 F. Clifton White and the group that had engineered Goldwater's nomination made overtures to Reagan.[25]

While the conservatives were regrouping after the 1964 defeat, the liberals began to self-destruct. In 1964 and 1965, Lyndon Johnson guided through Congress legislation that destroyed legalized segregation in the South, added Medicare and Medicaid to the welfare state structure, and began his War on Poverty with an array of Great Society programs. He made racial justice his highest priority and changed the focus of civil rights programs from establishing equal opportunity to insuring equal outcomes.

In those heady days Johnson seemed to be a political genius who would bring to completion the progressive-liberal reform agenda, and the Republican Party seemed unable to resist. Yet even in 1965, Johnson's support began to fracture, and in 1968 he had to withdraw from the presidential race to avoid almost certain defeat. Some blamed Johnson's troubles on racial disturbances, starting with the Watts riot in Los Angeles, on national divisions over the Vietnam War, and on Johnson's own arrogance and excesses. But as years passed and the conflicts of the 1960s deepened and widened, analysts realized that something more was at work. At the 1992 Republican Party convention, conservative political leader Patrick J. Buchanan proclaimed that the nation was locked in a cultural war, a war for "the soul of America." The culture war was fought to define America; it was a struggle for power by contending groups, each hoping to impose on the nation its moral system. Conservatives used the culture war, especially the so-called social issues involving race, family, and crime, to destroy the Roosevelt coalition by driving wedges between traditional New Deal constituencies. Reagan was at the center of the war, both as a product of it and as a general in it, commanding territory first seized by Goldwater, Nixon, and Alabama governor George C. Wallace.[26]

The politics of race underlay much of the cultural conflict. Urban riots and black militancy brought to northern cities and national politics an issue that many people thought had been confined to rural areas of the South. Racial politics drove the battles over welfare programs, forced busing to achieve racial balance in public schools, and, especially in the 1970s, affirmative action programs. The politics of race revolved around fairness issues, perceived threats to the family, and communities' rights to preserve local customs and control.

Political war over race took hold just as Americans confronted changes in the global economy. At the end of World War II, the United States produced nearly half of all the goods produced in the world. From the 1940s through the 1960s the American standard of living rapidly increased and encouraged the middle class to extend the welfare state safety net to more people. Then in the early 1970s the American economy stalled. Racked by high inflation and unemployment, economic performance sputtered. Middle-class people lost their feeling of security, and even if they continued to do well they feared that their children would not be able to duplicate their success. The politics of race took place in these straitened economic conditions, with the middle class increasingly intolerant of taxes and welfare programs that they believed took money from them to give to people whose lifestyle they condemned.[27]

Liberalism had weaknesses that had not been apparent in the 1960s. Many working- and middle-class members of the Roosevelt coalition had never been ideological liberals. They were socially conservative people who valued family, religion, and community and were Roosevelt loyalists because he had helped them economically. Roosevelt had carefully avoided dealing with race or abortion or other such issues that might have offended them. In August 1965, a few days after Lyndon Johnson signed the Voting Rights Act, which whites regarded as a major victory for black people, the Watts rebellion began and thirty-five people died. After that came racial explosions in other northern cities, including Chicago, Philadelphia, Newark, Cleveland, and Detroit. While many white liberals understood and sympathized with the rage that produced black militancy, many moderate and conservative Americans, especially middle- and working-class whites, did not. They believed that they were being asked to pay for an array of programs to benefit blacks who did not appreciate white people's sacrifices or their values. In the early 1960s most white Americans, watching television programs showing peacefully demonstrating blacks being attacked by southern white mobs, believed that white behavior was an important source of black problems. By the 1970s and 1980s, in one of the most important shifts of opinion in modern times, most white Americans believed that black people's behavior was mainly responsible for their problems.[28]

Although liberals dismissed white backlash against the civil rights revolution as simple racism, it was more complex than that. Racial change and conflict often occurred in the schools and neighborhoods of white working- and lower-middle-class people. It was their children, schools, and neighborhoods that were subjected to change, not those of affluent white liberals living in suburbs and sending their children to private schools. Reagan spoke to the anxieties of these Americans, like the carpenter in Brooklyn who said, "The rich liberals, they look down on my little piece of the American dream, my little backyard with the barbecue here. . . . But we've invested everything we have in this house and neighborhood."[29]

Conservative politicians quickly learned to tap this resentment. Reagan detested racism and bigotry. Still, he benefited from the politics of race. In most circles it had become politically unacceptable in the 1950s and afterward to express belief in biological racial inferiority of blacks. Politicians like Nixon, Reagan, and George Bush, however, learned to use a coded language to refer to race. In the context of the 1960s and afterward their attacks on welfare abuses, street crime, and affirmative action all had racial overtones. Democrat George Wallace devised an attack that proved to be a powerful weapon in Republican hands. He accused the liberal elite of engaging in "reverse discrimination," favoring blacks over whites. Nixon developed an additional strategy. He affirmed his belief in racial equality, but called for local enforcement of civil rights laws. Many whites responded to such messages.[30]

As liberal Democrats struggled with the politics of race, they blundered into a trap of their own making when John F. Kennedy escalated the cold war. As the "best and brightest" stumbled into the Bay of Pigs, recklessly endangered the world in the Cuban missile crisis, and sent troops into the Vietnam War, many young men and women moved leftward. Many in the New Left regarded liberal Democrats, not conservatives, as their particular enemy, because the liberals' imperialistic foreign policy was leading them to try to make the whole world into the American image and their timid welfare state programs mainly benefited upper- and middle-class people. Many young leftists concluded that the liberal elite initiated wars, the middle class paid for them in taxes, and poor whites and blacks fought them. Ironically, as liberal Democrats such as Eugene J. McCarthy, Robert F. Kennedy, and George S. McGovern turned against the war, the Democratic Party became identified with the antiwar New Left, even though most leftists detested the liberals.

The antiwar movement proved to be a trap for liberals. Most Americans, especially the working and lower middle classes, regarded the antiwar movement as a betrayal of the soldiers in Vietnam and as an unpatriotic attack on the nation. The sight of privileged young middle-class students shutting down colleges, desecrating the flag, and engaging in profane attacks on the police and national leaders appalled most older Americans. Many of them smothered their own doubts about the war, since opposing it meant, it seemed, supporting bearded radicals ridiculing values and myths that the middle class viewed as the source of American greatness. Middle-class people believed that they had played by the rules of society, had obeyed the law, and had lived by the work ethic. They believed that they had provided their families with opportunities for education that they themselves had not enjoyed, and that they had given their children the privileges and luxuries offered by the booming post–World War II economy. After enjoying those advantages, many young members of the so-called counterculture rejected their parents' way of life, and, verbally at least, scorned middle-class consumerism and materialism.[31]

Conflict over civil rights, the Vietnam War, and changing lifestyles set off a ferment of new ideas that led to questioning of almost every aspect of American life. Environmentalists, for example, fought to gain control of decision making on resource use. Feminists raised fundamental questions about traditional values and behavior and challenged patriarchal power in the family, education, government, and corporations. Economic pressures, such as inflation, forced millions of middle- and working-class women into the job marketplace and that, aside from feminism, had profound effects on gender roles and the traditional family structure.

Gays, Americans with disabilities, and other groups facing discrimination entered the arena to demand protection for their rights. In the 1970s and 1980s the culture war enveloped every level of the political system, from school boards to the presidency. Fights over abortion, gay rights, affirmative action, values taught in public education, multiculturalism in schools and other public institutions, and scores of other issues wracked a political system not designed to handle them. These came to be known as the "social issues," and they were often fought out in terms of the family. To many conservatives, patriarchal gender roles and family structure were ordained by God. Abortion, gay rights, and affirmative action all affected family values and were moral issues not subject to compromise.[32]

During the 1960s the Democratic Party increasingly fell into the hands of a liberal elite that had few ties to the less affluent white voters upon which Roosevelt had built his coalition. This elite, the "limousine liberals," did not understand that to many members of the Democratic coalition, Great Society programs violated deeply held beliefs in the work ethic and in traditional meritocratic values. Liberal intellectuals abandoned to conservatives serious discussion of issues concerning crime, family and community problems, need for welfare reform, and the relationship between individual responsibility and rights. Journalists Thomas B. and Mary D. Edsall, in describing the breakdown of the Roosevelt coalition, wrote, "For the white patrolman passed over for promotion to sergeant in favor of a black or Hispanic who scored lower on a test; for the elderly Catholic landlady required by law to lease the apartment on her third floor to a homosexual couple; for the night worker in New York who must ride the subway with the no longer confinable deranged; for the nurse assaulted in the hospital parking lot by a criminal out on bail; for the divorced secretary whose children were bused by court order to a school in a distant and unfamiliar neighborhood, the logic of social and racial liberalism was difficult, if not impossible, to grasp." The word "liberal," carried proudly by New Deal and Fair Deal Democrats running for office, now became a pejorative term that politicians used to attack opponents.[33]

In 1968, George Wallace, taking advantage of the growing discontent with racial unrest, antiwar demonstrations, and the rise of the counterculture, showed politicians the potential of a populist-oriented conservatism. He attacked the liberal elite in the name of the "little people" and based his political movement on a defense of the family and community. Nixon learned from Wallace and gave conservative politicians lessons in the politics of symbolism. His tough stand on "law and order" was heard as a call for suppressing racial disturbances and black militancy. He demonstrated the power of populist rhetoric, with his references to the "forgotten American" and the "silent majority," composed, he said, of people who loved their country, respected the family, prized individual initiative, and practiced decorum in behavior.[34]

Conservatism thrived in the 1970s. Conservative think tanks and publications made themselves felt in academia and in Washington. Neoconservative intellectuals invigorated political dialogue and, in the minds of many opinion makers, brought new respectability to the conservative drive for power and its attack on the state. Neoconservative leaders, often former liberal Democrats, included Irving Kristol, Nathan Glazer, Norman Podhoretz, Jeane J. Kirkpatrick, Ben J. Wattenberg, and Max M. Kampelman. Many of them had been cold-war liberals who had supported strong national defense and aggressive application of Truman's containment policy. They were horrified by George McGovern's antiwar campaign in 1972 and by what they perceived as President Jimmy Carter's weak foreign policy leadership. In domestic affairs, they believed that Great Society programs were inefficient and ineffective.[35]

The culture war continued, widening and deepening the splits in the American polity. As the civil rights movement waned and the Vietnam War ground down, new issues divided Americans, especially the fight over the Equal Rights Amendment (ERA), which would have provided a constitutional guarantee of gender equality. Conservatives often portrayed feminism as the product of an affluent liberal elite imposing its values on working- and middle-class women. Actually modern feminism had its roots far back in the nineteenth century, stemming from the effect on gender roles of the industrial revolution and from new ways of thinking unleashed by the French and American Revolutions. The biggest effect on gender relations in the late twentieth century came from the free-market system that pulled millions of married women into the workplace. Feminism did not change women's roles, as conservatives charged; rather, feminism responded to deep, long-term social and economic changes.[36]

By the end of the 1970s few politicians wanted to be tagged with the label "feminist" despite widespread support for the women's movement on many issues. Most Americans, for example, supported ERA and the 1973 Supreme Court decision, *Roe v. Wade,* that legalized abortions. Yet in 1980 they elected Ronald Reagan, who opposed abortion rights and ERA. Perhaps antifeminists felt more strongly on such issues than did profeminist voters, but more important, feminist issues came to be fought out over family values, and in the fight over the family, conservatives won. Conservatives learned to cast all issues in family terms: fighting crime, drugs, and pornography or opposing ERA, abortion, the welfare state (which they said financed divorce and illegitimate births). Most Americans wanted women to be treated fairly in the workplace, but they still felt ambivalent about the effect of changing gender roles on the family.[37]

In the 1970s the cultural war took on increased intensity because the American economy stagnated, and voters became more resistant to high taxes and expensive government programs. The United States share of gross world product had dropped from 40 percent in 1950 to 23 percent in 1970; its share of world trade dropped from 20 percent to 11 percent. Inflation increased, as did unemployment, and Keynesian methods of economic management no longer seemed to work. Global economic change shattered the assumption that Americans could expect a steadily increasing standard of living. Those changes again hurt the liberal Democrats, who since the Great Depression had portrayed themselves as the group best able to manage the economy.[38]

In the 1970s, the Republican mainstream moved rapidly to the right, and politicians who had once seemed conservative, like Gerald R. Ford, now came to be seen as suspiciously moderate or even liberal. Since the Great

Depression the Republican Party had been tagged as the party of big business. Now its leaders saw that it could become the party of family values and that they could use that tag to unite economic and social conservatives. Conservative Republicans understood the implications of the statement that most voters were "unyoung, unpoor, and unblack." In the 1950s they had tended to distrust the masses, but by the 1970s they were developing a right-wing populism. Populist, antiestablishment feeling in the United States had traditionally directed its anger at big business. Reagan redirected that anger and identified the establishment as the government. The enemy, he said, was the government, and he promised to get it off the backs of the people.[39]

The shock troops in the culture war in the 1970s came from the New Right, which made an explicit populist appeal. The New Right placed more stress on the social issues than had older conservatives, and leaders like Richard A. Viguerie, Howard Phillips, and Paul M. Weyrich were innovative and aggressive in using modern technology to get the conservative message out at a grassroots level. Jesse Helms (Rep., N. Car.), Newt Gingrich (Rep., Ga.), and Patrick Buchanan were sometimes labeled as New Right politicians. New Right allies included anti-ERA leader Phyllis S. Schlafly and television ministers Marion G. "Pat" Robertson and Jerry L. Falwell.

Much of the New Right's vigor and organizational base came from its alliance with the Religious Right. This was not merely a pragmatic political alliance. The New Right, like the Christian conservatives, believed that beneath liberal inefficiency and ineffectiveness lay moral relativism and secularism that threatened the nation. When Baptist minister Jerry Falwell called a meeting of conservative leaders, Weyrich suggested the name "Moral Majority" for the new organization they formed.[40]

The Religious Right included evangelicals and fundamentalists. Members of both groups usually considered themselves "born-again Christians," but fundamentalists tended to stress more than evangelicals the inerrancy of the Bible. They separated more than the evangelicals from "mainstream" Christian churches and from the political world, which fundamentalists regarded as a worldly place of sin and chaos, redeemable only by Christ's return to earth. Despite the assumption by many liberal scholars, the Religious Right was not confined to southern backwaters or to the poor and uneducated classes. Its members had proved able to cope successfully with modern society and prosper within it, while retaining their conservative religious beliefs. Their growing strength in numbers and confidence in their beliefs encouraged them to oppose actively the threat that secular society posed to their God-imbued lifestyle. Supreme Court decisions designed to limit religious activity to the home and private life inflamed the Religious Right because its members believed that religion should be the center of life, not removed to the periphery.[41]

Religious Right members were not monolithic, but they were more likely to be conservative on the social issues than the general public. The Religious Right represented millions of politically mobilized voters who brought new fervor to Republican ranks and brought a heavily theological content to party affairs. They made support for the social issues, like opposition to abortion, into the litmus test for politicians seeking election.[42]

Reagan had an unsurpassed ability to retain the support of these diverse groups of conservatives. He maintained his ties with the older groups of traditional, libertarian, and anticommunist conservatives and was seen as a populist conservative at a time when the New Right was moving in a populist direction. He displayed the same sensitivity to the rising power of the evangelicals and fundamentalists. He had formed ties with conservative Christians before they began to mobilize politically. In the 1950s his mother-in-law had introduced him to evangelist William F. "Billy" Graham and they became friends. In 1964 the Reagans began to attend the Bel Air Presbyterian Church and developed a close relationship with its evangelical minister, Donn Moomaw. When Reagan became governor of California he said he wanted to run the office according to the teaching of Jesus. He twice asked Graham to address the legislature and asked him to discuss with his California cabinet the second coming of Christ. Reagan frequently, privately and publicly, talked about God and the power of prayer. "I believe," he wrote, "our nation hungers for a spiritual revival." He believed that the Bible contained all answers to personal and social problems, that prayers were heard and answered, and that God had a personal plan for each individual. He was interested in Biblical prophecy and discussed the apocalypse in terms of nuclear war. In answer to the question of whether he was a "born-again Christian," Reagan said that term was not used in his Christian Church, but "I can't remember a time in my life when I didn't call upon God. . . . Yes, I have had an experience that could be described as 'born again.'" In 1980 he told a convention of evangelical and fundamentalist ministers that "I know you can't endorse me, but I want you to know that I endorse you and what you are doing."[43]

Conservative political organizations were awash in money in the 1970s. The New Right and Religious Right were innovative and aggressive in using new technology to tap grassroots funds. But big business also began to pour money into conservative political organizations. Many of the nation's largest firms had been part of the liberal corporate state and had been willing in good times to strengthen social harmony by agreeing to pay high wages and to support welfare state programs that sheltered workers from the full effect of the free workings of the capitalist marketplace. Many big business leaders easily accepted government regulation of the economy to protect consumers and workers and to guard the environment.

In 1973 and 1974, economic conditions changed and the economy stagnated. Corporate profits fell from a postwar-high average of 13.7 percent in 1965 to about 8 percent in the early 1970s; productivity growth almost ceased. The postwar age of affluence, the American economic empire, and the welfare state that had characterized a whole period of history, now all fell at the same time, said sociologist Jerome L. Himmelstein. While corporate leaders realized that a changing global economy accounted for most of their difficulties, they believed that high taxes, costly regulations, and expensive labor costs made their problems harder to solve. As economic stagnation worsened under Carter, the perception faded that the Democratic Party was the party of good times, and big business leaders brought the power of corporate America behind the conservative agenda. Corporations poured money into political action committees (PACs). In 1974 labor PACs outnumbered corporate PACs 201 to 89. By July 1980 there were 1,204 corporate PACs, while labor committees stayed about the same; big business poured $19.2 million into political activities in that year.[44]

Conservatism retained its base of traditional, libertarian, and anticommunist adherents, and added a populist cast from the New Right and the Religious Right, and reestablished a profitable relationship with a newly mobilized corporate community. Through all of these changes, Ronald Reagan remained one of the foremost spokesmen for conservatism, and by the 1970s he was the conservatives' choice for president. Reagan never had to make many adjustments in his standard pitch for the free marketplace and against communism. His speeches had always referred to the centrality of God in life and to the value of work, family, freedom, and community. He believed that liberalism threatened capitalism and eroded the moral foundations of society, but despite the dangers he described, he always ended his speeches with an optimistic vision of the future. He rejected the "root-canal conservatism" that had stressed sacrifice and limits to human achievement. He believed in progress because he believed that the United States was God's City on a Hill: "Into the hands of America God has placed an afflicted mankind. . . . I truly believe that to be an American is to be a part of a nation with a destiny[,] that God put this land here between the great oceans to be discovered by a special kind of people and that God intended America to be free."[45]

Reagan tapped into the resentment uncovered by Wallace and Nixon, but he mined it without expressing the anger and bitterness that often had characterized conservative leaders. He seldom attacked individuals or groups by name, and when he did criticize feminists, prochoice groups, or gay rights advocates, he presented them as misguided people who did not understand the consequences of their actions, rather than as evil individuals beyond redemption. He helped conservatives move beyond racism, bigotry, and McCarthyism. He tapped the middle- and working-class anxiety about changing gender and race relations but used inoffensive neutral language. He portrayed government as the main evil to be fought; it was big government that seduced big business and labor into transgressions against the free marketplace. He placed his attacks on big government in a theological context that pleased religious conservatives: "We are not to have graven images, or to have any other Gods before Him. Sometimes I fear that with the best of intentions, with only a desire to help those less fortunate, we are making a god of government. A Samaritan crossed over the road and helped the beaten pilgrim himself—he did not report the case to the nearest welfare agency."[46]

Reagan proved to be a man for all conservative seasons. He helped conservatives to develop positive and popular programs and to formulate an optimistic vision of the future, leaving behind the negative and ineffectual carping of many past Republican leaders. By 1966, he had his message honed to perfection and was ready to face the test of electoral politics.

4

Governing California, 1967–1974

Conservatives took Barry Goldwater's defeat in 1964 as a summons to seize control of the Republican Party. On 10 November 1964 Ronald Reagan attacked Republicans who had refused to support Goldwater. "We don't intend to turn the Republican Party over to the traitors in the battle just ended. We will have no more of those candidates who are pledged to the same goals of our opposition and who seek our support," he said. "Turning the Party over to the so-called moderates wouldn't make any sense at all."[1]

Reagan's campaign speeches for Goldwater convinced wealthy oil man Henry Salvatori and his friends that Reagan was the foundation on which to rebuild Republican conservatism. "We realized that Reagan gave the Goldwater speech better than Goldwater. He seemed steadier, less inclined to fly off the handle than Goldwater," said Salvatori. "He had more self-control, he could say the same things but in a more gentle way." In early 1965, Salvatori and his millionaire friends Holmes P. Tuttle and A. C. "Cy" Rubel urged Reagan to run for governor. They told him that he was the only candidate who could reunite the Republican Party and defeat Democratic governor Edmund G. "Pat" Brown. They wisely appealed to Reagan's sense of duty rather than to his self-interest. Reagan never would find it easy to admit that he wanted an office.[2]

Reagan agreed to spend several months touring California, speaking to different groups and gauging the political climate. In the meantime, Tuttle, Salvatori, and others, including Neil Reagan, asked political consultants Stuart K. Spencer and William E. Roberts to run Reagan's campaign. Since the political community regarded Spencer and Roberts as Republican moderates, their presence would help Reagan shed his image as an extremist, about which Richard Nixon had already warned him. In early 1965 Spencer and Roberts held several sessions with Reagan to convince themselves that he was not a "right-wing nut," and in May 1965 they agreed to manage his campaign. In January 1966 Reagan announced that he would run.[3]

Spencer and Roberts had the pleasant experience of running a campaign that had no money worries. The money establishment, said Spencer, was united behind Reagan. Roberts estimated that the Reagan campaign spent $4 million, $3 million of which came in blocs of over $4,000. Much of the remaining $1 million was "ideological money" coming from conservative true believers. In addition to Tuttle, Salvatori, and Rubel, Reagan had support from other wealthy business executives, including Taft B. Schreiber, Alfred S. Bloomingdale, Leonard Firestone, Justin Dart, Jaquelin Hume, and Reagan's personal lawyer, William French Smith. Hollywood supporters included Bob Hope, Jack Benny, Dinah Shore, George Burns, James Cagney, Jack Warner, Jimmy Stewart, Walt Disney, and John Wayne.

Some of Reagan's wealthy backers wanted Reagan to run for pragmatic reasons. Following the Goldwater debacle they wanted a conservative who could win, and Reagan seemed the most likely candidate. Justin Dart said about Reagan, "I don't think he's the most brilliant man I ever met . . . , but I always knew Ron was a real leader—he's got credibility. He can get on his feet and influence people." "We knew then, as we know now, that Reagan didn't have any depth," Salvatori said, "but he was sure good on his feet."[4]

Reagan proved to be an ideal candidate for Spencer and Roberts. As a studio-trained film actor, he had learned to trust producers, directors, and scriptwriters, and he now rather passively deferred to the judgment of his political handlers. Spencer and Roberts turned Reagan's ignorance about California issues and politics to advantage by portraying him as a citizen-politician whose inexperience was an asset, a man of the people who through courage and common sense would clean up the mess created by Sacramento's politicos. Reagan had often performed the role of citizen-reformer in films, and he played the part well because it exactly fit his self-image. In politics Reagan played himself and that gave his performance an authenticity that an actor's techniques could never achieve.[5]

Reagan's main primary opponent was moderate Republican George Christopher, former San Francisco mayor. He regarded Reagan as a political amateur who should be taken seriously only because he was an extremist. Christopher soon found that Reagan's masterly use of television made him a formidable opponent and that his inexperience in politics did not matter to voters disgusted with professional politicians. What struck Christopher as extremism put Reagan close to the mainstream of the California Republican Party, which was rapidly shifting to the right. Christopher also found it difficult to attack Reagan personally because the divisive 1964 campaign made unity the party's highest priority. Nixon had warned Reagan that any Republican "bloodletting" would give the election to the Democrats. Dr. Gaylord Parkinson, Republican state chair, enunciated the Eleventh Commandment: *Thou shalt not speak ill of any fellow Republican.* Reagan repeated the Eleventh Commandment so often that forever afterward it was associated with him rather than Parkinson. It had the practical effect of preventing Reagan's opponents from attacking him as an extremist. He promised Nixon, "I'll speak no evil (except about Democrats)."[6]

Reagan's well-financed primary campaign did not always go smoothly. In late February 1966 he became ill with influenza. Franklyn C. Nofziger, who joined Reagan's campaign as press agent and traveled with him in the day-to-day grind of politicking, said that the flu's aftereffects lasted a year and a half. Reagan became exhausted during the campaign because he resumed work too quickly and developed a lingering urinary tract infection that led to prostate problems and, finally, in 1967 to an operation. Nofziger believed that these continuing health problems were the source of Reagan's reputation for being lazy.

His exhaustion led to mistakes. On 12 March 1966 he stated that there had to be a commonsense approach to such environmental matters as preserving redwoods: "I mean, if you've looked at a hundred thousand acres or so of trees—you know, a tree is a tree, how many more do you need to look at?" Governor Pat Brown paraphrased that statement into "If you've seen one redwood, you've seen them all." Reagan denied that he made the statement and Nofziger did not play his boss the tape he had. "He was free to do one of the things he has always done best," Nofziger said, "convince himself that the truth is what he wants it to be." Reagan made a potentially serious mistake at a convention held by African-American members of the Republican Party. Christopher goaded Reagan with hints that he was a bigot, provoking him into an angry outburst. He stomped out of the convention, and the delegates thought he had walked out on them. Nofziger went to Reagan's home and persuaded him to return and smooth hurt feelings.

There would be countless more redwood-style bloopers in Reagan's future, but few of the lapses in judgment that he displayed by walking out of the black convention. As would be true throughout his political career,

Reagan's gaffes seldom hurt him badly with the public, and his mistakes did not help Christopher. Reagan got 1,417,623 votes to 675,683 for Christopher.[7]

California was the great American success story in the 1950s and 1960s. Its population growth dazzled the demographers, and its booming industrial, agricultural, and service sectors made it the sixth largest economy in the world. Pat Brown, Reagan's Democratic opponent in the fall election, was a two-term governor who had presided over that boom era. He was an innovative leader who initiated massive water, highway, and educational projects that kept up with the demands of the rocketing population increase. His political power seemed formidable, especially after he defeated Richard Nixon in the 1962 gubernatorial race.[8]

Brown believed that he could easily defeat Reagan. "We . . . rubbed our hands in gleeful anticipation of beating this politically inexperienced, right-wing extremist and aging actor in 1966," Brown wrote. Democratic Party leaders intended to link Reagan with right-wing extremists, especially with the anticommunist witch-hunters in the John Birch Society. Reagan's millionaire backers, however, helped convince the corporate establishment that he was not a right-wing "kook," and Spencer and Roberts lined up national support for him. Dwight D. Eisenhower telephoned liberal Republicans in California urging them to support Reagan, and Nixon came to California and raised $300,000 for him.[9]

Nixon undertook the delicate, and unsuccessful, attempt to mediate between Reagan and Republican senator Thomas H. Kuchel, who over the years had moved in a liberal direction and had angered California conservatives. Many Republicans accused Kuchel of betrayal because he had refused to support Nixon in 1962 and Goldwater in 1964 and now waffled on a Reagan endorsement.

Nixon arranged for an associate, John A. McCone, to visit Kuchel on Reagan's behalf. Reagan asked McCone to use the opportunity to clear up some misunderstandings. Kuchel had become a prominent opponent of the John Birch Society and other McCarthyite organizations. Reagan told McCone that he considered John Birch founder Robert H. Welch to be "utterly reprehensible" because he had accused various national leaders, notably President Eisenhower, of being communist sympathizers. Reagan, however, regarded pressure on him to condemn the entire society to be akin to McCarthyite witch-hunting. "Let me say, however," he told McCone, "that where members of the Society inject themselves into political activity and seek to subvert a political party to the purposes and goals of their organization, then they should be thrown out." Reagan told McCone that environmental issues, especially over preserving redwood forests, had become a point of contention between Kuchel and himself: "This doesn't mean in any way that I am not a conservationist. As a matter of fact I am an outdoorsman and bleed a little whenever a highway cuts through any of our scenery." He outlined a plan that would allow some development but would also protect the "best of the big trees." He also promised that as governor he would not interfere in party primaries and that he would support all Republican candidates in the general election, including Kuchel if he ran for reelection in 1968.[10]

McCone met with Kuchel twice in October 1966. McCone argued that Kuchel should endorse Reagan because he was going to win anyway and supporting him would help the two men later in dealing with patronage and policy matters. McCone reminded Kuchel of Reagan's overwhelming support within the party and said that the senator "should think a little of his own position in 1968." Kuchel resisted McCone's arguments and returned again and again to Reagan's refusal to repudiate the John Birch Society. In the second meeting, McCone told the senator that he thought that Reagan and Kuchel had so narrowed their differences that further delay in Kuchel's endorsement would be regarded as obstinacy and that Kuchel would bear the responsibility for dividing the party. Despite McCone's hardball pressure, Kuchel refused to endorse Reagan.[11]

Kuchel's endorsement proved irrelevant. Pat Brown realized that his campaign was in trouble, and he asked Democratic Party operative Frederick G. Dutton to come to California to evaluate what was wrong. Dutton reported that voters were tired of Brown. He had been in office for an eventful eight years, and people blamed him for every complaint that they had against government. Voters identified him as a Sacramento insider as they became disgusted with "politics as usual." Voter anger with politicians allowed Reagan to turn his inexperience to advantage. Brown had more experience than anybody, Reagan said: "That's why I'm running."[12]

Dutton reported that Reagan came across as a "plausible, persuasive 'good guy' whose synthetic packaging is not apparent." He had watched Reagan in eight appearances: "He is a 'natural' not only in the TV era but for the emerging cultural, psychological wave-lengths to which much of the country is attuned." Brown, on the other hand, came across as a figure from another era. A Democratic Party insider warned Brown that Reagan was seen as a hero in a white hat. "This sonofabitch is going to beat the shit out of you," he predicted.[13]

In the 1966 campaign, Reagan demonstrated a talent that would always baffle his liberal opponents. Conservatives had usually presented their message in pessimistic, dour terms and seemed to enjoy projecting a bleak future of limits and decline. Reagan sketched an optimistic vision of California blossoming under the freedom that would come with limited government and an unfettered marketplace. Brown learned that Reagan was a natural and adroit politician. In two books that Brown wrote about Reagan, he described the frustration that he felt because Reagan left him no target, no way to penetrate the "little worlds" of illusions that Reagan created through his speeches and television advertisements. Opponents always found that Reagan shed attacks in some indefinable way and that attacks on him invariably hurt the attacker. Reagan also learned something about himself: He loved campaigning and thrived on the competitive drive to win and to move people to action through speeches. Reagan the campaigner, Nofziger said, is "hell on wheels when the game begins."[14]

The biggest threat to Reagan was the extremist issue that Democrats had used to destroy Goldwater's candidacy in 1964. Brown's managers tried to make Reagan into a sinister figure with ties to the John Birch Society, but Reagan withstood the pressure and refused to renounce the Birchers. "Anyone who chooses to support me has bought my philosophy. I'm not buying theirs," he said. Brown could never make the extremist label stick because Reagan did not come across as a threatening person. He could express Goldwater's controversial positions in a low-key, commonsense way that made them seem reasonable. He could move an audience to near frenzy with a old-fashioned stump speech filled with patriotic rhetoric and slashing attacks on government, and on the evening television news it would seem cool and reasonable rather than demagogic and inflammatory. He struck voters as a pleasant and open man with a good sense of humor, not a stereotypically angry witch-hunter.[15]

The issues failed to work for Brown. He strongly supported the Vietnam War, which caused many young Democratic voters to stay home on election day. Voters were angry about disturbances in the black community. "The racial backlash in the state is . . . immediate, vocal and strong," Dutton reported. Reagan skillfully held Brown responsible for the Watts riot in 1965 and for later racial flare-ups in Los Angeles, San Francisco, Oakland, and Bakersfield. He portrayed Brown as soft on crime and presented himself as the law-and-order candidate, which carried the subtext of promising to crack down on black militants. Reagan also discovered a powerful issue that polls had not yet uncovered. In question-and-answer sessions he found that antiwar demonstrations and campus disturbances infuriated the middle class. The counterculture was just making itself felt on California campuses, and Reagan gave vivid descriptions of drug and sex orgies at state universities. Reagan knew his middle-class audience well. Hippies, he said, "act like Tarzan, look like Jane and smell like Cheetah."[16]

Brown could never find a winning issue. He recounted his accomplishments and compiled an ever-growing list of promises for his next term.

"Keeping up with Governor Brown's promises," Reagan said, "is like try-ing to read *Playboy* magazine while your wife turns the pages." One film clip showed a desperate Brown reminding schoolchildren that it was an actor that had assassinated Abraham Lincoln. Nothing worked for the gov-ernor, and on election day he suffered a humiliating loss, with 3,742,913 votes for Reagan and 2,749,174 for Brown.[17]

A few minutes after midnight on 3 January 1967 Reagan was inaugu-rated as governor of California. He lightened the solemn religious and patriotic ceremony by saying to former movie star, now senator, George Murphy, "Well, George, here we are on the late show again." He promised as governor to "squeeze and cut and trim until we reduce the cost of govern-ment." For years, he said, liberal bureaucrats had treated the people like children incapable of running government. Experts told the people that there were no simple answers to complex problems. "Well, the truth is, there are simple answers—but there are no easy ones."[18]

Roberts had taken a moment from his campaign duties to think ahead about Reagan's future: "That poor soul—what will we ever do if he gets to be governor!" After the victory, Nofziger exclaimed, "My God, what do we do now?" Reagan team members moved into Sacramento expecting that their conservative ideology would provide them with directions for cleaning up the mess they believed existed. They regarded career civil servants as enemies and resisted turning to them for help. Reagan later objected when a constituent referred to him as a politician: "I have repeatedly told my cabi-net and staff that we belong here only so long as we refer to government as 'they,' and never think of government as 'we.' " He soon confronted a reality more complex than he had anticipated. He was unprepared to run an institution that he had only criticized from the outside. He later admitted that nothing during his first year as governor went the way he planned: "I made lots of mistakes because of inexperience."[19]

Fortunately, Reagan had competent aides with him. Philip M. Battaglia, his executive secretary, acted as chief of staff. Nofziger managed press relations and handled various political chores, as did appointments secretary Thomas C. Reed. William P. Clark served as cabinet secretary. These men, joined by the heads of the major departments, composed Reagan's adminis-trative team. They were young (averaging less than forty years old), well-educated, white males. Reagan's millionaire backers had achieved most of what they wanted with his election and did not try to play a major role in decision making. Reagan felt comfortable with them and sought their reas-surance periodically, especially when he began new ventures in trimming programs. "It seemed like he'd change every time he'd come back from L.A.," a senior adviser recalled. "There would always be some new idea, like cutting welfare ten percent or something. Around the office we'd joke, 'Oh shit, the Governor's been talking to his grassroots again.' "[20]

Battaglia was a hardworking and brilliant young man who had graduated from the University of Southern California law school at age twenty. He quickly gained Reagan's confidence and became the governor's right-hand man. Some conservatives believed that Battaglia hungered for power and assumed responsibilities and made decisions that should have been left to Reagan. When Battaglia resigned in late 1967, William Clark became chief of staff, followed in 1969 by Edwin Meese III. Even those who had sharp disagreements with Clark and Meese regarded them as decent and fair men, as "honest brokers" who made sure that Reagan heard a variety of opinions on major issues. Clark and Meese would later serve Reagan in Washington, as did Caspar W. Weinberger, who headed the California Department of Finance. Michael K. Deaver became a Reagan family confidant, troubleshooter, and surrogate son to Nancy Reagan, smoothing her often troubled relationship with Reagan aides.[21]

Nancy, the most important member of Reagan's team, found the transition to Sacramento difficult. She enjoyed her wealthy socialite friends in Los Angeles and did not as a rule like politicians or mixing with average, everyday people. Her life became more difficult because she could not lead the cloistered private life in Sacramento that she had in Hollywood. She came under intense public scrutiny when she refused to live in the governor's mansion, which she regarded as a run-down firetrap. Ronald's wealthy friends purchased a suitable house and leased it to him, and the Reagans' living arrangements became a source of unending controversy.[22]

Reagan valued Nancy as an adviser because he believed that she had an extraordinary ability to judge people, while he was too trusting. She was more skeptical and, said Michael Reagan, had a frightening ability to see inside of people. Those who knew the Reagans believed that the rather passive Ronald had an absolute need for his wife's encouragement and guidance. "Ronnie Reagan had sort of glided through life," Deaver said, "and Nancy's role was to protect him." Ronald and Nancy remained absolutely devoted, with little room for others in their emotional life.[23]

As governor Reagan quickly established the management style that he would take with him to the White House. He believed that the governorship could be handled easily by bringing in the best people possible, setting general policy for them, and then leaving them alone. He regarded himself as the salesman and chief spokesman for the administration rather than as the manager of government operations. Clark and Meese grouped the more than forty departments and major agencies into four superagencies headed by secretaries. Those secretaries, along with the director of finance and

Reagan's executive assistants, formed the governor's working cabinet. Reagan held cabinet meetings once or twice a week, more often in times of heavy legislative activity.

Reagan's management style depended on his willingness to delegate authority. A consummate team player, he seemed to be without vanity or ego when it came to sharing credit. A motto on his desk read: "There's no limit to what a man can do or where he can go if he doesn't mind who gets the credit." Some aides, at first disconcerted when Reagan delegated responsibility to them and then left them alone with little guidance, blossomed under his trust. "Reagan accepts a person, figures his limitations and, honest to God, delegates," one assistant recalled. "You rise to heights you didn't know you could rise to."[24]

Reagan's hands-off management style had its critics. Some observers believed that he was lazy and had made the governorship into a nine-to-five job. They believed that his unwillingness to master details meant that he really did not grasp the essentials of his own administration. On 14 March 1967, when reporters asked him about his legislative program, he turned to his aides and said, "I could take some coaching from the sidelines, if anyone can recall my legislative program." Reagan's passivity meant that he did not look for ways to reach beyond the shell aides built around him. "He's a reactor, not an initiator," recalled an associate. His management system depended on his having honest brokers to make sure he received conflicting viewpoints, since he would not search for them.[25]

Reagan's cabinet routinely took up controversial issues without the governor's presence and after hammering out compromises would present them to Reagan for approval. Lou Cannon described a cabinet meeting held on 27 February 1967 when members discussed a proposal to put a nuclear power plant in the scenic Diablo Canyon. The Sierra Club and other environmental groups wanted to establish a park there. Reagan mentioned several times that the area sounded so beautiful that perhaps it should not be used for a power plant. Rather than ordering an investigation, he said, "I wonder if there is any possibility of finding out on this. I must say, they do make the Diablo Canyon sound very beautiful." As the meeting ended he said, wistfully, "I really was hoping that someone would say the canyon is just too beautiful for a plant." He seemed incapable of ordering his subordinates to come up with an alternative.[26]

If Reagan found managing the executive branch challenging, his relationship with the legislature was often nightmarish. The Assembly was in the hands of liberal Democrat Jesse Unruh, the "big daddy" of California politics, and several of Reagan's own Republican leaders were liberal supporters of New York governor Nelson A. Rockefeller. Reagan had angered many legislators during the campaign because he made clear his contempt for professional politicians. He did not enjoy their camaraderie and wanted to go home to spend evenings with Nancy rather than staying around, as Pat Brown had done, to gossip over a drink when the day's work ended. The 1967 legislature routinely killed Reagan's proposals to send him the message that the legislature had to be dealt with as an equal partner.

Reagan got the message. While he would never hang around Fat Frank's, the after-hours club frequented by Sacramento politicians, he learned to work with legislators and to invite them to his home for formal, usually somewhat stiff, dinners. They had to keep in mind Reagan's million-vote victory in 1966, and for his part Reagan came to understand that his own accomplishments rested on a successful working relationship with the legislature.[27]

In 1967 Reagan confronted an immediate fiscal crisis. Pat Brown had avoided raising taxes by using accounting tricks to hide an impending budget deficit, dumping the problem on Reagan's desk. The new governor initiated a highly publicized campaign of budget slashing: freezing state hiring, selling the state airplane, stopping out-of-state travel by public employees, halting the purchase of new state automobiles, and asking departments to reduce expenditures by 10 percent across the board. "The symbol on our flag is a Golden Bear; it is not a cow to be milked," he said.[28]

Reagan needed to make a show of budget cutting because he knew that he had to raise taxes. He decided to move quickly because he wanted people to remember that he had inherited the problem from Pat Brown. He worked out an agreement with Jesse Unruh that gave Californians property tax relief while raising their income and sales taxes. It was the biggest tax increase, $1 billion, that any state had ever imposed. In an early example of Reagan being the "Teflon" politician to which nothing unpleasant stuck, Californians blamed Brown for the increased taxes and gave Reagan credit for property tax relief.[29]

While struggling with budget and tax matters, Reagan became embroiled in a fight over higher education that led the usually polite governor to call a university regent "a lying son of a bitch" and, according to William French Smith, to grab a student demonstrator by the lapels and strike him. In the conflict, Reagan played his favorite role, representing the hardworking, middle-class taxpayer against, in his portrait, arrogant professors and university administrators and pampered, foolish students who allowed themselves to be manipulated by a small group of hardened radicals.[30]

The huge and expensive university system—with ten universities, nineteen state colleges, and eighty-five junior colleges—wielded tremendous political clout and had enjoyed large budgets that had allowed it to keep up with exploding enrollment numbers. In 1965, however, the Berkeley free speech movement led by Mario Savio and other New Left radicals began to erode higher education's privileged place in voters' priorities. Reagan had seized on campus unrest as a major issue in 1966 because he sensed the smoldering anger of taxpayers who resented student behavior. Reagan shared their contempt for the young militants. When student demonstrators shouted to him "We are the future," he scribbled a note and held it up to his limousine window: "I'll sell my bonds." He was visited by one student who told him that Reagan's generation could not understand young people because when older people were growing up they did not have satellites, computers, space travel, or instant communications. Reagan agreed: *"You're absolutely right. We didn't have those things when we were your age. We invented them."* His popularity soared when he told student rebels, Observe the rules or get out.[31]

In early 1967 the university board of regents presented the state with a budget request of $278 million. Reagan lowered its proposal by 15 percent and included the first tuition charge in state history. University of California president Clark Kerr tried to mobilize the educational lobby. He froze admissions, predicted that many of the best professors would leave, and warned that several campuses would have to close. Reagan dismissed this as scare tactics designed to stampede the public and legislature, and he turned Kerr into a symbol of intellectually arrogant but weak administrators who coddled student troublemakers. On 20 January 1967 the regents fired Kerr when he demanded and lost a vote of confidence.[32]

In 1968 student unrest spread to other schools beyond Berkeley. Reagan said that those who wanted an education would be protected by bayonets if necessary, and he occasionally used the highway patrol and National Guard to keep campuses open. The people supported him. In February 1969, 78 percent of Californians thought Reagan was doing a good or fair job and only 15 percent thought he was doing poorly. Pat Brown said Reagan could never be defeated as long as student demonstrations continued.

Reagan's highly publicized war with Kerr and with student dissenters led to charges that he had launched an anti-intellectual, right-wing onslaught against higher education. Despite these fears, state spending on higher education went up 136 percent during Reagan's eight years in office, and many professors came to appreciate the order that he imposed. A former chancellor in the state system concluded, as many liberal opponents would over the years, "His bark proved worse than his bite."[33]

During his first year in office, Reagan also had to cope with what came to be known as the "homosexual scandal." Nofziger and other aides began to suspect that a homosexual "ring" was operating in the governor's office.

They investigated without notifying Reagan and concluded that Philip Battaglia and one or two other staff members were involved. Nofziger, who resented Battaglia's influence over Reagan, later said that homophobic feelings did not influence him but that he feared a scandal might damage Reagan's chances for the presidency in 1968.

In August 1967 eleven Reagan aides descended on the Reagans while Ronald was recuperating in San Diego from a prostate operation. When they gave Reagan a report on the "ring," he turned pale and asked, "What do we do now?" Reagan was not homophobic, but, like most people in 1967, he considered homosexuality to be a mental illness, a neurosis, and believed that its practice should be illegal, even between adults. He probably would have accepted the position later described as "don't ask, don't tell."

After hours of discussion, he decided that the men would have to go. He turned the unpleasant task of getting rid of them over to Holmes Tuttle and Henry Salvatori, who asked Battaglia and one other aide to resign. Reagan clamped a lid on the story and for ten weeks reporters assumed that the men had resigned over an internal power struggle. The governor's office waited, almost paralyzed, and finally on 31 October 1967 nationally prominent journalist Drew Pearson broke the story.[34]

Reagan made a relatively minor incident worse by going into a press conference and denying Pearson's story. "He's a liar," Reagan said. Reporters asked Reagan if Nofziger had told some reporters that at least two aides had been dropped on moral grounds. Reagan said that nothing like that had happened and asked if Nofziger, standing beside him, would confirm it. Nofziger said, "Confirmed." Nofziger had, in fact, leaked the story to prevent Battaglia from starting a new career in Sacramento based on his work in the governor's office. Reagan's denial allowed Pearson to keep the feud going and hurt the governor's credibility because reporters knew he had lied.[35]

Despite the controversies of his first year in office, Reagan retained his popularity. He used conservative rhetoric to keep his right-wing supporters happy, but he often acted in a pragmatic manner that won him grudging admiration from some of his liberal critics. He revamped the system for selecting judges in California, substituting professional evaluation for patronage. He backed off his promise to repeal California's fair housing law when he understood how important symbolically it was to minority people. The feminist movement was just mobilizing politically when Reagan took office, and he brought no women into the highest level of the administration. "It isn't that we were deliberately sexist, just that we were naturally sexist," Nofziger said. Still, Reagan changed his previous position and made the temporary Commission on the Status of Women a permanent agency. He also signed a liberal bill that allowed abortion in cases of rape or incest and to save the life or health of the mother. His advisers assured him the law would be interpreted conservatively by physicians, but Reagan came to believe that he had made a mistake because some physicians accommodated women who wanted abortions by routinely declaring their health to be at risk. In 1967 there were 518 legal abortions in California, by 1980, 200,000. Reagan later concluded that liberalized abortion was "a license to murder and that we are committing murder on a wholesale scale."[36]

While he was struggling with the governorship, Reagan carefully watched national politics. A few days after the 1966 election, he met with his top advisers to discuss the 1968 presidential election. The group agreed that Thomas Reed would run an independent Reagan for President operation that would allow the governor to deny that he was running for office. Reagan would cooperate by speaking widely and keeping his options open to see what developed on the national scene.

In July 1967 Nixon met with Reagan at the annual Bohemian Grove gathering of political and business leaders. While they sat together under an oak tree, Nixon told Reagan about his plans to enter the primaries. He said he intended to unite the party and would not attack other Republicans. Reagan said that he would not enter the primaries, but, Nixon recalled, "Reagan said that he had been surprised, flattered, and somewhat concerned about all the presidential speculation surrounding him."[37]

Within months, Reagan reneged on the promise he had made to Nixon. In August 1967 he put out word among conservative leaders to "wait and see" rather than announcing for Nixon. Some conservative leaders, notably Barry Goldwater, worked to head off a Reagan challenge to Nixon. Goldwater told his friend Vice President Hubert H. Humphrey that he had talked with Reagan several times. "He said he told Reagan that this was not his time and that Reagan shouldn't kid himself into believing that he could beat Johnson," Humphrey recalled. "Goldwater said he told Reagan that the same little old ladies in tennis shoes that used to cheer and clap for him did the same thing for Bob Taft and Tom Dewey. In other words, don't be fooled by the enthusiastic response of a handful of hard-core conservative Republicans." Goldwater also told Humphrey that he did not think Reagan was ready for the presidency.[38]

Nixon rolled through the primaries winning victory after victory. When Reagan failed to withdraw his name from the Oregon primary, Nixon defeated him badly, taking 73 percent of the vote. Nixon did not, however, underestimate the governor. He envied Reagan's ability to stir Republican audiences. Patrick Buchanan gave Nixon a Reagan speech, saying that parts of it were remarkably good. Nixon sent it to one of his speechwriters and in a note said that while it was somewhat demagogic, it was effective. "He reaches the heart," Nixon wrote. "We reach the head. I know you may say he reaches only 22 percent—but do we not miss an opportunity in failing to reach the hearts—not just the heads?"[39]

Reagan's last hope for winning the nomination rested with liberal New York governor Nelson Rockefeller. As early as October 1967 Nixon received a message that a "buddy-buddy" relationship had developed between Sacramento and Albany. In July 1968, Emmet John Hughes, Rockefeller's "chief surrogate," secretly visited Reagan at his home in Los Angeles. They made no commitments, but Reagan assured the Rockefeller camp that he was in the race for keeps. If together they could stop Nixon, then they would battle each other for control of the party.[40]

Nixon had long before taken steps to shore up his southern flank where Reagan was strongest. After the Oregon primary he told journalist Theodore White that he was going to Atlanta to meet with southern leaders, saying, "I'm going to wrap up the whole campaign there." He met with Senator Strom Thurmond (Rep., S. Car.), Senator John G. Tower (Rep., Tex.), and other Southern leaders. He told them that he favored a strong military establishment, that in his administration civil rights activities would slow and would be enforced at the local level, that through his nominees he would tip the Supreme Court to the right, and that southern leaders would be included in decision making. At the convention Thurmond held the South steady, supported by tireless activity from John Tower, Barry Goldwater, and other Nixon conservatives. Theodore White talked with the Louisiana state chair, who cried as he described his love for Reagan but explained that he could not break his commitment to Nixon.[41]

On 8 August 1968 Nixon got 692 votes on the first convention ballot, enough to win the nomination. Rockefeller got 277 votes and Reagan, 182. When Nixon called Rockefeller to say that he understood his disappointment, Rockefeller laughed and said, "Ronnie didn't come through for us as well as we expected." To Reagan he said, "You didn't get as many votes as we counted on; we thought you'd stop Nixon for us."[42]

Nixon, with his remarkable ability to perceive political trends, established a relationship with Reagan that benefited them both. As president, Nixon gave Reagan needed foreign experience by sending him abroad on four missions, meeting heads of state in eighteen countries in Europe and Asia. Nixon gave the governor direct access to the Oval Office, which Reagan used sparingly but effectively. Nixon carefully explained his actions to Reagan as the president moved to normalize relations with China, and Nixon's care paid off. Reagan supported Nixon's China policy, and he backed Nixon when he began to withdraw troops from Vietnam. Reagan told his conservative supporters to trust Nixon to respond to international challenges without appeasing the communists. Reagan tried to help Nixon during the turmoil over the Watergate scandal that destroyed his presidency. Reagan said that the Watergate conspirators were not "criminals at heart," that a relatively minor transgression was being used by the president's political opponents to destroy him and to weaken the Republican Party.[43]

Reagan was also looking out for his own political future. In his campaign for reelection in 1970, he cranked up his right-wing supporters with rousing speeches, but acted moderately on specific issues. A Republican critic said, "Reagan charges up the hill by day and retreats under the cover of night." He presented himself as a citizen-politician, in the political world but not part of it. "I saw Reagan run for reelection as governor by running against the government," said Michael Deaver. "He campaigned as if he had not been part of it for four years. I can't explain it. . . . I only know that it worked." Stuart Spencer, who managed Reagan's campaign, said, "He ran against the . . . government he was running. I mean, he believes he's above it all. He believes it. That's why *they* [voters] believe it. I can't believe it. But they do."[44]

Reagan ran against Jesse Unruh, the "big daddy" of California politics, famous for his remark, "Money is the mother's milk of politics." Unruh was an easy target for the citizen-politician running against "politics as usual." Reagan ignored Unruh and attacked the New Left, Vietnam War protesters, and black power advocates. He put forward positive new programs as well, especially with his promise to overhaul the California welfare system. Although Unruh had deep support among traditional Democratic constituencies, Reagan won, with nearly 53 percent of the vote.[45]

During Reagan's second term he and his team worked to build a record of solid achievement. He reluctantly accepted a legislative proposal to establish a state income tax withholding system that made tax collection and financial planning more rational and efficient. Reagan had opposed withholding because he wanted people to feel the pain of writing out checks to pay taxes. With new forms of state aid, public school funding increased by 89 percent during Reagan's two terms (compared with 71 percent under Brown), while enrollment growth slowed. He signed over forty "law-and-order" bills that pleased his conservative supporters and helped them overlook the fact that under Reagan the state budget increased from $4.6 billion to $10.2 billion and state taxes per hundred dollars of personal income increased from $6.64 to $7.62.[46]

Reagan's good record on environmental issues surprised liberals. He saved Round Valley from a huge dam project, protected the John Muir Trail from highway construction, established an ecological reserve program to maintain critical wildlife habitat, established an Ecology Corps, and took important actions to maintain and improve air and water quality.[47]

During the 1970 campaign Reagan had promised welfare reform, claiming that California had 10 percent of the nation's people and 16 percent of its welfare recipients. The Aid to Families with Dependent Children (AFDC) caseload was increasing by forty thousand a month. His financial advisers warned him that welfare growth would force a huge tax increase by 1972. He also believed that the existing system destroyed initiative and undermined families by trapping them in a generational cycle of poverty and despair. At the same time, he believed that "truly needy" people's welfare benefits were too low to provide subsistence. In August 1970 Reagan announced that he was creating a task force to formulate a welfare reform program. "This study will place heavy emphasis on the tax-payer as opposed to the tax-taker; on the truly needy as opposed to the lazy unemployable," he vowed.[48]

In March 1971 Reagan submitted reform legislation to the legislature. Rather than eliminating entire programs as some states were doing, Reagan designed his plan to "purify" the existing system by removing those who "didn't belong there." It required those able to work to find jobs, intensified efforts to collect child support, and increased benefits for the "truly needy."[49]

Reagan fought hard for the bill. He spoke around the state and pressured the legislature by setting up welfare reform committees in every county in California. The Assembly Speaker, Democrat Robert Moretti, had kept the bill bottled up in committee, but finally in June 1971 he walked over to Reagan's office and told him, "Governor, I don't like you, and I know you don't like me, but we don't have to be in love to get something worked out around here, and if you're serious about accomplishing some things, let's sit down and let's do it."[50]

Moretti broke the impasse and the hard negotiations began. Reagan asked his aides to give him four sheets of paper, one listing what he had to have, another what he would like to have, a third what would be nice to have, and, finally, points that did not matter. Reagan and Moretti negotiated personally for a week, and then their aides worked for ten more days. Moretti found that Reagan was "interested more in accomplishing than he is in posturing, and if he has to compromise, he will."[51]

The welfare reform act was generally regarded as a success. It pleased conservatives because welfare rolls fell from 2,293,280 people in March 1971, to 1,941,096 by July 1973. At that time there were 785,000 fewer people on welfare than the experts had predicted and costs were $1 billion less. The caseload, which had been expanding by forty thousand people each month, started falling by eight thousand a month. Liberals applauded the bill because grants to the truly needy increased by 43 percent. Reagan's program attracted national attention and other states began adopting the California guidelines, including Nelson Rockefeller's New York.[52]

In 1973 the political future looked good for Reagan. Nixon's term would be up in 1976 and the Reagan strategists assumed that of the major contenders for the Republican nomination, he had the best chance. Watergate upset the political landscape and threw off all of Reagan's calculations. When Nixon resigned from the presidency in August 1974, party leaders assumed that the new president, Gerald R. Ford, automatically had a lock on the Republican nomination. Reagan would be sixty-five in 1976, and many of his disappointed supporters believed that he would be too old to run in 1980.

In May 1974, with Nixon battered but still holding on, Reagan met with his strategists. Holmes Tuttle and Justin Dart attended the meeting, as did Meese, Nofziger, Deaver, and several outsiders, including a young political consultant, John P. Sears. Most people there assumed that Nixon would survive the Watergate crisis and that if he did not the party would rally to Ford. Sears got Reagan's attention by saying, first, that Nixon would not last and, second, when Ford took over he would be an ineffective leader. Sears said Reagan should make his plans to run without regard to Nixon or Ford. Sears had planted a seed that would grow in the minds of the governor and his associates.[53]

When Reagan left office in January 1975, Deaver and his partner, Peter D. Hannaford, had set up a public relations business, with Reagan as their first client. They scheduled eight to ten highly paid speeches for him each month, arranged a newspaper column that appeared in 174 newspapers, and a daily radio commentary carried by over two hundred stations. Reagan kept his name and voice before Republican audiences and was well paid; Lou Cannon estimated he made more than $800,000 in 1975.[54]

Reagan regarded Ford as a caretaker without leadership ability. Ford destroyed his honeymoon with the American people when he pardoned Richard Nixon, and he infuriated conservatives by choosing Nelson Rockefeller as his vice president. The conservative indictment quickly lengthened: Ford had put forward an amnesty program for Vietnam War draft evaders; he had continued Henry Kissinger's policy of détente with the Soviet Union; and he had signed the Helsinki Pact that conservatives believed ratified the Soviet postwar takeover of Eastern Europe. For them, Ford was a government insider and part of the problem, not the solution.[55]

Still, Reagan's decision to run was difficult because if he damaged the Republican Party by dividing it, the fallout might destroy him politically. Ford did not like Reagan, and did not take him seriously. "I just never thought Reagan would run against me," Ford later said. Even the usually politically astute Nixon sent Ford a message on 25 September 1975: "RN feels that Ronald Reagan is a lightweight and not someone to be considered seriously or feared in terms of a challenge for the nomination." Tension mounted between the two normally calm and relaxed men. A Ford aide recalled, "Ford thought Reagan was a phony, and Reagan thought Ford was a lightweight, and neither one felt the other was fit to be President." On 20 November 1975 Reagan announced his candidacy for the Republican nomination.[56]

Reagan counted on establishing his credibility by winning the New Hampshire primary on 24 February 1976. He had support from popular former governor Hugh Gregg and other important figures in the state, and his conservative message was as popular in snowy New Hampshire as in California. Scarcely had he begun to campaign, however, than he was thrown on the defensive. In a September 1975 speech Reagan had promised to cut federal spending by $90 billion, balance the budget, and reduce personal income taxes by an average of 23 percent. The speech contained an addendum that explained that the $90 billion saving would come by transferring twenty-four programs back to the states, including welfare, education, housing programs, food stamps, and Medicaid. Ford's experts predicted that Reagan's plan would force some states and cities to raise taxes to pay for the programs shifted and this reverberated through New Hampshire, which had no personal income taxes.

Reagan's camp made other mistakes. He believed that he had the primary won and did not campaign in the state during the two days before the election, while Ford did. Reagan supporter Governor Meldrim Thomson claimed that Reagan would win outright. It was a shock, then, when Ford, the underdog, won by 1,317 votes. The vote was interpreted as a solid victory for Ford rather than as a remarkable showing by a challenger against an incumbent president.[57]

Reagan went on the attack, assailing Ford's record, especially on foreign policy issues, but in March he lost the Florida primary and then his home state of Illinois. Many journalists and politicians wrote Reagan off. He was running out of money, and party leaders began to demand that he withdraw in the interests of Republican unity.[58]

The 23 March North Carolina primary was crucial. Reagan was angry. He resented pressure on him to withdraw, and he fought back like a trapped lion. He focused on foreign affairs and charged that weak Ford leadership cost the United States power and prestige in the world. He pounded Ford over the proposed Panama Canal treaty that would return control of the waterway to Panama. He regarded the treaty as humiliating kowtowing by a great power to a Third World country. He told conservative southern audiences that the nation must keep the canal: "We bought it, we paid for it, it's ours, and we're going to keep it." Senator Jesse Helms fought Sears to get more television time for Reagan. Nancy Reagan backed Helms. "You'd better believe Miss Nancy puts her oar in," Helms said. "She's a very intelligent lady, very forthright; she's the best thing RR has going for him. Sharp as a briar." Of Reagan, Helms said, "Ultra-liberals in this country hate Ronald Reagan like the devil hates holy water."[59]

Reagan defeated Ford in North Carolina, and on 1 May took all ninety-six Texas delegates, followed a few days later by victories in Alabama, Georgia, and Indiana. Reagan and Ford battled it out state by state. Ford was angry and depressed at being forced into a contest for the nomination. His campaign staff divided between those who wanted Ford to stay in the White House and be presidential and those who wanted him to launch an aggressive attack on Reagan. One aide commented that the only Republicans who knew how to run a national campaign were Nixon people, and they were all in jail. Still, Ford won in Michigan, Kentucky, Tennessee, and other states. Some analysts later concluded that the outcome was settled before the North Carolina primary, when, with the campaign out of money, Sears decided not to contest Ford in some northeastern states, where Reagan could have picked up a few delegates that proved crucial.[60]

As the primary season closed and the party moved toward its mid-August convention in Kansas City, neither Ford nor Reagan had the nomination locked up. In the final week of July, the *New York Times* said that of the 1,130 delegates needed, Ford had 1,052, Reagan 995, with 141 uncommitted. The two men fought delegate by delegate. Strom Thurmond, a main figure in Reagan's defeat in 1968, now battled for him in the South, as did Jesse Helms and other southern leaders.[61]

Ford used his incumbency to advantage, inviting delegations to the White House, twisting the arms of individual delegates, and granting favors where he could. Momentum was with him, and the Reagan camp believed that the media was about to declare Ford the winner before the convention opened, which might stampede the uncommitted delegates into the president's camp.

Sears came up with a dramatic ploy that, had it worked, would have gone down as one of the most brilliant in modern politics. He, with Reagan's friend Senator Paul Laxalt (Rep., Nev.), decided that Reagan should announce his vice presidential nominee before the convention. On 23 July they stunned Reagan by recommending to him Senator Richard S. Schweiker of Pennsylvania, usually perceived as one of the most liberal Republicans in the Senate. Sears and Laxalt argued that the move would block the media from counting Reagan out. More important, they believed that it might break loose fifteen to twenty votes in Pennsylvania and would have an effect on other uncommitted delegates. Paul Laxalt assured Reagan that Schweiker was a fine man who had earned his liberal reputation mainly because of his votes on labor issues.[62]

On 24 July Reagan and Schweiker secretly met for a six-hour conversation, with Nancy, Sears, and Laxalt present. The two men quickly hit it off, and Reagan was surprised to find that they were close philosophically. Schweiker had been moving to the right. He opposed abortion, gun control, and mandatory busing, and he supported capital punishment and school prayer. Reagan liked him, and they agreed to announce that Schweiker was Reagan's choice for vice president.[63]

Reagan had time to talk to Schweiker and to understand that he had moved to the right. Reagan's supporters, however, did not have that opportunity and many regarded it as a cynical gesture. Representative John M. Ashbrook (Rep., Ohio) said it was "the dumbest thing I've ever heard of. . . . You can't trust any of them." Conservative representative Philip M. Crane (Rep., Ill.) said he went "berserk" when he heard about it. Most disappointing, Schweiker proved to have little influence within the Pennsylvania delegation. He was shocked at the harsh reaction his selection met and depressed at finding himself left without a following in his own delegation. He offered to withdraw, but Reagan said, "Senator, we came to Kansas City together and we're going to leave Kansas City together."[64]

Despite the uproar, most experts concluded that the Schweiker announcement did not affect things one way or the other. Most of those who came out for Ford after the announcement had already been counted for him anyway, and the Reagan people groused but remained steady behind their candidate. Still, there were not enough of them, and Ford eked out a first-ballot victory.[65]

As Ford began his acceptance speech, an emissary from the president told Reagan that Republicans remained divided and pleaded with him, for the good of the party, to come to the podium to speak. As Reagan made his way to the speaker's stand, one of his campaign advisers, Richard Whalen, said, "Ford has just given the future of the party to Reagan."[66]

The crowd stayed on its feet as Reagan delivered his six-minute talk, which he aimed at his conservative supporters. "Don't get cynical because, look at yourselves and what you were willing to do and recognize that there are millions and millions of Americans out there that want what you want, that want it to be that way, that want it to be a shining city on the hill." He paraphrased an old English ballad: "Though I am wounded, I am not slain. I shall rise and fight and fight again."[67]

Nixon congratulated Reagan on his brief address and said, "Having won a few and lost a few I can say that winning is a lot more fun!" But Reagan had conducted himself magnificently, Nixon said, and had again brought his eloquent message to millions of people. Reagan replied: "Nancy & I are at peace with ourselves & are enjoying a freedom we haven't known for some time. We remember with pleasure that where delegates had freedom to vote we did well. Defeat came in those three North East states where the party structure controlled the vote and I suspect 'Rocky' controlled the party structure." Reagan said that he was resuming his newspaper column and radio commentaries, "so I'll be doing business at the same old stand & for the same old cause."[68]

Reagan campaigned for Ford in the president's losing battle with Jimmy Carter, and although a few of Ford's disappointed supporters blamed Reagan for the Republican defeat, most did not. After 1976, the Republican Party continued its march to the right, and Reagan claimed its leadership as it prepared for the 1980 election. He kept his name before the public with his syndicated newspaper column and daily radio commentary. He maintained a busy speaking schedule, often campaigning for conservative Republican candidates, especially in states that would be the scene of 1980 primary contests.

5

Changing the National Agenda, 1981

"We've come in line with the American mainstream," a jubilant conservative exalted when Reagan came to the Republican convention to claim the 1980 presidential nomination. Liberal and moderate Republicans, who once would have been horrified at the thought of Reagan's leadership, accepted the prospect with equanimity. Race and taxes had continued to erode liberal power in both parties, moving the center closer to Reagan. He exploited racial resentments without opening himself to charges of bigotry. He attacked affirmative action on the grounds that it violated American principles of equal treatment of individuals. He portrayed himself as a conservative populist, who made equal opportunity a cornerstone of his beliefs. He upheld family values, which encompassed increasingly popular issues. His anti-Washington, outsider stance was more in favor than ever, and he proclaimed himself the father of the growing tax revolt. As President Jimmy Carter's popularity sagged, Reagan successfully presented himself as the leader who would rebuild the nation's economy and restore American pride and power.[1]

In early 1979, Reagan established a presidential exploratory team. Paul Laxalt served as national chair; John Sears became campaign manager and brought along James Lake and Charles Black. But the blend of Sears's team with Reagan's California associates—Michael Deaver, Edwin Meese, Martin C. Anderson, and Lyn Nofziger—did not work. The Californians distrusted Sears, believing that he wanted to force them out. They were right. First Anderson and Nofziger left, then on 26 November 1979, Thanksgiving Day, Nancy Reagan called Deaver and asked him to come to the Reagan home in Pacific Palisades. When he got there, he found the Reagans, Sears, Lake, and Black. Sears claimed that Deaver had failed in his fund-raising responsibilities and that he had overcharged Reagan for his services. They argued for hours and finally Nancy said to Ronald, "Honey . . . , it looks as if you've got to make a choice." Deaver interrupted, "No, governor, you don't have to make that choice. I'll resign." He walked out, with Reagan following. When Reagan returned, he was furious. "Damn it," he fumed, "you've just driven away someone who's probably a better man than the three of you are."[2]

Despite the fact that Deaver was a friend and confidant—sometimes said to be a surrogate son to the Reagans—Reagan acquiesced in his expulsion, but at a terrible cost to his peace of mind. Every time Reagan looked at Sears he was reminded of his own mistake: He had let down a friend in a moment of crisis.[3]

On 13 November 1979 Reagan became the tenth, and final, Republican to declare his candidacy. He aimed his announcement speech at middle-class Americans who yearned for strong and inspiring leadership. Instead of laying out a laundry list of promises, he described his vision of America's future. He expressed his belief in American exceptionalism, his belief that the laws of history did not apply to the United States: "If there is one thing we are sure of it is that history need not be relived; that nothing is impossible, and that man is capable of improving his circumstances beyond what we are told is fact." We are told today, he said, that the United States is in decline and we must learn to live with less. "I don't believe that. And, I don't believe you do either." American economic problems could be solved with sound leadership. The American people did not damage the economy, government did, by overspending and overregulating: "The key to restoring the health of the economy lies in cutting taxes." Conservation would not end the energy shortage, Reagan said; it just meant running out of resources less rapidly. Instead, the nation must produce more oil, coal, and nuclear power. In foreign affairs he said that the nation had "just drifted along with events, responding as if we thought of ourselves as a nation in decline." Peace must be the American goal and peace required military strength: "Negotiation with the Soviet Union must never become appeasement."[4]

Ten men entered the race for the Republican nomination, but the major challengers to Reagan were Representatives John B. Anderson and Philip M. Crane, both of Illinois, Senator Howard W. Baker of Tennessee, former director of central intelligence George Bush, and former governor of Texas John B. Connally. All the candidates except the liberal John Anderson fought on Reagan's battlefield, endorsing the positions he had been promoting since 1964: restoring American military power, cutting the size and scope of government, and providing incentives for business firms.[5]

Reagan started as the front-runner, but in January 1980 he stumbled in the Iowa precinct caucuses. He had appeared to have Iowa locked up. George Bush, who had a 0.3 percent name recognition when he began his campaign, spent nearly a day in Iowa for each hour that Reagan spent there. A mid-January poll found that Reagan's support had dropped 24 percent in one month, and Bush won the caucus votes. Paul Laxalt told Reagan not to rationalize his defeat: "You were sitting on your ass in Iowa," he chided.[6]

Reagan charged into New Hampshire as if he were the underdog. He abandoned his airplane for a bus and trudged through the cold and snow to meet voters individually. He did not have to prove his credentials in that conservative state; he mainly had to show the voters that he was still vigorous and capable. He defused the age issue by vigorous campaigning and by turning his sixty-ninth birthday into a statewide celebration. He claimed that Bush was a liberal who supported the ERA, welfare, abortion, and gun control. Reagan offered voters his sunny, optimistic view of unlimited possibilities, while Bush became tongue-tied any time he tried to express his vision of the nation's future.[7]

Bush frittered away his Iowa momentum. When the *Nashua Telegraph* offered to sponsor a debate between just Bush and Reagan, Reagan agreed to pay for the event and then invited the other candidates to participate. Caught by surprise, Bush at first refused to participate, and then sat silent while the audience hooted and hollered. When Reagan started to speak, Jon Breen, editor of the *Nashua Telegraph,* told aides to cut off Reagan's microphone. Reagan snapped, "I paid for this microphone." It was a galvanizing moment, like a scene from an old Reagan movie, with the forceful but calm and sure star standing up for a fair and open debate, while Bush seemed confused and paralyzed with fear. Journalist David S. Broder leaned over to Lou Cannon and said, "Reagan is winning this primary right now." Broder was correct. Reagan took 50 percent of the vote, with Bush trailing at 20 percent.[8]

As Reagan regained his footing in New Hampshire, he also resolved staff problems. He constantly had to explain to conservatives that contrary to rumors he, not John Sears, was setting policy. Sears had earlier pushed out Anderson, Nofziger, and Deaver and then tried to undermine Paul Laxalt and Edwin Meese. It was like an Agatha Christie mystery novel, Meese said, as "the original Reaganites kept disappearing." Reagan's nagging conscience, already festering with the loss of Deaver, exploded: "By God, you're not going to get Ed Meese! You guys have forced me to the wall." Although Nancy walked the halls in the evenings placating and mediating between warring camps, she finally decided that Sears, for all of his brilliance, was expendable. On election day in New Hampshire, before the votes were counted, Reagan asked Sears, Lake, and Black to resign. They did so gracefully and refrained then and in the future from criticizing Reagan.[9]

Before he dumped Sears, Reagan asked New York businessman William J. Casey to manage the campaign. Casey had served in the Nixon and Ford campaigns and got along with the Californians, working closely with Meese, who served as chief of staff in control of the campaign on a day-to-day basis. Deaver, Nofziger, and Martin Anderson soon rejoined the campaign, and Reagan rolled from victory to victory.[10]

His opponents soon began to drop out. John Anderson abandoned his quest for the Republican nomination and became an independent candidate. Bush scored points with his attacks on Reagan's "voodoo economics," but he never regained his momentum and on 26 May he dropped out. Reagan won twenty-nine of the thirty-three primaries he entered, taking about 60 percent of the total vote.[11]

The major drama at the Republican convention, which opened in Detroit on 15 July, came over Reagan's selection of a vice presidential running mate. Ford's and Reagan's relationship, cool since Reagan's 1976 attempt to wrest the nomination from the president, warmed in June 1980 when Reagan called on Ford at his home. After this initial pleasant meeting, insiders began to discuss a "dream ticket" of Reagan and Ford, a pairing that would heal wounds and reassure both wings of the party.[12]

Some major Republican figures believed that the dream ticket was unworkable, but when Reagan asked Ford to join him, Senator Howard Baker, Senator Robert J. Dole (Rep., Kans.), and others pushed Ford to accept. By Wednesday evening, 16 July, the convention was in turmoil. Some delegates questioned Reagan's competence, wondering why he had not settled such an important matter weeks before. After discussing the issue with Ford at 5:15 P.M., Reagan called him again at 9:00 and said he needed to act because rumors were getting out of hand. Ford said his "gut instinct" was not to accept but that he would have another talk with his advisers. Nancy Reagan called Betty Ford and told her that she would be delighted if Ford could join the ticket.

Finally at about 11 P.M. Ford told his wife that he did not think the ticket made sense. He went to Reagan's suite and told him his decision. Ford later said that the dream ticket failed to materialize because "there wasn't enough time." Reagan told publisher William Loeb that much of the hoopla surrounding the negotiations had been media "fairy tales." "On behalf of Jerry," Reagan wrote, "I must tell you that from the very first, he was opposed and the supposed bargaining was in reality efforts on the part of some of our Congressmen and Senators and others to persuade him to change his mind. . . . I think, also, that many of us came to realize as the day wore on that he was right in his feeling that he shouldn't do it."[13]

Reagan quickly chose Bush as his running mate. He later explained to a friend that by the time they got to Detroit, there was a "tidal wave" of support for George Bush, even from conservatives like Strom Thurmond and old Reagan allies like Holmes Tuttle, Justin Dart, and Jaquelin Hume. Reagan regarded Bush as wishy-washy on many issues, but he believed that he was superbly prepared for leadership and would help solidify moderate support for the ticket.[14]

In his acceptance speech, Reagan described his campaign themes: "Never before in our history have Americans been called upon to face three grave threats to our very existence, any one of which could destroy us. We face a disintegrating economy, a weakened defense and an energy policy based on the sharing of scarcity." He ridiculed Democratic leadership: "They say that the United States has had its day in the sun; that our nation has passed its zenith." Their vision was of sacrifice and lessened opportunity. "My fellow citizens, I utterly reject that view. The American people, the most generous on earth, who created the highest standard of living, are not going to accept the notion that we can only make a better world by moving backwards ourselves." Carter's foreign policy was "an equally sorry chapter" in his administration's record, Reagan said. A Soviet brigade trained in Cuba, the Soviet Union occupied Afghanistan, Iran had held Americans hostage for months, and United States military strength was at its lowest point in a generation. "I condemn the Administration's make-believe; its self-deceit and—above all—its transparent hypocrisy," he said. He ended with his vision of the City on a Hill: "Can we doubt that only a divine providence placed this land, this island of freedom, here as a refuge for all those people in the world who yearn to breathe freely[?]"[15]

Reagan made Carter's leadership the issue. Carter had stumbled badly from the beginning of his presidency. His economic program had failed. In 1976, he had used a misery index of 15.3 (the sum of the inflation and unemployment rates) to defeat Ford, but by the end of 1979 it had reached 19.3. Reagan turned the misery index into part of his scathing indictment of Carter's record.

Reagan had many other easy targets. In July 1979 Iranian revolutionaries had overthrown the shah, a longtime American ally, and turned the wrath of the Iranian people on the United States, the "Great Satan." In November 1979 a Tehran mob seized over fifty American hostages, and that was followed in December by the Soviets invading Afghanistan. At first, the American people rallied behind the president, but nightly newscasts ticked off the days that the hostages passed in captivity and as the days turned into weeks and then months, the hostage crisis eroded Carter's leadership image. In mid-July 1980, his approval rating fell to 21 percent. Patrick H. Caddell, Carter's own pollster, said that the public was hostile and sour: *"More to the point the American people do not want Jimmy Carter as their President."*[16]

Carter hoped that Reagan would self-destruct, and for a while that seemed possible. In July and August Reagan made mistakes that put him on the defensive. He called the Vietnam War a "noble cause." He suggested that creationism be taught in public schools along with evolution, and later in the campaign he blamed trees for air pollution, leading to jokes about "killer trees."[17]

Campaign managers limited media access to Reagan and reduced his schedule. His pollster, Richard B. Wirthlin, warned against assigning Reagan early-morning activities: "The Governor definitely is an 'afternoon person.'" Martin Anderson had organized nearly five hundred foreign and domestic policy experts into fifty task forces, and now the campaign began to draw on this "brain trust." Reagan soon recovered his balance. When he caused a flap by charging that the United States was in an economic depression, he told crowds: "They say I can't use the word 'depression.' Well, if the president wants a definition, I'll give him one. A recession is when your neighbor loses his job. A depression is when you lose *your* job. And recovery will be when Jimmy Carter loses *his.*"[18]

Reagan's candidacy unraveled the Roosevelt coalition by convincing many middle- and working-class white people—the silent majority—that the enemy was not wealthy Americans but "welfare queens" and liberal elitists. His tough law-and-order stand on crime and his attacks on "welfare queens" were coded messages that tapped white anxieties about blacks and other minority people. Reagan did not attack the welfare state directly, but when reporters asked him how he would cut taxes, raise military spending, and still balance the budget as he promised he would do, he answered that he would do it by eliminating waste, fraud, and abuse. Policy analysts knew that such waste amounted to only a tiny fraction of the federal budget, but the voters agreed with Reagan. A public opinion poll in late 1979 revealed that most people believed that fifty-two cents of every dollar spent by government was wasted.[19]

On 28 October Reagan and Carter held a televised debate. It was Carter's last chance to break Reagan's momentum. Carter looked tired and distracted as the debate began, while Reagan appeared vigorous and relaxed. Carter showed his legendary mastery of detail, and Reagan seemed well informed, with a good grasp of national problems and a clear sense of how he would solve them. Reagan's major vulnerability was that many voters believed that he endangered peace by being too belligerent in foreign affairs. In the first few minutes of the debate, he made his major point: "I'm only here to tell you that I believe with all my heart that our first priority must be world peace, and that use of force is always and only a last resort, when everything else has failed, and then only with regard to our national security." He said the United States had never gotten into a war because it was too strong. "I have seen four wars in my lifetime. I'm a father of sons; I have a grandson. I don't ever want to see another generation of young Americans bleed their lives into sandy beachheads in the Pacific, or rice paddies and jungles in Asia, or the muddy, bloody battlefields of Europe."

The line that most people remembered came when Carter attacked Reagan for wanting to change the Social Security system. With a wry smile and a shrug, Reagan said, "There you go again." With that gentle ridicule, and the audience's laughter, he diminished the president. If that line did not finish Carter, Reagan's closing remarks did. It was a brutally effective attack because it was direct and simple. He suggested that when the voters went into the polling booths, "it might be well if you would ask yourself, are you better off than you were four years ago? Is it easier for you to go and buy things in the stores than it was four years ago? Is there more or less unemployment in the country than there was four years ago? Is America as respected throughout the world as it was? Do you feel that our security is as safe, that we're as strong as we were four years ago?"[20]

Reagan won the debate and went on to defeat Carter in the election. He won 51 percent of the vote, Carter 41, and Anderson 7 percent. Reagan scored an electoral vote landslide by carrying forty-four states. Republicans took control of the United States Senate, and the Democrats lost thirty-three seats in the House.[21]

Looking back from a later perspective, conservatives saw the 1980 election as a giant step in the long swing toward conservatism that started in 1964. An ABC television exit poll found that 25 percent of the people who classed themselves as Democrats voted for Reagan, as did 52 percent of the independents. He got 44 percent of the vote of people eighteen to twenty-nine years old and carried a majority of those older than that. Fifty-four percent of males voted for him, as did 47 percent of females; he attracted 55 percent of white and 13 percent of black voters. He lost the vote of those with an annual household income below $20,000, but carried all income categories above that and got 60 percent of the vote of those making over

$30,000 a year. Forty-one percent of labor union families voted for him. His gains over Ford's 1976 vote came almost entirely from blue-collar Democrats.[22]

On election day Reagan named Meese as head of the transition, and Meese put one thousand experts to work to prepare for the conservative takeover. The theme that emerged from the transition task forces was that the administration should subordinate everything to its economic program. Reagan summarized the advice he received: "If we get the economy in shape, we're going to be able to do a lot of things. If we don't, we're not going to be able to do anything."[23]

The Reagan administration was, in the words of one observer, more ideological than partisan. The Reaganites did not want liberal Republicans any more than they wanted Democratic Party holdovers, and they established five criteria to guide them in personnel selections. Later, Reagan's team typically could recall only one of the five: loyalty to Reagan's conservative ideas and programs.[24]

Few presidents, perhaps none, have ever been as dependent on their immediate staff as Ronald Reagan was. He intended to set general policy and to act as administration spokesman to the people and Congress. He would leave it to his staff to turn his broad goals into specific policies and programs and often did not know about important actions taken in his name. Three aides—called the troika—acted almost as deputy presidents during Reagan's first term. He named Edwin Meese as counselor to the president with cabinet rank, James A. Baker III as chief of staff, and Michael Deaver as assistant to the president and deputy chief of staff. Baker, Bush's campaign manager, had gained Reagan's trust and admiration during the election campaign.

Although cynical observers predicted that power sharing would not work, the troika was effective. Meese assumed responsibility for White House relations with departments and agencies, for policy development, for cabinet administration, and for daily operations of the executive branch. The national security adviser reported to Reagan through Meese, and Meese was made a member of the National Security Council (NSC). Baker handled White House operations and relations with Congress and the press. Deaver supervised matters that affected the Reagans personally, including presidential trips, scheduling, and security matters. The First Lady's Office fell in his domain. All three shared oversight of personnel matters. The tripartite division fit Meese's interest in policy, Baker's expertise in politics, and Deaver's skill with media and his deep understanding of the Reagans' personal needs.[25]

Some observers divided Reagan's staff into the ideologues and the pragmatists. The ideologues, often men and women who had served with Reagan in California, were policy-oriented, conservative true believers and included Meese, Martin Anderson, Richard V. Allen, and Lyn Nofziger. The pragmatists, while conservative, were more willing to compromise on policy matters. Pragmatists included Baker and his associates Richard G. Darman and David R. Gergen. Michael Deaver often sided with Baker. The pragmatists were always vulnerable to the charge that they were compromising Reagan's conservative principles. The ideologues would raise the cry, Let Reagan be Reagan—but the division between the two camps fit Reagan's own personality. Rhetorically he was the most unbending of conservatives, but in practice he was a confident negotiator who understood that compromise was a necessary part of the political game.[26]

Meese, more loyal to Reagan's beliefs than Reagan was, turned the president's ideas and stances into policy and programs. Baker was more interested in political power and legislative success than in ideological purity. He was a cautious man who carefully cultivated the Californians, especially Meese and Deaver. Baker stayed in the background and established excellent relations with the media through such allies as Deaver and Gergen, and with Congress through the White House congressional lobbyists, Max L. Friedersdorf and Kenneth M. Duberstein. While Meese controlled an elaborate policy structure and the NSC, James Baker's power largely rested on the Legislative Strategy Group, directed by his chief ally, the brilliant Richard G. Darman. Darman's group became the White House "command center" because it, unlike Meese's elaborate apparatus, could react quickly to the political aspects of policymaking.

Michael Deaver's one major talent, some said genius, was his ability to manage the political image making that gave the Great Communicator much of his clout. "It was instinct," Deaver said, "just a God-given talent." Deaver was Reagan's producer and director, managing every scene, watching every detail of scripting, staging, and lighting. He was not interested in policy, but he participated in most substantive decisions because he was the expert at packaging administration goals for public presentation. Nancy Reagan trusted Deaver completely, and he, in turn, helped her achieve many of her goals, while delicately sidetracking her when her demands created problems for the administration.[27]

Reagan's national security team consisted of Secretary of State Alexander M. Haig, Secretary of Defense Caspar W. Weinberger, and Director of Central Intelligence William J. Casey. Reagan respected Haig, though some in the president's inner circle thought Haig had been too close to Nixon. On 11 December Reagan told Haig that he would be the administration spokesman on international relations, saying, "I'll look to you, Al." Reagan also made it clear to his personnel advisers that he intended for Weinberger to oversee a massive military buildup. Those who tangled with Weinberger over the defense budget soon learned the meaning of a plaque on his wall that read, "Never give in, never give in, never, never, never; in anything great or small, large or petty, never give in."[28]

William Casey wanted to be secretary of state, but Nancy Reagan and others in the inner circle did not think that the rumpled, mumbling, shuffling Casey looked like a secretary of state, and Richard Allen bluntly told him, "It's not going to happen." But Casey was not set aside. The Reaganites believed that the CIA had been damaged by investigations in the 1970s and counted on the tough, hard-driving Casey to put it back together.[29]

Reagan had already told his advisers that he wanted his friend and personal attorney William French Smith as attorney general. He selected Donald T. Regan, head of Merrill Lynch, as secretary of the Treasury. Reagan paid a debt to his loyal supporter Richard Schweiker by making him secretary of health and human services, and rewarded construction company owner Raymond J. Donovan, a major fund-raiser for the Reagan campaign, by making him secretary of labor. He named Andrew L. "Drew" Lewis as secretary of transportation. He had long been impressed by neoconservative Jeane J. Kirkpatrick's hard-line anticommunist thinking, and he named her ambassador to the United Nations. She was the only woman in Reagan's first cabinet. Reagan had his eye on David A. Stockman ever since the brilliant young congressman had stood in for Anderson and Carter in bruising debate preparations. He made Stockman director of the Office of Management and Budget (OMB), an important position in a year when the economy was the administration's first priority. He named William E. Brock, a major figure in the Republican party, the United States trade representative.[30]

Reagan deferred to his advisers on positions that did not interest him. Vice President George Bush had pushed businessman Malcolm Baldrige as secretary of commerce, and Senator Bob Dole had suggested John R. Block as secretary of agriculture. Samuel R. Pierce became the only black person in the cabinet, as secretary of the Department of Housing and Urban Development. Laxalt was the main supporter of James G. Watt as secretary of the interior. James B. Edwards and Terrel H. Bell took on the thankless task of heading departments that Reagan had promised to abolish, the Departments of Energy and Education, respectively.[31]

The cabinet was solidly conservative and all members were in fundamental agreement with Reagan's policy. On 8 January 1981 the president-elect met with them for the first time as a group. He warned them that civil service careerists would resist new policy and urged them to take firm control of their agencies. He said that if his team members started talking of government as "we" rather than "they," they had been in the job too long.[32]

On 20 January 1981 Nancy and Ronald Reagan took a quiet, tense ride with Jimmy and Rosalynn Carter to the inaugural ceremony held outside the Capitol. In his inaugural address Reagan sketched the harsh economic conditions confronting the nation, and said, "In this present crisis, government is not the solution to our problem; government is the problem." He promised that the United States would "again be the exemplar of freedom and a beacon of hope for those who do not have freedom." When he finished his speech, Reagan, the master of the politics of symbolism, went into the Capitol building and signed an order instituting a hiring freeze throughout the federal government.[33]

Reagan's first year in office was the most important of his presidency. The fight to institute his economic program, labeled Reaganomics, gave him several major victories and made him the dominating figure in Washington. The economic conditions that he inherited made his success possible. When he presented his economic program to the American people on 18 February 1981, the nation suffered from double-digit inflation and 20 percent interest rates. Almost eight million people were unemployed and millions more felt threatened by possible future layoffs. Workers had suffered a 5 percent decline in real hourly wages over the previous five years, while federal personal taxes for the average family had gone up 67 percent. The national debt was approaching $1 trillion.

Economic problems had been accumulating since 1965. Vietnam War financing had overheated the economy and allowed an inflation psychology to take root. At the same time the unemployment rate began to rise, and three recessions hit the nation from 1969 to 1980. The tax burden increased because of "bracket creep" that occurred when inflation pushed people into higher income tax slots. The productivity growth rate began to drop in 1973 and the American standard of living stagnated. Unemployment increased, while employment shifted from the high-paying, but declining, manufacturing sector into the expanding, but low-paying, service sector. Working- and middle-class wives flooded into the marketplace to try to maintain family income, and that movement increased disquiet because it challenged traditional conceptions of gender relations and family structure.[34]

By 1980, the American people had lost confidence in old ways of dealing with economic problems and were willing to try something new. After World War II, Keynesian economics had dominated policy. Government managers fought unemployment by beefing up the economy through spending increases and tax cuts or, in turn, battled inflation by cooling the economy with spending reductions and tax increases. But in the 1970s the

Keynesian consensus eroded. Stagflation—simultaneous rising unemployment and rising inflation—baffled economic managers because fighting one problem made the other one worse.[35]

Supply-side economists believed that they had the answers to deep-seated economic problems. They believed that Keynesian approaches had concentrated on demand and had neglected supply incentives to work and to invest. They believed that in the post–World War II era, government policy had increasingly eroded productivity by excessive government regulation that hampered business and added costs to American products trying to compete in the world economy. High progressive income taxes reduced the incentive to work harder and to invest more.

Supply-side proponents advocated a huge cut in marginal income taxes, embodied in legislation sponsored by Representative Jack Kemp (Rep., N.Y.) and Senator William V. Roth Jr. (Rep., Del.) that would cut personal taxes 30 percent over three years. Supply-side activists had deep faith in the dynamics of capitalism and in the self-regulating power of the free marketplace. Some supply-siders believed that the dramatic tax cut would so unleash the power inherent in the capitalist economy that it would quickly lead to an increase in tax revenue.[36]

Critics charged that Reagan had been brainwashed by a small supply-side group led by Kemp, journalist Jude Wanniski, and economist Arthur Laffer. John Sears had brought Kemp into contact with Reagan in preparation for the 1980 campaign. Sears believed that Kemp and his associates had a bold alternative (the Kemp-Roth plan to cut taxes by 10 percent each year for three years) to Carter's gloomy talk of limits. Reagan, like most Republican conservatives, had always feared and detested deficit spending, which he blamed on the Democrats. The supply-side approach, at least to an optimist like Reagan, promised that cutting taxes would not increase the deficit because the huge tax cut would be offset by a rise in revenue (as described in the "Laffer curve," named after Arthur Laffer). If the tax cuts were self-financing, as the supply-siders argued, allowing Washington to reduce taxes without slashing revenues, then Kemp-Roth would reduce the need for deep cuts in federal programs. Supply-side action, cutting taxes and maintaining high levels of spending, would provide an escape from the traditional Republican "root canal" economics that Kemp deplored. In January 1980, Kemp, Laffer, and Wanniski conducted a seminar for Reagan on supply-side theory. Wanniski described Reagan's reaction: "He has the concept of economic growth, as opposed to the Malthusian idea [of limits], in his bones and thus finds himself extremely comfortable with supply-side ideas." David Stockman said that when Reagan understood the Laffer curve, "He knew instantly that it was true and would never doubt it a moment thereafter."[37]

OMB director David Stockman became the main figure in the early months of the Reagan administration. "He would extract Reaganomics from Reaganism," wrote one journalist. Stockman over the years had zig-zagged in his ideological positions, and in 1976 he won a seat in Congress and then turned sharply to the right. Stockman came to regard his congressional colleagues as unthinking hacks whose major purpose was to serve special interests. An exception was Jack Kemp, who stood out "like a lighthouse in a sea of fog." One day Kemp gave Stockman a copy of *The Way the World Works,* by Jude Wanniski. "His book," Stockman wrote, "hit me with the force of revelation. It reordered everything I had previously known or thought about economics."[38]

Reagan and his advisers believed that it was essential to formulate quickly a comprehensive, highly visible economic program. Only Stockman seemed to have the physical energy and mastery of the material—especially of the huge federal budget—to do the job. Observers often described him as a moralist in the tradition of Old Testament prophets. He believed that expansion of federal activities and spending begun by the New Deal had led special-interest groups to warp government policy; raw power, rather than the search for justice, shaped programs. He believed that the growing economic crisis would allow Reagan to force the old-style politicians to the wall and make them dismantle bloated and wasteful activities or face national ruin.

Stockman later believed that he had been misled by Reagan's rhetoric: "The fact was, due to the efforts of myself and my supply-side compatriots, Ronald Reagan had been made to stumble into the wrong camp on the eve of his final, successful quest for the presidency. He was a consensus politician, not an ideologue. He had no business trying to make a revolution because it wasn't in his bones."[39]

Reagan's advisers agreed that all foreign and domestic policy had to be subordinated to economic goals, but they split on whether to concentrate on budget cuts or on tax reductions and on how much importance to place on a balanced budget. Stockman broke the impasse by setting a blitzkrieg schedule that allowed him to control decision making because no one else could keep up with him and the flood of constantly shifting economic numbers. The crisis atmosphere also allowed him to paper over the splits among the advisers. He became a star in the eyes of Reagan and his inner circle, none of whom knew much about economics, because he promised to produce a comprehensive package that could do all that Reagan had promised: cut taxes, reduce government spending, raise military spending, reduce inflation, and produce a balanced budget. Stockman realized early that the numbers did not add up, that economic reality would intervene and produce a huge deficit if Reagan tried to achieve everything that he had promised. Stockman assumed that when reality hit, panicked politicians would make an all-out assault on welfare state programs, reduce the size of the tax cut, and cut the rate of growth in military spending. He failed to realize that economic reality would always have to be filtered through political reality.[40]

On 7 January 1981 Stockman and the economic team met with Reagan, Bush, Meese, Baker, and others. Stockman made his major point: that the numbers indicated that spending would have to be cut by $75 billion a year, and possibly more, to balance the budget by 1984. Reagan's inner circle did not understand that budget cuts had to go beyond "waste, fraud, and abuse" and hit big programs with large, powerful constituencies. Nor did they understand that there would not be a Laffer curve bounce in revenues, since Stockman had already added recovered revenues to his projections. Rather than facing the reality that his program would not work as he had envisioned, Reagan's basic optimism convinced him that everything would turn out for the best. He did not like analysis and argument, and he let his boredom show. He set the policy and expected his experts to figure out how to do it. Reagan told Stockman that he agreed that there was an economic mess and that he would back up him and his economic team while they cleaned it up.[41]

After the 7 January meeting, Stockman presented Reagan and his advisers with proposals for large budget cuts. They accepted his suggestions without dissent. Reagan would say, "Okay, let's do it." These meetings fed the assumption that making the package work would be easy. What Stockman did not make clear was that the cuts, which sounded big, only dealt with a small part of the budget and did not touch defense, Medicare, Social Security, or veterans' benefits. Stockman won agreement to big cuts in Amtrak, education programs, synthetic-fuel subsidies, physician training programs, low-income housing, and scores of programs for community development, health, and social services.[42]

Despite the savings they had made on paper, the numbers required to balance the budget kept getting worse. Stockman and his team needed an accurate forecast on economic growth and inflation. That forecast would allow them to determine the spending reductions they needed to offset both the projected tax cuts and the increase in the military budget, and, finally, would give them the estimated size of the deficit. The experts could not agree on a forecast and, with time running out before Reagan's 18 February speech, just negotiated a compromise that predicted solid economic growth and a rapid fall in the inflation rate. That forecast came to be called the "Rosy Scenario," soon known as the highest placed lady in Reagan's administration.[43]

Even with the most optimistic forecast that people could reasonably accept, the numbers kept changing. The spending cuts they had agreed on no longer seemed enough. By 7 February the OMB computer was projecting deficits of $130 billion by 1984 and a five-year deficit of over $600 billion. Stockman devised another round of deficit-reduction measures, which he called Chapter Two cuts. These included measures that fell on upper-income people: user fees on private aviators and yachters, elimination of tax loopholes, including the oil depletion allowance, drastic curtailment of farm and business subsidies, and a cap on tax deductibility of home mortgage costs for those in the highest tax brackets. Chapter Two cuts would have provided $40 billion or more in savings by 1984 and made the whole package fairer. At the same time, Meese, worrying about the fairness issue, took the really big programs off the table and said they could not be touched: Social Security, Medicare, veterans' benefits, Head Start, and several other programs that benefited middle- and lower-income people. Reagan, in turn, would not allow defense spending to be touched.

On Wednesday, 11 February, Stockman presented his Chapter Two deficit-reduction package to the president. The usually passive Reagan quickly became enraged. He attacked the idea that the oil depletion allowance was a form of spending, a "tax expenditure": "We're not going to have any of that kind of thinking round here," he said. The trap began to close on Stockman. Meese had taken 40 percent of the domestic budget off the table, and Reagan had taken the defense budget off. Now Reagan forbade touching oil depletion and other tax breaks for the wealthy.[44]

Reagan's televised 18 February speech was one of the most important of his presidency. He presented a four-part program: reducing taxes, cutting government spending, eliminating unnecessary regulations, and pursuing an anti-inflationary monetary policy. He predicted that these actions would create thirteen million new jobs while controlling inflation. He claimed that his spending cuts would result in $49.1 billion in budget savings, by reducing eighty-three different programs. He estimated that his plan to reduce taxes 10 percent in each of the following three years would put $500 billion in the pockets of taxpayers over five years. Reagan's plan placed trust in the marketplace and promised to reward work and entrepreneurial risk taking, while reducing the role of government. "Spending by government must be limited to those functions which are the proper province of government. We can no longer afford things simply because we think of them." Government, he said, was the major cause of the nation's economic problems.[45]

After Reagan's speech he had to present a budget to Congress. His party controlled the Senate, but the Democrats, led by Speaker Thomas P. "Tip" O'Neill (Dem., Mass.), had a majority in the House. O'Neill and Reagan, two great Irish storytellers, liked each other personally, but O'Neill, the consummate insider, had barely concealed contempt for Reagan as a political leader. "You're in the big leagues now," he told the president, and O'Neill had a twenty-six-vote Democratic majority in the House. He was a liberal Democrat who considered Reaganomics unfair because it fell heavily on the less affluent and slashed programs reformers had been constructing since the days of Roosevelt. He bided his time, waiting for the enthusiasm that typically greeted a new administration to ease. In early spring he decided that it was time to go on the offensive, and he prepared a major attack on Reaganomics.[46]

On 30 March 1981, before O'Neill could act, Reagan left a Washington hotel where he had just spoken. He was approached by a mentally ill young man, John W. Hinckley, who sprayed the presidential party with gunshots, hitting the president, Secret Service agent Tim McCarthy, patrolman Thomas Delahanty, and gravely wounding the White House press secretary, James S. Brady.[47]

Reagan did not know he was hit. Secret Service agent Jerry Parr threw the president into his limousine and then fell on him. Reagan felt excruciating pain and thought that Parr must have broken his rib. He coughed into his hand, which filled with red, frothy blood. He told Parr that a rib must have punctured his lung. Parr directed the limousine to George Washington University Hospital. Reagan felt he was smothering and began to panic, going in and out of consciousness. Hinckley's bullet had ricocheted off the limousine, hit Reagan under the left arm, striking a rib, then penetrated his lung and stopped an inch from his heart. He was near death when he got to the hospital. Only quick, effective medical treatment saved his life.

Nancy Reagan and Reagan's inner circle hid the fact that the president was near death. Instead they treated the public to Reagan's heroic witticisms. To Nancy, he quipped, "Honey, I forgot to duck"; to a doctor as he prepared him for surgery, "I hope you're a Republican"; to a nurse who asked him how he felt, "All in all, I'd rather be in Philadelphia."[48]

The president's courage and grace raised him to a new level of popularity and added what Michael Deaver called the "Teflon coating" to his presidency. His popularity would go up and down over the years, but he was almost immune to personal attacks. The respect and affection most people felt for him was so enormous that opponents could attack his policies but not the man himself. But it was months before Reagan fully recovered, and there were lasting effects. Nancy's fears for her husband's safety made her more vulnerable to astrologers who would play an increasing role in shaping the president's schedule. The assassination attempt also encouraged the already detached and rather lazy Reagan to become even more disengaged from the details and operations of the White House. His team worked so well while he was on the sidelines that it taught him and those around him that he did not have to immerse himself in the work of his administration.[49]

If Reagan resisted mastering the operations of government, he worked hard as salesman. He realized that winning high-profile victories on his budget and tax plans would be crucial for the rest of his presidency. He addressed a joint session of Congress on 28 April. It was his first public appearance since the shooting, and he received a tumultuous welcome from Congress and the public. In the meantime, James Baker and the Legislative Strategy Group bargained with individual congressmen, and Reagan again did his part. During his first one hundred days in office, despite his wound, he met sixty-nine times with 467 congressmen, and he made countless telephone calls to individual legislators.[50]

A relatively new process called reconciliation helped Reagan in his fight for his budget. This procedure allowed the House and Senate Budget Committees to group budget proposals into one big package, avoiding individual votes on separate bills from each of the committees that supervised one part of the budget. Bargaining over the package was intense. Congressmen who regarded Reagan as an unbending ideologue learned that he could wheel and deal. He told Howard Baker: "Do what is necessary to get the program adopted. Don't back off. Find out what needs doing and do it. Period." Senator Orrin G. Hatch (Rep., Utah) protected the Job Corps, Jesse Helms guarded benefits for the tobacco program, Howard Baker defended the Clinch River Breeder Reactor, Strom Thurmond protected the Rural Electrification Administration. In a series of Senate votes, Reagan prevailed.[51]

In the House, James R. Jones (Dem., Okla.), chair of the Budget Committee, put together a centrist alternative to Reagan's budget. It included many of Stockman's cuts, but while the administration bill cut social programs an average of 25 percent, Jones's package reduced them 10–12 percent. He cut food stamps by $950 million rather than the administration's $1.6 billion; he lowered child nutrition programs by $1 billion, compared with the White House's $2 billion.

Stockman counterattacked, helping Phil Gramm (Dem., Tex.) and Delbert Latta (Rep., Ohio) put together a substitute for the Jones bill. With two plans on the table, Reagan went after the "boll weevil" Democrats, O'Neill's Southern conservatives. Insiders believed that Reagan needed about forty boll weevil votes to substitute Gramm-Latta for the Jones bill. Reagan wooed important members with invitations to state dinners, box seats to the Kennedy Center, and personal visits to his office. In early May sixty-three Democrats joined all the House Republicans to pass the Gramm-

Latta bill. "It's been a long time since Republicans had a victory like this," Reagan wrote in his diary.[52]

Gramm-Latta gave reconciliation instructions to the House committees. The actual spending cuts required legislation, which came in the Omnibus Budget Reconciliation Act of 1981 (OBRA), one of the most sweeping pieces of legislation in modern United States history. Reagan again led the fight. Congressmen lined up to make deals. Boll weevil John Breaux (Dem., La.), trying to protect sugar interests, spoke for many when he said, "I can't be bought, but I can be rented." The Reagan-backed bill passed on 27 July. On 31 July, after the conference committee worked out a final bill, both Houses passed OBRA.[53]

While the budget fight was taking place, Reagan guided his tax plan through Congress. It became the Economic Recovery Tax Act of 1981 (ERTA). In his 18 February 1981 address he had called for $53.9 billion in tax cuts in 1982, starting with a 10 percent cut in individual income tax rates on 1 July 1981, with the additional 10 percent cuts on 1 July 1982 and 1 July 1983. He also called for accelerated depreciation for businesses of the costs of purchasing new plants and equipment. He did not believe that his tax program threatened his military buildup and his goal of a balanced budget. Despite the denials of some of his associates, Reagan believed in the Laffer curve: "I wanted a balanced budget. But I also wanted peace through strength. My faith was in those tax reforms, and I believed we could have a balanced budget within two or three years—by 1984 at the latest."[54]

Treasury Secretary Donald Regan led the fight for the tax bill. He stressed the importance of a cut in marginal tax rates for individuals, the tax they had to pay for any increase in income. A cut in marginal rates, he told Reagan, would alter the behavior of taxpayers by giving them an incentive to work and invest. He also said that the administration tax bill mainly helped the middle class; people earning between $10,000 and $60,000 a year paid 72 percent of the taxes and would receive 73 percent of the tax-cut benefit. Stockman was more cynical. He said the goal was to bring down the top rates and that would have a beneficial "trickle-down" effect on less affluent people. To make a cut in upper rates politically possible, all the rates had to be lowered, "but, I mean, Kemp-Roth was always a Trojan horse to bring down the top rate," Stockman said.[55]

The battle was hard fought. Although many analysts assumed that the American people supported any tax cut, in fact polls indicated that they did not want tax reductions that led to bigger deficits. On 4 June, Reagan worked out a deal that he thought would attract the boll weevils. He accepted a bill proposed by Barber B. Conable (Rep., N.Y.) and Kent R.

Hance (Dem., Tex.). It provided for a 5-10-10 cut and delayed the first-year reduction until 1 October 1981. At a breakfast with the boll weevils, Reagan told them that while he could not prevent Republican challenges to their reelection in 1982, he promised that he would not campaign against those who supported his bill.[56]

On 27 July Reagan made an impassioned televised plea for the Hance-Conable bill. He asked the people to let their representatives hear from them, and telephone calls and letters flooded Congress. Representative Carroll Hubbard Jr. (Dem., Ky.), who had resisted the appeal of a state dinner invitation and personal pleas from the president, got 500 calls, 480 of them supporting Reagan. Hubbard voted for Hance-Conable. Reagan and his team bargained with individual congressmen. Minority Whip Trent Lott (Rep., Miss.) described the mood that swept the House: "Everybody else is getting theirs, it's time we got ours."

Reagan worked the telephones and invited fourteen waverers to a barbecue at Camp David (and got eleven of their votes). He made individual deals. Charles Hatcher (Dem., Ga.) got the administration to drop its opposition to peanut subsidies. William F. Goodling (Rep., Pa.) gave his support in return for a promise to keep open a military base in his district. Reagan gave Glenn English (Dem., Okla.) a handwritten note saying he would veto "with pleasure" any windfall tax on natural gas.[57]

Reagan nervously awaited the vote. On 29 July forty-eight Democrats joined all the House Republicans but one to give Reagan his tax bill, by a vote of 238 to 195. O'Neill once again was soundly defeated by the "amateur" from California. Reagan noted in his diary, "This on top of the budget victory is the greatest political win in half a century."[58]

On 13 August 1981, Reagan signed both the Economic Recovery Tax Act of 1981 and the Omnibus Budget Reconciliation Act of 1981. He said OBRA represented $130 billion in savings over the next three years and ERTA $750 billion in tax cuts over five years. Reagan's claim of savings by OBRA was probably too high, but the act clearly affected millions of people by making changes in AFDC, food stamps, unemployment compensation, subsidized housing, and many other programs.[59]

ERTA contained the 5-10-10 tax cut formula on individual tax rates, reduced the rate on investment income from 70 percent to 50 percent, reduced the maximum rate on capital gains from 28 percent to 20 percent, indexed individual income tax brackets to the consumer price index, provided business with an accelerated system of depreciation, and provided tax breaks for the oil industry.[60]

Time did not settle the debate over the meaning of Reaganomics. The economy slid into a deep recession just after Reagan signed the bills and then in later years the budget deficit reached levels hardly imagined possible when he took office. This confirmed to many critics that Reaganomics was a failure with disastrous consequences. Others believed OBRA and ERTA contained scores of needed reforms in reducing or eliminating flawed programs and in instituting needed changes in the tax code, such as bracket indexing. Some of the mistakes made in the tax code in 1981 would be revised in a new tax bill in 1982 and a major reform of the code in 1986. Reagan's supporters felt vindicated, because when the recession ended the United States entered the longest period of economic growth in American history. The debate continued. Reagan's supporters pointed to the fifteen million new jobs created during the period of economic expansion, while his opponents showed that half the positions paid below-poverty-level wages; jobs at Wendy's and McDonald's replaced those at Ford and General Motors.

One effect of Reagan's victory in winning OBRA and ERTA was clear. The outsider from California had established his domination in Washington to an extent that had eluded recent presidents. Reagan was surrounded by an aura of glamour and power that remained until the Iran-contra scandal placed him on the defensive during the latter half of his second term.

6

Managing Big Government, 1981–1985

Ronald Reagan's budget and tax victories in 1981 established him as a formidable political power and put Congress, liberal Democrats, and Republican moderates on the defensive for eight years. His victories convinced most Americans that Reagan had put the nation on the right track, and even during the severe recession of 1981 and 1982 he retained a solid base of supporters who believed, or hoped, that Reaganomics would eventually work the way he promised.

The "Reagan revolution" that his admirers believed he had begun in 1981 was more a matter of perception than reality. During the two decades prior to the Reagan presidency, for example, federal tax receipts had averaged about 19 percent of gross national product (GNP). Under Carter, Social Security tax increases and inflation-driven bracket creep pushed tax levels to 20.8 percent of GNP and were projected to rise to 24 percent by 1986. Reagan's tax cuts restored the federal tax share to about 19 percent of GNP, returning revenues to the level of the recent past. Reagan's reputation as a budget slasher was overstated as well. Spending rose under Reagan, even for many social welfare programs, but at a slower rate than under recent presidents. Reagan, said Martin Anderson, turned large planned increases into moderate ones.

But Reagan did bring change to Washington. He shifted the national agenda. During the liberal era reformers had responded to social and economic problems by starting government programs to deal with them. Reagan's huge tax cuts and his military buildup contributed to unprecedented deficits that for years after his presidency placed reformers on the defensive. Admirers of his foreign policy later said that Reagan had delegitimized the communist government of the Soviet Union, but he undermined the American government as well. For eight years he hammered home the message that government was the problem, not the solution. Faced with diminished expectations for the role of government in society, liberals concentrated on defending established programs and started no major new social welfare endeavors.[1]

Reagan's initial victories cushioned him when questions arose about his competence as president. While Washington insiders knew that his grasp of most issues was shaky to nonexistent, he was a master at presenting himself as a self-assured, forceful leader. Reagan believed that his major responsibility was to exert the inspirational, symbolic leadership that presidents alone could provide; he had underlings to look after administrative management and to take care of details. His duty, he thought, was to reinvigorate and defend traditional American values. Reagan was relaxed and serene in a city filled with driven workaholics. He loved almost every aspect of his job. He did not agonize over the presidency as the "loneliest job in the world" or suffer from existential despair. He made the presidency into a part-time position and still, in the judgment of most Americans, did the job well. He was a secure man, who confidently believed the Hollywood version of reality in which a citizen-politician could go to Washington and set things right.[2]

A few days before Reagan signed the budget and tax bills in August 1981, he entered into another battle that shaped public perceptions of him for the rest of his presidency. His high-profile stand against the Professional Air Traffic Controllers' Organization (PATCO) showed him to be tough, decisive, and confident. It provided an example of Reagan taking action that, according to one insider, most of his major advisers opposed, and it gave notice to business executives that it was acceptable to break the power of labor unions. Photographs of a union leader being taken away in chains even caught the attention of Kremlin leaders and impressed them with Reagan's resolve.[3]

PATCO members ran the sophisticated technology that controlled the nation's air traffic. They regarded themselves as highly trained professionals in stressful jobs, made worse by long hours and outmoded equipment. During the 1980 campaign Reagan held a secret meeting with PATCO president Robert E. Poli. Reagan promised that if he was elected he would take "whatever steps are necessary" to provide the best air traffic equipment available and to improve working conditions by hiring more controllers. PATCO endorsed him in his race against President Carter.[4]

After the election, Reagan had to act as the head of government rather than as a candidate seeking votes. The PATCO contract expired in March 1981, and Reagan's advisers warned him that the administration's position in those negotiations would send signals to several other unions, notably the huge postal union, whose contracts would expire in the first few months of 1981. One adviser wrote that a PATCO strike would show that Reagan was not easily pushed around and would moderate labor demands in both the public and private sectors. According to one analysis, PATCO had used six previous "disruptions" to win pay and benefits for its members that far exceeded those for other government employees. Critics regarded PATCO members, or at least its leaders, as pampered and arrogant. Reagan's advisers warned him, however, that a strike would cost $150 million a day in lost domestic commerce alone.[5]

Secretary of Transportation Drew Lewis, who led the negotiations, told Poli that he had three instructions from Reagan: to conduct no negotiations during a strike, to fire those who struck, and to offer no amnesty to those fired. Poli was about to learn that on some issues Reagan was unbending.[6]

In a press conference on 3 August, Reagan, joined by Drew Lewis and Attorney General William French Smith, announced that PATCO had struck at 7:00 A.M. Reagan gave striking workers forty-eight hours to return to work or be fired, and Lewis confirmed that there would be no change in the government offer to PATCO and no negotiations during the strike. He said that supervisory personnel, joined by 150 military controllers, had the system running at 50 percent capacity. On 5 August Reagan announced that 38 percent of PATCO members had returned to work, and on 13 August he said that about twelve thousand controllers had been fired and flight schedules had returned to 80 percent normal.[7]

The PATCO union was destroyed, and the administration did not flinch from predictions—erroneous as it turned out—that it would take two or three years to get the system back to normal. Reagan's legendary luck held. If there had been a major accident, the consequences for him politically could have been disastrous, but the air safety record actually improved. In early November, Richard Wirthlin's polls showed that 67 percent of the American people approved Reagan's actions, including 61 percent of blue-collar workers. On 9 December Reagan confirmed his position that fired controllers would not be rehired, although they could apply for other government positions. Reagan's action sent a powerful message to American business executives and labor leaders.[8]

Reagan also showed his toughness in pursuing his plan to build up American military strength. He told his associates that "if we can restore the strength of the military and get the economy healthy then everything else will become possible." As he had so often in public life, Reagan tapped a deep swing in public sentiment. The national security community was dismayed at the "Vietnam syndrome" that paralyzed American will to use its power. Nixon's détente policy with the Soviet Union and normalization of relations with China, and Carter's supposedly dovish defense policy, such as canceling the B-1 bomber program, convinced many that the United States had abandoned international leadership at the very time that the Soviet Union was expanding its military power. Analysts later concluded that the increase in Soviet military spending might have reflected that nation's inefficiency, which required higher expenditures just to maintain its relative position in relation to American power. While the Soviets could turn out impressive numbers of tanks and artillery pieces from their heavy-industry sector, they could not compete with the Americans in weaponry based on sophisticated technology. Still, toward the end of his presidency Carter responded to the perception that United States power had declined by beginning a military buildup.[9]

Reagan's defense program divided his advisers and displayed Reagan's decisive leadership on issues he regarded as basic. Secretary of Defense Weinberger and the defense establishment fought to increase Carter's already large increase in the defense budget, which promised a 5 percent increase in spending each year for five years. David Stockman, James Baker, and others believed that the huge impending deficits required the Department of Defense to moderate its spending plans. Other cabinet officers, concerned about cuts in their own programs, joined Stockman in demanding that Weinberger share their pain.

Weinberger doggedly fought even minor decreases, and Reagan backed him long after the public and Congress wanted to slow military spending. Reagan refused to judge defense spending in budgetary terms. He told his advisers, "The defense budget cannot be determined by other programs, what we spend on defense is what we must spend to maintain our national security, and how much we spend depends largely on what the Soviet Union does."

Weinberger and Reagan had decided to advance military spending by 7 percent a year, added to Carter's 5 percent increase. During Reagan's first five years in office, the military share of GNP grew from 5.7 percent to 7.4 percent. Military spending increased by over 50 percent in real terms, totaling nearly $1.5 trillion during those years, and growing from $143.9 billion in 1980 to $294.7 billion in 1985, which set the new standard for the defense budget in successive administrations.[10]

The results of the military buildup continued to be debated long after Reagan left office. Many critics believed that money flooded into the Pentagon so rapidly that much of it was wasted and did not add to American military power. Still, despite Pentagon waste, analysts concluded that Reagan's program dramatically improved the combat readiness of American forces. Edwin Meese and other Reaganites believed that it was Reagan's program that made possible the spectacular military performance in the 1991 Persian Gulf War. They also believed that it was Reagan's military buildup that forced Soviet premier Mikhail Gorbachev to accept the fact that his country could no longer compete with the United States militarily and to take actions to bring the cold war to an end.[11]

Reagan's victories in the tax and budget fights, his success in the PATCO strike, and his ability to carry out the largest defense buildup in history gave him a lasting public reputation for courage, boldness, strength, and competence. Yet this success took place alongside mounting evidence that Reagan paid little attention to much of the work of his government. Some observers wondered if someday scholars would uncover a "hidden-hand" Reagan presidency, as political scientist Fred I. Greenstein and other scholars discovered in the archives of the Eisenhower presidency. To his contemporaries, Eisenhower had seemed to be a pleasant and charming figurehead president who detested politics and turned many of his responsibilities over to his staff and cabinet. In fact, Greenstein found that Eisenhower was a masterly politician, a skilled behind-the-scenes puppetmaster who manipulated his subordinates and his public image to achieve his ends.

Reagan, like Eisenhower, succeeded in achieving a number of his goals, maintained his popularity over eight years, and exercised powerful political clout when he chose to intervene on specific issues. Was Reagan a cloaked Machiavellian figure who managed his administration in hidden-hand fashion? Almost certainly not. In terms of public leadership, in using the "bully pulpit" to build support for programs important to him, Reagan was one of the most skilled and active presidents of the twentieth century, on a par with Woodrow Wilson and Franklin Roosevelt. However, Reagan was often almost entirely absent from the nuts-and-bolts work of his administration's policy formulation. He concentrated his time and energy on a few major policy areas, and even there left the details to others. The administration worked effectively partly because Reagan provided such clear and emphatic ideological direction that his subordinates could make decisions in his name, confident he would approve.[12]

Reagan held to his priorities but was flexible on tactics. "He cajoled, he persuaded, he exhorted, and sometimes he threatened," wrote Martin Anderson. "He explored every possible means to achieve his ends. He would try one approach and if it did not work he would quickly give it up—with no apparent remorse or regrets—and move on to a new approach." He hid his compromises by his unmatched ability to present himself as the unbending defender of conservative principles and protector of the public good. Often at the very moment that he was giving in on an issue, he most strongly projected the image of being totally inflexible. Still, while his flexibility sometimes surprised opponents, he also often had a line that he would not cross, as Robert Poli found in the PATCO negotiations and as Mikhail Gorbachev would find at his summit meetings with Reagan. When he felt he had to make a decision, Anderson said, he "will never alter his course. . . . He never acts with malice and he never takes pleasure from the discomfort of others. But if it is necessary he will cause that discomfort, freely and easily." Reagan was, Anderson said, "a warmly ruthless man."[13]

Ordinarily, however, except for the limited number of issues that attracted his attention, Reagan was the most passive of modern presidents. His admirer Martin Anderson wrote: "He made decisions like an ancient king or a Turkish pasha, passively letting his subjects serve him, selecting only those morsels of public policy that were especially tasty. Rarely did he ask searching questions and demand to know why someone had or had not done something. He just sat back in a supremely calm, relaxed manner and waited until important things were brought to him. And then he would act, quickly, decisively, and usually, very wisely." NSC staff member Constantine Menges believed that Reagan's passivity stemmed from his trusting nature, from his belief that his aides would tell him what he needed to know without slanting the information. Donald Regan traced Reagan's passivity to his shyness. He was a diffident man who hesitated to show his ignorance by asking questions before people he did not know, and "thanks to the way his staff operated, nearly everyone was a stranger to this shy President except the members of his innermost circle."[14]

Reagan, a reactive decision maker shaped by his years as an actor, was used to performing the role worked out by his producer, director, and scriptwriter. Unlike other recent presidents he did not construct an informal network of outside confidants and advisers to insure that his staff did not hem him in. He never initiated contact with his subordinates nor checked to see if they had information for him. He trusted those around him to act as honest brokers and never understood that such people were rarely found.

He was more vulnerable than most presidents to his staff's attempts to protect him by building a wall around him. OMB staff member Fred Khedouri described self-censorship by the president's staff: "People wouldn't bring him something if they knew he would be averse to it." An associate, who disagreed with Reagan's opposition to *Roe v. Wade,* never discussed it with him: "Truthfully, I could not imagine ever raising an unpleasant subject with Ronald Reagan."[15]

Reagan's passivity raised questions about his intelligence. Clark Clifford dismissed him as an "amiable dunce." Carter's CIA director, Stansfield Turner, who briefed Reagan several times, described him as "stupid." In 1980, when Republican representative Henry J. Hyde of Illinois wondered why William Casey was supporting Ronald Reagan, a man who did not know anything, Casey defended Reagan by saying, "Don't forget, Henry—the guys who have the brains can't get elected, and the guys who get elected don't always have the brains." Later in Reagan's presidency Republican senator William S. Cohen of Maine said, "With Ronald Reagan, no one is there. The sad fact is we don't have a president."[16]

Some Reagan associates regarded him as highly intelligent, but recognized that he was not an intellectual who was capable of analytical thought or who enjoyed thinking through difficult concepts. He reduced complex ideas to anecdotes, often from his life in Hollywood, sometimes with little relevance to the subject at hand. Some found Reagan's intelligence displayed in his quick wit or his ability to read the American people and respond to their hopes and fears, and to use symbol and myth to accomplish his goals. Reagan was "no genius," said Lyn Nofziger, but his intellectual strength was his ability to see the "big picture." Speechwriter Peggy Noonan imagined that if she had asked Reagan why he was so odd, he would reply, "I'm only odd for a president." That was the conclusion Lou Cannon came to when he resolved his puzzle over Reagan's intelligence by reading psychologist Howard Gardner's theory of multiple intelligence. Cannon believed that Reagan was low in the logical-mathematical intelligence common in lawyers and politicians, but high in bodily kinesthetic, interpersonal, and linguistic intelligences. Thus, he was odd, indeed, only for a president.[17]

Even many admirers who believed Reagan was intelligent agreed that he was intellectually lazy. "Behind those warm eyes is a lack of curiosity that is, somehow, disorienting," said a friend. Tip O'Neill, who said that Reagan "would have made a hell of a king," concluded: "Ronald Reagan lacked the knowledge he should have had in every sphere, both domestic and international. Most of the time he was an actor reading lines, who didn't understand his own programs. I hate to say it about such an agreeable man, but it was sinful that Ronald Reagan ever became president." His conservative Republican associate, Representative Philip Crane, said, "Candidly, Reagan's problem is that he has not done his fundamental home work since the late 1950's." General Colin L. Powell, who served as Reagan's final national security adviser, agreed that since Reagan did not update his anecdotes, they decreasingly fit reality.[18]

Reagan's frequent misstatements of facts or reports of his laziness did not seem to bother the public. He was known as the Teflon president because blame did not stick to him. He was a genial man, completely free of meanness, and people, even cynical reporters, were seduced by his charm and wanted to protect him. His decisive actions in 1981, together with the White House's unparalleled ability to project the image it desired, allowed most people to retain their view of Reagan as a forceful leader who had the nation on the right track. His bloopers seemed to be irrelevant or even part of his charm. His anecdotes, even when they were inaccurate and off the point, often contained a moral that appealed to people. His little stories made facts come alive for his audiences and lodged his moral points in their memories.[19]

Reagan's staff tried in various ways to overcome his weaknesses. He typically received his briefings passively, making almost no verbal or physical response. Advisers like Clark and Meese worked hard at briefing, varying their voices, maintaining eye contact, switching subjects when the president's eyes glazed. The efficacy of whatever they tried in written and oral briefings depended on how willing Reagan was to work at it. His staff, worried about his performance, provided him with special briefing material before the 1983 international economic summit and gave it to him the night before the conference opened. The next morning James Baker found that Reagan had not opened the briefing book and asked why. Reagan replied, "Well, Jim, *The Sound of Music* was on last night."[20]

Reagan turned the presidency into a nine-to-five job, usually with Wednesday and Friday afternoons off. During his working hours his aides understood that they needed to keep his schedule light. If they did not understand that, Nancy Reagan made sure they learned it. When a friend remarked to Casey that he seemed to work harder at the CIA directorship than Reagan did as president, Casey said, "Are you kidding? . . . He barely works at the job." Reagan spent nearly a full year of his two terms at his 688-acre Rancho del Cielo in the Santa Ynez Mountains north of Santa Barbara, California. He enjoyed 183 weekends at Camp David. Reagan told Washington journalists, "It's true hard work never killed anybody, but I figure, why take a chance?"[21]

How did a physically and intellectually lazy man achieve so much? Part of the answer lay in the way Reagan organized his presidency to allow himself to act as chair of a board of directors. He was a team player who set the ideological boundaries for the board and acted as its public spokesman. This system fit both his personality and his strength as the Great Communicator, and it allowed his team to offset his personal weaknesses. The troika backed him with good political advice (James Baker), mastery of conservative policy positions (Edwin Meese), and astute understanding of Reagan's personality and personal strengths and weaknesses (Michael Deaver).[22]

Reagan, like virtually every modern president, started his administration by announcing that he intended to establish cabinet government, and he was one of the few who made cabinet government work reasonably well. Edwin Meese devised Reagan's cabinet council system as a way to provide team support for a president who did not want to deal with details (and to Reagan almost everything was a detail). Reagan initially established five cabinet councils: commerce and trade, human resources, economic affairs, national resources and environment, food and agriculture. Later he added councils on legal policy and on management and administration. The National Security Council oversaw foreign affairs and defense policy. Reagan chaired each council and named a chair pro tempore to direct the group when he was absent. Each council included the cabinet officers most affected by a particular set of policies. For example, Donald Regan was chair pro tempore of the Cabinet Council on Economic Affairs, and it included the secretaries of state, labor, commerce, transportation, the director of OMB, the U.S. trade representative, and the chair of the Council of Economic Advisers. Meese, Baker, Martin Anderson, and Vice President Bush were ex officio members of each council. The troika used the councils to initiate policy actions or to "park" items for further study.

The system worked reasonably well during Reagan's first term. It required minimum direction from the president, and it allowed the conservative ideologues in the White House to keep pushing his policy agenda. By 1985, the councils had met almost five hundred times. The system probably provided the closest thing to cabinet government possible in the modern presidency.[23]

Reagan was more dependent on staff than any other recent president. It was a family secret, William Casey said, that all the insiders understood: Reagan initiated nothing, gave no orders, decided nothing except in the sense of choosing among options presented to him by his advisers. It was a high-risk management style that worked well as long as the president had good staff around him. Secretary of State Haig claimed that the troika was the president: "You couldn't serve in his administration without knowing that Reagan was a cipher and that these men were running the government." Even self-directed individuals like Haig and Donald Regan found Reagan's hands-off approach disconcerting. Haig said Reagan's style created confusion: "To me, the White House was as mysterious as a ghost ship; you heard the creak of the rigging and the groan of the timbers and sometimes even glimpsed the crew on deck. But which of the crew had the helm? Was it Meese, was it Baker, was it someone else? It was impossible to know for sure." On 11 March 1981 Donald Regan wrote himself a note in which he said that so far he had not had even one minute alone with Reagan to discuss what the president expected from him at Treasury. He feared for the presidency: "This . . . is dangerous." Four years later he still had not seen Reagan alone and had never discussed with him economic philosophy or fiscal and monetary policy: "From first day to last at Treasury, I was flying by the seat of my pants. The President never told me what he believed or what he wanted to accomplish in the field of economics."[24]

Reagan had some insight into his management style, even if he did not see its dangers. A community college teacher wrote Reagan about a class he was teaching on leadership. The teacher had divided leadership into four categories: (1) telling, in which the teller initiates a plan and leaves it to subordinates to develop, (2) selling, by initiating policy and then following it through using communication and guidance to insure its implementation, (3) participating, with the participants immersed in group action, and (4) delegating responsibilities to others without deeply involving the leader himself. The teacher asked Reagan to describe himself. Reagan answered, "You have posed a rather difficult question. My initial reaction would be to place myself in the 'seller' category of leadership, because that is the way I would like to lead. However, given the enormous number of budgets and programs I must oversee in this office, I am frequently relegated to the 'delegator' category." He said that he could not, however, "quite" delegate his responsibility to anyone else.[25]

Most of Reagan's subordinates described him as a good boss. Ambitious, confident aides liked the freedom he gave them, and many believed that his trust in them made them live up to his expectations. There was, however, another side to Reagan's unfailing charm and courtesy. His friends and associates seldom knew how they stood with him, and they often discovered a veil or barrier beneath his kindness and good humor. Nancy Reagan told Lou Cannon, *"He's not an easy man, although he seems easy. To everybody he seems very easy, but he is more complex than people think."* His friend and personal lawyer William French Smith said that "Ronald Reagan requires more knowing than any man I have ever known."[26]

Most Reagan associates came to see this most charming and gregarious of men as a loner. He did not need other people, except Nancy. He let his aides manage him, said Lou Cannon, but he kept the managers out of his personal world: "Ronald Wilson Reagan believed in God, his luck, his mother, Nancy Reagan and the United States of America. His trust was in himself."[27]

He remained a mystery to his closest associates, and they discussed him endlessly, trying to figure him out. Perhaps the mystery largely stemmed from the expectations others held of him. Lyn Nofziger said what you saw publicly with Reagan was what you got: There was no private man or, rather, his private and public selves were one and the same. He puzzled his associates because they expected him to wear a public mask different from his private self. Perhaps, as Noonan said, Reagan was only odd for a president.[28]

While his associates regarded Reagan as the nicest of bosses to work for, a remarkable number of them turned out "kiss-and-tell" books that hurt his reputation. Reagan attached himself to causes, not people, which meant, said Martin Anderson, that he was "basically uncaring about the human feelings of those around him, 'a warmly ruthless man.'" He took his aides' work for granted and never patted them on the back, unless another aide told him to. He sometimes did not recognize major figures in his own administration, as when he confused housing secretary Samuel Pierce with a mayor. Nofziger described how brilliantly Reagan could work a crowd during a campaign, "but he never seems to remember that the people who work for him, both paid and volunteer, largely do so because they love and admire him and that they would be ecstatic if he would just drop by and say thanks once in a while. Which he almost never does of his own accord." It was a terrible shock to those who needed Reagan in some emotional way to realize that he did not need them. "I made a pact with myself long ago never to go before Ronald Reagan with my guts hanging out, hoping that he'd offer to put them back in," remarked an aide. "He just doesn't reach out like that." The most important members of the Reagan inner circle had departed or changed jobs by 1985, and they left without Reagan understanding the cost to himself.[29]

Speechwriter Peggy Noonan found that veterans of the Nixon administration believed that the Reagan White House was more punishing on the staff than Nixon's had been, when the enemy was outside the walls. Under Reagan the battlefield was within the White House, with aides backstabbing and knifing each other with gossip and leaks. "And you have to lay it on ol' Dutch," said an aide. "He wouldn't crack down. He should have stopped it. And he could have. But he didn't. It just wasn't his style to get involved." Reagan found it very difficult to fire anyone, which sometimes would have been the only way to end civil war among his subordinates. He was more inclined to let feuding aides slowly be ground up by bureaucratic warfare until they resigned.[30]

Reagan's success as president depended on his staff, which in his first term revolved around the troika. Meese, Baker, and Deaver surprised experienced Washington hands by making the three-way division of power work. George P. Shultz later looked back on the years of the troika as a "golden age," when the White House operated with special political "sensitivity and subtlety." Each morning Baker, Meese, and Deaver met at 7:30 for breakfast. They discussed the news of the previous twenty-four hours and planned the agenda for White House senior staff. At 8 A.M. they met the senior staff to discuss the day's events and ongoing problems and to make duty assignments. Then the troika briefed Reagan. Throughout the day one of the three men would be with Reagan in every meeting he attended.[31]

Meese's power was based on his long and close association with Reagan and his understanding of Reagan's conservative policy stands, but most analysts concluded that Baker, supported by Deaver, was the most powerful figure in the White House. If Meese's special influence with Reagan was based on their shared ideology, Baker's power came from his political sensitivity and good connections with Congress and the media. Baker showed the president how to implement his policy, which required compromise and political packaging. Deaver's title as deputy chief of staff and his responsibility for what seemed like mechanical activities—control over the president's schedule, advance operations, and the First Lady's Office—obscured his power. Deaver understood Ronald Reagan's personal needs, and he knew how to translate Nancy's wishes into action when appropriate or to deflect her when necessary. His special ability to project the media images that best benefited Reagan gave Deaver immense authority over policy and White House activities generally. Deaver was his era's supreme "spin doctor."[32]

Even the members of the troika would eventually be worn down, but one of the first Reagan aides ground up by internecine warfare was the loyal Reaganite national security adviser, Richard Allen. Allen had been placed in an impossible position because the White House had wanted to prevent the emergence of a powerful national security adviser in the mode of Henry Kissinger or Zbigniew Brzezinski. Allen did not report to Reagan directly, but through Meese, which resulted in inefficiency and confusion. When Allen was accused (later cleared) of mishandling some funds, Deaver lined up the support of Nancy Reagan, James Baker, and others to have him removed.[33]

In January 1982 Haig's deputy, William Clark, a Reagan associate from California, became national security adviser, with direct access to the president. Although Clark was inexperienced in foreign affairs, most people believed that he was an honest broker who made sure Reagan heard varying viewpoints. Clark, dismayed at finding Reagan uninformed on security matters, briefed the president once a day, sometimes twice, and had the CIA and Department of Defense prepare special material using visual images and films on subjects like the Soviet military threat.

Clark's reputation as an honest broker did not prevent him from being pulled into constant conflict with Weinberger, Casey, Haig, and Haig's successor, George Shultz. Deaver, joined by Nancy Reagan, began to undermine Clark because they felt that he was playing to Reagan's hard-line instincts in foreign affairs. They believed that with the military buildup under way, it was time for Reagan to become more flexible in foreign affairs and to prepare for a summit with the Soviets. By June 1983 Shultz found that the president "was uneasy with Bill Clark, and Nancy had no time for him at all."[34]

Clark, worn down by the White House infighting, decided to leave. When James Watt resigned in September 1983, Clark jumped at the chance to become secretary of the interior. Baker wanted the position as national security adviser, with Deaver replacing him as chief of staff. Bush, Nancy Reagan, and Shultz approved, but conservatives angrily confronted Reagan and he rejected the plan. Robert C. McFarlane became national security adviser. Reagan later concluded, "My decision not to appoint Jim Baker as national security adviser, I suppose, was a turning point for my administration, although I had no idea at the time how significant it would prove to be." Many Washington insiders believed that if the politically astute Baker had headed the NSC staff, the White House would not have blundered into the Iran-contra fiasco.[35]

The most spectacular turf battles involved the cabinet. Most observers believed that outstanding members of the early cabinet included Secretary of Transportation Drew Lewis and United States Trade Representative William E. Brock, both competent and politically astute men. Weinberger was a powerful force, especially in the early years when he directed the military buildup. Many considered Donald T. Regan to be the "star" in the early cabinet. He used the cabinet councils to forge a close relationship between his department and the White House and after the first few months replaced Stockman as the chief spokesman for economic policy. Attorney General William French Smith often proved to be an embarrassment, making damaging mistakes on civil rights and other policies. Samuel Pierce and Raymond Donovan proved most ineffective, with Pierce an uninspiring leader and Donovan drawn into long years of battles against criminal allegations, later dismissed.[36]

Alexander Haig's slow destruction showed other cabinet officers the fate of those who were not team players. It was easier to admire Haig than to like him. He was an intense man, often seemingly ready to explode in anger, sometimes pounding the table before the astonished, laid-back Californians. Haig later realized that from his first day in office he had violated the California sense of style and manners and had caused his colleagues to perceive him as power hungry. White House staff members toyed with the proud general, humiliating him in countless little ways, trying to drive him out.

Haig's fall also stemmed from clashes over policy. He was sensitive to the needs of the Western alliance and wanted to continue the ongoing arms talks with the Soviets, while some of those closest to Reagan wanted nothing to do with the "evil empire." Haig wanted to strengthen relations with China and was not as sensitive as some of the Californians to the interests of Taiwan. On the other hand, Haig wanted to break the "Vietnam syndrome," which he thought hindered the United States from properly exercising its power in the world, and he wanted to go on the offensive against communism in the Western Hemisphere, especially in El Salvador and Cuba. Haig's belligerent anticommunism frightened the Reaganites because he wanted action rather than hot rhetoric. At one meeting a participant claimed that Cuba was a source of terrorism in Central America, and Haig responded, "Give me the word and I'll make that island a . . . parking lot." After that, the troika insured that Haig never saw Reagan alone, which further undermined the secretary of state.[37]

Tensions mounted in 1982. Haig believed that he had lost Reagan's confidence because of the failure of his high-profile attempt to head off the Falklands War between Great Britain and Argentina. Reagan valued Haig's judgment in international matters but found him "utterly paranoid with regard to the people he must work with." Following one of Haig's many threats to resign, Reagan surprised him by accepting. On 25 June 1982 Reagan announced that Haig was leaving and that George P. Shultz had agreed to become secretary of state.[38]

Shultz became Reagan's most highly regarded cabinet member. He was experienced (this was his fourth cabinet position), highly intelligent, and straightforward. Shultz believed that Reagan had snapped the feeling of national malaise and that his military buildup had gotten the United States "back in business" as a world leader. He believed, however, that the administration's foreign policy needed clearer and stronger direction. Reagan and Shultz shared the belief that communism had failed and that the world was on the verge of historic change. Shultz believed that the communications revolution meant that totalitarian governments could no longer wall off their people from the world and that communist bloc countries would inevitability be forced to open their societies. That belief became a cornerstone of his Soviet policy.[39]

Shultz gave Reagan the firm direction he needed in foreign policy, but his presence created new conflicts. Weinberger and Shultz had served together in the Nixon administration and then as chief officers in the Bechtel Corporation. Despite their long association, perhaps because of it, they found it difficult to work together. Weinberger was tenacious and stubborn. He almost always took a conservative stand on issues and would not move, even if he was wrong. Once, when Admiral William J. Crowe considered admitting to having made a mistake as the best response to a particular news story, Weinberger flushed and said, "Do not do that. . . . Never, never, never, never, never admit you made a mistake."[40]

The Weinberger-Shultz fights sometimes paralyzed national security policymaking. National Security Adviser Clark—and his successors McFarlane and John M. Poindexter—were caught between the powerful and obstinate secretaries and were ground down by the pressure. When McFarlane urged Reagan to end the conflict, Reagan said that he could not fire either one: "If I were to fire George and put Cap over at State, I would get bad policy. So I'm not going to do that. George is the man I want there. But I'm not going to fire Cap. He's my friend." Reagan refused to settle the conflict by firing one of them, and he was too ill informed to act as arbitrator between his strong-minded advisers.[41]

The most controversial member of Reagan's cabinet was Secretary of the Interior James Watt, the Religious Right's highest-ranked member in the administration. The conflict between liberals and conservatives, Watt said, was a "moral battle," and he intended to give no ground. "I'm going for the long ball. . . . I'm Ronald Reagan's high-risk player." Watt had been a major leader in the western Sagebrush Rebellion, which Reagan endorsed. In the 1960s and 1970s environmentalists had scored many legislative victories, including passage of clean air and water acts and legislation to extend parks and wilderness areas. Watt placed himself in the tradition of conservationists who believed in the rational use, not preservation, of natural resources. The Sagebrush Rebellion pitted developers against preservationists, the ranchers, farmers, timber owners, miners, and real estate people against the environmentalists who wanted to leave resources untouched. The rebels portrayed environmentalism as a ploy of an upper-class elite that wanted to preserve its pristine playground at the expense of those who needed to use the nation's resources for survival. "They want food for the soul. *We* need food for the body," one said.

Watt came to Washington promising that under his stewardship the nation would mine more coal, drill more oil, and cut more timber. To Reagan, Watt admitted that he probably could not survive politically if he carried out the president's agenda. "You're going to have to back me and back me and back me," he said. "When you can no longer back me, you will have to fire me." Reagan, eyes sparkling with laughter, replied, "I will."[42]

Ronald Reagan loved the out of doors, and as governor of California he had a good record on environmental matters. Yet Reagan was a conservationist of the old school, not a preservationist. Like many westerners, Reagan supported development and did not see any end to wild nature in the vast western expanses. He ignored forecasts of environmental disasters because he would accept no limits on America's future, not even those set by nature. He had faith that when development encountered environmental restraints, the marketplace would call forth technological innovations to solve the problems.

Some politicians regarded as foolhardy Reagan and Watt's challenge to the environmental movement. However, while polls indicated widespread public support for environmentalist stands, it was a "passive consensus," with broad but not intense support. The environment was not a high-priority issue to most people. Most Americans were not very different from Reagan. They supported the environment, but they wanted jobs and economic growth even more. Reagan and Watt cast their attack on environmentalism in populist terms. Reagan wrote to a correspondent that the federal government had for years been engaged in a land grab, and it was not content with national parks that can be enjoyed by "people like you and me," but is turning it into wilderness areas, open only to those capable of hiking into them. The states were perfectly able to protect the environment, he said, and "I just can't believe that a little elite group in Washington has a conscience and that the people themselves do not."[43]

Watt believed that Reagan's election represented a mandate for development. He knew that he would provoke controversy, and made his agenda clear early. "You have to strike fast in this business," Watt insisted. "Influence is a very perishable commodity. You can lose it practically overnight. You have to use what you've got when you've got it. For me that's right now." During his first day on the job, he told Interior Department employees that he was immediately accepting the resignations of all Carter appointees. "The fact is that you were terminated on November 4. . . . I expect you to be prepared to depart at the end of work today." He urged all those who did not agree with the administration's policy to leave, and told department employees, "There is a place in the world for 'preservationists,' but it is not in the Department of the Interior during my tenure."[44]

Watt acted on his promise to use public land to pump more oil, cut more timber, and mine more minerals. He announced plans to begin processing mineral lease applications for mining development within the wilderness system and to increase grazing and strip-mining operations. In February 1982 the administration proposed selling thirty-five million acres of wilderness lands. Watt gave notice that he intended to lease one billion acres of oil and gas land on the outer continental shelf, a plan that caused him to be labeled an "environmental outlaw" by California governor Jerry Brown.[45]

"If you stick with me," Watt told his associates, "I guarantee you'll never have a moment's peace." He deliberately set out to delegitimize the liberal environmental movement. He ridiculed environmentalists as elitists who valued animals more than humans. He labeled them as extremists, and he argued that God had created the earth for human use, not to be locked away for enjoyment by the wealthy. He placed himself, and the Reagan administration, squarely in the tradition of such conservationists as Theodore Roosevelt and Gifford Pinchot. That tradition was, he said, to use natural resources, carefully and without waste, for the benefit of the people living now. The environmentalists struck back, depicting Watt as a crazed human chainsaw and tying up his initiatives in court. Watt was beloved by many conservatives, but he quickly became Reagan's least-popular cabinet officer.[46]

Watt's ally, Ann Gorsuch Burford, was another target of attack by the environmental groups. She had been an important young conservative legislator in Colorado and a leader of the Sagebrush Rebellion. As head of the Environmental Protection Agency (EPA), Burford had a high-profile responsibility for administering important environmental laws. When Watt interviewed her for the position, he expressed doubt that she was tough enough. Her explosion convinced him otherwise. What the administration had in mind was perhaps revealed by a question her deputy was asked during his job interview: "Would you be willing to bring EPA to its knees?"

Burford's critics claimed that she was deliberately sabotaging the environmental protection system built up in the 1960s and 1970s. The press's attack on her was ferocious and was made worse by the incompetence of Rita Lavelle, who was in charge of EPA's toxic waste cleanup. On 7 February 1983 Reagan, at Burford's insistence, fired Lavelle. The controversy continued, and on 9 March 1983, at White House insistence, Burford resigned. She felt betrayed by Reagan, who had abandoned her when she came under fire for carrying out his policy.[47]

The Lavelle and Burford media firestorm did not distract attention for very long from Watt. The Sierra Club gathered one million signatures petitioning for his removal. Former senator Gaylord Nelson, chair of the Wilderness Society, said, "It is time the white-coat people took him away." Watt's own tongue made him an easy target. For example, he angered Native Americans when he remarked that if people wanted to see the failure of socialism, they should visit Indian reservations. In August 1983 Watt spoke to the General Council of the Assemblies of God Church and compared abortion in the United States to the Holocaust. "What are the silent people doing while this destruction of human life is carried out?" he asked. "It is murder. Let's call it murder." The end came on 21 September 1983 when he addressed the United States Chamber of Commerce. He referred to a commission that he had recently appointed and said he had made it balanced: "We have every kind of mix you can have. I have three Democrats, two Republicans. I have a black, I have a woman, two Jews, and a cripple. And we have talent." He quickly apologized, but it was too late. Reagan tried to protect him, but the major figures in the Republican Party, including Paul Laxalt and other western senators, called on him to resign.[48]

William Clark took over the Interior Department, followed in 1985 by Donald P. Hodel. Clark and Hodel were more politically sensitive than Watt, but they did not break sharply with his policies. They were conservatives carrying out Reagan's policy of favoring development over preservation. Despite lawsuits and the delays that Congress tried to impose, Watt had challenged the ecological-preservationist consensus and brought development back into the decision-making process. After Watt's tenure, the environmental movement seemed more moderate and more cognizant of the need for a multiple-use resource policy. If Watt's push for all-out development was blunted, so was the preservationist drive.[49]

Despite the conflicts that tormented his subordinates, Reagan settled comfortably and happily into the presidency. His victories in 1981 gave him the aura of leadership and popularity that carried him through such problems as the recession that began in 1981 or the Watt controversy. He achieved this success without excessive physical effort or emotional stress. His staff did the heavy lifting involved in day-to-day governance, and associates like Watt took the heat for implementing Reagan's policies. The White House years were a happy time for Ronald Reagan.

Those years were not so serene and pleasant for Nancy Reagan. Ronald often returned to the White House living quarters to find her sitting in the bathtub talking to the wall and crying, her way of dealing with her misery. She described herself as experiencing the world through "intuitions and feelings." She never learned to shrug off personal criticism and remained "vulnerable, sensitive, and fearful of ridicule." She hid her vulnerability, she said, by a "hard exterior."[50]

She was controversial from her first days in Washington, starting with her $25,000 inaugural gown. Stories of her extravagances took on added bite as the nation slid into a recession. She seemed insensitive when she began expensive renovations of the White House at the same time that the president and Congress were slashing government budgets for the poor. Her plan to spend $200,000 in private funds on White House china was announced on the same day that the Department of Agriculture approved ketchup as a substitute for vegetables in school lunches. It was said that she was a Christian of the Dior persuasion.[51]

Nancy Reagan believed that critical articles by young female writers had shaped her public image. Feminists often presented her as a rather shallow person, more involved with style, fashion, and gossip than with public policy. She angered them because she opposed abortion rights and the Equal Rights Amendment. They resented her often-repeated statement that her life started when she married Ronald Reagan, and they ridiculed "the gaze," the stare she turned on her husband as he spoke, eyes wide and unmoving, mouth slightly open, as if awestruck by his very presence. She returned their contempt. "They're just ridiculous," she said, referring to feminists. "I really believe a woman's real happiness is found in the home with her husband and children. . . . That's where I think the women's libbers are in for trouble. God made men and women different and they have different needs. . . . I think a woman gets more if she acts feminine."[52]

After polls showed Nancy Reagan had the highest disapproval rating of any first lady in modern times, the White House public relations team began to work to transform her image. She downplayed her interest in style and fashion, and at the 1982 Gridiron dinner held by Washington journalists she performed in a skit that spoofed her interest in clothing and china. Her willingness to laugh at herself helped break the tension that had developed with the press. She also became a high-profile leader in a campaign against drug abuse. Many people admired her for her personal composure in 1987 when she had a mastectomy and used it as an opportunity to educate women about breast cancer.[53]

Nancy Reagan never entirely escaped controversy. While Ronald portrayed himself as the exemplar of family values, Nancy received most of the blame for Reagan family problems. Maureen, Michael, and Patti all publicly criticized her, and Michael's and Patti's estrangement especially became a source of public discussion. More damaging was the revelation in Reagan's second term that his wife was in almost daily contact with astrologer Joan Quigley. Both Nancy and Ronald believed in astrology, but Nancy became obsessed with it after John Hinckley shot her husband. She turned to astrology to protect Ronald and used it to schedule his trips, major speeches, and other events. Deaver translated Nancy's demands into action and kept her secrets. After Deaver left, Donald Regan tried to follow her directions, but he later made public her reliance on astrologers.[54]

Ronald Reagan loved Nancy. "The lights just don't seem as warm and bright without her," he wrote in his diary once when she was absent from the White House. Despite his love for her, his serenity in the White House partly depended on her discomfort. She was a lightning rod that helped make the Teflon presidency possible. She was seen as the "bad guy," she wrote, because "it's part of Ronnie's character not to confront certain problems, so I'm usually the one who brings up the tough subjects." She believed that he was too trusting of people around him and was too optimistic generally. She also believed that it was her duty to act as the bearer of bad news. White House aides who were reluctant to speak frankly to the president used her as a messenger to the Oval Office. Every president needs such a person, and Nancy played that role for Ronald Reagan, which pulled her into the White House civil wars. During the first term she was part of the Baker-Deaver alliance, often in conflict with Meese and Clark.[55]

Friends regarded Nancy as tougher and more realistic than Ronald. She was like a dog with a bone when she took up an issue, Deaver said, backing off on a rare occasion when Ronald flared up under her pressure but returning to the attack when she saw an opening. "The first lady never forgave aides for making her husband uncomfortable," Lou Cannon wrote, "unless they were doing so at her instigation." Her intervention in White House matters often showed in questions of personnel. She helped engineer the removal of Richard Allen, Alexander Haig, James Watt, Donald Regan, and many others.[56]

Nancy Reagan's involvement in personnel conflicts caught most of the headlines, but she also helped shape action on several major policy issues. She did not seem to be motivated by a policy agenda, conservative or liberal, but was concerned about Reagan's political future and his place in history. She pressured him to stop taking public stands on the abortion issue, to be responsive to concerns about the "fairness issue," to get out in front publicly by accepting responsibility during the Iran-contra scandal. Reagan's hard-line anticommunism especially concerned her because she believed it gave him the reputation of being a warmonger. She supported Shultz in his efforts to push her husband to begin the process that led to the Reagan-Gorbachev summits, and through such activity she contributed both to the president's place in history and to world peace.[57]

Ronald Reagan was not a cloaked puppetmaster skillfully running Washington from the Oval Office. Nancy Reagan more than the president ran a "hidden-hand" operation, although she seldom kept her activities hidden very well. She was not the power behind the throne, but she was one of the most influential first ladies in history. Over the eight years of Reagan's presidency, she was the most powerful figure around him. Of all those who compensated for Reagan's weaknesses, she was the most central to his successes and, at times, to his failures.

7

Facing Defeats, Winning Victories, 1982–1989

Ronald Reagan's 1981 tax and budget victories and his stand during the PATCO strike established his image of being a strong, confident leader with a clear vision of the future and helped him weather the severe recession that began in late 1981 and the ballooning budget deficits that followed. When he faced reelection in 1984, most Americans remained convinced that he had the nation on the right track. Although critics charged that he was lazy and neglected his presidential responsibilities, he had set a new direction for national political dialogue. Politicians worked at reducing spending and removing regulations rather than formulating new social and economic programs. Reagan's agenda provided the framework for congressional activity and would continue to do so long after he left office. His contention that government was the problem, not the solution, became part of mainstream discourse within both parties.[1]

Senate Majority Leader Howard Baker had described Reagan's economic program as a "riverboat gamble." Even before Reagan signed OBRA and ERTA on 13 August 1981, his advisers told him that the economic forecasts were changing and that the Rosy Scenario was losing its creditability. On 3 August, the troika, joined by Donald Regan, David Stockman, and other economic advisers, forced Reagan to listen. Stockman told the group that there was a "budget hemorrhage" that could wreck the president's entire economic program and threatened deficits of $60 billion to $100 billion a year for the next four years. Those numbers proved far too conservative, but in 1981 a $100 billion deficit seemed unbelievable. Reagan appeared stunned.

Stockman listed some options. Reagan could abandon his goal of a balanced budget in 1984. "Deficit spending is how we got into this mess," the president answered. Then, Stockman suggested, the administration could scale back the military budget. "There must be no perception by anyone in the world that we're backing down an inch on the defense buildup," Reagan responded. He later told Stockman, "On defense, we don't determine the budget. The other side does. You have no choice but to spend what you need." Stockman suggested raising taxes, and Donald Regan quickly squelched that option.[2]

In the end, Reagan accepted the deficit and did not flinch even when in February 1983 the Congressional Budget Office projected shortfalls of over $200 billion a year, far into the future. Reagan blamed Congress, ignoring the fact that he never once submitted a balanced budget to Congress and that his budget requests over eight years nearly equaled the amount passed by Congress.[3]

After Congress enacted Reaganomics in August 1981, the nation slid into a severe recession. By December 1981 the unemployment rate had reached 8.8 percent, with 9 million people out of work, and it peaked in January 1983 with 11.5 million unemployed. In the November 1982 elections the Democrats picked up twenty-six House seats, and Reagan's approval rating fell from about 60 percent in mid-1981 to 49 percent at the end of the year, dropping to 41 percent at the end of 1982. At that point many observers began to regard Reagan as a one-term failure.

In the first week in November 1981 Reagan met each day with his economic team. His advisers tried to push him toward realistic action, including a tax increase. The frustrated president protested, "I did not come here to balance the budget—not at the expense of my tax-cutting program and my defense program. If we can't do it in 1984, we'll have to do it later." With acute political insight, he told his worried advisers that if the administration got inflation down and employment up, then the average voter would discount the importance of the deficit.[4]

Meanwhile, David Stockman was in trouble. Starting in December 1980 he had met periodically with William Greider, the assistant managing editor of the *Washington Post,* to discuss the budget and tax battles with Congress. After the bills passed, Greider published an article entitled "The Education of David Stockman," which exhibited the budget director's disillusionment with Washington's inability to deal responsibly with national problems. Stockman also revealed that the White House had deliberately given Congress misleading and incorrect information, and, most damaging, he described supply-side theory as new packaging for the old Republican trickle-down economics. Reagan's tax cut was a "Trojan horse," he said, that reduced rates on the less affluent in order to achieve its real goal: lowering taxes for the wealthy.

Many Reaganites felt Stockman had betrayed the president. James Baker saved Stockman's job but his mystique was shattered. He was reduced from being the presidential economic point man, one person said, to being a budget technician. Some in Washington never trusted him again. Representative David Obey (Dem., Wis.) told him: "I have no questions for you because very frankly, I wouldn't believe any answers you gave."[5]

Stockman remained an important figure because he knew the budget better than anyone else in the White House. The growing deficit figures frightened Washington and created a sense of crisis. Congress greeted Reagan's 1982 budget with the message that it was "dead on arrival." On 22 February, Reagan met with Republican congressional leaders. "They are really antsy about the deficit and seem determined that we must retreat on our program—taxes and defense spending," he wrote in his diary. He refused to budge from his earlier decision: "I told our guys I couldn't go for tax increases. If I have to be criticized, I'd rather be criticized for a deficit rather than for backing away from our economic program."[6]

Reagan's stubbornness did not change the worsening economic numbers, and he finally gave the troika permission to seek a compromise, agreeing to trade slight defense cuts and some tax increases for domestic spending reductions. Negotiations were intense. On 28 April Reagan met with Tip O'Neill to try to break the deadlock. After three hours of haggling, they had made no progress. At one point, O'Neill said that Reagan's budget was unfair and inequitable. "I've heard all that crap," Reagan snapped. "You had a depression when I took over." He promised himself that if talks deadlocked and he had to go on television, "there will be blood on the floor."

He soon decided that the fight was not "bloody, just messy." The House wrestled with seven competing budgets and the Senate considered several additional versions. Reagan went to work lobbying. He spent long, frustrating hours on the telephone. He wrote in his diary, "A compromise is never to anyone's liking; it's just the best you can get and contains enough of what you want to justify what you give up."[7]

When the compromise budget bill passed in June 1982, Reagan immediately went to work for what became the Tax Equity and Fiscal Responsibility Act (TEFRA). Meese, Nofziger, and other Reaganites came to believe that Reagan's accepting TEFRA was his worst presidential decision. He, however, believed that it was a necessary compromise with Congress, and he claimed victory because he preserved his 5-10-10 tax cut on individual rates. Many analysts regarded TEFRA as an important achievement. It included reforms in the code that tax experts had wanted for years. It also took back some windfalls that corporations got in the 1981 tax reduction act, although business still came out an overall winner. Senator Robert Dole, who guided the bill through the Senate, held Reagan in line by telling him that he had to accept increased taxes on business or lose his third-year cut in individual rates. According to Reagan's numbers, over three years the tax bill increased revenues by about $98.3 billion in return for promised budget cuts of $280 billion. He later felt that Congress betrayed him by not following through on the cuts.[8]

These budget and tax actions did not resolve the deficit problem. On 2 November 1982 Reagan wrote in his diary, "We really are in trouble. Our one time projections, pre-recession, are all out the window and we look at $200 billion deficits if we can't pull some miracles." The miracle did not happen, but Reagan was correct in his political analysis: When economic recovery started, voters ignored the deficits.[9]

In mid-1983 rapid economic recovery began, and it turned into the longest period of economic growth in American history. By 1988 unemployment had fallen to 5.4 percent; GNP grew at an average annual rate of about 4 percent from 1982 to 1988; inflation stabilized at around 4 percent. Reagan's opponents had blamed him for the recession and now had to watch helplessly as he claimed success for Reaganomics.

Reagan did not cause the recession, and most economists did not find a direct link between his policy and the recovery. Federal Reserve Board chair Paul A. Volcker's war on inflation was probably the main cause of the recession. Reagan backed Volcker when many politicians panicked as the Fed pushed interest rates to around 20 percent. Whipping inflation was Reagan's, and Volcker's, clearest and most important economic success.[10]

In addition to the budget deficit and the recession, the administration faced another potential catastrophe. The Social Security system was going broke; its revenues fell far short of the amount paid out to the elderly. It was an explosive issue because workers resisted higher taxes and older citizens fought bitterly against any cuts in benefits. Neither political party wanted to take sole responsibility for reform. On 16 December 1981 Reagan announced the creation of a fifteen-member National Commission on Social Security Reform, chaired by Alan Greenspan and balanced carefully to represent the interested parties. Greenspan put together a compromise that boosted the payroll tax on employees and employers, gradually raised the retirement age from sixty-five to sixty-seven, taxed the benefits of high-income recipients, and delayed payment of the annual cost-of-living increase. Experts said the plan would stabilize the system until about the year 2000. On 20 April 1983 Reagan signed into law the Social Security Amendment of 1983.[11]

One of Reagan's major goals was to reduce the regulatory burden on business. He agreed with the supply-side economists who thought excessive regulation contributed to stagflation and believed that regulatory relief, paired with tax reduction, would restore the free marketplace and release capitalism's dynamism. On 29 January 1981 Reagan ordered all agency heads to postpone implementing new regulations until the administration had time to review them. He appointed Vice President Bush to chair the Task Force on Regulatory Relief. In August 1983 Bush's group claimed that by lifting unnecessary regulations it had saved business, consumers, and state and local government $150 billion over a ten-year period. On 17 February 1981 Reagan issued Executive Order 12291, which required agencies to estimate the cost and benefits of proposed major regulatory rules and to pick the least costly alternative. In 1985 Executive Order 12498 required agencies to submit yearly reports showing how their regulatory goals fit administration policy. The OMB had authority to kill regulations that violated White House guidelines.[12]

Experts found it difficult to gauge the Reagan administration's effect on the regulatory state. Ford and Carter had already begun to deregulate major industries, including transportation. Reagan's people scrapped thousands of rules but many were of minor significance. Analysts often used the *Federal Register* as a crude index to regulatory activity. Its size declined each year during Reagan's first term, after having steadily grown for two decades, and by 1986 its pages had been reduced by 45 percent. The OMB estimated that by 1987 the administration had cut the annual paperwork burden on the American public by more than 600 million hours. Reagan slowed the regulatory state by placing hostile administrators in charge of key agencies, where they willingly accepted budget cuts. By 1985 the regulatory agencies had lost 12 percent of their personnel and funding. The Federal Trade Commission had its personnel reduced from 1,665 in 1981 to 1,075 in 1985; the Consumer Product Safety Commission dropped from 855 to 502 positions. The federal courts and Congress stopped or slowed some changes, but the administration successfully eliminated many regulations and placed the burden of proof on those proposing new regulations.[13]

Reagan ridiculed mindless rule making that resulted in regulatory overkill, but his administration at times engaged in mindless deregulation, which in one case led to a financial disaster for American taxpayers. For years the staid savings and loan industry had acted primarily to provide mortgage loans for home purchasers. In the 1970s high interest rates and competition from banks and other financial institutions battered the industry. Under Carter, Congress removed caps on interest rates that savings and loan firms could pay to depositors, loosened reserve requirements, and raised federal deposit insurance coverage from $40,000 to $100,000. The Reagan administration, through the Garn–St. Germain Depository Institutions Act of 1982, allowed savings and loan firms to go beyond housing loans into more speculative investments. When Reagan signed the act on 15 October 1982, he said, "All in all, I think we hit the jackpot."

Thieves thought so too. They looted and left insolvent hundreds of institutions. The Garn–St. Germain act, said one writer, resulted in "the biggest heist in history." The White House labeled subordinates who warned of impending disaster as disloyal "re-regulators." Reagan remained oblivious to the problem, and by the time President Bush took action in 1989, the disaster was costing taxpayers $35 million each day. In July 1996, the General Accounting Office estimated that the savings and loan bailout costs had reached $480.9 billion and eventually would total several times that figure. The bailout cost taxpayers many times more than the Vietnam War had, and was by far the most expensive scandal in world history.[14]

Reagan's major foreign policy initiatives came in his second term, but several specific incidents played a role in the 1984 election. On 8 March 1983 Reagan thrilled the anticommunists when he spoke to the National Association of Evangelicals. He described the immorality of the communist state and expressed hope that someday the Soviets would find God, but until they do, he said, "they are the focus of evil in the modern world." The Soviet Union was an "evil empire," and it could not last: "I believe that communism is another sad, bizarre chapter in human history whose last pages even now are being written."[15]

Despite his harsh rhetoric, Reagan intended to negotiate with the Soviets, but only after his military buildup had restored American power. One aspect of Reagan's defense program took the nation in a new and controversial direction. The United States relied for protection from Soviet nuclear attack on the doctrine of mutual assured destruction (MAD). MAD rested on the ability of either superpower to absorb a first strike from the other side and still be able to launch a massive counterattack. Since both sides knew that launching an attack would bring an immediate nuclear response, they would, presumably, be deterred from aggression. Deterrence rested on the assumption that superpower leaders were rational individuals: "No matter how ideological they are, they are not crazy," said one Soviet expert.

Anticommunist conservatives, however, found it difficult to regard the Soviets as rational beings who thought in the same ways as Americans, which was precisely what MAD required them to do.

On 23 March 1983 Reagan shocked the world, and his own administration, by proposing the Strategic Defense Initiative (SDI), labeled "star wars" by its opponents. He envisioned placing a defensive umbrella over the United States that would intercept and destroy in space intercontinental ballistic missiles. To supporters, his proposal promised protection from nuclear destruction. To opponents, SDI opened the frightening prospect of destabilizing the deterrence system that they believed had so far prevented nuclear war.[16]

Reagan, who seldom claimed credit for his administration's activities, made sure that the record was clear that SDI was his idea. To Reagan SDI was a shield against Armageddon, which he believed was predicted in the Bible and would take the form of nuclear war. "I thought that [MAD] was the most ridiculous thing I had ever seen," Reagan said. "It's like two guys with guns pointed at each other's heads and cocked and thinking that neither one of them will take a chance and pull the trigger." "There had to be a better way," he wrote.

Reagan recalled that after he became president he received a briefing that gave him the most startling information he had ever heard (it is startling that he had not heard it until he became president). He learned that even if the United States won a nuclear war, 150 million Americans would die, with the survivors breathing poisoned air and living in a destroyed civilization. Reagan's optimistic nature rebelled against the helplessness and despair over the human condition that he saw embodied in MAD. "He was a romantic, a radical, a nuclear abolitionist," wrote journalist Strobe Talbott.[17]

Reagan needed military support for an idea that would be vulnerable to ridicule from the defense establishment and arms control experts. The Joint Chiefs of Staff (JCS) had also been rethinking some fundamental assumptions. Ford and Carter had struggled unsuccessfully with the question of how to base MX intercontinental ballistic missiles—a new, highly accurate missile that carried ten warheads each—to best protect them from Soviet nuclear attack. JCS member Admiral James D. Watkins, a nuclear engineer with moral qualms about the arms race and MAD, felt that the world was moving into a "strategic valley of death." He believed that the Soviets could overcome any MX basing mode that the United States could devise and that building land-based missiles gave Moscow an advantage by neglecting the field that the United States clearly dominated: advanced technology. On 5 February 1983 Watkins briefed his Pentagon colleagues on the possibility of constructing a defensive system. Weinberger opposed it, but he believed

Reagan should hear the presentation. On 11 February the JCS briefed Reagan and each chief endorsed the idea. Army chief John W. Vessey said to Reagan, "Wouldn't it be better to protect the American people rather than avenge them?" The Great Communicator instantly interjected to his aides, "Don't lose those words."[18]

On 23 March 1983 Reagan gave a televised speech on national defense. He promised to pursue arms reduction talks with the Soviets, but he said that the world would still rely on mutual terror to keep the peace, "and that's a sad commentary on the human condition. Wouldn't it be better to save lives than to avenge them?" He claimed that after "careful consultation" with the JCS he had a better way: "It is that we embark on a program to counter the awesome Soviet missile threat with measures that are defensive. Let us turn to the very strengths in technology that spawned our great industrial base and that have given us the quality of life we enjoy today." He asked, "What if free people could live secure in the knowledge that their security did not rest upon the threat of instant U.S. retaliation to deter a Soviet attack, that we could intercept and destroy strategic ballistic missiles before they reached our own soil or that of our allies?" It was a formidable technical undertaking that might not be accomplished before the century's end, but he was ordering a comprehensive program to begin to develop a defensive system. "My fellow Americans," the president pledged, "tonight we're launching an effort which holds the promise of changing the course of human history."[19]

Reaction from within the national security community was generally negative, as was world opinion. George Shultz briefed Soviet ambassador Anatoly Dobrynin a few hours before the speech. Dobrynin cautioned that SDI would open a new phase in the cold war. Soviet premier Yuri V. Andropov warned that it was starting down "an extremely dangerous path." European allies feared that it would destroy deterrence and might provoke the Soviets into a preemptive strike before the shield was built.[20]

Some critics who scoffed at SDI rethought their position when they realized that the Soviets took it seriously indeed. British prime minister Margaret Thatcher reconsidered her initial opposition: "President Reagan's Strategic Defence Initiative, about which the Soviets and Mr. Gorbachev were . . . so alarmed, was to prove central to the West's victory in the Cold War," she wrote in her memoirs. "Looking back, it is now clear to me that Ronald Reagan's original decision on SDI was the single most important of his presidency."[21]

The SDI speech showed Reagan taking strong action over the objection of many of his most trusted advisers. His mixture of strength and passivity was seen in other national security matters during his first term. Reagan dueled for years with Libya's Muammar al-Qaddafi, whom Reagan regarded as a madman and a major sponsor of world terrorism. The American Sixth Fleet had traditionally held maneuvers in the Gulf of Sidra, but Carter had canceled them when Qaddafi had claimed the gulf as Libyan territory. After Reagan became president, Qaddafi threatened action if the fleet entered the Gulf of Sidra. Reagan ordered the maneuvers to be held, and during an August 1981 cabinet meeting he authorized using force if the Libyans fired on or interfered with United States ships. The room hushed as a cabinet officer asked if American planes could pursue Libyan planes that harassed fleet vessels. Reagan replied, "All the way into the hangar." On 19 August 1981 Libyan airplanes fired on two American fighter jets in the Gulf of Sidra, and the American pilots shot down two planes. Explaining the action, Reagan wrote that he "wanted to send a message to others in the world that there was a new management in the White House."[22]

The verbal war between the Americans and Soviets heated up after Reagan's March 1983 "evil empire" speech. Late that summer one of the most ferocious propaganda battles of the cold war occurred. On 1 September 1983 a Soviet pilot shot down Korean Air Lines flight 007 (KAL 007), killing 269 people, including 61 Americans. Reagan unleashed a verbal attack, referring to Soviet violation of civilized standards of behavior, to its "barbaric" acts and "brutality," to its "massacre" of innocent people. He asked Congress to condemn the Soviet action, forbade the Soviet airline Aeroflot entering the United States, and suspended several bilateral arrangements with the Soviets. He proclaimed 11 September a day of national mourning, in memory of the dead passengers.

Later reports revealed that on the day after the KAL 007 disaster, the United States had intelligence information showing that the Soviets had thought they were tracking an American spy plane and had failed to identify it properly before they shot it down. Rather than recognizing the tragedy as a mistake resulting from incompetence, the Reagan administration used it as proof that the Soviet Union was an "evil empire." The Soviets remembered Reagan's reaction when on 3 July 1988 the United States shot down an Iranian airliner with 290 people on board, and he said that it was a regrettable mistake. To Reagan, Americans made mistakes; the Soviets committed sins.[23]

Reagan also joined the ranks of every president since Harry Truman who tried and failed to become the Middle Eastern peacemaker. He later said that the American intervention in Lebanon had been "my greatest regret and my greatest sorrow." The Lebanese civil war, which started in 1975, had led to nearly one hundred thousand deaths by 1982. The once beautiful and prosperous small country had long been divided ethnically and religiously among Muslim, Jewish, and Christian populations. The tiny nation was also caught between two implacable enemies, Israel and Syria. The mix became more volatile in the 1970s when Jordan expelled the Palestine Liberation Organization (PLO), which then moved its base to Lebanon.

By the time Reagan took office, Israeli and PLO forces were striking at each other across the Israeli-Lebanese border. In July 1981 American ambassador Philip C. Habib negotiated a cease-fire. In Israel, Prime Minister Menachem Begin and Defense Minister Ariel Sharon chafed under the restraint, and on 6 June 1982 Israel invaded Lebanon. Begin assured the Reagan administration that his forces would penetrate only a few miles to destroy some PLO strongholds along the border. In fact, the Israeli forces continued the attack against both PLO and Syrian forces, driving forward to the outskirts of Beirut.[24]

In the meantime, Haig had resigned, and on 16 July 1982 George Shultz was sworn in as secretary of state. State Department objectives were ambitious: to obtain a cease-fire, lay the groundwork for sending in a multinational peacekeeping force, negotiate a PLO withdrawal from Beirut, keep Israeli troops out of the city, remove all foreign forces from Lebanon, and, finally, get the country back on its feet and have it establish stable relations with Israel.[25]

Although Lebanon was not of vital national interest to the United States, Reagan sent troops there twice. He felt compelled to play peacemaker, but his inability to unify his own administration led to disaster. Debates within the administration revolved around United States participation in a multinational force. Pentagon leaders still felt betrayed because they believed that the nation had put American troops into Vietnam and then failed to support them. In a speech on 28 November 1984 Weinberger laid out six tests that the military wanted met before American troops were committed into crisis situations. Troops should only be committed to combat if United States or allied vital interests were involved, if the nation intended to win, if political and military objectives were clearly defined before intervention, if the relationship between objectives and force size were continually reevaluated and adjusted, if there was reasonable assurance of public and congressional support. Finally, and most important, troops should be committed only as a last resort.[26]

Lebanon did not meet Weinberger's test for using military force, and he and the JCS vigorously opposed American intervention. The State Department and the NSC often took more bellicose and aggressive stances than did the Department of Defense. Weinberger said that the NSC staff spent its time dreaming up "ever more wild adventures for our troops." General Colin L. Powell, Weinberger's military aide, said military force should be used when it made sense, "but Beirut wasn't sensible and never did serve a purpose. It was goofy from the beginning."[27]

By early August 1982 the PLO was willing to evacuate Lebanon and Habib worked out an agreement. Syria agreed to withdraw its troops; a multinational force, including eight hundred American marines, would land; and the PLO military forces would evacuate, starting on 21 August. The evacuation was carried out peacefully, and on 23 August Bashir Gemayel, a Christian leader friendly to the United States, was elected president. On 7 September Habib returned to Washington and received the Medal of Freedom. Weinberger withdrew the United States Marine contingent on 13 September.[28]

Meanwhile, Shultz had been secretly developing a broad new plan for a negotiated Israeli-Arab settlement, which would allow Reagan to be the peacemaker in the Holy Land. The Camp David process begun under Carter had stalled, and Shultz felt that it would die if the Americans did not revive it. On 1 September 1982 Reagan laid out his proposal for a "fresh start" and suggested that a final accord might include an autonomous Palestinian territory federated with Jordan. Israel would give up most of the territory it had grabbed during the 1967 Six-Day War, and, in return, the Arab states would recognize Israel's right to exist. Begin and Sharon reacted angrily, but Arab and Israeli moderates supported the "fresh start."[29]

As had often occurred in Middle Eastern negotiations, the euphoria of breakthroughs disappeared in new rounds of conflicts. On 14 September, as American marines were withdrawing, President-elect Bashir Gemayel was assassinated, and Israel immediately occupied Beirut. Washington reacted with horror when it learned that Israeli forces had allowed Gemayel's soldiers to enter two PLO civilian camps and massacre seven hundred unarmed men, women, and children. When Ambassador Moshe Arens said that any insinuation that Israel was responsible for the massacre would cast a "shadow" on the United States–Israeli relationship, Shultz bluntly told him, "You bear responsibility."

After a bitter struggle between Weinberger and Shultz, Reagan sided with Shultz and on 20 September announced that marines would return to Beirut. Under intense pressure from the United States, the Israeli government agreed to withdraw from Beirut. On 21 September Amin Gemayel, Bashir's brother, was elected president.[30]

At first the threat of anarchy rallied some support for Amin Gemayel, but as the weeks passed he came to be seen as a weak man, partial to Lebanese Christian factions and dependent for survival on the United States. The American government remained divided over its objectives. Shultz wanted a broad agreement that would remove all troops from Lebanon, while Weinberger wanted to force a unilateral Israeli withdrawal. Weinberger counted twenty-six different armed factions in Lebanon and thought the situation was hopeless and dangerous. Reagan reminded him that marines did not cut and run.[31]

By mid-1983 Lebanese Arabs regarded American marines as props for Gemayel's unpopular government rather than as neutral peacekeepers. On 10 September 1983 special envoy Robert C. McFarlane, who had replaced Habib, urged Washington to allow the marines to use naval and air power to keep the Lebanese army from crumbling. The next day Reagan agreed to the use of force, ending any pretense of American neutrality.

At an 18 October NSC meeting Weinberger told Reagan that the Lebanese saw the marines as combatants and that the JCS unanimously recommended removing them. McFarlane, back in Washington as the new national security adviser, replacing Clark, sided with Shultz in opposing withdrawal. Reagan employed the "falling dominoes" analysis so often used by American policymakers during the cold war. He wrote New Hampshire governor Meldrim Thomson that the Lebanese situation "is only one facet of the whole middle east problem. Mel is there any way the U.S. or the Western World for that matter can stand by & see the middle east become a part of the Communist bloc? Without it our West Europe neighbors would inevitably become Finlandized and we'd be alone in the world."

Finally on 23 October 1983 a young Muslim man detonated a bomb-loaded truck near the marine barracks, killing 231 Americans. Reagan tried to maintain the mission in Lebanon, but in February 1984 Gemayel's government collapsed. As chaos spread, Bush, James Baker, and Republican congressional leaders united to coax Reagan into agreeing to withdraw, while carefully avoiding that word.[32]

Reagan's Lebanon policy had as much to do with his self-image of "standing tall" and not "cutting and running" as it did with a close analysis of United States national interest. It turned into a disaster partly because he did not master the situation well enough to set clear objectives and to provide matching resources. The marines did not have enough troops to engage effectively in peacekeeping and yet their halfhearted gestures made them active players. They huddled at the Beirut airport, exposed to hostile forces, to satisfy Shultz's desire for intervention, but, in deference to Weinberger's opposition to their being in Lebanon, they were too few to shape events.

Reagan's resounding success in the tiny Caribbean island of Grenada helped him deflect the political consequences of his failed Lebanese policy. He sent an invasion force into Grenada ostensibly to rescue about a thousand Americans, including eight hundred medical students, living on the island. His real objective was to overthrow its leftist government. On 23 October the Beirut bombing occurred, and on 24 October Reagan gave final approval to the invasion of Grenada and tried to placate a furious Margaret Thatcher when he told her that he was going to order an invasion of a Commonwealth nation. Thatcher regarded it as an unnecessary overreaction by a great power, a frustrated response to the Beirut bombing.

Nineteen Americans were killed during the invasion, along with over one hundred people from Cuba and Grenada. World opinion was negative but Reagan's popularity soared at home. His political opponents were handcuffed when one of the students disembarked from the airplane, knelt before the television cameras, and kissed the earth. In a televised address, Reagan briefly discussed the Beirut bombing, then let the patriotic rhetoric flow when he described the Grenada invasion.[33]

As Reagan began to prepare for the 1984 presidential election, he continued to hold together the disparate conservative movement. Young entrepreneurs, stereotypically greedy and self-centered, respected him as did the older conservatives who valued stability, family, and community. He gave conservatives renewed pride in their country and optimism for the future, and they overlooked the growing deficits, inaction on the social issues, and an economic program that benefited the wealthy more than it did Reagan's middle-class supporters. He gave conservatives SDI, the defense buildup, patriotic rhetoric, and largely symbolic actions as in Grenada, which did not really challenge the "Vietnam syndrome" that limited the use of American power in the world.

If Reaganomics united large blocs of conservatives, the social issues—including abortion, school prayer, and mandatory school busing—tended to be divisive. Many libertarian-oriented conservatives opposed the social issues agenda. When Jerry Falwell opposed Sandra Day O'Connor's nomination to the Supreme Court and said all "good Christians" should oppose her, Barry Goldwater responded, "Every good Christian ought to kick Falwell right in the ass." Most Americans did not rate the social issues high in importance, but those who did were well funded and articulate.[34]

Reagan had to proceed carefully. He had spoken forcefully on the social issues over the years, but he always subordinated them to Reaganomics. He kept his Religious Right followers happy through rhetoric and symbolic gestures, rather than through effective action on their agenda. "We want to keep the Moral Majority types so close to us they can't move their arms," said a White House aide. Reagan favored conservative religious leaders with invitations to the White House, with special private briefings, and with speeches to their national conventions. He validated their organizations and aims by paying attention to them. He constantly spoke against abortion and ERA. He supported a school prayer amendment, and his wife participated very publicly in the antidrug campaign. Because it involved taking a stand on sexual behavior and practices, Reagan stayed away from the AIDS issues until Surgeon General C. Everett Koop persuaded him in his second term at least to recognize the plague's existence.

Reagan most pleased the Religious Right by his recognition in numerous offhand remarks, formal statements, and major speeches of the centrality of God and God's mission for the United States. Billy Graham told Reagan, "I would think that you have talked about God more than any other president since Abraham Lincoln."[35]

Reagan did not keep all conservatives happy. The biggest blowup on the right came in July 1982 when Richard Viguerie, publisher of the *Conservative Digest,* devoted an entire special issue to articles discussing the question, "Has Reagan deserted the conservatives?" New Right leader Paul Weyrich, Senator Jesse Helms, and others contributed to the attack. Reagan was irritated, dismissing Viguerie and Weyrich as "narrow ideologues," but he also stepped up his effort to hold conservative allegiance. Most conservatives appreciated the limitations imposed on Reagan by the necessity of keeping a broad coalition happy. When they did express their dismay at some action or inaction, they often blamed the "pragmatists" around him, especially James Baker. Reagan's fire-breathing conservative rhetoric hid from many the fact that he was a very skillful politician who placed winning above ideological purity.[36]

Of the people around Reagan, conservatives probably most mistrusted Bush. Bush knew that his future in the conservative-dominated Republican Party depended entirely on Reagan. He subordinated himself to the president and worked carefully and successfully to win his trust. Bush headed various special task forces, went on many foreign missions for the president, and often substituted for Reagan in ceremonial and Republican Party events. By May 1988 Bush had spent 1,475 days outside Washington, usually acting as a stand-in for Reagan. There was never any serious doubt that Reagan would select Bush for the ticket again in 1984.[37]

As Reagan prepared for the 1984 elections, he faced special problems with black voters and many women. In 1980 Reagan received the lowest percentage of African-American votes of any candidate in history, and in 1984 he broke his own record. His presidency was the most hostile toward civil rights of any administration since the early 1950s. Some critics characterized the administration's policy as "benign neglect" but that ignored the activist nature of Reagan's attempt to redefine civil rights activity. His administration did not create the hostile environment toward the civil rights movement, but it catered to growing white racism. In the 1960s, most white Americans believed that white racism and white-dominated institutions were mainly responsible for African-American social and economic problems. In the 1970s and 1980s most whites came to believe that black people's behavior was mainly responsible for their problems. This shift had dramatic implications for government programs. Whites were decreasingly willing to pay for government programs or make other sacrifices that they regarded as designed primarily to benefit black people.[38]

Nothing made Reagan angrier than to imply that he was a racist. His parents had taught him that racism was wrong. He had defied the racial code by having black football players in his home in Dixon, and in Hollywood he had spoken out against racism and anti-Semitism. But Michael Deaver pointed out that Reagan had little personal experience with blacks and could be remarkably insensitive to their concerns. When he talked with black leaders he often dwelled on his defiance of racial mores in the 1920s and 1930s and seemed unaware that his anecdotes had little relevance to life in modern inner cities. He revealed his insensitivity in a 1983 press conference when he seemed to validate charges that Martin Luther King Jr. was a communist sympathizer. He signed a bill making King's birthday a national holiday, but privately explained that he had to do so because the "perception of too many people is based on an image, not reality."[39]

The heart of the Reagan administration civil rights policy was its rejection of affirmative action. Attorney General William French Smith and head of the Justice Department Civil Rights Division William Bradford Reynolds opposed offering any special group protections or remedies based on past discrimination against that group. They opposed in the courts any busing plan or other mandated effort at school desegregation, even those voluntarily arrived at in negotiations between local school boards and civil rights groups. The administration cut budgets for such programs as legal services that had played special roles in helping black citizens. It filled the Equal Employment Opportunity Commission with members hostile to its mission, and it engaged in a nasty and protracted fight to pack the United States Commission on Civil Rights with a conservative majority that opposed affirmative action.[40]

Reagan wrote off the African-American vote, but the gender gap proved worrisome. In 1980 men had favored Reagan over Carter 54 percent to 37 percent, while women had supported Reagan over Carter 47 percent to 45 percent. Throughout Reagan's years in office, men gave him about 9 percent higher approval than women. The gender gap was partially a product of Reagan's antiabortion and anti-ERA stands, but it also appeared on a variety of peace, economic, and environmental issues, apparently because while women had not changed much in their positions on policy issues, men had moved in a Republican and conservative direction. Reagan did not have a women's problem, one person said, but the Democrats had a men's problem.[41]

Reagan could be personally insensitive. He referred to Secretary of

Health and Human Services Margaret Heckler as a "good little girl." In 1982, he explained that unemployment resulted from women flooding into the workforce. He provoked groans when he told a women's organization, "I happen to be one who believes that if it wasn't for women, us men would still be walking around in skin suits carrying clubs." Women who dealt with Reagan personally did not find him to be sexist, but their issues were not a high priority to him. Lyn Nofziger said that in California Reagan had placed few women or minority people in high positions, but that "these weren't deliberate slights, they were matters of indifference." In the White House, Reagan had no women or minority people in his inner circle. "I haven't figured out yet why there were no women," wrote Nofziger, "except that there never had been, and Reagan probably figured, if he bothered to figure at all, that that's the way it was supposed to be." Speechwriter Peggy Noonan said of the White House, "I had entered a place where men were completely in charge." Helene von Damm, a Reagan associate since the California years, heard White House males make fun of Secretary of Transportation Elizabeth H. Dole for being "schoolmarmish" and dismiss hard-hitting presentations by Jeane Kirkpatrick as a product of her "time of the month."[42]

The Reagan administration's problems with minority people and women came together to form the fairness issue. Senator Bob Packwood (Rep., Ore.) warned against trying "to build a party on white Anglo-Saxon males over forty. There aren't enough of us left." Congressman John L. Napier (Rep., S.C.) put it more simply: "There are a lot more little people than there are rich people." By the end of 1982, with the recession continuing, journalists identified the fairness issue as the administration's point of vulnerability. The 1982 elections were a warning. The GOP held its 54-to-46 majority in the Senate, but lost twenty-six House seats.[43]

Many critics believed that the administration waged its war against inflation by driving up unemployment and that the administration's fight against deficits resulted in budget cuts that fell heaviest on the least affluent. Senator Howard M. Metzenbaum (Dem., Ohio) told Stockman that he had performed brilliantly in cutting the budget, "but I also think you've been cruel, inhumane and unfair." The changes in Social Security and income taxes during Reagan's first term left families with income under $10,000 a year with a $95 net loss, while families making from $75,000 to $100,000 gained $403 and those with income above $200,000 gained $17,403. Families that made less than $10,000 annually lost $1,340 in benefits; those making between $40,000 and $80,000 gained $390. By 1983, 408,000 people had lost AFDC eligibility and 299,000 more had their benefits cut. At Reagan's urging, Congress cut $2 billion from the $12 billion food stamp budget and $1 billion from the $3.5 billion school lunch program. Spending on Medicaid dropped 3 percent in fiscal year 1982 and 4 percent in 1983. Between 1982 and 1985, unemployment insurance spending dropped 6.9 percent, AFDC 12.7 percent, food stamps 12.6 percent, child nutrition programs 27.7 percent, housing assistance 4.4 percent, and low-income energy assistance 8.3 percent. Washington slashed federal funds for cities nearly in half.[44]

Despite the fairness issue 80 percent of Americans thought they were better off as a result of Reagan's four years in office. When he announced his candidacy on 29 January 1984, he promised to continue his policy. "America is back and standing tall," he claimed. "You cannot beat an incumbent president in peacetime if the nation is prosperous," political pro Richard Nixon said about the 1984 election. Walter F. Mondale, Reagan's Democratic opponent, admitted later that there were only two or three days during the entire campaign when he thought that he might win.[45]

Baker tightly controlled the election campaign, placing Edward J. Rollins in charge of operations. They mounted the most professional, mistake-free campaign in history. They had little trust in the seventy-three-year-old Reagan's mental agility and kept him away from the press and from un-scripted appearances. Their fears were confirmed on a few occasions. In one case, he was warming up before giving a radio address and spoke into an open microphone: "My fellow Americans. I am pleased to tell you I just signed legislation outlawing Russia forever. The bombing begins in five minutes." For the most part the public never saw him in 1984 except in tightly controlled patriotic settings based on the campaign theme, "America is back."[46]

Reagan strategists portrayed Mondale as an old-fashioned "tax-and-spend" liberal, beholden to an array of special interests, especially labor. Mondale opened his campaign with two high-risk gambles designed to demonstrate bold leadership. He chose Geraldine A. Ferraro as his running mate, the first woman to be nominated for vice president by a major party. That move backfired to an extent because the Republicans engaged in a ferocious attack on her. She brought excitement to the campaign, but drawn-out controversies surrounding her husband's finances and business activities distracted the campaign.[47]

Mondale made another valiant attempt at boldness during his 19 July acceptance speech before the Democratic convention. He launched a scathing attack on the Reagan record, reminding voters that when they elected Reagan in 1980, they did not vote to run a $200 billion deficit or to turn "the heavens into a battleground" with SDI. "You did not vote to destroy family farming. You did not vote to trash the civil-rights laws. You did not vote to poison the environment." After that telling attack Mondale said that

Reagan's deficits would have to be paid for: "Let's tell the truth. Mr. Reagan will raise taxes, and so will I. He won't tell you. I just did."

Mondale was gambling that such forthrightness would make him look bold and honest and would force Reagan into a debate on the deficit. In fact, it made him look like the "tax-and-spend Democrat" that Reagan said he was. Reagan quickly nailed Mondale: "My opponent has spent his political life supporting more taxes and more spending. For him, raising taxes is a first resort. For me, it is a last resort."[48]

Reagan's advisers believed he was most vulnerable to attack on the fairness issue. According to one estimate, Reaganomics had changed the effect of taxes and spending so that by 1984 the income of the top 0.2 percent of people had increased by 21–26 percent, while those at the median point gained about 3.5 percent, and families under $10,000 a year lost more than 15 percent of their income. Mondale's South Carolina campaign manager said, "For a textile worker to vote for Ronald Reagan is like a chicken voting for Colonel Sanders." Such attacks did not stick. Reagan, the master of the politics of symbolism, engaged in slick image productions designed to show blue-collar workers that he understood their fear of crime and deteriorating neighborhoods, their despair over eroding moral values and crumbling family structures, their anger and frustration because their hard-earned money was being redistributed to those who did not deserve it. Journalist David Broder found surprising support for Reagan in Michigan, a state hard hit by the economic downturn. He regarded as typical a young couple who agreed that Mondale sided with average people like themselves, while Reagan benefited the rich, and that Mondale would be more likely than Reagan to keep the peace. They still intended to vote for Reagan, however, because he brought the country together and gave them pride in being Americans.[49]

Two televised debates between the candidates, the first on 7 October, gave Mondale his only chance to break Reagan's dominating lead. Anticipating danger, Stockman prepared Reagan by engaging in mock debates with him. Some believed that Stockman enjoyed mauling Reagan and exposing his ignorance. At one point Reagan shouted "Shut up!" at him, an uncharacteristic loss of composure. As Reagan struggled, an aide realized with surprise that the president had become an old, frail man.

Patrick H. Caddell, a Mondale adviser, also believed that Reagan had aged and deteriorated mentally. He advised Mondale to surprise Reagan and attempt to throw him off stride. During the debate, Mondale treated the president with deference but launched an unrelenting attack on the president's record. Nancy Reagan watched in horror as her husband reeled under the assault. The debate was a nightmare, she said: "Right from the start, he was tense, muddled, and off-stride." Rather than offering his soaring vision of the past and future, Reagan appeared defensive and bogged down in statistics.

Mondale himself was flustered by Reagan's performance. He found the president to be so weak mentally and physically that it was frightening. "When I said hello to him I knew he wasn't going to make it," Mondale said. At one point he was afraid that Reagan was going to physically collapse. He told an aide as he came off the stage, "This guy is gone. It's scary. He's really not up to it." He told advisers, "The President's not all there. His eyes were wandering, he seemed shaky. The President is out to lunch." He privately used the word "senile" to describe Reagan and said, "It was scary. . . . He just *left*."[50]

Mondale's earlier attempt to use the age issue—referring to "leadership by amnesia"—had not worked. Now age became the issue. In the week following the debate, each television network brought up the age issue and played film clips showing Reagan's loss of concentration. They went to the archives to find film footage showing him dozing off in the presence of Pope John Paul II and Nancy whispering to her husband answers to a reporter's question. They interviewed physicians and psychologists to discuss senility. Richard Wirthlin's polls showed Reagan's lead shrinking from nineteen points to twelve, with young voters' support slipping twenty-five points.[51]

Some Reagan aides found him so dispirited that they were afraid he could not finish the race. Nancy Reagan understood that first and last Reagan was a performer and that his performance depended on his self-confidence and sunny disposition. She, Paul Laxalt, and others, including even Richard Nixon, carefully worked to restore Reagan's self-assurance as he prepared for the second debate. They reduced his preparatory sessions and brought in political consultant Roger E. Ailes to watch the process. Ailes realized that the American people wanted Reagan as president and would watch the debate just to see if he was still capable of leadership; they did not care if he was shaky on the details. All Reagan had to do was stay on his feet and not be kayoed, said one aide.[52]

During the second debate, held on 21 October 1984 in Kansas City, Missouri, Reagan seemed better able than before to project his vision of the nation's future, always his great strength, and to use his one-line quips to fend off attacks. Halfway through the debate journalist Henry Trewhitt brought up Reagan's age and asked if he had any doubts about his ability to function in all circumstances. "Not at all, Mr. Trewhitt," Reagan replied, "and I want you to know that also I will not make age an issue of this campaign. I am not going to exploit, for political purposes, my opponent's youth and inexperience." The audience burst into laughter and applause.

Nancy relaxed, and Mondale and Ferraro later said that they realized the election was over.

In the last few minutes, Mondale watched Reagan fading, just disappearing in front of his eyes, Mondale said. The president's closing statement seemed rambling and pointless. Still, he had survived an aggressive attack and most people remembered only his quip about the age factor, which the networks replayed often in the next few days. Most polls gave Reagan the debate. "I guess my response had satisfied them that I wasn't senile," Reagan wrote.[53]

Reagan carried every state but Minnesota, taking 59 percent of the popular vote to 41 for Mondale. Mondale got only 25 to 27 percent of the vote in the former Democratic stronghold of the South. Southern conservatives reacted positively to Reagan's patriotic and religious message, as well as to his racial policy. Reagan carried almost every category of people: 63 percent of the white vote, including 61 percent of white female voters, 65 percent of the middle-class vote, 71 percent of white Protestants, and 55 percent of white Catholics. Only 9 percent of black voters supported Reagan, and he lost the Jewish vote. People who made under $10,000 a year voted against him, but all other income categories supported him. Young people voted for Reagan, perhaps because they had entered the job market during the stagnant 1970s and appreciated the economic boom. They also responded to his patriotic themes and to his optimistic vision of the future.[54]

Most presidents lucky enough to be reelected had found their second term to be more difficult than their first one, and Reagan was no exception. His feel-good campaign had played on patriotic themes without building a mandate for new programs. Most important, Reagan had never understood how dependent he was on a strong staff, and he let the troika break up after the 1984 election. Meese left the White House to become attorney general, and Deaver established a Washington lobbying firm. James Baker became secretary of the Treasury, and Donald Regan replaced him as chief of staff. Regan was intelligent, hardworking, and completely loyal to Reagan and his ideas, but he was not politically skilled and his abrasive manner cut him off from experienced White House hands who might have helped him. He also had little understanding of Nancy Reagan and soon made an enemy of her.[55]

In his second term, Reagan stressed as his major domestic achievement the continuation of economic growth, with low inflation and unemployment. He offered one major new domestic initiative. In late 1983 Treasury Secretary Regan, who had been forced to determine what Reagan wanted by watching his body language, believed that the president might support a major overhaul of the tax system. Understanding how Reagan's mind worked, Regan told the president that he had a story for him. Reagan

1927. Ronald Reagan as lifeguard at Lowell Park in Dixon, Illinois. During his seven years as lifeguard, Reagan won acclaim in his community by saving seventy-seven people from drowning in a treacherous stretch of Rock River.

1930s. Reagan won regional fame and honed his communication skills at WHO radio station in Des Moines, Iowa.

Ronald and Nancy Reagan in the early 1950s at the Stork Club in New York. The Reagans usually avoided the nightclub scene and settled into quiet domestic life in the Hollywood film colony.

4 March 1952. Ronald and Nancy Reagan cut their wedding cake at the home of their actor friend, William Holden.

Barry Goldwater and Ronald Reagan, probably in 1964. Reagan first came to national attention as a political figure by his dramatic 1964 speech for the conservative senator from Arizona. Goldwater was sometimes said to be Reagan's John the Baptist.

Nancy and Ronald Reagan, probably in the early 1960s. After a decade of marriage the romance continued, as it did throughout their life together. The American flag would become the most common backdrop for Ronald's photographs.

January 1967. Judge Marshall McComb in a private ceremony swears in Reagan as governor of California.

Reagan's first cabinet, 4 February 1981. *Seated, left to right,* Secretary of State Alexander Haig, President Ronald Reagan, Vice President George Bush, Secretary of Defense Caspar Weinberger. *Standing, left to right,* Secretary of Labor Raymond Donovan, Secretary of Treasury Donald Regan, Secretary of Education Terrel Bell, Director of the Office of Management and Budget David Stockman, Secretary of Transportation Drew Lewis, Secretary of Housing and Urban Development Samuel Pierce, Attorney General William French Smith, Secretary of the Interior James Watt, U.S. Ambassador to the United Nations Jeane Kirkpatrick, Counselor to the President Edwin Meese, Secretary of Energy James Edwards, Secretary of Commerce Malcolm Baldrige, U.S. Trade Representative William Brock, Secretary of Health and Human Services Richard Schweiker, Secretary of Agriculture John Block, Director of Central Intelligence William Casey. Despite the high turnover in personnel, Reagan's cabinet and staff acted as a necessary and effective team to support their disengaged president.

The troika, 2 December 1981. *Left to right,* James Baker, Edwin Meese, and Michael Deaver. Although the experts said shared power could never work, the three men formed a team that made good use of Baker's political skills, Meese's grasp of Reagan's conservative ideology, and Deaver's understanding of Ronald and Nancy Reagan.

David Stockman and Ronald Reagan in the Oval Office, 6 October 1981. The dynamic and intelligent budget director spearheaded the drive to formulate the 1981 Reaganomics program. Shortly after this photograph was taken, Stockman's private conversations with a journalist became public and his revelations about the inner workings of Congress and the executive branch undermined his power.

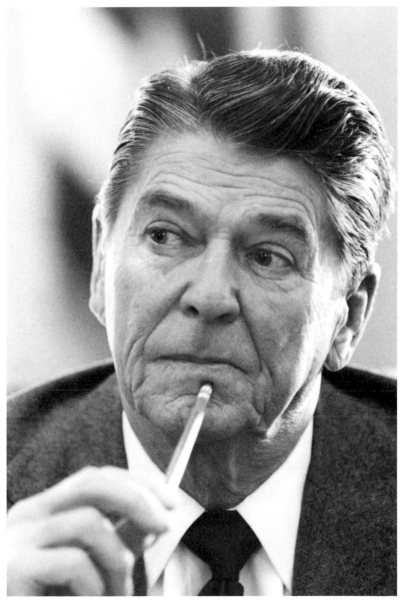

1 November 1983. The impassive mask that greeted Reagan briefers. Reagan's subordinates, often reduced to reading his body language to gauge his thinking, wondered how much he was absorbing of what they were saying.

7 October 1984. Walter Mondale and Ronald Reagan, during their first debate. Reagan's poor performance raised the age issue and gave Mondale a moment of hope before Reagan's strong performance in the next debate cemented the election for him.

The Great Communicator on 4 June 1986. His optimistic vision of the United States as God's chosen land helped renew the national pride and confidence of millions of his countrymen. Many of his supporters believed that was his most important legacy.

Reagan displaying the persona that best fit his self-image as a cowboy-Cincinnatus, a citizen-politician from the American West who took time from his "real life" to clean up the mess left by professional politicians.

Ronald Reagan and Mikhail Gorbachev on 19 November 1985, in their meeting in the boathouse at the Geneva summit. The warmth and trust they established in their first private meeting gave them the confidence in each other that allowed them during the next few years to make breakthroughs in nuclear arms negotiations and in easing cold war tensions.

The generally friendly relationship between Reagan and Gorbachev had moments of conflict. Here, on 12 October 1986, the two men angrily confronted each other as the Reykjavik summit broke up. During the gloomy ride back to the American embassy, the disappointed president told Donald Regan, "We were *that* close to an agreement," measuring a slight distance with his thumb and forefinger.

On 18 June 1985 Reagan met with several advisers who became key players in the Iran-contra affair. *Left to right,* Donald Regan, Reagan, George Bush, Robert McFarlane, and John Poindexter.

25 November 1986. *Left to right,* Caspar Weinberger, George Shultz, Edwin Meese, Donald Regan, and Ronald Reagan. Reagan's worried advisers gathered around him a few minutes before he revealed to the public that some of his subordinates had secretly diverted profits from Iranian arms sales to Nicaraguan contra forces.

26 February 1987. *Left to right,* Ronald Reagan, Edmund Muskie, John Tower, and Brent Scowcroft. Reagan held the Tower Board report on Iran-contra before the glum panel that had come to understand the fragility of the Reagan presidency. Reagan's rapid decision to call on these respected outside investigators allowed him to overcome a potentially devastating scandal.

29 October 1987. *Left to right,* Reagan, Frank Carlucci, and Colin Powell. "My God, we didn't sign on to run this country!" Carlucci once remarked to Powell after they briefed the impassive and unresponsive president. A few days after this photograph was taken, Reagan made public his selection of Carlucci as secretary of defense and Powell as national security adviser.

On 31 May 1988 Reagan and Gorbachev met in Red Square, the heart of the ''evil empire.'' His productive summit meetings with Gorbachev helped Reagan leave office as one of the most popular presidents in history.

brightened. The secretary asked Reagan what his old corporate sponsor, General Electric, had in common with Boeing, General Dynamics, and fifty-seven other big corporations. Reagan leaned forward, smiled, and waited for the answer. Regan said the president's personal secretary paid more in federal taxes than all those corporations together. Reagan flushed and said that he did not believe it. It was true and it was wrong, Regan told the president, who agreed.

Regan took that as a mandate to formulate a plan to overhaul the entire tax system, and in his 1984 State of the Union address Reagan proposed a "historic reform" of the tax code to achieve fairness and simplicity and to promote economic growth. He announced that he had asked Regan to submit a plan to him in December 1984.[56]

Regan's Treasury Department team worked on a plan that would be revenue neutral, shifting but not raising or lowering tax revenues. Under Regan's guidance they lowered the rates, raised the personal exemption for taxpayers, reduced the number of tax brackets from fourteen to three, and closed some major loopholes that benefited special groups, while retaining deductions for medical expenses, home mortgage interest, and other broad tax benefits that especially benefited the middle class.

Reagan submitted the plan to Congress and then battled for it throughout 1985 and 1986. Regan played a crucial role in holding the White House behind the bill after he became chief of staff. From Treasury, James Baker and Richard Darman managed the negotiations with Congress and special interests. In 1985 political analysts pronounced the bill dead again and again, and conventional wisdom said tax reform was impossible. Ronald Reagan refused to give up and pushed reform in countless meetings with business and other groups and with Congress. On 28 May 1985 he delivered a major television address, placing his fight in the tradition of the revolutionary generation's fight against taxation without representation. His willingness to lead and to share the heat encouraged Congress to keep working.

Congress surprised itself, and shocked conventional wisdom, by passing the Tax Reform Act of 1986, which Reagan signed on 22 October 1986. It reduced the brackets to three, cut the maximum rate for individuals from 50 percent to 28, nearly doubled the personal exemption, and destroyed thousands of shelters. The new code took six million people off the tax rolls and lowered the rate on low-income and many middle-income people. A single parent with three children and an income of $12,000 paid $1,200 less in income taxes, getting an 83 percent tax cut; a couple with two children and $15,000 received a cut of $826. If many corporations lost previous windfalls, business generally gained because overall rates fell. Wealthy business owners and executives also benefited from the bill because it reduced personal income tax rates.[57]

Reagan's victory on tax reform helped obscure the fact that the administration had run out of new ideas. Reagan's personal agenda had largely been accomplished: tax cuts, the defense buildup, and budget reductions for many liberal programs. His leadership on domestic issues became increasingly sporadic in the second term. The White House received a body blow in the 1986 elections, when the Republicans lost control of the Senate and Reagan could no longer use it as a wedge to force House Democrats to compromise.[58]

That setback was followed almost at once by the Iran-contra scandal (discussed in chapter 9). Scandals had plagued the administration from the beginning. William Casey had difficulty winning confirmation as CIA director because of questions about his financial dealings. Richard V. Allen had been forced to leave as national security adviser. Secretary of Labor Donovan had been indicted and later cleared. Reagan's old associates Lyn Nofziger and Michael Deaver both were indicted and convicted of violating lobbying laws after they tried to capitalize on their White House connections, although Nofziger's conviction was later overturned. According to one study, over 190 Reagan administration officials were indicted or convicted of illegal activities. Reagan did not regard government service as an honorable profession, and he never established an ethics code for his administration or discussed ethics in his speeches.

Meese came under investigation from the moment Reagan nominated him as attorney general. Most people who knew Meese well believed that he was an honest and honorable man who was careless with his personal finances and too trusting of his friends. Questions about ethics held up his confirmation and then continued after he took office. He was caught up in investigations of Wedtech—called the "most corrupt little company in America"—whose founder Reagan had called one of the "heroes for the eighties." In July 1988 independent counsel James C. McKay said that Meese had probably violated the law on four occasions, but he declined to prosecute. The federal prosecutor, with the approval of United States Attorney Rudolph Giuliani, publicly labeled Meese "a sleaze." Several top officials in the Department of Justice resigned in protest against Meese's tenure. On 5 July 1988 Meese announced that he would resign. He was replaced by former Pennsylvania governor Richard Thornburgh.[59]

Reagan faced other problems. Relations with conservatives frayed during the second term. After a blowup between Paul Weyrich and the White House staff, Weyrich had a personal meeting with Reagan. Afterward, Weyrich told a friend, "The good news: The President is not senile. He was vigorous and sounded fully engaged by the topics discussed. The bad news is that he is almost completely misinformed; the worst news is that he does not know this and appears to doubt it." Reagan retained widespread appeal among conservatives, who respected him as an aging warrior who had successfully led them in winning many battles. As his last year in office began, Wirthlin found that Reagan had a 72 percent approval rating from "very conservative" Americans.[60]

Conservatives smarted over the loss of the fight in 1987 to place Robert H. Bork on the Supreme Court to replace retiring justice Lewis F. Powell. Powell had been a moderate who had provided the fifth vote for liberals on abortion and affirmative action cases. Civil rights and women's organizations made defeating Bork their highest priority, while conservatives regarded his confirmation as the opportunity to nail down their majority on the Court. To them, Bork was a heroic figure who for years had been laying the intellectual foundation for a conservative legal revolution. Opponents used that extensive record of publications and speeches to portray Bork as an ideologue who would twist the law to fit his preconceived ideas. Reagan and the White House staff fought hard for Bork, but the administration had been complacent and got into the fight late, while Reagan was weakened by the loss of the Senate and by the decline in his popularity following the Iran-contra scandal. In October 1987 Bork lost the confirmation vote.[61]

Despite conservative disappointment over the Bork defeat, Reagan left a legacy that continued to benefit the right wing long after he left office. His concerted packing of the federal judiciary kept the New Right and Religious Right happy despite few legislative victories for the social agenda. The administration had come to Washington with "revolutionary zeal," recalled Attorney General William French Smith, determined to place "right-thinking" judges in positions they would continue to fill long after the administration ended its work. The Reaganites believed that since the liberal court of Earl Warren in the 1950s and 1960s, judicial activists had twisted the Constitution out of shape, extending rights never envisioned by its authors to women, minorities, criminals, and homosexuals, while eroding traditional rulings on abortion and school prayer. The administration set up an elaborate procedure to find "right-thinking" judges. Reagan's aides kept his spirits up in his difficult last two years in office by providing him with examples of how his judges were chipping away at the liberal legal edifice. Conservative judges were imposing longer sentences on criminals, an aide told him, and were leading a turn against judicial activism, and knocking down race and gender quotas.[62]

Reagan had a major effect on the Supreme Court. Many people in the Religious Right and New Right were furious at Reagan's first appointment. On 7 July 1981 he announced that he was nominating Sandra Day

O'Connor, the first woman placed on the Court. Some conservatives thought that she was soft on the abortion issue, but Reagan carefully worked to still any doubts, and she was easily confirmed. She turned out to be conservative chief justice William H. Rehnquist's most faithful ally, voting with him about 87 percent of the time in her first six years on the bench. In 1986, Reagan named Rehnquist, then associate justice, to replace retiring chief justice Warren E. Burger, and chose the rigorous conservative thinker Antonin Scalia to take Rehnquist's seat. Finally in 1988, after Bork's nomination failed, Reagan placed respected conservative Anthony M. Kennedy on the Court. The Court Reagan shaped was conservative, chipping away at earlier positions it found offensive, but it was not revolutionary and did not try quickly to overthrow the legal framework it had inherited and that had been evolving over half a century.[63]

By June 1988 Reagan had appointed nearly half of all federal judges, and by the time he left office he had placed nearly four hundred judges on the bench, having only three nominees rejected. His candidates were younger than the average of other administrations, because he wanted "right-thinking" judges in action as long as possible. He also appointed a much higher than average number of nominees from law schools and legal think tanks, rather than from the ranks of sitting judges, in the expectation that they would be less bound by the precedents of the Warren and Burger Courts.[64]

Reagan was in the peculiar position of having gained most of his major domestic goals within a few months of his taking office. His early victories cushioned him through mistakes he made, as in Lebanon, and during the long recession that began in 1981. The economic recovery that followed helped him win one of the greatest landslide elections in history. It became obvious as his second term opened that Reagan had few domestic initiatives left to offer, but by that time he had turned his attention to negotiations with the Soviet Union. His summit meetings with Mikhail Gorbachev led to some of the president's major achievements.

8

Engaging the Soviets, 1981–1985

In foreign affairs Ronald Reagan used the rhetoric of realpolitik, but he was, said one analyst, a "hard-line romantic" who envisioned possibilities for change that many experts ridiculed. His entire foreign policy, wrote CIA deputy director Robert Gates, was aimed at reversing history. He was a hard-line anticommunist, yet he joined with Mikhail Gorbachev to bring the cold war to an end. He directed the biggest defense buildup in history, yet he disconcerted his arms control experts by envisioning a world free of nuclear weapons and by taking the first important steps toward achieving that goal. It was ironic, wrote Press Secretary Marlin Fitzwater, that Robert Kennedy rather than Ronald Reagan paraphrased the lines, "I dream things that never were and ask 'Why not?' "[1]

Reagan spoke with patriotic fervor, but he acted cautiously. He understood the American need to "stand tall" in the world, but he also responded to the public fear of getting involved in another Vietnam-style disaster. Observers divided his national security team into pragmatists and ideologues, or, to some, the accommodationists and the "crazies." The pragmatists, led by George Shultz, included Robert McFarlane, Michael Deaver, James Baker, Nancy Reagan, and George Bush. The ideologues included Caspar Weinberger, William Clark, William Casey, Jeane Kirkpatrick, Richard N. Perle, and Edwin Meese. Such labels as pragmatists and ideologues obscured the fact that all members of both groups were conservative anticommunists who supported Reagan's military buildup. Pragmatists wanted to capitalize on that power as a basis for bargaining with the Soviets. Hard-liners believed that negotiations with the "evil empire" promised few benefits to Americans.[2]

Warring conservative camps turned the Reagan administration into a battlefield, and Reagan often did not have the knowledge to impose his will on those who spoke in his name. The "scandal" of the administration, agreed Casey and Jeane Kirkpatrick, was Reagan's ignorance. After a Latin American tour Reagan told reporters, "And you'd be surprised, yes, because, you know, they're all individual countries." He was surprised as well to find that Soviet nuclear power was primarily in land-based intercontinental ballistic missiles, and that bombers carried nuclear weapons. He was happy to learn that French president François M. Mitterrand, a socialist, was anticommunist, since he thought socialism and communism were the same thing. When Mitterrand heard Reagan's tales about communist infiltration of SAG and his battles with a KGB-trained priest, he said to Canadian prime minister Pierre E. Trudeau, "What planet is that man living on? Does he really believe that the Soviets would bring an American priest to Moscow in order to send him back to be a spokesman for Actors of Equity?" Trudeau liked Reagan but had little respect for him: "I think it fair to say that Reagan could be pleasant company for social conversation but was not a man for thoughtful policy discussion."[3]

Reagan sometimes seemed to believe that the cold war resulted from misunderstandings that could be cleared up quickly by face-to-face conversations. He was amazed when he realized that the Soviets really feared United States aggression. In a statement that ignored the history of American blacks, Native Americans, Mexicans, and others, he wrote, "I'd always felt that from our deeds it must be clear to anyone that Americans were a moral people who . . . had always used our power only as a force of good in the world." When he realized that the Soviets might have a view of the United States different from his own, Reagan wrote, "I was even more anxious to get a top Soviet leader in a room alone and try to convince him we had no designs on the Soviet Union and Russians had nothing to fear from us." He liked longtime Soviet ambassador Anatoly Dobrynin and his wife, but he seemed amazed that they, two communists, loved each other and had been married for forty years. "They are a most likable couple," he marveled. "In fact, so much so you wonder how they can stick with the Soviet system." In 1986 he learned that Dobrynin was returning to Moscow to take a high position in the Communist Party. "Is he really a communist?" Reagan asked. Dobrynin wrote, "The sentiments underlying his question surely were complimentary, but the question itself revealed that we were not dealing with an ordinary politician."[4]

Reagan was even less able than in domestic affairs to give his foreign policy subordinates clear directions. His foreign policy structure, wrote James Baker, "was often a witches' brew of intrigue . . . and separate agendas." Reagan's physical and mental energy, not high in his first term, declined significantly in his second term. General Colin L. Powell, deputy to National Security Adviser Frank C. Carlucci, recalled: "The President's passive management style placed a tremendous burden on us. Until we got used to it, we felt uneasy implementing recommendations without a clear decision. . . . One morning after we had gotten another decision by default on a key arms control issue, Frank moaned as we left, 'My God, we didn't sign on to run this country!' "[5]

Franklin D. Roosevelt provoked conflicts among his staff to force subordinates to come to him for decisions to break deadlocks. Reagan, on the other hand, was perfectly willing for others to act for him if they stayed in line with his general policy. His advisers usually served him well, but since they sometimes based their understanding of his wishes on nothing more than reading his body language, they often disagreed on what he wanted. Stalemate frequently resulted, broken sometimes, as in the case of Iran-contra, by people acting in the president's name without his knowledge.

George Shultz gave Reagan important support. Shultz had failures. His Middle Eastern peace initiatives did not get far during the Reagan years; he was largely excluded from Iranian policy; some believed that he turned Central American policy over to Casey and the hard-liners to gain a free hand in other parts of the world. His great success came in Soviet-American relations. He was a strategic thinker with a grand vision, and a careful tactician. Shultz respected Reagan's intelligence, if not his knowledge, and he often reminded himself and others that Reagan, not they, had been elected president. He clearly understood, as Weinberger did not, that Reagan intended his defense buildup to be a prologue to negotiations with the Soviets. Shultz used his skill in bureaucratic infighting to move the administration toward the negotiations that began in 1985. During the bruising battles from 1982 to 1985, he had the support of Baker, Deaver, and Nancy Reagan, as well as the trust and respect of Ronald· Reagan, although the president found himself unable to resolve the conflicts that often undermined Shultz and threatened his control of foreign policy.[6]

Shultz's major opponent within the administration was the dogged and indefatigable Caspar Weinberger. Weinberger had little interest in negotiating with the Soviets. Even after Reagan and many other conservatives had decided that Gorbachev was a new type of Soviet leader, Weinberger held to his belief that the Soviet Union was an evil empire out to take over the world.

The conflict between Weinberger and Shultz was irreconcilable. "You know, it's pointless to try to do business with you, Cap," Shultz told him. "You don't analyze things. You take stances. If you're going to govern, you have to listen and analyze to figure out the right thing to do. But you don't ever do that, Cap." The conflict was costly. It paralyzed policymaking and distracted some senior officials and encouraged others, as during the Iran-contra affair, to go outside of channels. It also wore down the two men. Shultz several times offered to resign, and Weinberger, who seldom displayed stress, and who idealized Reagan, suffered emotionally as well. Once in a darkened airplane returning with Colin Powell from an exhausting tour, Weinberger, whom Powell had thought was asleep, broke the silence, his voice coming out of the darkness: "This is a lonely life. You make real enemies but few real friends. It exhausts a man in body and spirit. I try to serve the President as faithfully as my strength permits. But gratitude does not always come easily to him or his wife."[7]

Infighting and paralysis among senior officials ground up the national security advisers. Lacking firm presidential direction and backing, they were tempted to overcome stalemate by running foreign policy operations from the White House. Reagan had six national security advisers during his eight years in office. Richard Allen and William Clark could do little to settle conflicts among Weinberger, Haig, Kirkpatrick, Casey, Shultz, and other major figures. Robert McFarlane served as national security adviser during the crucial time that the administration began serious discussions with the Soviet Union. He also played an important role in the Iranian operation that came back to haunt the administration after he left. McFarlane, who found that Reagan's grasp of foreign affairs did not go much deeper than the slogan "peace through strength," was a hardworking, dedicated man who tried to bring coherence to national security policy. By the fall of 1985, he was nervous and exhausted by the infighting and his inability to get the president to make hard decisions. His deputy, Admiral John M. Poindexter, an intelligent but narrowly educated naval officer, took over. Poindexter had little understanding of politics, Congress, or the press and was worn down by conflict and overwork. Frank Carlucci took over the NSC staff after the Iran-contra scandal and instituted reforms to get the agency back on track. He, like his predecessors, found that Reagan practically forced him to operate periodically as surrogate president. In late 1987 Carlucci replaced Weinberger as secretary of defense and Colin Powell became national security adviser. For the first time Reagan had a national security team that worked well together. During that final year, Powell,

Shultz, and Carlucci, often propping up the president, prepared the nation to enter the confusing post–cold war era.[8]

A generation of scholars analyzed the origins of the cold war without reaching a consensus on its causes. A new generation will find the story of the end of the cold war equally complex. Most analysts believed that the cold war had ended by 1988 and that a new era of history was opening as Reagan left office. Colin Powell spent part of the night of 22 April 1988 thinking about a question a smiling Mikhail Gorbachev had asked him that day, "What are you going to do now that you've lost your best enemy?" Powell realized that the "old verities" that had guided his thinking about international politics had collapsed, and leaders began to talk of an emerging "new world order."[9]

A variation of history's age-old "great man" debate quickly began. Some viewed the end of the cold war as a waltz led by Gorbachev, danced to music he composed and conducted, with Reagan lagging a step behind. Reagan's supporters, on the other hand, claimed that he was the first Western leader to understand that the Soviet Union verged on collapse and that he formulated and coordinated a comprehensive strategy to force it to surrender. Others, who disparaged the claim that Reagan won the cold war, gave credit to the aged cold warrior's ability to respond so quickly, against the advice of many White House hard-liners, to Gorbachev's overtures. Still other interpreters stressed the convergence of forces and events that brought the conflict to an end, with the two leaders hastily improvising to stay up with change that was beyond their control; only with hindsight did it seem that they had, separately or together, worked from a well-planned, coherent design to end the cold war. Forty years of bipartisan effort, wrote Henry Kissinger, and "seventy years of communist ossification" ended the cold war.[10]

Reagan, his admirers said, understood a simple but profound truth: the Soviet Union's collapse was inevitable. He gave it a hard push, they believed, to hurry the process. On 8 June 1982 Reagan predicted, in a most public forum, the Soviet fall. He told the British Parliament that the Soviet Union "runs against the tide of history," that its economic failure was "astounding," and that its political and economic system was being rejected throughout the world. Communism belonged to the "ash-heap of history," he proclaimed.

It is possible, however, that rather than having some deep insight into the Soviet Union Reagan was fortunate enough to be in power when that nation changed for reasons that he did not understand and did not influence. George Shultz said that Reagan's belief that the USSR was collapsing "was not based on a detailed learned knowledge of the Soviet Union; it was just instinct." CIA deputy director Robert Gates said that Reagan's understanding of Moscow may have been "primitive" but happened to coincide with reality.[11]

Most conservatives admired Reagan as the coldest of the cold warriors. George Shultz understood another part of Reagan's vision: Reagan intended to open serious negotiations when American strength and Soviet vulnerability converged to bring Moscow to the bargaining table. Toward the end of Reagan's presidency, Robert McFarlane congratulated Reagan on the "vindication of your seven year strategy" that had resulted in his triumphant summit conferences with Gorbachev. McFarlane summarized Reagan's strategy: "The truth is that the American economic renewal under your leadership combined with your commitment to make a major investment in high technology, compelled the Soviet Union to take a hard look at whether, and if so how, they could possibly compete and keep up. And after doing that, they had to recognize that they couldn't! . . . *You* . . . forced the Soviet Union to face the reality that they simply had to change their system or face inevitable decline."[12]

The major reasons for Moscow's taking action to end the cold war were found within the Soviet Union. In August 1985 Mikhail Gorbachev held a revealing discussion with *Time* magazine editors. He told them that foreign policy was a continuation of domestic policy and that he intended to institute a "grandiose program" of domestic reform. He asked them, therefore, to ponder what his domestic plans would require in terms of "external conditions." Gorbachev adviser Anatoly Chernyaev later spelled out the implications of Gorbachev's statement: "When Gorbachev became the leader of the Soviet Union, his main concern was to have resources for domestic reform, for 'perestroika,' and he could only get those resources by stopping the arms race. That was the only way, and stopping the arms race was only possible if he could change the nature of relations between the Soviet Union and the United States." "It sounds simple," Chernyaev added, "but it was an extraordinarily difficult task."[13]

The cold war ended mainly because the Soviet Union had to change internally to save itself. Communism had failed to live up to its promise to find "an alternative road to modernity." As Gorbachev and his associates took power in the mid-1980s they struggled to achieve the promise of the "Khrushchev thaw," a failed attempt at liberalization and economic development led by premier Nikita S. Khrushchev. During Leonid I. Brezhnev's long reign, the old guard had choked off that attempt at liberalization. When the younger generation finally took power, they found the world had changed. Measured by the goals that Khrushchev had set for it in 1961, the USSR was successful. By 1984, the Soviet Union was producing 80 percent more steel than the United States, 78 percent more cement, 55 percent more fertilizer, many times more tractors, iron ore, pig iron, and metal-cutting lathes. The central planners had set a goal and had deployed labor, capital, and raw materials to achieve it. Had the world remained the same, the Soviet Union would have been an economic giant, but by the 1980s "the West was living in an entirely different economic system, a post-industrial world in which the new sinews of wealth were microchips rather than pig-iron, plastic rather than steel, and where conservation in the use of raw materials was becoming more important and more profitable than crude production."

Détente, rather than strengthening the Soviet Union as the Reaganites believed, had opened the communist bloc to trade, travel, and intellectual exchange, and citizens there realized that they had less freedom and fewer consumer goods than those in Western and many Asian countries. Many talented young people experienced an "inner migration" in which they withdrew their support from the system.

Gorbachev scrambled to find a solution to these problems. His *perestroika* reforms aimed at restructuring the nation's economy, and his *glasnost* program attempted to democratize and liberalize Soviet society. As he struggled to deal with crushing domestic needs, he moved at an incredible speed to change relations with the West. In the end, change came too late to deal with the massive problems stemming from seventy years of failed promises. Gorbachev would prove unable to control the process of change that he had initiated, and he proved too wise and humane to keep the lid on by using the harsh methods of his predecessors.[14]

While the Soviet leaders took action for domestic reasons to end the cold war, Reagan kept all the pressure on Moscow that he could exert from the outside. He saw the American defense buildup as the key to producing change within the Soviet Union. He believed that SDI was the specific military program that pushed Moscow into submission, for although many American scientists and defense experts dismissed SDI, Gorbachev took it seriously. SDI posed many threats to the Soviets. If it was only partially successful, it would enhance the American second-strike capability in a nuclear attack. Even if it could not be built as Reagan dreamed, the incredibly sophisticated and expensive research program might lead to technological breakthroughs that would raise the arms race to an entirely new level. SDI challenged the Soviets in advanced technology, where the Americans had a clear advantage. If Gorbachev tried to compete, it would take valuable resources away from his *perestroika* program. "SDI was a Soviet nightmare come to life," wrote Robert Gates. Several Soviet officials later confirmed that SDI seemed to be an extraordinary threat that hit them just as they were beginning to comprehend the extent of their nation's economic and social disaster. "It frightened us very much," one said.[15]

In addition to his military buildup, Reagan formulated an extensive "silent campaign" against the Soviet Union, embodied in several secret National Security Decision Directives (NSDD). He signed NSDD-32 in March 1982, NSDD-66 in November 1982, and NSDD-75 in January 1983. NSDD-32, said Edwin Meese, formally abandoned Roosevelt's Yalta accords with the Soviets. National Security Adviser Clark, who helped write the directive, said, "In NSDD-32, Ronald Reagan made clear that the United States was not resigned to the status quo of Soviet domination of Eastern Europe. We attempted to forge a multipronged strategy to weaken Soviet influence and strengthen indigenous forces for freedom in the region." It responded to Soviet pressure on Poland by offering covert support to underground resistance movements in Eastern Europe, intensifying psychological warfare campaigns in the region, and using trade and diplomacy to try to erode Moscow's hold over the area. NSDD-66 outlined a campaign by the United States and its allies of economic warfare against the Soviet Union.[16]

Soviet expert Richard E. Pipes described NSDD-75 as the administration's decision to reject détente and coexistence and to go beyond the containment strategy. "NSDD-75 was a clear break from the past," Pipes explained. "It was the first document which said that what mattered was not only Soviet behavior but the nature of the Soviet system. NSDD-75 said our goal was no longer to coexist with the Soviet Union but to change the Soviet system." It declared that the United States would resist Soviet imperialism in the international arena and pressure the Soviet Union to move toward a more "pluralistic" political and economic system. The United States should exploit Soviet vulnerability in Eastern Europe and Afghanistan, work to decrease Cuban influence in Central America and Africa, and weaken the Soviet links to the Third World while promoting democracy in those countries.[17]

These documents, along with Reagan's speeches, especially his 9 May 1982 speech at Eureka College and his 1985 State of the Union address, were said to constitute the Reagan Doctrine, based on Reagan's City on a Hill vision that the United States's mission was to lead the world to democracy and freedom. "We cannot play innocents abroad in a world that's not innocent; nor can we be passive when freedom is under siege," he said in his 1985 State of the Union address. "We must stand by all our democratic allies. And we must not break faith with those who are risking their lives— on every continent, from Afghanistan to Nicaragua—to defy Soviet-supported aggression and secure rights which have been ours from birth." Henry Kissinger summarized the Reagan Doctrine: "America would not wait passively for free institutions to evolve, nor would it confine itself to resisting direct threats to its security. Instead, it would actively promote democracy, rewarding those countries which fulfilled its ideals and punishing those which fell short—even if they presented no other visible challenge or threat to America."[18]

Poland was a country that the Reagan administration began to focus on even before inauguration day in 1981. It was there that the Soviet empire seemed to be fraying. The Solidarity trade union movement had turned into a general challenge to communist rule. In 1981 General Wojciech Jaruzelski became premier, determined to bring Poland under control, and Washington feared that the Soviet Union would intervene militarily to stabilize Jaruzelski's communist regime. Haig warned the administration to act with restraint. He believed Poland was a *casus belli* for the Soviet Union, an issue on which it would go to war with the United States. The old Soviet leader, Vyacheslav M. Molotov could remember conversations about Poland going all the way back to the days of Roosevelt and Truman. "We cannot lose Poland," Molotov said on 4 December 1981. "If this line is crossed they will grab us, too."

A few days later, Moscow directed Jaruzelski to impose martial law. Reagan reacted furiously. "Something must be done," he told his advisers. "We need to hit them hard, and save Solidarity." Despite heated verbal exchanges, both Moscow and Washington acted with some restraint. The Soviets, for example, did not use military force to restore order as they had in Eastern Europe in the past. The Reagan administration also carefully avoided giving any encouragement to a Polish uprising. On 29 December 1981 Reagan announced sanctions against the Soviet Union, including stopping Soviet airline service to the United States, prohibiting certain kinds of trade, and suspending various ongoing negotiations between the two nations. In February 1982 Reagan ordered Casey to provide money, communications equipment, and intelligence information to Solidarity. By early 1985 the United States was covertly spending $8 million a year to keep Solidarity going while its leadership was in jail.[19]

The Reagan administration also conducted a silent campaign of economic warfare against the Soviet Union. On 26 March 1982 Reagan summarized a briefing he had received that day, saying the Soviets "are in very bad shape and if we can cut off their credit they'll have to yell 'Uncle' or starve." Reagan wanted to accelerate Soviet distress, and he had an eager ally in CIA director Casey. Casey believed that the CIA had been geared only toward assessing Soviet strengths; he wanted to know its weaknesses, where to attack. He brought in journalist Herbert E. Meyer to make "vulnerability assessments" to guide American economic warfare. Meyer concluded that the Soviet Union was an empire in an advanced stage of decay. It contained within its borders over one hundred nationality groups, each chafing under Russian domination. Its economy was stagnating and perhaps shrinking. Food was short outside Moscow; five of seven main communicable diseases (including hepatitis and diphtheria) were out of control; infant mortality was increasing and life expectancy declining; a deep pessimism was spreading among the people; Soviet leaders had lost confidence that history was with them. The Soviet empire had entered its terminal stage, Meyer wrote. These "vulnerability assessments" became part of Reagan's nightly reading. "We can do them in," Casey gloated.[20]

Casey, Weinberger, and others drew up a comprehensive strategy to "do them in," including prohibiting important technology transfers to the Soviet Union and denying it and its allies economic credit. The administration quietly warned financial circles about the risk in investing and loaning money within the Soviet empire. Casey courted Saudi Arabia. He supported arms sales to the Saudis, shared intelligence information on matters that were important to the Saudi royal family, and promised American support against any attack on their government. His goal was to win Saudi cooperation in lowering oil prices. Casey estimated that a one-dollar-a-barrel increase in oil prices pumped $1 billion in hard currency annually into the Soviet Union from oil exports. Weinberger later said that the reason the White House fought hard against the Jewish lobby's opposition to selling sophisticated arms to Saudi Arabia was to encourage the Saudis to lower oil prices. In July 1985 Reagan gave this message directly to King Fahd. Finally, in August 1985, Saudi Arabia opened the oil spigot, raising production from less than two million barrels a day to almost nine million. Oil prices plummeted, from about thirty dollars a barrel to around twelve dollars, and reduced Soviet hard currency income by half. "A stake was driven silently through the heart of the Soviet economy," wrote one analyst. "It was a catastrophic event," recalled a Soviet official.[21]

Reagan and Casey had early agreed on covert aid to the *mujahideen* "freedom fighters" in Afghanistan, where Casey had determined the Soviets were especially vulnerable. The administration funneled weapons and other supplies to the *mujahideen* through Pakistan. In January 1985 Reagan told his advisers, "Do whatever you have to to help the *mujahideen* not only survive, but win." By late 1986, when the Politburo began to explore ways to withdraw from Afghanistan, the war was costing the Soviet Union $4 billion a year and thousands of lives.[22]

The Soviet Union obsessed Reagan. He often described world politics in Manichaean terms of a struggle between good and evil, which pleased Paul Nitze, one of the post–World War II authors of the containment policy. He liked Reagan because "his distrust of the Soviets was complete, and his reflex in the area of defense was to build more of everything no matter what the cost." Vice President Bush, on the other hand, who found Reagan's ideas about international relations "almost unimaginable," was "simply amazed to see to what extent Reagan was dominated by Hollywood cliches and the ideas of his wealthy but conservative and poorly educated friends from California."[23]

There was, however, another side to Reagan's thinking, one that led him to undertake a series of summit meetings with Mikhail Gorbachev. Ambassador Dobrynin speculated that Reagan's hatred of nuclear weapons ultimately overcame his "visceral anticommunism." Reagan was shocked, he later wrote, to find that some people at the Pentagon thought that a nuclear war was winnable: "I thought they were crazy." If war started, he wrote, "it would be like two spiders in a bottle locked in a suicidal fight until both were dead." Beneath his often frightening anti Soviet rhetoric, Reagan had a different vision. "My dream," he said, "became a world free of nuclear weapons."[24]

To achieve his dream, Reagan would have to negotiate with the hated Soviet communists. While one part of his mind contained images of an implacable Soviet drive to take over the world, another part believed that after the United States rebuilt its military power, the Soviets could come to the bargaining table and begin serious talks. His optimism convinced him that however evil communism was, people everywhere were the same and that they never wanted war. He wrote, "I felt that if I could ever get in a room alone with one of the top Soviet leaders, there was a chance the two of us could make some progress in easing tensions between our two countries. I have always placed a lot of faith in the simple power of human contact in solving problems." This optimism and his belief in the myth of the City on a Hill, his faith that all people of goodwill wanted to be like Americans, led him to the view that while communism was wrong, Gorbachev was a different kind of communist.[25]

Both sides of Reagan's thinking were evident during his first three years in office. On 29 January 1981, at his first press conference, in answer to a question from journalist Sam Donaldson, Reagan thrilled conservatives and appalled liberals. He said détente had been a one-way street and that every Soviet leader since the revolution had stated that the Soviet goal was a global communist state. Soviet leaders "have openly and publicly declared that the only morality they recognize is what will further their cause, meaning they reserve unto themselves the right to commit any crime, to lie, to cheat, in order to attain that," he said. Dobrynin had his first official visit with Haig that same day, and asked if the administration was looking for a pretext for confrontation. "How is he going to do business with us?" Dobrynin wondered. "What is the purpose of all that? Why should he set such a tone for the new administration from the very beginning?" Haig told Dobrynin that Reagan had called him after the press conference and assured him that his statement about the Soviet Union was not meant to offend anyone in Moscow but just expressed his deep convictions. "This clarification only made things worse," Dobrynin responded dryly.[26]

The softer side of Reagan also showed itself in 1981. During an introspective period after the assassination attempt in March, Reagan wrote Brezhnev a personal letter, which disconcerted the professionals in the State Department. He reminded Brezhnev of their meeting years before at San Clemente, California, and their discussion of their hopes for peace. The world's people share that hope, Reagan wrote, and they share other things: the right to control their own destiny, to work at jobs of their own choosing, to raise their families in peace. "Is it possible that we have permitted ideology, political and economic philosophies, and governmental policies to keep us from considering the very real, everyday problems of people?" Haig had not wanted Reagan to send the letter, but Reagan told Deaver that he had decided in the hospital that he had been spared for a purpose and intended to follow his instinct.[27]

Paul Laxalt told Dobrynin that the important thing was not what Reagan's letter said but the "psychological stride" he had made in writing it. Dobrynin thought it odd that Reagan believed that a personal private gesture could cancel his aggressive public statements. Still, he concluded that the Kremlin had made a mistake in returning a stiffly worded formal reply rather than responding to the psychology of the wounded Reagan tentatively reaching out his hand.[28]

In 1982 an important change in leadership occurred when George Shultz replaced Haig as secretary of state. Shultz seemed moderate in comparison with Weinberger, Clark, Casey, and other unbending hard-liners, but he was a tough negotiator who believed that Soviet behavior in the world was unacceptable. He also believed, however, that Soviet leadership was rational and would make and abide by agreements in its interest. His primary foreign policy goal was to open constructive dialogue with the Soviets. Knowing that his major battles would come with his colleagues in Washington rather than his opponents in Moscow, he noted that "I would have to be deft, but I was determined not to hang back from engaging the Soviets because of fears that 'Soviets win negotiations.' "[29]

In November 1982 Brezhnev died and Yuri V. Andropov replaced him. Dobrynin believed that had Andropov lived, he might have made a breakthrough with the Americans. He was an intelligent man who recognized that the Soviet economy was a disaster and that the Soviet Union was overextended internationally. In August 1982 Andropov had told a visiting delegation from Poland that the Soviet economy was not in much better shape than the Polish one, which was near collapse. He initiated 110 studies of problems his nation faced. These studies provided the foundation that Gorbachev would use to begin his comprehensive reform programs. In Andropov's first few weeks in office, he suggested a summit with Reagan, proposed a nonaggression pact, and made major positive offers for nuclear arms reduction.[30]

In 1983 Shultz tried to pull Reagan directly into dialogue with the Soviets. "When he's engaged, he's good," Shultz said. He opened the year with a memorandum to the president proposing opening dialogue on a four-part program that became the United States agenda with Moscow for the rest of Reagan's years in office: human rights, arms control, regional issues (the war in Afghanistan, for example), and bilateral relations between the two nations. Although the "ideologues" around the president savaged Shultz's memorandum, Reagan authorized him to begin a dialogue with Dobrynin.[31]

On Saturday, 12 February 1983, a snowstorm hit Washington and the Reagans could not go to Camp David. Instead, they asked Shultz and his wife to the White House for an intimate dinner. A year before in a similar setting Billy Graham, a Reagan family friend, had found that Ronald Reagan was hesitant about opening a dialogue with Moscow but that Nancy was eager to do so. She regarded a breakthrough toward normalizing relations with the Soviet Union as a way for her husband to become a truly historic figure. Now, Shultz discovered that Reagan was much more willing to open relations with the Soviets than the secretary of state had realized. He also understood that Reagan felt captive to his hard-line staff and by his own past anti-Soviet rhetoric. Shultz told Reagan that he was meeting with Dobrynin on the following Tuesday and suggested that he bring the Soviet ambassador in to talk with the president. Reagan agreed.[32]

When Dobrynin called on Shultz on 15 February, the secretary whisked him to the White House for a secret meeting with Reagan, held in the family quarters. This was the first business session that Reagan had held with a Soviet official. They talked for two hours, with about a third of the time spent on overall Soviet-American relations, a third on arms control, and a third on human rights. Reagan seemed prepared and fully engaged. He told Dobrynin that the Soviet people probably regarded him as a "crazy warmonger," but he wanted peace. He proposed making a "fresh start."

He raised with Dobrynin the plight of several Pentecostal Christians who in 1978 had sought sanctuary in the American embassy in Moscow. It was the kind of human interest story that appealed to Reagan. When career diplomat Jack F. Matlock Jr. visited the president following a tour of duty in Moscow, Matlock was surprised because the first thing Reagan asked about was not Brezhnev's arms control policies but the Pentecostals. After Reagan brought the matter up with Dobrynin, the ambassador pushed Moscow hard to respond. It seemed strange to the Kremlin leaders that after years of hostility, Reagan's first personal request related to seven Pentecostals. It may sound a little "bizarre," Bush told Dobrynin, but it was "a kind of a litmus test" with Reagan. By mid-July the Pentecostals were free to leave the Soviet Union.[33]

The internecine warfare within the administration now became more intense. Before a 10 March 1983 White House meeting on Soviet-American relations, Reagan took Shultz aside and told him he did not want those present to know about his session with Dobrynin. The president was a prisoner of his own staff, and the internal warfare was so vicious that Shultz's position within the administration was constantly at risk. His main allies were Nancy Reagan, with her eye on her husband's place in history, and Michael Deaver, who believed improved relations would help Reagan politically. With their help, Shultz maintained his personal access to Reagan, notwithstanding constant sniping from the hard-liners.[34]

Despite several positive exchanges of letters between Andropov and Reagan, 1983 turned out to be one of the harshest years in the entire cold war. On 8 March Reagan, speaking to the National Association of Evangelicals, gave a speech that rattled the Soviets (and many Americans), and disturbed them for the rest of his presidency. He said it was an "elementary fact" that Moscow did not accept any morality unless it furthered class warfare. The Soviet Union was the "focus of evil in the modern world" and was an "evil empire." Nancy and others encouraged him to tone down his rhetoric, and he never used such harsh words again; but then he did not need to—the message was clear and the words unforgettable.[35]

Still, a positive exchange of letters between Reagan and Andropov followed in July and August, then ended in the sharpest flare-up of propaganda warfare in decades. On 1 September 1983, a Soviet fighter jet shot down a Korean airliner, KAL 007, carrying a United States congressman and sixty other Americans. Reagan reacted with fury, while the Soviets stonewalled and denied responsibility. "I thought both sides had gone slightly crazy," Dobrynin said, with the Kremlin handling the disaster in a crude, insensitive way and the White House making unsubstantiated charges.[36]

There were other conflicts in 1983. In 1977 the Soviet Union had begun to deploy SS-20 ballistic missiles in Europe. These were intermediate-range missiles that could strike Western Europe but could not reach the United States. Their deployment posed an insidious threat to the Western alliance. Many Europeans thought it unlikely that the United States would bring nuclear destruction on itself by responding to a Soviet attack on Europe.

West German chancellor Helmut Schmidt said that the Americans must deploy intermediate-range missiles in Europe or get the Soviets to remove theirs; otherwise the alliance would be subject to nuclear blackmail. Reagan fulfilled Carter's promise to deploy American missiles, beginning in November 1983. Reagan and the Western allies unflinchingly held to this policy despite intense Soviet pressure and opposition from a strong Western European peace movement. It was a "gut-wrenching" experience for the Americans and Europeans, but once the United States began deployment, the alliance was internally stronger and more confident than ever. In response to the deployment, the Soviets walked out of the arms talks in Geneva, and for the first time in fourteen years, no arms control talks were under way.[37]

Diplomatic activity was paralyzed. Dobrynin was so depressed that he considered "giving up" and transferring back to Moscow. Even routine NATO war exercises in November 1983 triggered Soviet fears that the Americans were planning a nuclear strike. Moscow had hoped that Reagan's anti-Soviet rhetoric was campaign theatrics that would be discarded when he assumed the presidency. They understood that hard-line anticommunists like Nixon had more freedom to negotiate than liberals, and hoped Reagan would follow that path. Now they were disillusioned. "Reagan is unpredictable," Andropov said. "You should expect anything from him." He complained that history had given him Reagan to deal with, calling it "just my bad luck." Dobrynin believed that Reagan's anti-communist language and action strengthened Kremlin hard-liners, and he feared that Soviet leaders were beginning "to absorb Reagan's own distinctive thesis that Soviet-American relations could remain permanently bad as a deliberate choice of policy."[38]

Despite the deteriorating relationship, George Shultz continued to operate on the assumption that the president wanted to open a dialogue with the Soviet leaders. Since Reagan was unwilling to impose that decision on his subordinates, Shultz had to fight Clark, Casey, Weinberger, and others to carry out the president's policy. Shultz's hand was strengthened in late 1983, because the American economy was expanding rapidly and the Reagan military buildup had poured hundreds of billions of dollars into the Pentagon. Renewed economic and military power gave Reagan confidence in dealing with Moscow. In addition, Robert McFarlane had taken over as national security adviser, and he shared Shultz's belief that it was time to go to the bargaining table with the Soviets. They were supported by Nancy Reagan, concerned with her husband's place in history, and by James Baker and Michael Deaver, who were looking toward the 1984 election. Reagan had his own special reasons for wanting negotiations. Shultz told his associates in the State Department, "Every meeting I go to . . . the president talks about abolishing nuclear weapons. I cannot get it through your heads that the man is serious."[39]

On 16 January 1984 Reagan delivered a major address on Soviet-American relations. Dobrynin said that although the Kremlin greeted it with mistrust, in retrospect he recognized that it marked a real shift in Reagan's thinking. Jack Matlock, a Soviet expert who would become United States ambassador to the Soviet Union and who drafted most of the speech, agreed with Dobrynin's assessment. Matlock said the speech established the agenda for the Soviet-American dialogue for the rest of Reagan's presidency and laid the foundation for the principles on which the cold war would end.

Reagan said that the United States was strong and confident and ready to establish a constructive relationship with the Soviet Union, based on "credible deterrence and peaceful competition." He said that the two nations might concentrate on reducing armament stockpiles, cooperating to end the use of force in regional conflicts like the Middle East, Afghanistan, and Central America, establishing better bilateral relations, and respecting human rights. "In working on these tasks, our approach is based on three guiding principles—realism, strength, and dialog." Reagan ended his speech with a little fantasy that he wrote himself. He imagined an Ivan and Anya and Jim and Sally spending time together, talking about their children, their work, their hopes for the future. They would find, Reagan said, a common human connection and a shared abhorrence of war.[40]

On 31 January Dobrynin met with the ambassadors from communist countries and all except Cuba reported that the United States had adopted a more conciliatory attitude toward their countries. At about the same time, Reagan met President Mika Spiljak of Yugoslavia, former ambassador to the Soviet Union, and "picked his brains." Spiljak believed that the Soviets were insecure and frightened, Reagan wrote in his diary, and added, "He also believes that if we opened them up a bit, their leading citizens would get braver about proposing changes in their system. I'm going to pursue this."[41]

Before Reagan could push further for an opening, Andropov died, and on 13 February 1984 Konstantin U. Chernenko became general secretary. Although ill, audibly gasping for breath after every few words in his speeches, Chernenko slowly moved Reagan away from the dead end that their nations had reached by 1983. The Soviets did not know if Reagan was sincere in his "Ivan and Anya" speech or if he had his eye on the November election. When Lawrence S. Eagleburger left the State Department in May 1984, he described Reagan to Dobrynin as a man very proud of his "inborn instinct" but without many new ideas. His grasp of foreign policy was still "mediocre," said Eagleburger, and he was not interested in details. While he wanted better relations with Moscow, his inner circle did not know how to construct a dialogue with the Soviets. Later in the year, Bush described Reagan to Dobrynin as rather uninformed but said that the president's desire for improved relations was sincere.[42]

By late summer Kremlin leaders decided that Reagan was going to be reelected and that they would have to deal with him. On 28 September 1984 Foreign Minister Andrey A. Gromyko, who had dealt with American presidents from Roosevelt on, accepted an invitation to meet with Reagan at the White House. The talk was blunt, and Reagan searched Gromyko's granite-like face for any reactions. He described the meeting in his diary: "The big day—Andrei Gromyko. . . . I opened with my monologue and made the point that perhaps both of us felt the other was a threat, then explained by the record we had more reason to feel that way than they did. . . . I kept emphasizing that we were the two nations that could destroy or save the world. I figured they nurse a grudge that we don't respect them as a super power. All in all, three hours including lunch were I believe well spent."

Gromyko described the conversation as "edgy." Reagan displayed no "frostiness," but Gromyko did not see any readiness to move in a more "positive" direction. His report did amuse his colleagues in the Kremlin. At lunch he asked Nancy Reagan to whisper "peace" in Ronald's ear each night. She agreed but said she also would whisper it in Gromyko's ear.[43]

After Reagan told Shultz to push hard to open a dialogue with Moscow, administration infighting intensified. Some conservatives told the president that Shultz had "gone soft," and they wanted the president to fire him; in return, "I told them, that was utter nonsense." He wrote in his diary: "George sounds like he wants out. I can't let that happen. Actually George is carrying out my policy. I'm going to meet with Cap and Bill [Casey] and lay it out to them. Won't be fun but has to be done." When Reagan suggested to Chernenko that Gromyko and Shultz meet in January 1985, the hard-liners resisted. Reagan finally told Weinberger, "Cap, we can't know where it will all come out, but we are going to engage the Russians. So George, go over there and get it started, without giving anything up."[44]

On 11 March 1985 Reagan learned that Chernenko had died. How could he make peace, a frustrated Reagan asked, "if they keep dying on me?" When Shultz went to the Soviet embassy to express condolences, he told Dobrynin that he had talked to Reagan earlier that day and the president said that the two nations were facing "a new situation with new opportunities . . . and it would be unforgivable not to take advantage of it, although the outcome was hardly predictable." Vice President Bush attended the funeral in Moscow and gave the new leader, Mikhail Gorbachev, a letter inviting him to a summit. Gorbachev responded positively and said that in the meantime both sides had to work to build trust and to avoid harsh public attacks. Reagan took the hint. He wrote in his diary that he intended "to lean on the Soviets one on one, not in the papers."[45]

Gorbachev led impatient young reformers who had long recognized that the Soviet Union was in crisis. They soon found that the problems were deeper than they had guessed. Gorbachev was a committed communist who wanted to reform the existing system, but as he struggled with the catastrophe that his nation faced he improvised changes "on the march," and reform turned into revolution. Gorbachev proposed both restructuring the Soviet economy to build in market mechanisms and democratic reform to allow more freedom of expression and give the alienated public a stake in society. Time ran out for Gorbachev and his nation long before his dramatic reforms took root. "In 1985, . . . when I said there was going to be a revolution, everybody cheered," he told George Bush. "They said, yes, we needed a revolution. But by 1987, our revolution was on, and the cheering began to die down. Now in 1988, the revolution still goes on, but the cheering has stopped."[46]

Gorbachev's "number one preoccupation" was the economic cost of the cold war. His aide Anatoly Chernyaev said Gorbachev realized that "we had to put an end to the Cold War." American ambassador to the Soviet Union Jack Matlock said that the cold war ended because Gorbachev accepted as his own program the four-part agenda that Reagan had proposed: resolving nuclear arms issues, regional conflicts, bilateral questions, and human rights problems. The Americans did not impose this agenda on the Soviets, Matlock said; Gorbachev came to see that ending disputes on these matters were a necessary part of his own reform program. The cold war ended because by the late 1980s the interests of the superpowers coincided.[47]

When Gorbachev and Reagan agreed to hold a summit in Geneva in November 1985, they did so against a backdrop of arms control negotiations that had suddenly become more meaningful. In 1981, arms control talks had not been a high priority. Weinberger and his main assistant for arms control matters, Richard Perle, did not trust the Soviet Union to abide by agreements anyway, and despite the horror inspired by those weapons, the arms control community believed that the nuclear arsenal had maintained stability and peace for forty years.[48]

The administration believed that the Strategic Arms Limitation Treaty (SALT II), limiting long-range missiles, was deeply flawed. Negotiated during the Carter years, it had not been ratified because of the uproar over the Soviet invasion of Afghanistan. Reagan, one of the few members of his administration who believed the world would be safer without nuclear weapons, decided to abide by the terms of the treaty without ratifying it.

Debate in 1981 and 1982 thus centered on intermediate-range missiles, which the United States was preparing to deploy in Europe. Richard Perle, backed by Weinberger, formulated what they called the zero-zero option. The United States would give up its 1983 deployment if the Soviets would eliminate from Europe their intermediate-range missiles. Many State Department officials suspected that the zero-zero option was a Weinberger-Perle ploy to kill any agreement because it required the Soviets to give up five weapons systems, while the Americans would give up nothing since deployment had not yet occurred.

On 18 November 1981 Reagan spoke to the National Press Club and endorsed the zero-zero option for intermediate-range missiles. On long-range missiles, he proposed that the superpowers continue to abide by SALT II but suggested that they open new talks aimed at actually reducing strategic weapons rather than controlling their growth. He labeled these proposed negotiations START, for Strategic Arms Reduction Talks. Although many analysts considered Reagan's proposals as devious attempts to sabotage arms talks, the United States and the Soviet Union signed an intermediate-range treaty in 1987 and finished work on START during the Bush administration.[49]

The ups and downs of Soviet-American relations in 1983 buffeted the arms control talks, and they were suspended altogether when the Soviets walked out after Americans began deploying missiles in Europe. In 1984 both sides began to edge toward breaking the stalemate, and when Gorbachev came to power he quickly grasped the importance to Reagan of arms reductions. Shultz had earlier told the arms negotiating team that Reagan wanted to eliminate nuclear weapons. "So think more about the theme of elimination of nuclear weapons," Shultz had said. "Everyone thinks it is rhetoric, but rhetoric said often enough by important people tends to wind up with an operational character to it."[50]

As the two sides prepared for the summit in Geneva, Gorbachev pushed Reagan to adopt new thinking on nuclear arms control and other matters. In April he announced a moratorium on further Soviet deployment of intermediate missiles, and in October he announced that the Soviets would reduce the number already deployed. By the time in November 1985 that Shultz visited with Gorbachev and the new Soviet foreign minister, Eduard A. Shevardnadze, the Soviets had clearly signaled their interest in redefining the Soviet-American relationship.

Shultz enjoyed the intellectual challenge that Gorbachev invariably offered and, in turn, he tried to educate Gorbachev and Shevardnadze on basic global changes that he saw in their future. Computer and communication technology was transforming the world and opening a new era of history, he warned, and if the Soviet Union did not keep up it would permanently fall behind the rest of the world. The age of information, he argued, required an open society with political and economic freedom, which meant that the Soviet Union, in its own self-interest, had to accept the human rights agenda. Closed societies could not cope with this new technology, Shultz told the two men. Rather than being offended, Gorbachev beamed and told Shultz he should take over the Moscow planning office. Gorbachev made some of these themes part of his vision of the future as he began his reform program.[51]

Reagan prepared carefully for the summit. He had dreamed of meeting a Soviet leader face-to-face to convince him that the Americans meant his nation no harm and that the two of them could work to create a more peaceful world. In his mind it was like a scene in the movies, with two men of goodwill meeting, breaking through on human terms, and confounding all the nay-saying experts. It promised to be the performance of a lifetime. "Lord, I hope I'm ready," he nervously wrote in his diary.[52]

Vice President Bush told Dobrynin not to expect a breakthrough in Geneva because Reagan was not ready to accept any limit on SDI, which was Moscow's highest priority. "After some hesitation," Dobrynin wrote, "Bush mentioned another of Reagan's congenital peculiarities: the president found it hard simultaneously to think and to express his own ideas. This meant that whenever Reagan was ardently advocating an idea be it right or wrong, he hardly grasped what his opponent was saying, Bush said. He needed some time to digest the ideas and arguments coming at him from the other side. For that reason, Bush believed the first summit should above all put into Reagan's head some different ideas from the ones that he held so tenaciously."[53]

The two men met first at 10 A.M. on 19 November 1985. Dobrynin had warned Gorbachev that first impressions were critical to Reagan and that the president would need to see Gorbachev in "human terms" even when they were disagreeing. It boded well for future relations when Reagan instantly felt warmth and humanity from Gorbachev. Gorbachev responded similarly. He looked into Reagan's eyes, he told historian Edmund Morris, and "I had a sensation of sun and open sky. I saw at once that he was authentic." Both men had already changed many of their previous conceptions about each other, their countries, and possibilities for change. "I understood the irony of what happened that morning under the overcast Geneva sky," Reagan wrote. He had spent much of his life as an anticommunist leader. "Now, here I was opening negotiations with the Kremlin, and, while doing so, I had extended my hand with warmth and a smile to its highest leader."[54]

The most dramatic event on the first day came when Reagan asked Gorbachev if he would like to walk down to a boathouse on Lake Geneva, away from their advisers. Gorbachev jumped up ready to leave before Reagan finished his sentence. Ronald and Nancy had carefully selected the meeting place and had a fire laid in the fireplace. Reagan now could act out the dream that he had visualized like a scene from a film, and proceeded to do so. "Here you and I are, two men in a room, probably the only two men in the world who could bring about World War III. But by the same token, we may be the only two men in the world who could perhaps bring about peace in the world." He said that distrust was driving the arms race. It was important to talk about arms reductions, Reagan urged, "but isn't it also important that you and I should be talking about how we could reduce the mistrust between us?" Perhaps images from the 1951 film *The Day the Earth Stood Still* went through his mind as he told Gorbachev that it would be easy to work together "if there was a threat to this world from some other species, from another planet, outside in the universe. . . . We'd forget all the little local differences that we have between our countries, and we would find out once and for all that we really are all human beings here on this Earth together." He also told Gorbachev, "We can agree to reduce arms—or we can continue the arms race, *which I think you know you can't win*. We won't stand by and let you maintain weapon superiority over us. But together we can try to do something about ending the arms race."

One of Reagan's main objectives at Geneva was to arrange for another summit. As they walked back from the boathouse, he invited Gorbachev to come to Washington the following year. Gorbachev agreed and invited Reagan to come to Moscow for a third summit, which Reagan accepted. The two men returned, relaxed and smiling, to their delegations.[55]

The first day did not consist entirely of smiles and plans for the future. The Americans welcomed Gorbachev's presentation on the need for constructive engagement at all levels and his talk of withdrawing from Afghanistan. "As I listened," Shultz recalled, "I thought to myself, Gorbachev could be reading right out of the president's own briefing book." Reagan had given Gorbachev a short document on arms control proposals. It proposed a 50 percent reduction in strategic arms, an interim agreement on intermediate-range weapons with the goal of eliminating all such missiles, and an accord allowing development of defensive systems (that is, SDI). Gorbachev accepted the first two items as the basis for negotiations, but he concentrated his fire on SDI. If SDI was developed, Gorbachev said, "only God himself would know where it would lead." Before the summit Reagan had decided that under no conditions would he trade away SDI to win concessions. If Gorbachev was adamant on the issue, Reagan said, "Well, this will be a case of an irresistible force meeting an immovable object."[56]

On the second day of the summit Gorbachev and Reagan engaged in verbal brawls that burned themselves into onlookers' memories. Gorbachev said he could not understand why the Americans wanted the SDI system unless it was to pour $600 billion to $1 trillion into the military-industrial complex. When Reagan tried to explain that SDI was a defensive system, not offensive, Gorbachev answered, "I hear your arguments, but I'm not convinced. . . . It's emotional . . . part of one man's dream." Reagan promised to share SDI technology with Moscow, but Gorbachev responded, "Why should I accept your sincerity on your willingness to share SDI research when you don't even share your advanced technology with your allies?" He said he wanted compromise and offered important concessions on arms reduction, "but SDI has got to come to an end." A long silence followed, finally. broken by Gorbachev. "Mr. President, I don't agree with you, but I can see you really mean it," and he added, "maybe this has all grown a little bit heated. I was just trying to convey to you the depth of our concern on SDI."

The summit ended on the third day, 21 November. The two sides issued a communiqué in which they agreed on a 50 percent reduction in strategic arms, with the details to be worked out at the arms control table, an interim intermediate-range missile agreement, additional summits, cultural and scientific exchanges, and other moves to reopen Soviet-American dialogue. The communiqué included the statement that nuclear war could not be won and must never be fought.[57]

Dobrynin believed that history might regard the Geneva summit as the beginning of the end of the cold war. Gorbachev came away believing that Reagan "wasn't terribly bright or very knowledgeable" and told his associates "ideologically this man is a dinosaur." On the other hand, Gorbachev had learned that Reagan was not the "bogeyman" Kremlin hard-liners believed. There was a "spark of mutual trust" between them, Gorbachev said, like an arc between two electric poles. Several of his aides said he came away confident that there could be a trust between the two countries, and this trust would allow him room to deal with Soviet internal problems. When Gorbachev returned home he shocked Kremlin hard-liners with a statement that had startling implications for the future: "It is my profound conviction that we would gain nothing from United States insecurity vis-à-vis the U.S.S.R. since this would result in mistrust and breed instability."[58]

Reagan was transformed as well. "I bet the hardliners in both our countries are bleeding when we shake hands," he remarked to Gorbachev. Although he would engage in isolated instances of Soviet-bashing in the next few years, he no longer led the anticommunist crusade as he had in the past.

Shultz told Dobrynin that Reagan had come to understand that not all Soviet statements and proposals should be read as propaganda ploys, as he had believed in the past. He told his cabinet he believed that the Soviets wanted to work with Washington "to get something done, and to get things straightened out."[59]

Reagan and Gorbachev soon found themselves embroiled in debilitating domestic struggles. Gorbachev grappled with the continuing slide of his country toward social, economic, and political disaster, and even while Reagan was at Geneva, his administration was engaged in a foreign policy adventure, Iran-contra, that crippled him politically and endangered his ability to govern. When the beleaguered leaders met in future summits, they worked to solve long-standing international problems, and they also found that they could use each other to try to rebuild their public images and slippery political positions.

9

Coping with Scandal, Exiting with Honor, 1985–1989

The Iran-contra scandal, which marred the last years of Ronald Reagan's presidency, was composed of several separate operations. First, the United States secretly sold weapons to Iran, a terrorist state, to which such sales were prohibited by American law. These sales violated Reagan's own highly publicized Operation Staunch, an international campaign to stop all countries from selling arms to Iran. Second, the United States government violated an American law, the Boland Amendment, by secretly aiding the contra rebels in their war against the leftist Sandinista government of Nicaragua. Third, these two covert ventures became entangled because National Security Council staff members, especially Lieutenant Colonel Oliver L. North, managed both operations. Fourth, North secretly diverted profits from the Iranian arms sale to fund the contras.

The causes of the Iran-contra affair varied. Some Reagan advisers wanted to open relations with Iranian moderates, hoping that when the Ayatollah Ruhollah Mussaui Khomeini died the United States would be in a position to counter Soviet mischief making in the region. Reagan himself twisted that strategic opening into a straight arms-for-hostages operation, counting on moderates in Tehran to help free kidnapped Americans held by radical groups in Lebanon. The contra part of the affair occurred because the White House, frustrated at the restraints placed on the executive branch after the Vietnam War, wanted to counter Soviet and Cuban influence in Central America and to undermine the Sandinista government. On 1 March 1985 Reagan said that the contras were the "moral equal of our Founding Fathers," and on 29 April 1985 he claimed that members of Congress who opposed contra support "really are voting to have a totalitarian Marxist-Leninist government here in the Americas." When Congress tried to end United States government aid to the contras, Reagan told National Security Adviser Robert McFarlane, "I want you to do whatever you have to do to help these people keep body and soul together." To men often forced to read Reagan's wishes by his body language, that was an emphatic, ringing order.[1]

National Security Advisers Robert McFarlane and John Poindexter were military men, attentive to their commander in chief's wishes. They believed that the president had authority under the Constitution to carry out foreign policy without interference from the other branches of government, and they chafed under the restrictions imposed by Congress after the Vietnam War. The 1973 War Powers Act tried to restrict an "imperial presidency" from engaging in military adventurism. The 1974 Hughes-Ryan Amendment required the president to "find" that a covert action was important to national security and to report such actions to Congress in a "timely fashion." By 1981 the process required a presidential finding to be in writing and "timely" was interpreted as a few days, not months or years. Patriotic NSC staff officials, who believed that a strong president in charge of foreign affairs best served the national interest, had to interpret laws that they believed hampered the chief executive and weakened the nation.[2]

Each of the three investigatory bodies that later examined Iran-contra concluded that Ronald Reagan was mainly responsible for it. The congressional investigating committee, for example, said, "If the President did not know what his National Security Advisers were doing, he should have." Independent counsel Lawrence E. Walsh concluded, "President Reagan created the conditions which made possible the crimes committed by others by his secret deviations from announced national policy as to Iran and hostages and by his open determination to keep the contras together 'body and soul' despite a statutory ban on contra aid."[3]

Reagan confronted a divided government in formulating Central American policy, and he was unwilling to impose a coherent policy. The internal conflicts, George Shultz recalled, made "trying to forge policy ... like walking through a swamp." Many anticommunist hard-liners, fearing that Marxism was making gains in Central America and the Caribbean, wanted to take action. Reagan, however, was deterred by Latin American sensitivity to United States interference. He believed in the Monroe Doctrine, he assured a conservative supporter, "but I've learned even our best friends in Central & and South Amer. would turn on us [if I reaffirmed the Monroe Doctrine]. It has too much of the gunboat diplomacy aura around it. We're making progress in the Hemisphere but it has to be on a partnership basis not the 'big colossus' of the North giving orders." Reagan also had to be sensitive to the "Vietnam syndrome" that made many Americans fearful of adventurism that might entangle the nation in another war.[4]

The contra part of Iran-contra began to unfold quickly in 1981. After Nicaraguan dictator Anastasio Somoza fell in July 1979, Daniel Ortega Saavedra, who led the most extreme leftists within the Sandinistas, began to consolidate his position and push more moderate elements aside. He established close ties to Moscow and allowed weapons to flow from Nicaragua to rebel groups in El Salvador. That gave the administration activists the cover they needed. They would argue that they were not trying to overthrow the Sandinistas but to stop the export of arms and revolution. Nicaragua posed a difficult problem for Washington, however, because the leftist Sandinista government operated under a liberal constitution and in 1984 held democratic elections. Administration hard-liners believed that the Sandinistas were committed communists intent on using Nicaragua as a base to spread revolution, but moderates and liberals believed that the young revolutionaries had begun needed reforms in their country and that through negotiations could be induced to stop exporting arms and revolution to neighbors.[5]

Weinberger, Haig, Kirkpatrick, Casey, Shultz, and other major figures pulled Reagan back and forth and policymaking deadlocked. McFarlane later said that he did not have the "guts" to stand up and tell Reagan that he should examine the legalities of the contra operation: "To tell you the truth, probably the reason I didn't is because if I had done that, Bill Casey, Jeane Kirkpatrick and Cap Weinberger would have said I was some kind of a commie." Deadlock within the administration, heated battles with Congress over Nicaraguan policy, and Reagan's order to keep the contras together body and soul created "a highly ambiguous legal environment," concluded the Tower Board, which investigated the Iran-contra affair.[6]

Reagan sat like a "remote sort of king . . . just not there," said Jeane Kirkpatrick, while she, Casey, Clark, Shultz, and others engaged in savage, consuming battles over policy. Reagan did, however, make several important decisions. Based on an NSC discussion on 16 March 1981, he signed NSDD-17, authorizing nearly $20 million to build the contras into an effective guerrilla force. During a meeting with his senior advisers on 1 December 1981, Reagan decided to sign a finding to cover the secret operation, formally beginning the covert war against the Sandinistas that would kill thousands of people and cost hundreds of millions of dollars. When Elliott Abrams, assistant secretary of state for inter-American affairs, later argued to Shultz that the CIA could not effectively conduct a major military operation, Shultz replied, "Yeah, but Cap [Weinberger] won't touch it with a ten-foot pole, and Bill Casey wants it, so that is how it is going to be."[7]

In the fall of 1982 the press began to uncover United States support for the contras, and members of Congress raised questions about American activities and goals. From the controversy came the first Boland Amendment, sponsored by Edward P. Boland (Dem., Mass.), which Reagan signed on 21 December 1982 after it passed the House 411 to 0. It prohibited the CIA and the Department of Defense from using any funds to overthrow the Sandinista government. The administration promptly said its goal was not to overthrow the Sandinistas but to support the contras as a way to encourage the Nicaraguan government to establish peaceful relations with its neighbors.[8]

The NSC staff intensified covert military operations as the year ended, and Lieutenant Colonel Oliver North began to direct contra matters. North had served in Vietnam and had won a Bronze Star, Silver Star, and two Purple Hearts. His war experience had scarred him emotionally, many of his associates believed, making him cynical and contemptuous of Congress. He was an attractive, articulate, gung-ho Marine. He was a workaholic who did his assignments without asking for guidance; "the problem was, he needed it," an NSC colleague said. North exuded competence and self-confidence, but his operations often took on a Keystone Kops character. He was a self-dramatizing figure who had trouble telling the truth. Even those who realized that his stories at best exaggerated events still enjoyed listening to him. "God, the man could speak a blue haze of bullshit," a CIA official said. He loved to tell associates about his personal relationship with Reagan—"The old man loves my ass," he said—but the president later told associates he would not have known North if he had walked into the room, and office logs showed that Reagan never saw North alone, met him only four times, and spoke to him once on the telephone.[9]

In 1984 the NSC largely took over from the CIA covert operations in Nicaragua. When North estimated that contra funding would run out in June 1984, the administration requested a $21 million supplemental appropriation. Speaker Tip O'Neill said the request was dead on arrival. It was at this point that Reagan directed the NSC staff to hold the contras together "body and soul." McFarlane passed Reagan's instructions to North and the two of them began to pursue third-country funding for the contras. In June Saudi Arabia agreed to contribute $1 million a month to the contras, upped to $2 million a month in 1985. When McFarlane told Reagan about the Saudi contributions, the president expressed satisfaction and told McFarlane to keep it secret. North also set up a network of associates to raise money from private donors. He provided private briefings for big contributors and at times arranged appearances by Reagan.[10]

On 12 October 1984 political pressure forced an angry Reagan to sign Boland II, which tried to close loopholes in the earlier bill and prohibited the CIA from providing even nonmilitary support for the contras. Reagan did not withdraw his mandate to support the contras body and soul, and CIA director Casey told North: "Okay, you have got it all." Although Boland II seemed clearly to prohibit any government support to the contras, North and others argued that it did not apply to the NSC staff.

North brought an arms dealer, retired Air Force major general Richard V. Secord, and his partner, Albert Hakim, an Iranian-American businessman, into the contra supply operation. With the millions of dollars that North had raised from private sources, he and Secord set up "the Establishment," a miniature, private CIA that "you could pull off the shelf and use at a moment's notice." North used his network of supporters in the NSC staff, CIA, and Departments of State and Defense to help the Establishment pass military maps, intelligence, and other information to the contras. North and Secord soon had at their disposal a ship, munitions, airfields, airplanes and pilots, and sophisticated communications equipment.[11]

In late summer 1985 journalists began to uncover aspects of NSC staff operations in Nicaragua and mentioned North in their stories. The House intelligence oversight committees asked McFarlane if NSC was conducting operations in Nicaragua, and McFarlane said no. North told a colleague, "Bud McFarlane just perjured himself for me—God bless him."[12]

On 16 March 1986 Reagan supported his request for $100 million for the contras by giving what was referred to as his "red tide" televised speech, a throwback to the heated anticommunist rhetoric in the days of McCarthyism. He said that a mounting danger in Central America threatened United States security. Nicaragua was a Soviet ally located only two hours flying time from the United States. "Using Nicaragua as a base, the Soviets and Cubans can become the dominant power in the crucial corridor between North and South America. Established there, they will be in a position to threaten the Panama Canal, interdict our vital Caribbean sealanes, and, ultimately, move against Mexico. Should that happen, desperate Latin peoples by the millions would begin fleeing north into the cities of the southern United States or to wherever some hope of freedom remained." He said that already in Nicaragua there were thousands of Cuban military advisers, as well as contingents from East Germany and the Soviet Union and other elements of international terrorism, all acting on "the old communist slogan," "The road to victory goes through Mexico."[13]

Reagan's pressure worked. In June 1986 the House authorized $100 million in military and humanitarian aid for the contras. Then, on 5 October 1986, one of Secord's planes was shot down in Nicaragua, and the Sandinistas captured one man, Eugene Hasenfus, alive. North and Casey prepared for the operation to be exposed, and North began shredding files. On 8 October Poindexter briefed Reagan about the flight and said he did not know exactly who was involved, "but I think you should be careful about denying any U.S. role." Yet that same day Reagan publicly said about the crew, "While they're American citizens, there is no government connection with that at all." This was the first of many public misstatements that Reagan would make in the next few months.[14]

In November 1986 while the administration was trying to finesse the contra story, the Iranian covert operation exploded into headlines. Under Shah Mohammad Reza Pahlavi, Iran had been a loyal American ally. In early 1979 the followers of the Ayatollah Khomeini overthrew the shah and as relations between the two nations spiraled downward, Iranian radicals took hostage the American embassy staff in Tehran. While Iranian fundamentalists portrayed the United States as the Great Satan, the Americans demonized the Ayatollah, equating him with Hitler. Although Washington left an arms embargo in place on Iran even after it released the hostages, other nations freely sold Tehran arms, and in 1983 Iran took the offensive in its long and bloody war with Iraq. The administration launched Operation Staunch to choke off international arms sales to Iran, and in January 1984 Shultz officially designated Iran as a sponsor of international terrorism and Reagan referred to it as "Murder Inc." On 30 June 1985, in a statement that came back to haunt him, Reagan said, "The United States gives terrorists no rewards and no guarantees. We make no concessions; we make no deals."[15]

National Security Adviser Robert McFarlane played an important role in the early part of the Iranian operation. McFarlane had fought in Vietnam, had a master's degree in international relations, and had been Alexander Haig's "right arm" in the State Department until William Clark brought him to NSC as his deputy. McFarlane saw himself as a national security adviser in the mold of Henry Kissinger and Zbigniew Brzezinski. He took strong stands on policy issues, while trying to ensure that Reagan heard all viewpoints. He took pride in his ability to see the strategic implications of the global chess game, but he found it emotionally difficult to stand up under the pounding he received from Weinberger and other conservatives, who regarded him as an ally of Shultz. With the administration so often deadlocked, the conscientious, overworked McFarlane was forced to guess what Reagan wanted him to do. Some observers believed that by the time McFarlane resigned in 1985, he was suffering from a nervous breakdown. His feeling of guilt over his role in the Iran-contra affair later led him to attempt suicide. Michael Deaver visited him while he was recovering and tried to console him. "You've got nothing to be ashamed of," Deaver told McFarlane. "Ronald Reagan used you."[16]

McFarlane was troubled in 1984. He feared that when the aged Khomeini died, there would be a succession crisis that the United States could not influence. With the United States ousted from Iran, not capable of influencing events there, he feared the Soviets could cause mischief in a region affecting American strategic interests. He looked for a way to re-establish relations with Iran.[17]

The impetus for the White House to seek a "strategic opening" to Tehran came from outside Washington. In November 1984 Manucher Ghorbanifar met with former CIA agent Theodore G. Shackley, who reported the conversation to Washington. Ghorbanifar, an exiled Iranian businessman and arms dealer, said that he was a nationalist who feared that Iran was going to fall into Soviet hands. He said that Iranian destiny depended on the United States and that there were moderates like himself within Iran who wanted to restore good relations with Washington. He wanted, he said, to establish his "bona fides" with the moderates by arranging an arms sale to Iran and with the Americans by helping gain the release of United States citizens held hostage in Lebanon.

Ghorbanifar was a con man with a genius for understanding people and telling them what they wanted to hear. He offered McFarlane and Casey access to Iranian moderates and a chance to counter Soviet activities; Reagan would become obsessed by fanciful opportunities to free the hostages; some businessmen would see an opportunity to make big profits by selling arms to Iran, and Oliver North would recognize the chance to skim off money for the contras; Israelis saw the possibility of reopening relations with Iran and reestablishing American power in the region; the Iranians sought arms to help in their war with Iraq. Each time the fast-talking Ghorbanifar was exposed as a liar, he would produce just enough of his promises to keep the operation going.[18]

Israeli intelligence forces believed that there were moderates within Iran and that Ghorbanifar had access to them. McFarlane and other Americans had an inordinate respect for Israeli intelligence and discounted the CIA's more pessimistic view of Ghorbanifar and his story of Iranian moderates. When in May 1985 Israeli prime minister Shimon Peres informed McFarlane that Iran had recently asked Israel to sell it arms and that Israel would make the sale if Washington agreed, the game began. Shultz exploded in anger at the report, believing that Tel Aviv would skew its intelligence to fit Israeli, not American, interests, and McFarlane, in the first of many of the NSC staff's misleading statements, told Shultz that he was rejecting the Israeli initiative, "turning it off entirely."[19]

McFarlane kept pushing. In mid-June 1985 he circulated a draft order that would have ended Operation Staunch, hoping that lifting the arms embargo would be the first step in improving relations with Iran. Shultz opposed the proposal "forcefully." He downplayed the supposed advantage that Moscow had over the United States in the region. He also pointed out that selling arms to Iran would alarm Saudi Arabia, Iraq, and the Persian Gulf states. Weinberger was less diplomatic. Under no circumstances should the United States lift its arms embargo on Iran, he said, and wrote General Colin Powell, "This is almost too absurd to comment on. . . . The assumption here is 1) that Iran is about to fall & 2) we can deal with them on a rational basis—It's like asking Quadhaffi to Washington for a cozy chat."[20]

Shultz and Weinberger often thought they had stopped the Iranian initiative, but McFarlane and Poindexter, with Reagan's approval, excluded the secretaries of state and defense from the Iranian "information loop" to the extent possible. Shultz and Weinberger fought the Iranian operation, but they also allowed themselves to be excluded. They made their opposition clear but did not want to keep nagging Reagan on the issue. CIA official Robert Gates said that the "dirty little secret" of the Iran affair was that "no one thought it was that big a deal." Shultz and Weinberger regarded it as a "wacko" NSC staff operation that inevitably would fail. They did not regard it as an issue important enough to trigger their resignations.[21]

Indeed, it was Ronald Reagan who kept the Iranian initiative alive and who twisted McFarlane's concern for creating a strategic opening into an arms-for-hostages trade. Reagan assumed that the hostages were held in Lebanon by radical groups who looked to fundamentalist Iran for leadership. When Reagan started his trading, terrorists held five American hostages; when he left office they held eight men. As his experts had warned, trading arms to gain the release of kidnapped victims created an incentive to take more hostages.

Reagan's aides had tried to keep him away from hostage families because they knew he was vulnerable to emotional appeals. On 28 June 1985 Reagan met in Chicago with relatives of the passengers of a TWA airliner held hostage by Hizballah guerrillas. Also attending was the family of Father Lawrence Jenco, a hostage held in Lebanon. Father Jenco's family demanded of the shaken president why he was willing to make concessions to terrorists to win the TWA passengers' release and had forgotten the

Lebanese hostages. Donald Regan believed that after the Chicago meeting Reagan, the former actor, placed himself in the role of a man sitting alone and abandoned in a dark cell. He became obsessed with the hostages, opening practically every national security briefing by asking what was being done about them. Reagan's "driving me nuts" about the hostages, the self-dramatizing Oliver North told a colleague.[22]

On 3 July 1985 David Kimche, the director general of the Israeli Foreign Ministry, told McFarlane that the Israelis believed that they had established contact with moderate forces in Iran—the contact was Ghorbanifar—who wanted to avert chaos when Khomeini died. To show their seriousness, the moderates would win the release of American hostages; in turn, as a token of good faith, they wanted Israel to sell Iran one hundred TOW antitank missiles.

Reagan had been admitted to the hospital for cancer surgery, which took place on 13 July. And on 18 July McFarlane met with Reagan and Donald Regan at the hospital. In a meeting that lasted twenty-three minutes, McFarlane briefed the president about the Israeli proposal and asked for guidance. Each man later provided several different versions of what took place. It seems clear that Reagan approved pursuing the contact with Iranian moderates. Donald Regan told investigators that Reagan had said to McFarlane "open it up" and had approved further talks. Reagan expressed hope that the Iranians might help with the hostages, but he told McFarlane that the United States could not approve selling arms, although that might come later if discussions built trust among the parties.[23]

When Reagan left the hospital he told McFarlane to call a meeting of the national security team to talk about the Iranian initiative. On Monday, 22 July, McFarlane briefed the group on the proposed Israeli sale of TOW missiles to Iran. Shultz and Donald Regan questioned it, and Weinberger was emphatically opposed, saying it was bad policy and probably illegal. Casey, however, backed the initiative, which fit in with his desire to counter Soviet power everywhere. Reagan told McFarlane to keep the discussion with Israel open, although he did not at the meeting approve of the arms transfer.

On Saturday, 27 July 1985, Reagan called McFarlane from Camp David. The president said that the more he thought about the "Israeli thing," the more he liked it. "Couldn't you use some imagination and try to find a way to make it work?" he asked. McFarlane reminded the president that Shultz and Weinberger opposed it. "I know," Reagan replied, "but I look at it differently. I want to find a way to do this." On 2 August Kimche called on McFarlane, explained the proposition, and said that Israel did not want to proceed without Washington's specific approval.[24]

Events became murky after this, and participants later evidently confused several different meetings or discussions among the top national security advisers. On 6 August in a meeting held in the president's private quarters, McFarlane explained the operation to Reagan, Bush, Shultz, Weinberger, and Regan. The goal was to open a dialogue with Iranian moderates, he said. Israel would sell Iran one hundred TOW missiles, and Iran would produce four or more hostages. Shultz said it was an arms-for-hostage deal and was a bad idea. Weinberger agreed and said it violated Operation Staunch. They warned that the deal would leave Reagan vulnerable to blackmail from those who knew of it. Donald Regan recalled that Reagan told McFarlane to "go slow" and be sure that they were not dealing with the Ayatollah's terrorists.

Although the meeting was fateful for Reagan's presidency, he conducted it in an offhand manner and kept no official record. As was often the case with Reagan, people left without being sure what, if anything, he had decided. Weinberger and Shultz left thinking the initiative was dead. McFarlane, on the other hand, believed that Reagan had approved the deal and wanted to be careful that the arms did not go to Khomeini's men. Reagan's advisers were often reduced to reading body language. Weinberger, for example, wrote, "It seemed to me clear, although the President did not state so there, that the President agreed that we should not proceed with this matter."

McFarlane said that shortly after the meeting Reagan called him to the Oval Office and told him, "Well, I've thought about it . . . and I want to go ahead with it. I think that's the right thing to do." McFarlane reminded him of Shultz's and Weinberger's opposition, and Reagan replied, "Yes, I understand how they feel. But I have to think about what's at stake here. I believe it's the right thing to do." He told McFarlane that he would take the heat for the decision.[25]

Donald Regan later disputed McFarlane's claim that Reagan had given prior approval to the Israeli transfer of TOW missiles to Iran. The Tower Board and the congressional investigating committees, which had information they could not publicly divulge, including Reagan's diary, accepted McFarlane's version. Independent counsel Lawrence Walsh, who had access to contemporary notes made by the principals, found that they verified much of what McFarlane said, and he concluded that Reagan had given prior approval to the missile sale.[26]

On 20 August 1985 Israel sent ninety-six TOW missiles to Iran. Ghorbanifar and his business associates handled the financing, using a Swiss bank account. No hostage was released. Instead, Iran demanded additional missiles, and on 14 September Israel sold Iran 408 more missiles. One hostage, Benjamin Weir, was released. The "strategic opening" had deteriorated into a strict arms-for-hostage transaction, and neither the Americans nor Israelis knew who in Tehran was receiving the missiles.

Officials in Tehran now realized that despite Reagan's harsh rhetoric about terrorists and Washington's holding its allies to Operation Staunch, the administration would trade hostages for arms. In October Iran proposed another trade, this time for more expensive and sophisticated Hawk missiles. McFarlane became concerned that the Americans were losing sight of the goal of making a strategic opening to Iranian moderates. Even Ghorbanifar warned that the negotiators were in danger of becoming "hostages to the hostages." Still, when Israeli defense minister Yitzhak Rabin came to Washington and asked if Reagan approved another arms shipment to Iran, McFarlane said that he did. In his diary on 20 November Weinberger noted a conversation that he had with McFarlane: "Told him we shouldn't pay Iranians anything—he s[ai]d President has decided to do it through Israelis." Reagan's diary entries mentioned "an undercover thing" to get the hostages "sprung."[27]

North later recalled the November 1985 arms transfer as "a bit of a horror story." Israel was going to make the transfer from Tel Aviv through Portugal to Iran. Portuguese officials, trying to enforce Washington's Operation Staunch, refused to allow use of Portugal's airports. McFarlane then told Oliver North to handle the problem. North asked if Reagan knew of the operation, and McFarlane replied, "Yes, just go take care of it." North intermingled the Iranian and contra operations, considered unprofessional by covert action experts, by bringing in Secord to handle operational details.

McFarlane informed Shultz in November while the secretary of state was at the Geneva summit meeting. In a note made on 22 November, Shultz told his advisers that McFarlane "says he's cleared [the exchange] with the President." Shultz said he was appalled by the operation, and McFarlane recalled that the secretary of state told him that "you're skating on thin ice here. . . . This is very high risk, could do a lot of damage to the President." Shultz realized that it was a straight arms-for-hostage deal, but he also realized that Reagan had approved it. He told McFarlane that he hoped some hostages got out, but in fact no hostages were freed.[28]

In late November 1985 McFarlane resigned, and his deputy, John Poindexter, took over. Poindexter was a superbly educated graduate of Annapolis and held a doctorate in nuclear physics. In 1984 he had been offered command of the Sixth Fleet but had chosen to stay at the NSC. He was a highly disciplined, hardworking man, but he had little political skill. He seemed contemptuous of Congress and its constitutional role in foreign policy and military affairs. He was totally loyal to his commander in chief, even to the point, some investigators later concluded, of acting in his name to protect him from potentially embarrassing disclosures.[29]

Before McFarlane left the NSC, he tried to end the Iranian operation. He told Reagan that it was not working, that they had set out to open dialogue with Iranian moderates and had ended up dealing with arms merchants. Reagan had him call a meeting of his national security team, which was held on 7 December 1985. Reagan, McFarlane, Poindexter, Donald Regan, Weinberger, Shultz, and CIA deputy director John N. McMahon attended. McFarlane traced the history of the Iranian operation and argued that it had gone astray.

Reagan must have felt besieged by his advisers. McMahon, sitting in for the usually supportive Casey, said that he "was unaware of any moderates in Iran, that most of the moderates had been slaughtered by Khomeini, that whatever arms we give to these so-called moderates . . . will end up supporting the present Khomeini regime." Donald Regan, who had supported the initiative, and would again, argued against it in the December meeting. He believed the earlier transfers had gone wrong. "Cut your losses and get out," he said. Shultz made the prophetic statement that "ultimately, the whole story will come out someday and we will pay the price." Shultz, who was usually economical in his praise for Weinberger, later told investigators that the secretary of defense was forceful and effective in his opposition. Weinberger recalled that he ran through every argument he could think of, including the fact that if the operation became public it would anger the allies and if it remained secret it would expose the United States to blackmail from those who knew of it. He also argued that the operation was bad policy and illegal and "washing" it through Israel would not make it legal.

Reagan told his advisers that the American people would never forgive him if he passed up a chance to free hostages. The usually passive president felt so strongly about the issue that he defied his advisers. He said that he was not paying ransom to kidnappers but was rewarding a third party, Iran, which might be able to intervene with the kidnappers. At one point he said that, legalities aside, he had to take action to free the hostages. "Visiting hours are Thursday," he quipped, recognizing the possible illegal nature of the operation. Most participants in the meeting realized that Reagan was very disappointed by their opposition, but they believed that by the end of the meeting he had submitted to the consensus. Weinberger told a colleague that he and Shultz had "strangled" the "baby in its cradle."[30]

The much abused baby had often been strangled yet still lived. Reagan's diary showed that he still regarded the operation as viable. He sent the recently resigned McFarlane as his personal representative to London to meet with North, Secord, Ghorbanifar, and representatives from Israel. In his diary on 9 December Reagan said the "purpose" of McFarlane's mission was "to free our hostages first and then we'd supply the weapons."

McFarlane told the men that Washington wanted to open a political dialogue with Iran but not to trade any more arms. North was clearly unhappy with the message, and Ghorbanifar "went ballistic." "Are you crazy?" he shouted. The moderates were too weak to open such a dialogue, he argued, they needed weapons to build their prestige before they took power. He said that if he took McFarlane's message to his colleagues they might say "To hell with the hostages! Let the Hezbollah kill them!" That was the blackmail that Shultz feared, and it was an argument designed to have an effect on Reagan.

On 10 December McFarlane reported on his trip to Reagan, Weinberger, Casey, Donald Regan, and Poindexter. Reagan seemed disappointed and pensive. He told the group that the nation was "going to spend another Christmas with hostages there" and that he was "looking powerless and inept" because he could not free them. In his diary Reagan revealed that Ghorbanifar's message, which McFarlane suspected might have been constructed by North, had found its mark. He wrote about the London meeting, "Their top man said he believed if he took that proposal [to stop arms transfers] to the terrorists they would kill our people."

As was typical with Reagan meetings, participants left this one unclear about what the president had decided. Casey probably best understood Reagan's thoughts: "As the meeting broke up, I had the idea that the President had not entirely given up on encouraging the Israelis to carry on with the Iranians. I suspect he would be willing to run the risk and take the heat in the future if this will lead to springing the hostages."[31]

On 2 January 1986 Amiram Nir, Peres's adviser on terrorism, came to Washington and presented a proposal to ship four thousand TOW missiles to Tehran. All American hostages were to be released, with Israel simultaneously releasing twenty to thirty imprisoned members of the radical Hizballah organization. The NSC met on 7 January 1986 to discuss Nir's proposal. Reagan, Regan, Bush, Shultz, Weinberger, Meese, Casey, and Poindexter attended. Shultz and Weinberger again fought the arms transfer, but no one else joined them. Shultz wrote, "I had an uneasy, uncanny feeling that the meeting was not a *real* meeting, that it had all been 'precooked.' I had the sense that a decision had already been made, though none was explicitly stated. I was bewildered and distressed by this turn of events."[32]

Shultz was correct. The day before Reagan had signed a finding, presented to him in draft form, that approved the deal. He signed another finding on 17 January 1986. Neither finding was transmitted to the congressional intelligence committees. Reagan understood his decision and noted in his diary, "I agreed to sell TOWs to Iran."[33]

In February 1986 a Secord crew delivered one thousand TOW missiles to Iran. No hostages were released. On 8 March Ghorbanifar said that "they've" decided they did not want TOW missiles; they wanted Hawk spare parts instead. McFarlane wrote North, "Gorba [Ghorbanifar] is basically a self-serving mischief maker. Of course the trouble is that as far as we know, so is the entire lot of those we are dealing with." Poindexter, disgusted, seemed willing to scrap the operation, but Reagan wanted it to go forward and North was willing to handle it.[34]

In May 1986 the slipshod Iranian operation became positively bizarre. Reagan sent McFarlane, North, and several men on a secret trip to Tehran. They used false passports, took along a chocolate cake and two pistols as gifts, and carried suicide pills to take as needed. McFarlane had expected a motorcade to meet him in Tehran to take him to a meeting with top government officials, but after they waited at the airport for awhile, Ghorbanifar arrived with several broken-down vehicles and took the party to a suite of guarded hotel rooms where they met with lower-ranking officials, obviously frightened even to be talking to the Americans. McFarlane told the Iranians to think big, to consider reestablishing good relations between their nations. He soon learned that the Iranians had little interest in a strategic opening: They wanted weapons to use in their bloody war with Iraq. It also became apparent that whatever influence they might have with the Lebanese kidnappers, they could not produce freed hostages on demand. McFarlane broke off the talks and returned to the United States. North tried to encourage the disappointed McFarlane by telling him, "It's not a total loss, at least some of the money from this deal is going to Central America." That was the first that the startled McFarlane knew of the diversion of funds.[35]

By this time 1,508 TOW missiles, 18 Hawk missiles, and Hawk spare parts had been shipped to Iran. The Americans had also supplied the Iranians with intelligence information on the Soviet threat and on the Iran-Iraq War. The operation continued. In May and October 1986 the United States shipped additional supplies to Tehran. In July Father Jenco was released, followed by David P. Jacobsen in November. Reagan wrote in his diary, "This release of Jenco is a delayed step in a plan we've been working on for months. It gives us hope the rest of the plan will take place. We'd about given up on this." More hostages were taken, however, and when the operation ended there was one more hostage held than when Reagan began it.[36]

There had been warnings that the Iran and the contra operations were unraveling. In October 1986 the North-Secord airplane was shot down and Eugene Hasenfus captured in Nicaragua. In mid-October Iranian students distributed leaflets describing McFarlane's visit to Tehran. On 3 November 1986 the story broke into the open when a Lebanese magazine, *Al-Shiraa,* published a description of McFarlane's activities. While one group of reporters began digging into the contra–NSC staff connection, a larger group pursued the convoluted tale of hostages and arms trades.[37]

Many people in the Reagan White House had served under Nixon and had watched his presidency destroyed by Watergate. Some remembered that it was not the break-in that had undone Nixon but the cover-up that followed. They advised Reagan to get the whole story out quickly, admit mistakes, and assume responsibility. Reagan, however, did not believe that he had made mistakes, and, in any case, he did not feel responsible since he had always left details to his subordinates. The White House public relations people hindered matters by telling Reagan what he wanted to hear. As late as 5 December 1986 Pat Buchanan told Reagan that increasing evidence indicated that Iran-contra was an "inside-the-Beltway" story.[38]

A senior White House official said of Reagan, "He has this great ability to build these little worlds and then live in them." But the outside world began to shatter those "little worlds." Reagan's face flushed when Donald Regan told him that only 14 percent of the people believed his version of the Iranian operation. Reagan scheduled a press conference for 19 November. On the evening of 18 November an obviously troubled George Bush told his house guest, New Jersey governor Tom Kean, that reporters would rip Reagan up at the press conference. Bush said that he had gone "to the mat" with Reagan, but "Reagan didn't see what all the fuss was, thought he'd just go out there and say what he'd done. He didn't understand!"[39]

Shultz tackled Reagan the next day. He made a detailed presentation on how Iranian-backed terrorism still continued and told Reagan that three more hostages taken in September and October had been seized by Lebanese groups associated with Iran. Reagan was surprised, saying, "This is news to me." "You must not continue to say we made no deals for hostages," Shultz argued. "You have been deceived and lied to." Reagan repeated, "You're telling me things I don't know." "Mr. President," Shultz replied, "if I'm telling you something you don't know—I don't know much—then something is terribly wrong here!" Shultz realized that he had failed to get the message through. Poindexter was misleading Reagan, Shultz believed, but Reagan wanted to be deceived.[40]

Reagan paid a high cost for not listening to Shultz and Bush. His success as a communicator had depended on his credibility with the American public, and he damaged it badly in the press conference. He denied Israel had been involved in arms shipments, and he claimed, incorrectly, that all the shipments together could fit easily in one airplane with plenty of room left over, that more hostages could have been freed if it had not been for the recent publicity, that Washington had not given arms to Khomeini's followers but to moderate factions.[41]

Shultz, knowing that he was in danger of being fired, decided he had to press ahead because he realized that Reagan was being misled. He met with Reagan on 20 November and detailed the false and misleading statements he had made in his press conference. It was a "hot and heavy" session, Shultz wrote: "I never thought I would talk to a president of the United States in such a direct and challenging way." Reagan refused to admit there was a problem. "I didn't shake him one bit," Shultz told an aide.[42]

The following day, the president tried to end the confusion over what had happened during the Iranian operation by asking Ed Meese to investigate and report the facts to a meeting of senior advisers scheduled for Monday, 24 November. Poindexter, who had been present when Reagan asked Meese to make his investigation, quickly warned North, and when North saw McFarlane later that day he told him that there would be a "shredding party" that weekend.[43]

Despite Meese's initial mistake in not sealing NSC staff records, he quickly uncovered the outlines of the story, and his rapid action perhaps saved the administration from slow disintegration. He put together a Justice Department investigating team of William Bradford Reynolds, John N. Richardson Jr., and Charles Cooper. On Saturday, 22 November, Reynolds and Richardson visited North's office to examine his records. North, who had spent the night shredding documents, was not in when the two men arrived. Reynolds found a surviving paper that indicated that money from the Iranian arms sales had been used to help the contras. Meese, shocked at the information the two men brought him, realized the dangers this diversion of funds presented to the administration. On Sunday, the next day, North confirmed to Meese that the diversion had occurred. Meese, based on his face-to-face conversations with Casey that weekend, did not believe that he had directed North's activities, but Casey had a devastating stroke on 15 December 1986 and, suffering from a brain tumor, died on 6 May 1987. It was only after Casey's stroke, when he could no longer refute their charges, that North and others began to paint the director as the shadowy figure behind Iran-contra.[44]

On late Monday afternoon, 24 November, Meese briefed Reagan on what he had discovered. Donald Regan said the color drained from Reagan's face and he turned pasty white. Regan believed that was the first moment that the president had heard of the diversion. A little later, Nancy found him "pale and absolutely crushed." The furious first lady called Donald Regan and told him that there had to be a housecleaning, starting at the top. Regan knew that meant him.

Poindexter's head was the first to fall. He confirmed to Meese that he had known of the diversion. Poindexter said that he had been so furious at Congress because of its treatment of the contras that "he just decided to let it happen." When he came into the Oval Office to resign, Reagan asked him no questions.[45]

On Tuesday, 25 November, Reagan appeared before the press, accompanied by Meese. One observer said the president "looked stricken and suddenly old." Reagan said that Meese had reported to him the results of an investigation about matters involving Iran and the contras. He now understood, he said, that he had not fully been informed about activities involving his administration. He announced his appointment of a Special Review Board to investigate the role of the NSC staff. He announced that Poindexter had resigned and North had been relieved of his duties on the NSC staff. Meese then took over. There was an audible gasp as he described the diversion.[46]

Reagan agreed with Meese that he had to get the whole story out quickly. On 26 November 1986 the president formed the Special Review Board, chaired by former senator John Tower and including former senator Edmund S. Muskie and former national security adviser Brent Scowcroft. On 2 December Reagan asked for the appointment of an independent counsel to investigate the matter, and on 19 December a panel of judges named Lawrence E. Walsh to that position. On 4 December the House and Senate announced plans to appoint select committees to investigate the Iran-contra affair.

Morale in the White House plummeted while it waited for the Tower Board to report. Reagan, as depressed that winter as his optimistic nature allowed him to be, still believed his policy was correct, but his confidence in his greatest skill, communicating with the people, was shattered because he could not convince them that he was right. A 2 December *New York Times*/CBS poll found that his approval rating had fallen from 67 percent to 36 percent, and the Gallup organization said that his drop in popularity was the sharpest ever recorded. Shultz found the president to be "tentative and deferential, humbled."

With Reagan barely able to go through the motions of governing, Nancy stepped into the vacuum. Her first task was to get rid of Donald Regan. She blamed him for allowing Iran-contra to happen and for not having the political skills to cope with its aftermath. Regan had long resented her interfering with White House operations and using astrological charts to schedule the president's activities. The feud became public and dragged on for weeks.

The end was brutal. The Tower Board intended to report on 26 February 1987. Regan told the president, "If I go before that report is out, you throw me to the wolves. I deserve better treatment than that." His resentment at Nancy flared. "I thought I was Chief of Staff to the President, . . . not to his wife," he told Reagan. "I have to tell you, sir, that I'm very bitter about the whole experience. You're allowing the loyal to be punished." Reagan promised that they would send Regan off in "good fashion," and they agreed that he would leave a few days after the board reported. Instead, Regan saw on a televised newscast that the White House had already chosen former senator Howard Baker as his successor. Regan sat down, wrote a brief resignation note, and left the White House without seeing the president.[47]

Howard Baker helped pull the Reagan administration together. He brought in good people, worked to rebuild morale, and carefully began to restore Reagan's self-confidence. He built on other personnel changes. Marlin Fitzwater replaced Larry Speakes as press secretary, and Fitzwater developed a good relationship with the press. Patrick Buchanan resigned as director of communications and was replaced by Baker aide Thomas Griscom. Baker brought in Kenneth Duberstein as his deputy, and the competent Duberstein took over as chief of staff when Baker left in 1988.[48]

Shultz assumed firm control over foreign policy. Public respect for the calm, steady secretary rose as the details of the Iran-contra affair became public. After Casey resigned in late January 1987, Reagan replaced him with the highly respected William H. Webster. Frank Carlucci became national security adviser and brought Colin Powell with him as his deputy. In October 1987 Weinberger resigned, and Carlucci became secretary of defense. Colin Powell replaced him as national security adviser.[49]

Meanwhile, the three Iran-contra investigations proceeded. The Tower Board was composed of three highly respected and responsible members of the Washington establishment. Tower, Muskie, and Scowcroft wanted to get at the truth, but they did not intend to destroy the Reagan presidency. They were shocked, however, wrote Lou Cannon, because their investigation exposed them to the "real Reagan," the man usually seen in unguarded moments only by his closest aides. The Tower Board members came to understand the fragility of the Reagan presidency.

Reagan first testified to the Tower Board on 26 January 1987. By that time, McFarlane had testified to Congress that Reagan had given prior approval to Israel's August and September 1985 shipments of TOW missiles to Iran. Donald Regan, in contrast, had consistently said that the president had not known of the shipment until after it was completed. Reagan told the board that he had approved the arms sale in advance, confirming what McFarlane had said. Tower noticed that Reagan was "working off" staff notes and McFarlane's public testimony, highlighted in yellow. Tower recalled, "I had ample experience with the president's tendency to ramble on and tell stories, and I tried to gently guide him back to the main point."

White House counsel Peter J. Wallison, who had prepared Reagan before he testified, was surprised at what he heard Reagan tell the Tower Board. "In our earlier discussions the Pres. had no recollection of having approved this sale, and now he seemed to have a pretty clear recollection that he had done so," Wallison wrote. "I could not figure out how he had come to that view, which put him at odds with Regan, the rest of the cabinet, and the written record." Reagan's initial statement was, in fact, correct.

On 28 January Wallison gave Reagan a memorandum summarizing what the president had told the Tower Board, and Reagan said it seemed accurate. Two days later, Wallison and Donald Regan confronted Reagan and asked if he remembered approving the August 1985 shipment beforehand or if he had approved it later. Reagan did not seem to have a memory of it one way or the other. Then, according to Wallison's note, Regan intervened to say that he remembered "McF. [McFarlane] telling the Pres. that the Israelis had sent the weapons without our approval, and that the Pres. was surprised and displeased. Regan said the Pres. said something like 'What's done is done,' but was not happy. As he listened to this, the Pres. seemed to have a recollection of this event. He said to me [Wallison] 'You know, he's right' referring to Regan."

On 11 February Reagan met with the Tower Board again. "I, for one, was shocked at what I was hearing," Tower wrote. "The president was recanting his previous testimony." He recanted by reading from a memorandum that Wallison had prepared for him. Wallison had written it in the second person, and Reagan read it without even changing the "you's" into "I's." Wallison realized that board members would conclude that Reagan's aides had tampered with his recollections. It was obvious, Tower wrote, that "words were being put into his mouth." The Tower Board members left the meeting quietly and pensively. Tower broke the silence. "What the hell are we going to do now?" he asked. It was a question that related both to their investigation and to the last two years of Reagan's presidency.

Board members realized that Reagan's testimony was worthless. Reagan confirmed this on 20 February, when he again changed his testimony. In a letter to the board, he said that he had let other people influence his memory, and he did not have notes or records to clarify the matter, and that "My answer therefore and the simple truth is, 'I don't remember—period.' "[50]

The Tower Board found that Donald Regan, William Casey, and others should have been more vigilant in making Reagan aware of the dangers in his policy, but that the president was responsible for executive branch operations. The board found that Reagan did not ensure legal vigilance in determining how those operations could be carried out within the law. Tower met with Nancy and Ronald after the board released its report. Reagan tried to defend the Iran arms sales as valid, and Tower bluntly said, "Mr. President, that just won't wash." Whatever he believed, his closest advisers told him, he had to accept publicly that he had made an error of judgment.[51]

However much he fumed inside, on 4 March 1987 Reagan made the first big step in getting the administration back on track. In a nationally televised speech, carefully crafted to accept responsibility while shedding blame, he said that he had carefully studied the board's report. "First, let me say I take full responsibility for my own actions and for those of my administration. As angry as I may be about activities undertaken without my knowledge, I am still accountable for those activities. As disappointed as I may be in some who served me, I'm still the one who must answer to the American people for this behavior. And as personally distasteful as I find secret bank accounts and diverted funds—well, as the Navy would say, this happened on my watch." He went on to say, "A few months ago I told the American people I did not trade arms for hostages. My heart and my best intentions still tell me that's true, but the facts and the evidence tell me it is not." The Tower Board concluded that the Iranian initiative had deteriorated into an arms-for-hostages operation. "There are reasons why it happened," he said, "but no excuses."[52]

The House and Senate each created select committees to investigate. They worked ten months, reviewed three hundred thousand documents, interviewed five hundred witnesses, and held forty days of joint hearings. The committees, guided by the Watergate hearings, narrowed their focus to a hunt for a "smoking gun," for evidence that Reagan had known of the diversion of funds to the contras. Interest in the hearings faded when Poindexter testified that he had approved the contra diversion himself without telling Reagan. Still, the final report placed responsibility for Iran-contra squarely on Reagan: "If the President did not know what his National Security Advisers were doing, he should have."[53]

Independent counsel Walsh's investigation dragged on for years. Walsh charged fourteen people with criminal violations. All were convicted, except one man whose case was dismissed on national security grounds and two who were given pretrial pardons by President Bush. The Supreme Court overturned Poindexter's and North's convictions on technical grounds. In 1994, in a carefully worded final report, Walsh concluded that Reagan's conduct "fell well short of criminality which could be successfully prosecuted." He said that it "could not be proved beyond a reasonable doubt that President Reagan knew of the underlying facts of Iran/Contra that were criminal or that he made criminal misrepresentations regarding them." Criminality aside, Walsh concluded: "President Reagan created the conditions which made possible the crimes committed by others by his secret deviations from announced national policy as to Iran and hostages and by his own determination to keep the contras together 'body and soul' despite a statutory ban on contra aid." In a press conference, Walsh said that if Congress had had the facts that he had uncovered, it should have considered impeachment.[54]

Public focus on the diversion of funds helped Reagan. No surviving document indicated that he had known of the diversion, and Poindexter testified under oath that he had not told him. Poindexter said he had deliberately chosen not to tell Reagan to protect him if the operation became public. Some believed that Poindexter lied to protect Reagan, and that Reagan allowed the lie to stand. Others believed that Poindexter had told him but that the inattentive president had not understood or had forgotten. Poindexter may have told Reagan in a passing way, McFarlane said, "and with the attention span of a fruit fly, it would have been out of his mind in about thirty seconds." In any case, the public's narrow focus on diversion deflected attention from the broader story of the president's contra policy and of his trading arms for hostages. Oliver North became a public hero, and most people ignored the questions raised by his and his colleagues' contempt for the law, Congress, and constitutional and democratic processes.[55]

While the investigations continued, Howard Baker carefully rebuilt White House morale and Reagan's self-confidence. Baker worked with his many friends in the media and Congress to project an image of a president putting his administration back on track. Baker united the cabinet behind the president, planned events that showed Reagan acting presidential, and promoted splashy media events, such as Reagan's proclamation in July 1987 of an Economic Bill of Rights. The White House worked hard to create a positive image of continuing achievement. In truth, however, Reagan's last two years were at best a holding action in the domestic arena.[56]

The story was different in the foreign policy arena. Reagan and Gorbachev, both in trouble at home, helped each other during Reagan's last two years in office. On 15 January 1986 Gorbachev proposed eliminating all intermediate-range weapons from Europe, and then called for an arms reduction plan that would rid the world of all nuclear weapons by the year 2000, contingent on the United States giving up SDI. Shultz understood that Gorbachev and Foreign Minister Eduard Shevardnadze had opened a new era: "The Soviets were awake. We had to engage them."[57]

At the Soviet Union's Twenty-seventh Party Congress, held in February and March 1986, Gorbachev took a step that CIA deputy director Robert Gates called the beginning of the end of the cold war. Shevardnadze called

Gorbachev's keynote address an ideological bombshell because it abandoned the idea of international class struggle. Modern weapons made it impossible for a nation to defend itself by military means alone, said Gorbachev. Each superpower must have security: "The highest wisdom is not in worrying only about oneself, or, all the more, about damaging the other side; it is necessary for all to feel that they are equally secure." Genuine security depended not on each side building the biggest arsenal possible, Gorbachev argued, but in maintaining the arms balance at the lowest level possible, with nuclear weapons excluded altogether. There was no alternative to cooperation between capitalist and communist nations, he said.[58]

The Soviet-American dialogue took a new turn with the Reykjavik summit held in Iceland on 11–12 October 1986, just before Iran-contra began to unravel. Reykjavik was a turning point in world history, Gorbachev said later, and Shultz said it was the most "remarkable" meeting ever held between the two nations.

The Soviets asked for the meeting. Gorbachev had become obsessed with SDI. He believed that it would force the Soviets to invest such vast amounts of scarce resources to build a Soviet defensive system that it would destroy his plans for economic and social rebuilding. Gorbachev told Dobrynin that he intended to offer Reagan such deep cuts in strategic arms that he would give up SDI.[59]

When Reagan and Gorbachev met on 11 October, Shultz was astonished as Gorbachev began to lay "gifts at our feet." He proposed a 50 percent reduction in heavy offensive missiles, accepted the zero-zero option on intermediate-range missiles in Europe, and agreed to a number of other items the Americans had been urging. Paul Nitze, who had been dealing with the Soviets for four decades, said it was the best Soviet proposal that he had ever seen. In what some described as an atmosphere of giddiness, Reagan and Gorbachev started raising the ante, building on the already dramatic breakthroughs they had made. They both agreed, in principle, to destroy all ballistic missiles over a ten-year period, and then they went on to agree to eliminate all nuclear weapons during that time. Reagan's dream of a nuclear-free world seemed at hand.

But Reagan's hopes crashed. He had suspected from the beginning that Gorbachev's real goal was to destroy SDI. Gorbachev finally said that all the proposals he had made depended on scrapping SDI. "I couldn't believe it and blew my top," Reagan recalled. A Gorbachev aide remembered watching Reagan at the meeting, seeing him not as an actor or as the president but as a human being torn by what to do, wavering, but finally deciding that SDI was not a bargaining chip. After heated exchanges, Reagan said to Shultz, "The meeting is over. . . . Let's go, George, we're leaving." A senior Gorbachev aide told Henry Kissinger that they had planned for contingencies, but "we had thought of everything except that Reagan might leave the room." As they were leaving a stricken Gorbachev said, "I don't think you want a deal. . . . I don't know what more I could have done." Reagan replied, "You could have said yes."[60]

For the next few weeks Washington and its Western allies were in turmoil as they struggled to understand the meaning of Reykjavik. To Margaret Thatcher it felt like "an earthquake beneath my feet." It seemed to threaten the whole system of deterrence that had kept the peace for forty years. It destroyed all certainty in the alliance, she said: "There was no place where you could put your political feet, where you were certain that you could stand." At home, Bush barely hid his disgust at the unscripted wheeling and dealing over such fundamental issues. The Joint Chiefs of Staff informed Reagan that scrapping all ballistic missiles would be a risk to national security.

Various spokesmen tried to deny that Reagan had agreed in principle to eliminate all nuclear weapons within ten years. Poindexter, who believed eliminating all nuclear weapons would be a catastrophe, told Reagan that they had to clarify what he had agreed to. Reagan said that he had agreed to eliminate all nuclear weapons. "No," Poindexter protested, "you couldn't have." "John," insisted Reagan, "I was there, and I did." His advisers soon "clarified" the record, however, to indicate that Reagan had agreed to eliminating ballistic missiles, not all nuclear weapons.[61]

As time passed, Reykjavik came to be seen as beginning a new era. Margaret Thatcher regarded it as having deeper significance than she had perceived at the time. She believed it was the point in the arms race at which the Soviets surrendered, at which they accepted the reality that they could not compete technologically and economically with the United States. Reykjavik broke superpower dialogue through into a different dimension. According to Gorbachev, "What happened in Reykjavik irreversibly changed the nature and essence of the debate about the future world." "The genie was out of the bottle" and future relations would take place on an entirely different level. Reagan wrote of Reykjavik, "I think history will show it was a major turning point in the quest for a safe and secure world."

At Reykjavik, Gorbachev and Reagan had settled the major remaining problems on an intermediate-range missile agreement, and they would sign the Intermediate Nuclear Forces (INF) Treaty the following year. They had also settled some big issues relating to the START talks on long-range missiles. They reached other understandings overlooked at the time, including Moscow's accepting human rights matters as part of the Soviet-American agenda in future negotiations.[62]

In 1987 Shultz and Reagan began to sense that an international "sea change" was under way and that it favored the United States. Gorbachev was in trouble at home. His concessions to the Americans angered many hard-line communist officials, and his reforms did not move fast enough to keep the general public happy. Reagan's stubbornness over SDI and his lack of knowledge of policy details irritated Gorbachev, yet he came to realize that it was in his interest for Reagan to be powerful and popular. As Gorbachev's support eroded at home, he could make himself look good by helping Reagan look good.

Reagan was a visionary capable of making "great decisions," Gorbachev told Dobrynin. Gorbachev came to believe that SDI should not block all progress in arms talks. He realized that with its ballooning budget deficit, the United States would not spend the huge amounts required for SDI if he took steps to reduce cold-war tensions. In other words, he could in effect kill SDI by winding down the cold war, reducing the threat that Americans felt. In 1987 he "unlocked" SDI from agreements on intermediate- and long-range missile agreements.

Gorbachev's willingness to make concessions continued to anger conservatives in Moscow, but he understood that he was running out of time. Shultz said it was clear to him by early 1987 that the Soviet leaders knew their system was failing but did not know what to do about it.[63]

Historian John Lewis Gaddis said that in one sense Reagan and Gorbachev's failure in Reykjavik was not that they looked too far ahead but that they did not look far enough, beyond eliminating nuclear weapons, toward ending the cold war. Increasingly in 1987 and 1988 that became the driving force behind Soviet-American talks. When Reagan stood before the Brandenburg Gate in June 1987 and pleaded with Gorbachev to tear down the Berlin Wall, he believed, as many of his advisers did not, that real changes were taking place within the Soviet Union. The end of the cold war was at hand, but neither he nor Gorbachev fully grasped that point in 1987.[64]

On 8 December 1987 Gorbachev joined with Reagan to open the Washington summit. "Gorby fever" swept the capital as the Soviet leader worked the crowds like a sophisticated American politician. He touched a deep yearning in people for peace by telling them that profound changes were at hand. At 1:45 P.M. on 8 December Reagan and Gorbachev signed the INF Treaty, eliminating a whole category of nuclear weapons, the American and Soviet intermediate- and short-range nuclear missiles. The treaty, in line with Reagan's zero-zero proposal of 1981, required the Soviets to abandon many of the objections to it that they had raised in the past. It included an intrusive verification procedure that Washington had long demanded from the Soviets.

During Gorbachev and Reagan's initial meeting in Washington, Gorbachev was well prepared, showing his remarkable mastery of the specifics of arms control and other matters, referring to chemical weapons production in Pine Bluff, Arkansas, for example, and mentioning details of weaponry that even General Colin Powell did not know. He gave the Americans an important report on his progress in implementing *perestroika* and *glasnost.* Suddenly Reagan interrupted and began to relate an anti-Soviet anecdote that had no relevance to the discussion. Gorbachev stared ahead without expression, while the American delegation looked away in embarrassment.

Afterward Shultz told Reagan, "Mr. President, that was a disaster. That man is tough. He's prepared. And you can't just sit there telling jokes." A contrite Reagan promised to do his homework, and his staff gathered around to protect him in the next few days, making sure that he had a script for every occasion. Next day Reagan was businesslike, and the two men discussed a wide range of issues and gave a boost to the START talks, agreeing on overall principles.[65]

The INF Treaty was the first time in history that nations had agreed to destroy nuclear weapons rather than just slow down the arms race. It was a step toward "demilitarization of human life," Gorbachev said. The fight for ratification was difficult, pitting Reagan against many conservative Republicans, but he won the battle in May 1988 and signed the immensely popular treaty. The INF Treaty made the world safer. The cold war seemed to be easing, and Reagan's presidency was ending in a dignified and productive manner.[66]

In January 1988 Reagan's approval ratings were high—67 percent in the *Los Angeles Times* polls. If he did not quite set off "Ronnie mania" when he visited Moscow in May 1988, he was extremely well received in the Soviet capital and honored at home. The Moscow summit did not result in major substantive agreements, but it continued the momentum in the START talks and, more important, in the unwinding of the cold war. Many realized a new day was at hand when they saw images of Reagan, symbol of hard-line anticommunism, being welcomed by smiling Kremlin leaders and enjoying himself with crowds of Muscovites. *Glasnost* had started to take effect in the Soviet Union, and Reagan, allowed to speak freely, delivered several notable speeches.[67]

In mid-November 1988 that most realistic of cold warriors, Margaret Thatcher, declared that the cold war was over. In December 1988 Gorbachev came to New York to deliver a speech at the United Nations. He asked Reagan to visit him, which was the final meeting between the two men before Reagan left office. Perhaps nothing signaled the beginning of a new era as much as Gorbachev's speech did. The Bolshevik revolution of

1917 belonged to history, he said, and a new era required nations to recognize the interdependence of all humanity and to free international relations from the grip of ideology. Neither force nor the threat of force should be an instrument of foreign policy, he proclaimed: "Freedom of choice [by nations] is a universal principle. It knows no exception." Finally, he announced that Moscow was unilaterally reducing the Soviet army by five hundred thousand troops, and withdrawing fifty thousand men and five thousand tanks from Eastern Europe. More would follow, he promised.

The New York meeting was a grand send-off for the aged and tiring Reagan. Gorbachev's major battles lay before him. When President-elect Bush asked him what it would be like in the Soviet Union in three or four years, Gorbachev laughed and said, "Mr. Vice President, even Jesus Christ couldn't answer that question!"[68]

10

Evaluating Reagan

Ronald Reagan and Mikhail Gorbachev met twice after Reagan left the presidency. Their pleasant reminiscences about their spectacular summit meetings were held against a tortuous backdrop. When they met in 1990 historical circumstances had changed with startling rapidity. Reagan had left office as an honored and popular elder statesman, while Gorbachev was losing his struggle to maintain stability and support until his reform program took hold. He shared Reagan's ability to exercise dramatic, visionary leadership, but he lacked the American's legendary good luck.

When Reagan finished his presidency in 1989, most Americans believed that it was time for new leadership, but they continued to admire and respect him as the chief executive who had placed the nation back on the right track. Popularity polls gave him a 70 percent approval rating, a record high for a retiring president. He was the first president since Eisenhower to complete two terms and was one of the few in the twentieth century to pass his office along to a chosen successor. George Bush won the Republican nomination in 1988 largely because of the sanction Reagan gave to his loyal vice president among suspicious conservatives, and Reagan's surging popularity in late 1988 fueled Bush's campaign against the Democratic nominee, Michael S. Dukakis. The *New York Times* exit polls attributed Bush's victory to his status as Reagan's heir.[1]

Reagan found his final days in the White House to be a "bitter sweet time." He had enjoyed his eight years as president, but he was eager to return home to California. On 20 January 1989 Colin Powell gave Reagan his final national security briefing: "Mr. President, . . . the world is quiet today." Reagan left Bush a note on the president's Don't Let The Turkeys Get You Down memoranda pad: "You'll have moments when you want to use this particular stationery. Well, go for it."[2]

After Bush's inaugural address, the new president escorted the Reagans to a helicopter that took them to the airport for their flight to California. The helicopter pilot circled the Capitol and then descended to give the Reagans a final view of the White House. "Look, honey, there's our little shack," Ronald told Nancy.[3]

They moved to the Bel Air section of Los Angeles, an exclusive area that offered privacy to its many wealthy and famous residents. During the next few years Reagan settled into a routine of working at his ranch, golfing, and visiting friends. He became the highest-paid speaker in the world, receiving $2 million for a few appearances in Japan. In 1990 he published his memoirs and in 1991 held the dedication of the Ronald Reagan Library, housed in a beautiful Spanish-style structure set by itself atop a mountain in Simi Valley, California. Reagan continued to conduct ceremonial occasions with his usual grace and charm, as in his speech at the 1992 Republican convention, his last high-profile public appearance.[4]

Reagan, seventy-eight years old when he left the presidency, seemed in good health. He had had serious injuries and illnesses in his life: damaged hearing, a shattered leg, and viral pneumonia during his Hollywood career, a prostate operation while he was governor, the nearly fatal assassination attempt in 1981, a serious cancer operation on his colon in 1985, another prostate surgery in 1987, a minor operation on his hand just before he left the White House. In 1989 he fell from a horse during a visit to Mexico and suffered a subdural hematoma that was removed surgically at the Mayo Clinic in Minnesota. Despite such episodes Reagan seemed healthy and vigorous, able to recover from physical problems rapidly and completely.[5]

In November 1994 Reagan shocked Americans by releasing a handwritten letter revealing that he had been diagnosed as having Alzheimer's disease. He said that at the moment he felt fine and intended to live out his life enjoying his remaining years with Nancy and his family and friends.

> Unfortunately, as Alzheimer's Disease progresses, the family often bears a heavy burden. I only wish there was some way I could spare Nancy from this painful experience. When the time comes I am confident that with your help she will face it with faith and courage.
> In closing let me thank you, the American people, for giving me the great

honor of allowing me to serve as your President. When the Lord calls me home whenever that may be, I will leave with the greatest love for this country of ours and eternal optimism for its future.

I now begin the journey that will lead me into the sunset of my life. I know that for America there will always be a bright dawn ahead.

Thank you my friends. May God always bless you.[6]

In mid-1996 family members reported that Reagan's mental deterioration had slowed and that he surprised many people with his ability to carry on conversations, at least on subjects of his choosing. He retained his elegance and charm and kept to his routine of going each morning to his office in nearby Century City. He received visitors, who would be preceded by an aide who told Reagan his guest's name and relationship to the president. He usually played a few holes of golf or took long walks with Secret Service agents before returning home. He retained his serenity and optimism, but the disease took its toll. Nancy Reagan called Alzheimer's disease "the long goodbye." In September 1996 she decided to sell Rancho del Cielo and revealed that Ronald had not been there in two years.[7]

Reagan's announcement set off speculation about how long he had suffered from Alzheimer's disease. For a year before the public announcement his doctors had been considering diagnosing him as having the disease, and Reagan's friends had noticed his mental deterioration at least two years earlier, although they did not understand its cause. Reagan's videotaped deposition in the 1990 Poindexter trial had caused comment because it revealed that he remembered little about major figures and events of his administration. Some people believed that he had exhibited symptoms of the affliction earlier, even during his presidency. It was difficult to determine if Reagan's mental lapses as president were the result of some form of dementia or just the real Reagan, who had little memory for details that did not interest him. His management style allowed his aides to carry much of the everyday burdens of the presidency, and White House public relations experts and his fiercely protective wife carefully managed the president's image to show him as a strong leader in charge of his administration. Some observers who saw evidence of the president's mental impairment assumed that they were seeing the normal lapses that any elderly man might experience, especially when he was tired. Many people had experiences similar to that of Lou Cannon. In July 1981 Cannon, who had a private conversation with Reagan when they were returning from an economic summit, found the physically exhausted Reagan nearly incoherent.[8]

Walter Mondale privately used the word "senile" to describe Reagan after the Democratic nominee's three hours of unscripted face-to-face exchanges with the president during the 1984 election. Journalist Elizabeth

Drew reported during that time that close observers had noticed that Reagan had slowed in his ability to react, that his anecdotes were off the mark more than in the past, that he was more stubborn, and that he had on days and off days. Others reported that by 1985 or 1986 Reagan was showing signs of mental impairment and that he was an "intermittent force" in the administration. After Reagan announced that he had Alzheimer's disease, Dr. Steven Miles revealed that he was one of several geriatricians who in the middle of Reagan's second term, noting the president's inability to speak lucidly outside tightly controlled settings, had considered jointly suggesting through the *New York Times* that the president be evaluated for Alzheimer's disease.[9]

Doctors did not test Reagan for Alzheimer's disease while he was in the White House, and most people assumed his behavior was typical of that of an elderly man. Even during his last year in office, Reagan at times seemed fully competent. In early 1988 the Department of Justice indicted Panamanian dictator Manuel A. Noriega for drug trafficking. The State Department negotiated a deal by which Noriega would leave Panama in return for the United States not pushing for his arrest. The story leaked to the press, and many people, especially members of Congress and the law enforcement community, were infuriated at the idea of making a deal with a drug lord. George Bush, in the midst of his presidential campaign, fought any deal and was backed by Attorney General Meese, Treasury Secretary James Baker, and most other top officials. George Shultz later published transcripts of tense meetings in which Reagan engaged in head-to-head battles with his closest friends and supporters. Reagan wanted to seize the opportunity to get rid of a dictator without killing young American or Panamanian soldiers. He stood firm in the face of furious opposition and held his own during hours of heated and draining unscripted exchanges. Reagan told his team that he was going to make the deal (which later fell through) and that he would assume responsibility for explaining it to the American people.[10]

The nature and extent of Reagan's mental impairment while he was president remained unclear and added to the many controversies surrounding his presidency. "He is the most mysterious man I have ever confronted," said Edmund Morris, Reagan's official biographer. That mystery, added to his long and varied career and to the intense feelings he generated among both supporters and opponents, generated a flood of Reagan articles and books. In late 1996 an electronic database counted nearly two thousand books under the subject "Ronald Reagan." Hundreds of scholars and journalists began to evaluate his administration.[11]

After Reagan won his budget and tax victories in 1981, many of his conservative supporters proclaimed the beginning of the "Reagan Revolution." But as budget deficits grew and most of Franklin Roosevelt's New Deal programs remained untouched, the Reagan era seemed less revolutionary than it did initially. Conservatives did not achieve most of their major goals, not even a reduction in the size of government. The number of government employees grew at a faster rate than under Jimmy Carter, and spending as a percentage of gross domestic product averaged 23 percent in Reagan's first term and 21.8 percent in his second term, compared with 21.1 percent under Bill Clinton. While the American people expressed great skepticism about the government in the abstract, they continued to support specific programs that they considered important to themselves and to the nation. Americans were pragmatists. They responded to Reagan's message that government was the problem and they showed little interest in major new federal initiatives, but they did not want to destroy existing programs.[12]

The Reagan years disappointed some conservatives. They appreciated his symbolic gestures, such as hanging portraits of William Howard Taft and Calvin Coolidge in the cabinet room, but supply-side economics, and its promise to cut taxes while retaining high spending levels, sounded too good to be true to many conservatives, who were horrified by mounting deficits. Still, most conservatives, even those disappointed at lack of action on the social agenda, remained loyal to Reagan. They saw him as an old warrior who had led them in many important battles, as a dynamic leader who attracted young people into the movement, and as a visionary who left conservatives with an optimistic, forward-looking populist message that placed them squarely in the mainstream where the voters were. Most agreed with Jerry Falwell's claim that conservatives in the 1980s owed everything to one man, Ronald Reagan.[13]

Most journalists and political contemporaries, even if they disliked his policies, believed that Reagan was a major president in terms of his impact on history. Historians, however, did not seem to agree. A major survey of historians found that an overwhelming majority of them blamed Reagan for the economic problems of the 1980s and gave him little credit for gains; 66 percent believed that he was very or somewhat racist and 19 percent said that he was mildly racist; over 70 percent believed he was very or somewhat sexist; 92 percent thought that the general public overestimated him. A sizable majority, 62 percent, ranked Reagan in the "below average" category, between Zachary Taylor and John Tyler.[14]

Despite this preliminary evaluation by historians, Reagan was a president of consequence. He moved the nation's political center to the right and changed the nature of Washington's "policy talk" by ushering in an age of diminished expectations in people's attitude toward government. He transformed both political parties. In 1988 and afterward Republicans of all persuasions scrambled for the Reagan mantle. Reagan also had an impact on the Democratic Party. Bill Clinton's victories in 1992 and 1996 showed that Democrats could win, but they could no longer do so by marching proudly under the New Deal banner, and Clinton had to protect himself from charges that he was a "closet liberal." The "New Democratic" party that Clinton trumpeted was his attempt to come to terms with post-Reagan America.[15]

Presidents Bush and Clinton both had to cope with "Reagan's revenge." They faced a massive budget deficit that forced them to concentrate on cutting or holding down the growth of programs and left them little room for policy innovations. For eight years Reagan had hammered home the message that taxes were evil and that government was the problem. His successors struggled under the burden of that legacy. For example, Bill Clinton's health reform program foundered under the impact of "Reagan's revenge." The first Reagan legacy, hatred of taxes, prevented Clinton from proposing the tax increase necessary to fund the kind of program he believed the nation needed. He then tried to substitute government regulation of the health system for adequate financing and that ran into the second Reagan legacy: distrust of government. While Reagan was delegitimizing the Soviet government, "he was also hollowing out our own Government, denying its claims upon the citizenry," wrote Garry Wills.[16]

The flood of material analyzing aspects of the Reagan administration concentrated on his communication skills, management style, Reaganomics, and foreign policy. Most analysts recognized Reagan as one of the most persuasive speakers in American history, and Reagan was most confident in his role as the Great Communicator. When one of his aides, impressed by Reagan's knowledge of esoteric aspects of federal-state relations, said that the White House needed to find some way to get his expertise into his speeches, Reagan thanked him for the compliment. "But you know," he said, "I've been selling things for a long time. I know what I'm doing."[17]

Nelle and Jack Reagan and Disciples of Christ minister Ben Cleaver taught Reagan how to tell a good story. Growing up in the American heartland gave him values and images, such as the City on a Hill myth, that he used with great power in his political career. Reagan's life spanned most of the twentieth century, and he used his experiences to evoke varying, even conflicting, images: his identification with small-town America, Hollywood, and the White House; his years as a union leader followed by his stint as spokesman for corporate America; his advocacy of traditional values and his faith in technological progress; his association in people's minds with images of the West, sports, the Great Depression, World War II. His life had been rooted in "various national yesterdays" that could still be evoked by his power to use symbols, images, and words that sounded familiar and true. He revalidated the American dream by living it out publicly, and he verified to many that America remained young with all of its promise before it, still a frontier nation with unlimited possibilities. He spoke in symbolic terms of a vision of the future rooted in the American past—but a cleaned up, Disneyland kind of past, free of a dark side of poverty-blighted dreams, racial oppression, or imperialistic wars.[18]

White House professional speechwriters found that Reagan remained the best craftsman among them. He set a few rules for them: use short sentences, do not use words of two syllables if one would do, never reach for eloquence at the cost of convolution, frame ideas in terms of striking images, use examples in place of sermons. His speechwriters learned to avoid negatives: "I'll never forget" became "I'll always remember." Reagan relied on his writers to churn out the millions of words his job demanded, but he sometimes surprised them. For example, in his speech on Grenada and Lebanon in October 1983, he extensively edited the entire speech and then added nine full pages of handwritten changes and additions. He wrote the phrase that many remembered most from the speech: "I will not ask you to pray for the dead, because they're safe in God's loving arms and beyond need of our prayers."[19]

Reagan presented himself as a citizen-politician, as an average American, unusual only because of his special access to the "bully pulpit." He, like a mirror, reflected the people back to themselves, tapping the "attic of imagery" already present in their minds. He knew that a good story never grew old and that its purpose was not so much to teach as to remind listeners of what they already knew. He used self-deprecating humor to establish bonds with the people, and he did not seem to be trying to generate emotions in his audience as much as sharing his own feelings with them. He spoke in terms of traditional values that seemed threatened in the modern world: the work ethic, family, community, faith in God. He proudly displayed his patriotism and never questioned the belief, unfashionable in intellectual circles, that God had selected Americans as a chosen people with a special mission. He contemptuously dismissed the idea that the United States was in decline; the best days were still ahead, it was always morning in America, he believed. Reagan reiterated the central core of American mythology that had been told and retold through the years back to the Jamestown and Plymouth settlements. What he said struck people as right because it was based on beliefs handed down through the generations as simple truths. He knew, like Dr. Johnson, "that people more often need to be reminded than informed." Reagan never got "off-message." He presented a consistent vision of America's past and its future, a message based on national traditions and common sense.

Reagan appealed to a spiritual and mythic side of Americans but also to their materialism, and he saw no more contradiction between spiritual values and material hunger than did most of his countrymen. He easily combined his glorification of the past with unquestioned faith that technological progress would make a better future. Speechwriter Peggy Noonan believed that Reagan also understood that loneliness was a major problem for people living in modern urban, industrialized society and that he spoke directly to isolated individuals, enveloping them into a community based on a shared vision of the American past and its future.[20]

With the Great Communicator at its head, the White House mounted the most effective public relations operation in history. Reagan husbanded his appearances, carefully avoiding overexposure. In 1981, the decisive year for establishing his administration's goals, he delivered only four major televised addresses to the nation. He held forty-two press conferences in his eight years, averaging fewer than six a year, which minimized the mistakes he was prone to making and allowed his handlers to control the image that he presented. When he had to appear in unscripted situations, his team left as little to chance as possible. When he held press conferences his aides placed friendly reporters to his right and told him that if he got in trouble to recognize reporters in that direction. The press managers even planted questions among reporters to shout at Reagan when he left the White House to walk to his helicopter. Press Secretary Larry Speakes later admitted that at times he made up Reagan quotations and gave them to reporters as the president's own, including the famous line Reagan supposedly uttered at the Geneva summit: "There is much that divides us, but we believe that the world breathes easier because we are talking here together."[21]

Both the White House and the press agreed that Reagan was treated more generously than any modern president. Journalists always had to remember that most of the general public liked Reagan personally and wanted his presidency to succeed. The White House was also skilled in manipulating the press. "You don't tell us how to stage the news," Larry Speakes admonished the press, "and we don't tell you how to cover it." No administration had ever been so sophisticated in its understanding of how the media worked and how to manage it. When CBS reporter Lesley Stahl contrasted Reagan's appearance at the Handicapped Olympics with his cuts in programs that helped such Americans, Richard Darman thanked her for the Reagan "commercial." She protested that he must have misunderstood what she said, and Darman told her that no one had heard her words: "They just saw the five minutes of beautiful pictures of Ronald Reagan. They saw the balloons, they saw the flags, they saw the red, white and blue. Haven't you people figured out yet that the picture always overrides what you say?" The press and White House formed a mutually beneficial relationship. After a terrorist incident that killed an American citizen, a *New York Post* editor telephoned the White House and said that he had a great headline that he would like to use. Reagan's aides wrote it down and had Reagan mouth it: "You can run but you can't hide." The newspaper had its headline, and its readers saw a heroic and strong leader in action.[22]

The Great Communicator had his critics. Some believed that Reagan represented the increasing dominance in the modern world of image over substance. Journalist Fred Barnes found Reagan to be an unusual politician in that he was a more interesting person in public than he was in private; the performance was everything and, like the Wizard of Oz, there was not much impressive going on behind the scenes. Some believed that Reagan, the least cynical of individuals, fed public cynicism, because of the gap he left between the image he projected of leading a revolution and the reality that little had changed. Other critics charged that he devalued words and rational discussion and analysis. He "educated America down to his level," said Robert Hughes. "He left his country a little stupider in 1988 than it had been in 1980, and a lot more tolerant of lies, because his style of image-presentation cut the connective tissue of arguments between ideas and hence fostered the defeat of thought itself." Just as Iran-contra revealed Reagan's contempt for constitutional processes, some critics thought that his communicative techniques undermined democracy. His stance of treating critics as beyond contempt sapped debate, and his Congress bashing and his message that government was the problem undermined confidence in national institutions.[23]

Despite such criticism, most analysts gave Reagan high marks as the Great Communicator. His economic program received mixed reviews, however. From 1940 to 1973 Americans had become used to healthy economic growth and a rapidly expanding standard of living. That golden age ended as the United States confronted an increasingly competitive global economy and had to pay the cost of its own economic mismanagement and bear the economic consequences of playing global policeman during the cold war. When Reagan defeated Carter, the prime interest rate was over 15 percent, the inflation rate exceeded 12 percent, and civilian unemployment topped 7 percent. By 1989 interest rates had fallen below 10 percent, inflation under 5 percent, and unemployment ran about 5 percent. During that time GNP had nearly doubled and per capita disposable income had grown from $9,722 to $11,326. The fabled misery index (the sum of the rates of unemployment and inflation) that Reagan had used with devastating effect against Carter had dropped by half. Under Reagan the United States experienced the longest peacetime economic expansion in United States history; the sense of malaise snapped as the era of stagflation ended; and the United

States led the world toward renewed faith in free market economies. As communist systems collapsed and socialist governments cut back on social welfare activities and searched for ways to incorporate market incentives, there hardly seemed a challenge left to capitalism.

But critics of Reaganomics had their own statistics. Budget and trade deficits mounted to frightening levels in the 1980s. Reagan and Bush added more national debt than all previous presidents put together, and Reagan presided over the transformation of the United States from the world's largest creditor nation into the world's largest debtor. Inflation and unemployment rates did indeed fall under Reagan and productivity increased, but the inflation, unemployment, and productivity record lagged behind previous postwar decades. Most of the economic gains of the 1980s were raked off by the very wealthy, and economists found that the huge tax cut of 1981 did not lead to increased investment in the American economy. Critics charged that the Reagan era of prosperity stemmed from citizens enjoying the benefits of massive spending financed by borrowing from the next generation rather than taxing themselves. A Reagan administration economist said that the deficit reflected the American people's preference for federal spending of about 23 percent of GNP and taxes at about 19 percent of GNP. "Something must give," he said. Nothing did and deficits ballooned.[24]

Reaganites took pride in the long period of economic growth that began in 1983 and in the seventeen to eighteen million new jobs created during Reagan's presidency. Critics pointed out, however, that many of those jobs were minimum-wage positions that often left the workers in poverty and forced both husbands and wives to enter the workforce to maintain their family income level. Real GNP growth averaged 3.0 percent during the Reagan years, compared with 3.2 percent in 1971–78 and 3.0 percent during the Carter years of stagflation. The economy of the 1970s provided almost as many jobs as that of the 1980s. Reaganites applauded the huge 1981 tax cut on individual income taxes and corporations, but critics pointed out that the 1981 reduction was followed by five "revenue enhancements" and that a major result of the changes was to shift the tax burden from upper- to middle-income people.[25]

Political scientists Joseph White and Aaron Wildavsky rejected the common assumption that the Reagan tax cut was the main source of the deficit. His reductions had moved the tax level back to the "normal" 19 percent of GNP, down from the 20.9 percent that had helped destroy Carter politically. Nor did Reagan's increase in military spending cause the deficit. Before Reagan took office, leaders in both parties agreed that defense spending had to increase; Reagan just pushed expenditures further and faster. The deficit mainly resulted from decisions political leaders made before 1973. Politicians made commitments on social welfare spending, especially the entitle-ment programs, based on assumptions that had been realistic in the decades after World War II. After the "silent depression" that began in 1973, they made few new commitments. Reagan and Congress got caught in a "fiscal tidal wave" generated long before, argued White and Wildavsky: "Most of the increase in spending after 1979 constituted old commitments hitting the beach of a new economy." The huge deficits would have come without Reagan because the politicians who reduced taxes, raised defense spending, and retained high spending levels on domestic programs accurately repre-sented their constituents' wishes.[26]

If Reagan did not reduce the level of government spending, as his con-servative followers thought he intended to do, he did change its composi-tion. "The press is trying to paint me as now trying to undo the New Deal," he complained in his diary on 28 January 1982. "I remind them I voted for FDR four times. I'm trying to undo the 'Great Society.' It was LBJ's war on poverty that led us to our present mess." Real federal government spend-ing was 7.7 percent of GNP in 1980 and 8.2 percent in 1988. The largest shift in dollar amounts came in national defense. National defense outlays in 1982 dollars had increased by 68.3 percent in 1989 compared with 1980; Social Security had increased 46.5 percent and Medicare 97.8 percent. The growth rate in spending on AFDC, veterans' benefits, food stamps, child nutrition, and other such "welfare" programs slowed, however. According to one estimate discretionary domestic spending fell as a percentage of GNP to about the same level as before the Great Society.[27]

The 1980s were often labeled as years of greed and selfishness, a surpris-ing indictment in a materialistic nation that had long glorified the "self-made man." The United States had always had a high degree of inequality in wealth and income, but it became more extreme in the 1980s, partly due to Reagan's tax changes and spending reductions. Economist Robert Reich, soon to be secretary of labor, in 1991 estimated that the average income of the poorest fifth of American families decreased by about 7 percent in the 1980s, while that of the richest fifth increased by about 15 percent. Econo-mist Mark Levinson found that the income of the bottom 20 percent of Americans fell 6 percent in the 1980s and the income shares of the next 60 percent were the lowest since 1947.[28]

Rising poverty rates and income inequality fell hardest on women, blacks, and other minority groups. Unions, too, were in their weakest posi-tion since World War II. Reagan's breaking of the PATCO strike and his packing the National Labor Relations Board with corporate lawyers hostile to unionization signaled business that it could be as tough on organized labor as was the national administration. In 1983, 45 percent of the members of the moderate and prestigious Conference Board's Personnel Forum said that their main labor goal was to be union free. Union membership fell from 23 percent of the labor force in 1980 to less than 17 percent by the time Reagan left office, the lowest rate since the 1930s.

Although lower- and middle-income people often fought a losing struggle to maintain their standard of living during the 1980s, Reagan retained widespread support among voters in those income groups. A public school teacher on Long Island, New York, a third-generation Italian-American, described himself as a former liberal who had become a devout Reaganite. He said that people like him knew that Reagan's policies hurt them economically—"We are not fools," he said—but he loved Reagan because the president had given him what he valued more than economic gains: renewed pride in being an American and restored confidence in the future.[29]

While analysts divided on their assessment of Reaganomics, almost all agreed that Reagan was a poor manager. He had strengths: he delegated easily, did not second-guess actions by himself and his subordinates, and made cabinet government work fairly well. He did not, however, manage his team well. He was a passive man without much curiosity. He trusted aides to know what he wanted and to act honestly in his name. He did not check on subordinates or build an intelligence apparatus independent of his staff. He delegated easily but did not supervise those to whom he delegated; he delegated supervision of his staff to his staff.

Reagan established clear ideological direction on a few issues—cutting taxes and building up the military, for example—but otherwise he failed to establish well-defined guidelines and to make straightforward decisions. Colin Powell described National Security Adviser Frank Carlucci's first briefing of Reagan:

> President Reagan listened carefully and asked a few questions, but gave no guidance. This became the pattern almost every morning when we briefed him. We would lay out the contrasting views of various cabinet officers and Congress and wait for the President to peel them back to get at underlying motives. It did not happen. Most unnerving, when Carlucci presented options, the President would say little until Frank gave him his recommendation. And then the President would merely acknowledge that he had heard him, without saying yes, no, or maybe. Frank and I would walk down the hall afterward with Frank muttering, 'Was that a yes?' We eventually assumed that the President knew we had balanced competing views and had given him our best judgment. He evidently felt it unnecessary to do more than acknowledge what we would be doing in his name. That, at least, was our optimistic interpretation.[30]

Reagan was not, however, a mere front man to be manipulated by a staff who set policy and sent him out to sell it. He had deep beliefs that he stuck to, in season or out. He was more than a performer; his performance served his beliefs. His harshest critics described him as an "empty suit." Yet Howard Baker believed that Reagan's success came from his central core of unwavering convictions: "He knew who he was, he knew what he believed, and he knew where he wanted to go." On matters that Reagan considered important he set the agenda and established the priorities. He exhibited leadership in the face of staff opposition on tax policy; he horrified traditional Republicans by deciding to accept the deficit rather than give up his tax cut and military expansion; he pushed the military buildup after the indefatigable Caspar Weinberger faltered; he overrode two of the men he liked best and respected most, Weinberger and George Shultz, on Iran-contra matters; he quickly responded to Gorbachev's overtures despite the opposition of the anticommunist hard-liners that surrounded him; he pushed SDI and nuclear arms reduction over many of his arms control advisers; he overruled his military advisers by sending troops to Lebanon and invading Grenada. He reestablished the prestige of the presidency after a string of failed administrations and provided inspirational leadership at a time of national self-doubt. He reaffirmed for Americans many of their fundamental beliefs about the value of work, family, community, and America's place as God's City on a Hill. "My view is that he should go down in history as a very superior president on the main issue," said Paul Nitze. "The main issue was eloquently defending the value system of the United States."[31]

Commentators singled out other parts of Reagan's legacy for praise or blame. He was a major symbol of the free-market economics that seemed to be establishing itself around the world. He put a conservative stamp on the federal judiciary that continued to be felt long after he left office. His New Federalism program generally disappointed its advocates but did result in reforms that benefited states. "Whether you agree with President Reagan or not, he has made Governors important again," said Arkansas governor Bill Clinton. Despite Reagan's harsh attack on terrorists as "cowardly, skulking barbarians," he was not more successful than other presidents in finding a solution to the problem of terrorism. His bombing attack on Libya pleased Americans, as did his approval of a plan to force down on Italian soil an Egyptian airliner carrying suspected terrorists. Still, as one of his conservative critics pointed out, "It would be hard to imagine a case where there is a larger gap between words and action in Administration policy."[32]

There was also a huge gap between Reagan's rhetoric and his actions in trade policy. Reagan believed in free trade and carried that message to the yearly economic summits he attended with leaders of Western industrial nations, all of whom expressed their agreement with his free-trade views. "But the plain truth was that all of us were protectionist to some extent,"

Reagan noted in a rare moment of recognition of the difference between his ideology and his practice. Major pressure for protection came from the American automobile industry, which was reeling from the competitive challenge offered by Japan's high-quality products. At American insistence, the Japanese entered into a voluntary restraint agreement that limited exports to 1.68 million cars per year for three years and to a slightly higher level beginning in 1984. That agreement, according to one estimate, cost American consumers $1 billion per year. In contrast, on 2 January 1988 Reagan achieved a significant victory for freer trade when he signed the United States and Canadian Free Trade Agreement and worked out the framework for a similar agreement with Mexico, which George Bush and Bill Clinton concluded as the North American Free Trade Agreement (NAFTA).[33]

The end of the cold war will become the focus of historians' interest in the Reagan administration's record on foreign policy. Reagan and Gorbachev were a fascinating pair of world leaders. It could be truthfully said of both of them that, in Max Kampelman's phrase, they were "event-making men." The usually passive Reagan could exert great leadership on matters central to his vision of the future. Many people knew more about world affairs than Reagan, said Jesse Jackson, but like other great leaders, once he moved and set the pace and sent the word out, people said, "Well, now, *that's* what time of day it is."[34]

Reagan did not have a coherent foreign policy when he entered the White House; he had a few fundamental beliefs. He believed that democracy and free-market economies provided the necessary foundation for a peaceful and prosperous world. He believed that nuclear weapons were evil and should be removed from the world. He believed that peace depended on strength and that before he could initiate major foreign policy changes he had to rebuild United States military power. His fundamental belief was in American exceptionalism, the vision embodied in the myth of the City on a Hill. Every president had spoken of American moral superiority and its destiny to transform the world, said Kissinger, but "what rendered Reagan's particular variant of American exceptionalism unique was his literal interpretation of it as a guide to the everyday conduct of foreign policy."[35]

Reagan believed that communism was an inherently evil and expansionist system and he believed that it had to fall because it violated God's will and human nature. He believed that the Soviets had had one overriding goal since 1917: to establish communism across the world by destroying the Western democracies. He refused to accept as valid the Yalta accord's division of Europe into eastern and western blocs, and he rejected his sophisticated advisers' assumption that the Soviet Union was a big and dangerous but still ordinary nation-state that was here to stay. Reagan did not believe that the Soviet Union had a right to exist, at least in the form it had taken since 1917. There was no moral equivalence between the superpowers; morally the Americans were right and the Soviets wrong. To Reagan calling the Soviet Union an evil empire was stating the obvious.[36]

Those captivated by the "great man" approach to history quickly began to argue over whether Reagan or Gorbachev had ended the cold war. "I came in with a plan," Reagan told Martin Anderson. He had to convince the Soviets, first, that nuclear war was unthinkable and could not be won and, second, to reduce nuclear stockpiles. His strategy was to brand the Soviet Union as an evil empire to highlight the struggle as a moral battle between good and evil. His next step was relentlessly to rebuild American military power, later adding SDI to the buildup: Whatever his experts thought, Reagan believed that the Soviet Union would break under the pressure. He was confident enough in his views that in June 1982 he proclaimed in a speech to the British Parliament that Soviet communism was doomed. It was a remarkable speech, wrote Margaret Thatcher, that "marked a decisive stage in the battle of ideas which he and I wished to wage against socialism." Many of Reagan's admirers believe that the president understood a simple but profound truth, that the Soviet Union's collapse was inevitable. He gave it a hard push.

Even those who reject the claim that Reagan won the cold war must still give credit to the aged cold warrior's ability to respond so quickly, against the advice of many White House hard-liners, to Gorbachev's overtures. Reagan was fortunate to have George Shultz at his side. Shultz understood that despite Reagan's evil empire rhetoric he intended to open serious negotiations when American strength and Soviet vulnerability converged to bring Moscow to the bargaining table. Both Shultz and Gorbachev came to understand that Reagan had a radical vision: to achieve a world free of nuclear weapons. Eventually Reagan and Gorbachev understood that such a breakthrough required an end to the cold war, another radical vision.[37]

Moscow led in taking action to end the cold war. Gorbachev realized that he had to begin a rapid and drastic reform program. He told his wife just before he took office in 1985 that he would have to accept the position of general secretary if his colleagues offered it to him because he had to try to change things. *"We can't go on living like this,"* he told her. Gorbachev quickly moved to restructure his nation's economy and liberalize Soviet society. "As a first step," Gorbachev recalled, "we had at least to clear up the 'snow-drifts' left over from Cold War times and to alleviate the pressure that had borne down on us due to our involvement in conflicts all over the world." He did not have a detailed plan of action, but he understood that

Soviet progress depended on rejoining the West and making the USSR part of an increasingly interdependent world. He also understood that for the Soviet Union to feel safe enough to change itself internally, the West also had to feel secure, and that meant Moscow had to take action to reduce world tensions. He believed that he had to focus his peace campaign on Reagan and the United States or his efforts would be seen as communist intrigue designed to split the Western alliance.[38]

By 1988 it had begun to sink in on many world leaders that the cold war had ended, and they began to talk of an emerging new world order. When he attended the Moscow summit a reporter asked Reagan if the Soviet Union was still an evil empire. "No," he replied, "I was talking about another time, another era." There was a surprising lack of euphoria at the end of the half-century-long cold war, partly, perhaps, because the new order remained vague and ill defined and seemed to carry dangers of its own. John le Carré's spy George Smiley spoke for many people in the West: "We won. Not that the victory matters a damn. And perhaps we didn't win anyway. Perhaps they just lost. Or perhaps, without the bonds of ideological conflict to restrain us any more, our troubles are just beginning." Henry Kissinger believed that the cold war had especially fit the American mind: it offered a clear moral, military, and ideological threat and provided Americans with an arena in which their beliefs in democracy, capitalism, and individual freedom seemed most relevant. With the threat gone, Americans, always tempted by isolationism, had to chose what, if any, role they wanted to play in a suddenly messy world. George Bush expressed many of his countrymen's doubts. While welcoming the new era, he seemed almost to feel nostalgia for 1945 and the beginning of the cold war. "Nineteen forty five provided the common frame of reference, the compass points of the postwar era we've relied upon to understand ourselves. And that was our world until now."[39]

Ronald Reagan shared few of these feelings of disquiet. He knew that the world was safer than when he took office and that a bright future lay ahead. Historians rank Ronald Reagan too low. He did not destroy the liberal Democrats' standing among lower- and middle-class Americans; his political success was a product of that change. Over a period of several decades liberals had eroded their base among middle-class voters. For the American political structure to maintain stability, the powerful American middle class must get most of what it wants most of the time. Reagan gave them that without much pandering or trimming of his message. If he fooled his countrymen, as some of his liberal critics charged, it was because they wanted to be fooled, which is the majority's privilege in a democracy. Reagan adjusted details in his conservative message as times changed and he surrounded it with new visual images, but the tune never changed much: America was God's chosen nation destined to create his City on a Hill; the nation's best days lay ahead in a future unbounded by limits; government was the problem, not the solution; Americans were overtaxed and overregulated; hard work, family, and community were the essential foundation of a healthy society; peace depended on strength; and the communist Soviet Union was an evil empire. His countrymen said that Reagan made them feel proud to be Americans, and by their votes they indicated that that pride was more important to them than any deleterious effects they saw in his economic program. In any case, most Americans could easily say in 1989, as Ronald and Nancy Reagan boarded their airplane to return to California, that in terms of the misery index, at least, they were economically better off than they had been in 1980, and that they lived in a safer world.

Notes

Chapter 1: Growing Up in the Heartland, 1911–1937

1. Edmund Morris, "Ronald Reagan as Metaphor," audiotape of a lecture presented at the Hofstra University Conference on Ronald Reagan, 22 April 1993.

2. Lou Cannon, *Reagan,* 27; Anne Edwards, *Early Reagan,* 23–32, 571–72; see also Patricia M. White, *The Invincible Irish: Ronald Wilson Reagan, Irish Ancestry, and Immigration to America.*

3. Quotation in Ronald Reagan and Richard G. Hubler, *Where's the Rest of Me?* 8–10; Ronald Reagan, *An American Life,* 21–22; Garry Wills, *Reagan's America: Innocents at Home,* 11–13; Edwards, *Early Reagan,* 26–28.

4. Edwards, *Early Reagan,* 28, 32–38, 40–46.

5. First quotation in Reagan and Hubler, *Where's the Rest of Me?* 13; second quotation in Jane Mayer and Doyle McManus, *Landslide: The Unmaking of the President, 1984–1988,* 30; third quotation in Mark Twain, *Adventures of Huckleberry Finn,* 160; Wills, *Reagan's America,* 7.

6. Reagan and Hubler, *Where's the Rest of Me?* 7–9; Lou Cannon, *President Reagan: The Role of a Lifetime,* 207–9; Reagan, *An American Life,* 33–34; Wills, *Reagan's America,* 33–35.

7. Reagan, *An American Life,* 20–23, 32–33; Edwards, *Early Reagan,* 35–40, 104–5; Nancy Reagan and William Novak, *My Turn: The Memoirs of Nancy Reagan,* 107–8; Maureen Reagan, *First Father, First Daughter: A Memoir,* 62–64; Stephen Vaughn, *Ronald Reagan in Hollywood: Movies and Politics,* 9; Wills, *Reagan's America,* 22–25, 34; Reagan and Hubler, *Where's the Rest of Me?* 8–10; Lou Cannon, *Ronnie and Jesse: A Political Odyssey,* 4; Cannon, *President Reagan,* 212.

8. Reagan and Hubler, *Where's the Rest of Me?* 9; Reagan, *An American Life,* 25; Ed-

wards, *Early Reagan,* 36, 67, 92; Robert E. Gilbert, *The Mortal Presidency: Illness and Anguish in the White House,* 178; Cannon, *President Reagan,* 210–12; Peggy Noonan, *What I Saw at the Revolution: A Political Life in the Reagan Era,* 153–54, 161; Patti Davis, *The Way I See It: An Autobiography,* 21–23.

9. First and second quotations in Reagan and Hubler, *Where's the Rest of Me?* 13–16, 40; third quotation in Reagan and Novak, *My Turn,* 105; Reagan, *An American Life,* 28; Cannon, *Ronnie and Jesse,* 3–4; Cannon, *President Reagan,* 32; Cannon, *Reagan,* 18–19; Ronald Reagan interview, 13 December 1980, Frank van der Linden papers, Hoover Institution, Stanford University, Stanford, California.

10. First quotation in "Ronald Reagan's Boyhood Home," Reagan Homes folder, Dixon Public Library, Dixon, Illinois; second quotation in Reagan, *An American Life,* 29; third quotation in Noonan, *What I Saw,* 146–47, 152; Reagan and Hubler, *Where's the Rest of Me?* 17; Reagan, *An American Life,* 27–28; Edwards, *Early Reagan,* 47–49; see also Suzanne Hanney, "Reagan Home Resembles Others," no folder, loose in Reagan file cabinet, Dixon Public Library, and Norman E. Wymbs, *A Place to Go Back To: Ronald Reagan in Dixon, Illinois.*

11. Quotation in Reagan, *An American Life,* 23, 31; Cannon, *President Reagan,* 213.

12. First quotation in Edwards, *Early Reagan,* 62–63; second quotation in Reagan and Hubler, *Where's the Rest of Me?* 12, 15; Vaughn, *Ronald Reagan in Hollywood,* 6; Reagan, *An American Life,* 24; Cannon, *Ronnie and Jesse,* 3, 5; Cannon, *President Reagan,* 213–16.

13. Reagan, *An American Life,* 36–40; Edwards, *Early Reagan,* 51–53; Reagan and Hubler, *Where's the Rest of Me?* 17–21; Wills, *Reagan's America,* 30–31; Cannon, *President Reagan,* 214–16; see lists of local newspaper stories on Reagan in Reagan Homes folder, Dixon Public Library.

14. First quotation in Reagan, *An American Life,* 34–35, 37, 40–43; second quotation in Cannon, *President Reagan,* 216–17; Reagan and Hubler, *Where's the Rest of Me?* 21–22, 37–38; Edwards, *Early Reagan,* 82; Colin L. Powell and Joseph E. Persico, *My American Journey,* 371.

15. Quotation in David E. Harrell, *Quest for a Christian America: The Disciples of Christ and American Society to 1866,* 4–7, 39–44, 46–47, 60–61, 63, 68; Wills, *Reagan's America,* 18–22, 38; Vaughn, *Ronald Reagan in Hollywood,* 10–13; see also Winfred Ernest Garrison, *An American Religious Movement: A Brief History of the Disciples of Christ.*

16. First quotation in Reagan, *An American Life,* 56, 168, 374; second quotation in Vaughn, *Ronald Reagan in Hollywood,* 15; third quotation in Frank van der Linden, *The Real Reagan: What He Believes, What He Has Accomplished, What We Can Expect from Him,* 26–27; Wills, *Reagan's America,* 16–18; Cannon, *President Reagan,* 34, 212; Edwards, *Early Reagan,* 58–60; Helene von Damm, *At Reagan's Side,* 61; Lyn Nofziger interview, 5 January 1978, A. James Reichley papers, Gerald R. Ford Library, Ann Arbor, Michigan; Robert Walker, oral history interview, Bancroft Library, University of California at Berkeley, Berkeley, California. All oral history interviews are from the Bancroft Library unless otherwise noted.

17. Edwards, *Early Reagan,* 79–82, 97; Reagan and Hubler, *Where's the Rest of Me?* 22–24; Cannon, *President Reagan,* 220–21; Wills, *Reagan's America,* 39–40; see also the Ronald Reagan exhibit in the Donald B. Cerf College Center, Eureka College, Eureka, Illinois.

18. First quotation in Edwards, *Early Reagan,* 83, 86–88; second quotation in Vaughn, *Ronald Reagan in Hollywood,* 21–22; Ronald Reagan and Gladys Hall, "How to Make Yourself Important"; Reagan, *An American Life,* 53–54.

19. Quotation in Reagan and Hubler, *Where's the Rest of Me?* 26–30; Edwards, *Early Reagan,* 83–86, 88–94; Cannon, *Reagan,* 34–36; Wills, *Reagan's America,* 38–51.

20. Quotation in Wills, *Reagan's America,* 51–52; Joel Kotkin and Paul Grabowicz, *California, Inc.,* 57.

21. Quotation in Edwards, *Early Reagan,* 88, 94; Reagan, *An American Life,* 57–58; Reagan and Hubler, *Where's the Rest of Me?* 29; Cannon, *Reagan,* 36–37.

22. Quotation in Reagan to J. Byron Flanders, 29 August 1983, ID: 165721, WHORM:

Subject: FG, Reagan presidential papers, Ronald Reagan Library, Simi Valley, California; Cannon, *Reagan,* 31, 42–43; Reagan and Hubler, *Where's the Rest of Me?* 41–45; Edwards, *Early Reagan,* 95–96; Cannon, *President Reagan,* 217–20; Reagan and Novak, *My Turn,* 114; Reagan, *An American Life,* 57–59.

23. First quotation in Reagan and Hubler, *Where's the Rest of Me?* 45–52, 54; second quotation in Vaughn, *Ronald Reagan in Hollywood,* 23; Reagan, *An American Life,* 20; Cannon, *Ronnie and Jesse,* 18–19; Cannon, *Reagan,* 44.

24. Wills, *Reagan's America,* 58–61, 68, 70–71; Edwards, *Early Reagan,* 128–29; Reagan and Hubler, *Where's the Rest of Me?* 52–54; Cannon, *Reagan,* 32; Reagan, *An American Life,* 68–69; Michael K. Deaver and Mickey Herskowitz, *Behind the Scenes,* 37.

25. Cannon, *Reagan,* 44–47; Wills, *Reagan's America,* 98–100, 102–6, 132–37; Cannon, *President Reagan,* 33, 221–23; Reagan, *An American Life,* 71–72; Reagan and Hubler, *Where's the Rest of Me?* 59.

26. Wills, *Reagan's America,* 109–11, 115–24, 138; Reagan, *An American Life,* 72–73; Reagan and Hubler, *Where's the Rest of Me?* 58–60.

27. Cannon, *Reagan,* 43–44, 47–48; Edwards, *Early Reagan,* 98–99, 131–36, 141–43; Wills, *Reagan's America,* 107, 111–12; Reagan and Hubler, *Where's the Rest of Me?* 45; Reagan, *An American Life,* 75–76.

28. Reagan and Hubler, *Where's the Rest of Me?* 63–64; Edwards, *Early Reagan,* 133, 142–44; Reagan, *An American Life,* 66–67. For Reagan's early interest in politics, see the item by Melissa Williams and Utley Noble, Reagan folder, Dixon Public Library.

29. Kenneth J. Gergen, *The Saturated Self: Dilemmas of Identity in Contemporary Life,* 6–7, 201–5; Robert Jay Lifton, *The Protean Self: Human Resilience in an Age of Fragmentation,* 1–3, 8–9, 32, 74–75, 87–89, 115, 120.

30. First quotation in Reagan, *First Father, First Daughter,* 402; second quotation in photocopy of Reagan's handwritten letter reproduced in Patti Davis, *Angels Don't Die: My Father's Gift of Faith,* 124; see Reagan poem "Life" in Reagan folder, Dixon Public Library; Reagan and Novak, *My Turn,* 108; Deaver and Herskowitz, *Behind the Scenes,* 41.

31. Quotation in Reagan and Novak, *My Turn,* 106; Edmund Morris, "This Living Hand," *The New Yorker,* 16 January 1995, 68; Cannon, *President Reagan,* 33, 174–76.

32. First quotation in Edwards, *Early Reagan,* 99; second quotation in Bob Woodward, *Veil: The Secret Wars of the CIA, 1981–1987,* 403–4; Cannon, *Reagan,* 26; Cannon, *President Reagan,* 17, 180.

33. Reagan and Novak, *My Turn,* 104.

34. Quotation in Noonan, *What I Saw,* 151; Deaver and Herskowitz, *Behind the Scenes,* 104.

35. Cannon, *Reagan,* 19; Deaver and Herskowitz, *Behind the Scenes,* 177; Franklyn C. Nofziger, *Nofziger,* 45.

36. First quotation in William French Smith, *Law and Justice in the Reagan Administration: The Memoirs of an Attorney General,* 11; second quotation in Joseph E. Persico, *Casey: From the OSS to the CIA,* 186; third and fourth quotations in Noonan, *What I Saw,* 151, 199–200; Selwa "Lucky" Roosevelt, *Keeper of the Gate,* 199; Martin Anderson, *Revolution: The Reagan Legacy,* 51, 279, 341; Laurence I. Barrett, *Gambling with History: Ronald Reagan in the White House,* 25; Reagan, *First Father, First Daughter,* 318; Cannon, *President Reagan,* 106; Elliott Abrams, "Reagan's Leadership: Mystery Man or Ideological Guide?" 99; Barry M. Goldwater and Jack Casserly, *Goldwater,* 393; Paul Beck, oral history interview; Robert Carleson, oral history interview; Gaylord B. Parkinson, oral history interview.

37. Cannon, *President Reagan,* 137–39; Howard Gardner, *Frames of Mind: The Theory of Multiple Intelligences,* 73–98, 205–76.

Chapter 2: Finding Fame and Fortune in Hollywood, 1937–1966

1. Reagan, *An American Life,* 76–81; Reagan and Hubler, *Where's the Rest of Me?* 69–77; Doug McClelland, *Hollywood on Ronald Reagan: Friends and Enemies Discuss Our*

President, the Actor, 154, 156, 178–79; Ronald Reagan, "The Making of a Movie Star," *Des Moines Sunday Register,* 13 June 1937.

2. Edwards, *Early Reagan,* 156–57.

3. Ibid., 161, 165; Reagan, *An American Life,* 116. For descriptions of each Reagan movie and other information on his entertainment career, see Edwards, *Early Reagan,* 495–525; Tony Thomas, *The Films of Ronald Reagan;* and Arthur F. McClure, C. David Rice, and William T. Stewart, *Ronald Reagan: His First Career, A Bibliography of the Movie Years.*

4. Reagan, *An American Life,* 116–18; Thomas, *Films of Ronald Reagan,* 9.

5. Ronald Reagan, *Public Papers of the Presidents of the United States: Ronald Reagan, 1981,* 1023; Reagan and Hubler, *Where's the Rest of Me?* 75–77; Edwards, *Early Reagan,* 164–65.

6. Reagan and Hubler, *Where's the Rest of Me?* 77–80; Thomas, *Films of Ronald Reagan,* 31–34; "Dutch Is Hit in First Film," *Des Moines Sunday Register,* 22 August 1937; Vaughn, *Ronald Reagan in Hollywood,* 41–44, 46–47, 51, 67–68, 79.

7. Edwards, *Early Reagan,* 174.

8. Dialogue transcribed by author from film, *Sergeant Murphy* (1938); for a discussion of racial issues and Reagan's films, see Vaughn, *Ronald Reagan in Hollywood,* 56–58, 66.

9. The articles ran in the *Des Moines Sunday Register* from 13 June to 3 October 1937.

10. Quotation·in Ronald Reagan, "The Role I Liked Best," 67; Edwards, *Early Reagan,* 184–85; Vaughn, *Ronald Reagan in Hollywood,* 30.

11. First quotation in McClelland, *Hollywood on Ronald Reagan,* 150, 233; second quotation in Reagan and Hall, "How to Make Yourself Important"; Cannon, *President Reagan,* 33, 46, 53; Cannon, *Reagan,* 66; Wills, *Reagan's America,* 178–79; Vaughn, *Ronald Reagan in Hollywood,* 72; Edwards, *Early Reagan,* 187, 232; Laurence Leamer, *Make-Believe: The Story of Nancy and Ronald Reagan,* 97–98.

12. Joe Morella and Edward Z. Epstein, *Jane Wyman,* 26–27; Edwards, *Early Reagan,* 188–92.

13. McClelland, *Hollywood on Ronald Reagan,* 24, 26, 66; Reagan and Hubler, *Where's the Rest of Me?* 201; Morella and Epstein, *Jane Wyman,* 27, 37, 79; Wills, *Reagan's America,* 145; Edwards, *Early Reagan,* 188–94; Cannon, *Reagan,* 60–61.

14. Quotations in Edwards, *Early Reagan,* 205, 226–27, 229; McClelland, *Hollywood on Ronald Reagan,* 26, 28.

15. Quotation transcribed by author from the film; Cannon, *Reagan,* 54–56; Pat O'Brien, *The Wind at My Back: The Life and Times of Pat O'Brien,* 240; Reagan and Hubler, *Where's the Rest of Me?* 90–95; Rudy Behlmer, ed., *Inside Warner Bros., 1935–1951,* 113–15.

16. Wills, *Reagan's America,* 120–21, 411; Vaughn, *Ronald Reagan in Hollywood,* 81–86; Reagan, *Public Papers, 1981,* 431–35.

17. Quotation in Reagan and Hall, "How to Make Yourself Important"; Thomas, *Films of Ronald Reagan,* 109–14; Vaughn, *Ronald Reagan in Hollywood,* 87–91.

18. Cannon, *Reagan,* 56; Edwards, *Early Reagan,* 206–9; Vaughn, *Ronald Reagan in Hollywood,* 36–37; David Ogilvy, *Ogilvy on Advertising,* 159.

19. Thomas, *Films of Ronald Reagan,* 128–32; Behlmer, *Inside Warner Bros.,* 137–39; for a critical analysis of the film, see Wills, *Reagan's America,* 174–77, 418 note 7.

20. Vaughn, *Ronald Reagan in Hollywood,* 105–8; Edwards, *Early Reagan,* 261, 267–68; Cannon, *Reagan,* 57.

21. Morella and Epstein, *Jane Wyman,* 4, 57, 77; Vaughn, *Ronald Reagan in Hollywood,* 104–5, 112–18; McClelland, *Hollywood on Ronald Reagan,* 28–50.

22. Edwards, *Early Reagan,* 255, 290–91; Reagan and Hubler, *Where's the Rest of Me?* 140–41.

23. Thomas, *Films of Ronald Reagan,* 145–55; Vaughn, *Ronald Reagan in Hollywood,* 219; Edwards, *Early Reagan,* 322–25.

24. Quotation in McClelland, *Hollywood on Ronald Reagan,* 30, 32, 62, 74; Wills, *Reagan's America,* 172–73; Edwards, *Early Reagan,* 279–83, 290; Morella and Epstein, *Jane*

Wyman, 109; Michael Reagan and Joe Hyams, *On the Outside Looking In,* 20; Reagan, *First Father, First Daughter,* 44–45.

25. Edwards, *Early Reagan,* 325–32, 353–55; Morella and Epstein, *Jane Wyman,* 122–26; June Allyson and Frances Spatz Leighton, *June Allyson,* 96; Cannon, *Reagan,* 62–64; Cannon, *President Reagan,* 226–28.

26. First quotation in Cannon, *President Reagan,* 228; second quotation in Reagan and Hubler, *Where's the Rest of Me?* 201; third quotation in Dan E. Moldea, *Dark Victory: Ronald Reagan, MCA, and the Mob,* 78; Cannon, *Reagan,* 64–65; Edwards, *Early Reagan,* 229–30, 254–55, 320–21; Michael Freedland, *The Warner Brothers,* 201; Morella and Epstein, *Jane Wyman,* 62; Robert Perrella, *They Call Me the Showbiz Priest,* 130–31.

27. Cannon, *Reagan,* 72; Reagan and Hubler, *Where's the Rest of Me?* 130–32; Edwards, *Early Reagan,* 295–97, 351; Wills, *Reagan's America,* 215–22, 423 note 13.

28. Reagan and Hubler, *Where's the Rest of Me?* 132–33.

29. Ibid., 176–77; Edwards, *Early Reagan,* 231, 435, 494; David F. Prindle, *The Politics of Glamour: Ideology and Democracy in the Screen Actors Guild,* 4–5, 8, 31.

30. Quotations in Moldea, *Dark Victory,* 65–69; Wills, *Reagan's America,* 224–30, 232–44, 251–53; Cannon, *Reagan,* 72–76; Cannon, *President Reagan,* 284–85; Vaughn, *Ronald Reagan in Hollywood,* 134–43; Reagan and Hubler, *Where's the Rest of Me?* 126–30, 133–38, 142–57, 159–62; Edwards, *Early Reagan,* 311–17. For a discussion of organized crime in Hollywood, see George Murphy and Victor Lasky, *"Say Didn't You Used to Be George Murphy?"* 219–24; for a history of the formation of SAG, see Prindle, *Politics of Glamour,* 16–36, 39–50; for internal politics in Hollywood guilds, see Nancy L. Schwartz and Sheila Schwartz, *The Hollywood Writers' Wars,* 248–51.

31. Edwards, *Early Reagan,* 172–73, 230, 292–93; Thomas, *Films of Ronald Reagan,* 9; A.E. Hotchner, *Doris Day: Her Own Story,* 121; McClelland, *Hollywood on Ronald Reagan,* 158, 194, 228.

32. Quotation in Ronald Reagan, "Fascist Ideas Are Still Alive in U.S.," 6; Kotkin and Grabowicz, *California, Inc.,* 58; Reagan and Hubler, *Where's the Rest of Me?* 139–42; Edwards, *Early Reagan,* 293, 295; Ingrid Winther Scobie, *Center Stage: Helen Gahagan Douglas, A Life,* 220, 227, 236; Helen Gahagan Douglas, *A Full Life,* 323; Vaughn, *Ronald Reagan in Hollywood,* 4, 121–22, 171–72.

33. Vaughn, *Ronald Reagan in Hollywood,* 122–32, 157–59, 162–70, 175–81, 290 note 4; Edwards, *Early Reagan,* 302–4, 417–18; Wills, *Reagan's America,* 72–77, 145–49; Ronald Brownstein, *The Power and the Glitter: The Hollywood-Washington Connection,* 106–11; Reagan and Hubler, *Where's the Rest of Me?* 166–69.

34. Reagan to Antonio L. Reed, 28 September 1981, ID: 046810, WHORM: Subject: BE, Reagan presidential papers, Wills, *Reagan's America,* 245–46, 257–50, Cannon, *Ronnie and Jesse,* 158; Allyson and Leighton, *June Allyson,* 95–96, 139–40; Edwards, *Early Reagan,* 196–97, 228, 273; Kotkin and Grabowicz, *California, Inc.,* 60–62; Ronald Reagan, "Motion Pictures and Your Community," 25.

35. William E. Pemberton, *Harry S. Truman: Fair Dealer and Cold Warrior,* 71–77, 96–99, 107, 109–10, 150–56.

36. First quotation in Reagan and Hubler, *Where's the Rest of Me?* 158–59, 162–65, 169; second quotation in Reagan, *An American Life,* 114–15; Murphy and Lasky, *"Say,"* 279–96; Lary May, "Movie Star Politics: The Screen Actors' Guild, Cultural Conversion, and the Hollywood Red Scare," 143–44, 148; Edwards, *Early Reagan,* 297–99; Harvey Klehr, John Earl Haynes, and Fridrikh Igorevich Firsov, *The Secret World of American Communism,* 9; Wills, *Reagan's America,* 247–49; Larry Ceplair and Steven Englund, *The Inquisition in Hollywood: Politics in the Film Community, 1930–1960,* 201–3, 206.

37. Quotations in Eric Bentley, ed., *Thirty Years of Treason: Excerpts from Hearings before the House Committee on Un-American Activities, 1938–1968,* 144–47; Gordon Kahn, *Hollywood on Trial: The Story of the Ten Who Were Indicted,* 59.

38. First quotation in Moldea, *Dark Victory,* 78–79; second quotation in Kotkin and

Grabowicz, *California, Inc.,* 59–60; Edwards, *Early Reagan,* 304–7; Wills, *Reagan's America,* 249–50; Reagan and Hubler, *Where's the Rest of Me?* 169–71; Reagan, *An American Life,* 111.

39. Ceplair and Englund, *Inquisition in Hollywood,* 328–31, 338–39, 445; Vaughn, *Ronald Reagan in Hollywood,* 153–55; Cannon, *Reagan,* 85–86.

40. Quotation in Victor S. Navasky, *Naming Names,* 87, 124; Wills, *Reagan's America,* 254–55, 258; Cannon, *President Reagan,* 286–87; Prindle, *Politics of Glamour,* 55; Schwartz and Schwartz, *Hollywood Writers' Wars,* 282; Vaughn, *Ronald Reagan in Hollywood,* 146, 206–17; Michael P. Rogin, *Ronald Reagan, the Movie: And Other Episodes in Political Demonology,* 32; May, "Movie Star Politics," 145. On Anne Revere, see Edwards, *Early Reagan,* 335–36, 350–51. For Reagan's comments on the blacklist, see Robert Scheer, *With Enough Shovels: Reagan, Bush, and Nuclear War,* 254–55; Brownstein, *Power and the Glitter,* 112–16; and Helene von Damm, ed., *Sincerely, Ronald Reagan,* 15. For a study of the blacklist, see Stefan Kanfer, *A Journal of the Plague Years.*

41. Edwards, *Early Reagan,* 425–28.

42. Vaughn, *Ronald Reagan in Hollywood,* 182–83; Moldea, *Dark Victory,* 75–76; Cannon, *Reagan,* 87; Scheer, *With Enough Shovels,* 255; Edwards, *Early Reagan,* 404.

43. Prindle, *Politics of Glamour,* 71–74.

44. Quotation in Moldea, *Dark Victory,* epigraph, see also 2–3, 13–19, 22–30, 62; Brownstein, *Power and the Glitter,* 179–83; Edwards, *Early Reagan,* 211–13.

45. Wills, *Reagan's America,* 266; Timothy R. White, "Hollywood's Attempt at Appropriating Television: The Case of Paramount Pictures," 145–49; Prindle, *Politics of Glamour,* 78.

46. Quotation in Moldea, *Dark Victory,* 177–78, 182–83; Brownstein, *Power and the Glitter,* 183; Wills, *Reagan's America,* 263–66; Prindle, *Politics of Glamour,* 78–80.

47. First quotation in Moldea, *Dark Victory,* 103; second quotation in Brownstein, *Power and the Glitter,* 183 note.

48. Moldea, *Dark Victory,* 3; Brownstein, *Power and the Glitter,* 183–84; Wills, *Reagan's America,* 266.

49. Prindle, *Politics of Glamour,* 80–82; Edwards, *Early Reagan,* 435–40; Wills, *Reagan's America,* 278; Moldea, *Dark Victory,* 101–4, 203.

50. Wills, *Reagan's America,* 268–70; Brownstein, *Power and the Glitter,* 186–87, 220–21.

51. Moldea, *Dark Victory,* 139, 142–43; Edwards, *Early Reagan,* 467–72; Wills, *Reagan's America,* 275–77; Reagan and Hubler, *Where's the Rest of Me?* 276–77; for the views of an older actor, see Mickey Rooney to Reagan, 30 March 1981, ID: 017815, WHORM: Subject: BE, Reagan presidential papers.

52. Quotations in Moldea, *Dark Victory,* 167–185; Moldea printed the entire verbatim testimony. See also Wills, *Reagan's America,* 270–75; Edwards, *Early Reagan,* 441.

53. Kitty Kelley, *Nancy Reagan: The Unauthorized Biography,* 19, 22–28; Reagan and Novak, *My Turn,* 33, 66–67, 72–75, 82–83; Cannon, *Reagan,* 141–42; Edwards, *Early Reagan,* 386–87; Loyal E. Davis, *A Surgeon's Odyssey,* 231. For contrasting studies of Nancy Reagan, see Leamer, *Make-Believe;* James S. Rosebush, *First Lady, Public Wife: A Behind-the-Scenes History of the Evolving Role of First Ladies in America Political Life;* and Frances S. Leighton, *The Search for the Real Nancy Reagan.*

54. Reagan and Novak, *My Turn,* 83–88; Cannon, *Reagan,* 89–90; Edwards, *Early Reagan,* 375–76, 392–93.

55. Edwards, *Early Reagan,* 377–79, 420 (for Nancy Davis's film and stage credits, see 532–36); Wills, *Reagan's America,* 180–88; Reagan and Novak, *My Turn,* 89–92; Leamer, *Make-Believe,* 167; Dore Schary and Charles Palmer, *Case History of a Movie,* 42–45.

56. Quotation in Reagan and Novak, *My Turn,* 123; Reagan and Hubler, *Where's the Rest of Me?* 208; Cannon, *Reagan,* 89; Reagan, *An American Life,* 123.

57. Quotations in Reagan and Novak, *My Turn,* 93–96, 100, 103; Mervyn LeRoy and Dick Kleiner, *Mervyn LeRoy: Take One,* 192–93; Edwards, *Early Reagan,* 394, 400–403.

58. First quotation in Reagan to Ethel M. McHenry, 13 June 1984, ID: 236827, WHORM:

Subject: FG, Reagan presidential papers; second quotation in Reagan, *An American Life,* 123; Reagan and Novak, *My Turn,* viii, 35.

59. Quotation in von Damm, *Sincerely, Ronald Reagan,* 121–22; Cannon, *Ronnie and Jesse,* 160–61.

60. Reagan and Hubler, *Where's the Rest of Me?* 241; Reagan and Novak, *My Turn,* 179.

61. Reagan and Novak, *My Turn,* 146–47, 149.

62. Reagan and Hyams, *On the Outside,* 14–15, 32–33, 52, 71, 76–77; Reagan and Novak, *My Turn,* 151–61; Edwards, *Early Reagan,* 255; Cannon, *President Reagan,* 228.

63. Quotations in Davis, *Way I See It,* 15, 18–20, 29–30, 33–41, 51–54, 90, 134; Reagan and Novak, *My Turn,* 169–76; see also the novel by Patti Davis and Maureen S. Foster, *Home Front.*

64. Quotation in Cannon, *Reagan,* 65–66; Reagan and Hubler, *Where's the Rest of Me?* 185–86; Edwards, *Early Reagan,* 409–10, 444; Wills, *Reagan's America,* 173–74.

65. First quotation in Behlmer, *Inside Warner Bros.,* 314–15; second quotation in Cannon, *Reagan,* 66–67; third quotation in Edwards, *Early Reagan,* 405–8.

66. Reagan and Hubler, *Where's the Rest of Me?* 216–17; Cannon, *Reagan,* 67–68; Edwards, *Early Reagan,* 396–97.

67. Thomas, *Films of Ronald Reagan,* 169–72; Edwards, *Early Reagan,* 370.

68. Thomas, *Films of Ronald Reagan,* 193–97; Edwards, *Early Reagan,* 428.

69. First quotation in McClelland, *Hollywood on Ronald Reagan,* 227; second quotation in Brownstein, *Power and the Glitter,* 219–20.

70. Quotation in Moldea, *Dark Victory,* 106–9, 189–99; Edwards, *Early Reagan,* 447 (for Reagan's television credits 526–31); Reagan and Novak, *My Turn,* 124–30; Wills, *Reagan's America,* 262–63; Cannon, *Reagan,* 92; Deaver and Herskowitz, *Behind the Scenes,* 40.

71. Quotation in McClelland, *Hollywood on Ronald Reagan,* 134; Vaughn, *Ronald Reagan in Hollywood,* 232.

Chapter 3: The Turn toward Conservatism, 1947–1980

1. Melvin J. Thorne, *American Conservative Thought since World War II: The Core Ideas,* 4–7; Alan Brinkley, "The Problem of American Conservatism," 409–10, 414–22.

2. William B. Hixson, *Search for the American Right Wing: An Analysis of the Social Science Record,* xxvi, 306; Leo P. Ribuffo, "Why Is There So Much Conservatism in the United States and Why Do So Few Historians Know Anything About It?" 438–39, 442–47; Alexander M. Haig, *Caveat: Realism, Reagan, and Foreign Policy,* 20–25.

3. Thorne, *American Conservative Thought,* 8–10. See also David G. Green, *The New Conservatism: The Counter-Revolution in Political, Economic, and Social Thought;* and J. David Hoeveler, *Watch on the Right: Conservative Intellectuals in the Reagan Era.*

4. Thorne, *American Conservative Thought,* 10–11; George H. Nash, *The Conservative Intellectual Movement in America since 1945,* 86; Paul Gottfried, *The Conservative Movement,* 3–5; Jerome L. Himmelstein, *To the Right: The Transformation of American Conservatism,* 13–24; William C. Berman, *America's Right Turn: From Nixon to Bush,* 2; David W. Reinhard, *The Republican Right since 1945,* 2–4; Fred Siegel, "Liberalism," 654–55.

5. Nash, *Conservative Intellectual Movement,* 4–18, 20–31, 33–35; Himmelstein, *To the Right,* 45–50; Gottfried, *Conservative Movement,* 5–10.

6. Nash, *Conservative Intellectual Movement,* 36–46, 49–53, 55–56, 58–67, 77–82; Thorne, *American Conservative Thought,* 11–12; Gottfried, *Conservative Movement,* 7, 17–18, 20, 23; Wills, *Reagan's America,* 381–82.

7. von Damm, *Sincerely, Ronald Reagan,* 213.

8. Nash, *Conservative Intellectual Movement,* 84–105, 109–17, 119–23, 292–93; Hixson, *Search for American Right Wing,* 46–47; Gottfried, *Conservative Movement,* 11–16; Thorne, *American Conservative Thought,* 12; Sara Diamond, *Roads to Dominion: Right-Wing Movements and Political Power in the United States,* 19–20, 37–38, 307; Himmelstein, *To the Right,* 44–45.

9. Reinhard, *Republican Right,* 115–58; Hixson, *Search for American Right Wing,* 52–60; Nicol C. Rae, *The Decline and Fall of the Liberal Republicans: From 1952 to the Present,* 46–48, 79–80, 86–87, 118–20; Mary C. Brennan, *Turning Right in the Sixties: The Conservative Capture of the GOP,* 7–18.

10. Reagan to Nixon, 27 June 1959, Reagan folder, Richard M. Nixon prepresidential papers, National Archives, Pacific Southwest Region, Laguna Niguel, California.

11. Reagan and Hubler, *Where's the Rest of Me?* 139; Reagan, *An American Life,* 134–35; Cannon, *Reagan,* 91; Cannon, *President Reagan,* 108; Barrett, *Gambling with History,* 56–58.

12. Quotations in Ronald Reagan, Address, "America the Beautiful," 9–13; Barrett, *Gambling with History,* 30, 51–52.

13. Quotation in John S. Saloma, *Ominous Politics: The New Conservative Labyrinth,* 64; Cannon, *Reagan,* 92–93; Reagan, *An American Life,* 127; Reagan and Hubler, *Where's the Rest of Me?* 257–59; Wills, *Reagan's America,* 283.

14. Quotations in Kurt Ritter and David Henry, *Ronald Reagan: The Great Communicator,* 14; Reagan to Mr. Hansen, 19 September [1961], Reagan (GE and Reagan) folder, Drew Pearson papers, Lyndon B. Johnson Library, Austin, Texas; Cannon, *Reagan,* 94; Cannon, *President Reagan,* 88–93; Reagan and Hubler, *Where's the Rest of Me?* 259–60, 266–68; Reagan, *An American Life,* 128–29. See also Ronald Reagan, *A Time for Choosing: The Speeches of Ronald Reagan, 1961–1982.*

15. Ronald Reagan, Address, "Encroaching Control."

16. Patrick Buchanan to RN [Nixon], undated handwritten note, Campaign of 1968 Research Files Ronald Reagan folder, PPS 500.105.24.1, Richard M. Nixon papers, Richard Nixon Library, Yorba Linda, California; Barrett, *Gambling with History,* 47–48.

17. Quotation from transcript, *CBS Reports,* "What About Ronald Reagan?" 12 December 1967, Miscellaneous Speeches and Scripts folder, Press Unit, Reagan gubernatorial papers, Hoover Institution, Stanford University, Stanford, California; Ritter and Henry, *Ronald Reagan,* 23; Reagan and Hubler, *Where's the Rest of Me?* 268–72; Cannon, *Reagan,* 95–96; Navasky, *Naming Names,* 227; Moldea, *Dark Victory,* 223–24; Cannon, *Ronnie and Jesse,* 69–70.

18. Cannon, *Reagan,* 96–97; Cannon, *Ronnie and Jesse,* 69–70; Reagan and Hubler, *Where's the Rest of Me?* 272–73. For an argument that the program was canceled because Reagan was called before the grand jury investigation on MCA, see Wills, *Reagan's America,* 284–85; for General Electric's description of its relationship with Reagan, see M. M. Masterpool to Newspaper Editors, 23 September 1966, Reagan (G.E. and Reagan) folder, Pearson papers.

19. Quotations in Nixon to Reagan, 18 June 1959, and Nixon to Reagan, 6 July 1959, Reagan folder, Nixon prepresidential papers; Brennan, *Turning Right,* 19–20; Reagan, *An American Life,* 132–34.

20. Reagan to Nixon, 15 July [1960], Reagan folder, Nixon prepresidential papers.

21. First quotation in Robert A. Goldberg, *Barry Goldwater,* x, 118–25, 145, 181, 217–18, 336; second quotation transcribed by author from Goldwater's introduction to the videotape of Ronald Reagan, Address, "A Time for Choosing"; Nofziger, *Nofziger,* 12; Anderson, *Revolution,* xviii–xix; Brennan, *Turning Right,* 82, 85–86; E. J. Dionne, *Why Americans Hate Politics,* 180–83.

22. Goldberg, *Barry Goldwater,* 181, 234–36; Brennan, *Turning Right,* 41–43, 103; Dionne, *Why Americans Hate Politics,* 184–86; Berman, *America's Right Turn,* 5–6.

23. Quotations transcribed by author from videotape of Reagan Address, "A Time for Choosing"; Reagan, *An American Life,* 139–41; Cannon, *Ronnie and Jesse,* 71–72; Cannon, *Reagan,* 13; Wills, *Reagan's America,* 291; Stephen Shadegg, *What Happened to Goldwater? The Inside Story of the 1964 Republican Campaign,* 252–53.

24. Ritter and Henry, *Ronald Reagan,* 24; Reagan, *An American Life,* 141–43.

25. Quotation in Reinhard, *Republican Right,* 208–9; Goldwater and Casserly, *Goldwater,* 388; Goldberg, *Barry Goldwater,* 237.

26. Quotation in Diamond, *Roads to Dominion,* 1; Patrick J. Buchanan, *Right from the*

Beginning, 275; James Davison Hunter, *Before the Shooting Begins: Searching for Democracy in America's Culture War,* 5, 8–10, 15–17, 19–21, 30–32; James Davison Hunter, *Culture Wars: The Struggle to Define America,* 42, 52–53; Charles W. Dunn and J. David Woodard, *American Conservatism from Burke to Bush: An Introduction,* 171; Dionne, *Why Americans Hate Politics,* 12.

27. Berman, *America's Right Turn,* 164–65; Thomas B. Edsall and Mary D. Edsall, *Chain Reaction: The Impact of Race, Rights, and Taxes on American Politics,* ix–x.

28. Jonathan Rieder, "The Rise of the 'Silent Majority,' " 243, 245–47; Jack W. Germond and Jules Witcover, *Wake Us When It's Over: Presidential Politics of 1984,* 22–27; Andrew Hacker, *Two Nations: Black and White, Separate, Hostile, Unequal,* 50–64, 200–202; Diamond, *Roads to Dominion,* 66–67, 90–91; Frederick F. Siegel, *Troubled Journey: From Pearl Harbor to Ronald Reagan,* 162–67; Dionne, *Why Americans Hate Politics,* 90; Edsall and Edsall, *Chain Reaction,* 7–9; James L. Sundquist, *Dynamics of the Party System: Alignment and Realignment of Political Parties in the United States,* 352.

29. Quotation in Dionne, *Why Americans Hate Politics,* 92–93, 95–97; Rieder, "Rise of the 'Silent Majority,' " 253–57; Siegel, *Troubled Journey,* 167–68; Edsall and Edsall, *Chain Reaction,* 3–5, 48–49.

30. Siegel, *Troubled Journey,* 169–70; Edsall and Edsall, *Chain Reaction,* 75–78; Dionne, *Why Americans Hate Politics,* 90–91, 121.

31. Andrew N. Greeley, "Turning Off 'the People,' " attachment to Chester Finn to Ed Morgan et al., 23 June 1970, untitled folder, Chester E. Finn papers, Hoover Institution; Siegel, *Troubled Journey,* 110–11, 131–49, 151, 179; Dionne, *Why Americans Hate Politics,* 31, 38–44, 50–54; Edsall and Edsall, *Chain Reaction,* 262–63; Michael P. Riccards, *The Ferocious Engine of Democracy: A History of the American Presidency,* 363.

32. Cannon, *Reagan,* 273–74; Hixson, *Search for American Right Wing,* 179; Dunn and Woodard, *American Conservatism,* 160–61; Hunter, *Culture Wars,* 34–51, 53–57, 62–64, 67–72, 77–97, 108–16, 120–26, 128–31, 136–52, 159–60, 163–68, 173, 176–77.

33. Quotation in Edsall and Edsall, *Chain Reaction,* 5, 14–16, 165; Dionne, *Why Americans Hate Politics,* 12–14, 16–22, 75–76, 78–80; Berman, *America's Right Turn,* 1; Rieder, "Rise of the 'Silent Majority,' " 258; Shelby Steele, "How Liberals Lost Their Virtue over Race," 41–42; Siegel, *Troubled Journey,* 175–76; William G. Mayer, *The Changing American Mind: How and Why American Public Opinion Changed between 1960 and 1968,* 337–38. For a study of Democratic Party's shift to the right, see Randall Rothenberg, *The Neoliberals: Creating the New American Politics.*

34. Hixson, *Search for American Right Wing,* 122–23; Stephan Lesher, *George Wallace: American Populist,* xi–xii, 311–13, 491; Rieder, "Rise of the 'Silent Majority,' " 249–51; Berman, *America's Right Turn,* 7–11; Brennan, *Turning Right,* 128, 134–37; Siegel, *Troubled Journey,* 202–3. See also Dan T. Carter, *The Politics of Rage: George Wallace, the Origins of the New Conservatism, and the Transformation of American Politics.*

35. Saloma, *Ominous Politics,* 7–21; Dionne, *Why Americans Hate Politics,* 55–75, 144; Gottfried, *Conservative Movement,* 31–35, 78–90, 151; Dunn and Woodard, *American Conservatism,* 12–13, 40–41; Wills, *Reagan's America,* 340–42; Berman, *America's Right Turn,* 64–66; Diamond, *Roads to Dominion,* 178–80, 185, 195–98. See also Peter Steinfels, *The Neoconservatives: The Men Who Are Changing America's Politics.*

36. Siegel, *Troubled Journey,* 207–9; Dionne, *Why Americans Hate Politics,* 104–7.

37. Dionne, *Why Americans Hate Politics,* 108–15; Hixson, *Search for American Right Wing,* 323–24.

38. Berman, *America's Right Turn,* 12–14; Siegel, *Troubled Journey,* 230–37, 267–68, 271–72.

39. Quotation in Dionne, *Why Americans Hate Politics,* 199–200, 204–8; Brennan, *Turning Right,* 3–4; Frederick F. Siegel, "Conservatism," 222–23; Patrick Buchanan interview, 13 September 1977, Reichley papers; Michael P. Federici, *The Challenge of Populism: The Rise of Right-Wing Democratism in Postwar America,* 25–27, 37–39, 94; Michael Kazin, "The Grass-Roots Right: New Histories of U.S. Conservatism in the Twentieth Century," 136–46;

Michael Kazin, *The Populist Persuasion: An American History,* 246–48, 250, 253.

40. Federici, *Challenge of Populism,* 75–89; Berman, *America's Right Turn,* 28–30, 61–63; Himmelstein, *To the Right,* 64–65, 77, 80–93; Gottfried, *Conservative Movement,* 97–100, 105–9, 111–13; Diamond, *Roads to Dominion,* 110, 127–28, 135–37; Hixson, *Search for American Right Wing,* 177–79, 183–86, 211, 227, 231; Dionne, *Why Americans Hate Politics,* 228–31; Jerry Falwell, *Strength for the Journey,* 358–65; Kazin, *Populist Persuasion,* 247. For a collection of essays on the New Right, see Robert W. Whitaker, *The New Right Papers.*

41. Erling Jorstad, *Holding Fast/Pressing On: Religion in America in the 1980s,* 1–5, 54, 57–58; Matthew C. Moen, *The Christian Right and Congress,* 4, 10–30, 34–35; Steve Bruce, *The Rise and Fall of the New Christian Right: Conservative Protestant Politics in America, 1978–1988,* 13, 23, 29–34, 40–41, 44, 46, 76–79, 81–82, 168–70; Himmelstein, *To the Right,* 97–98, 100–105, 108–20, 126–28; Hixson, *Search for American Right Wing,* 242, 244–46; Leo P. Ribuffo, "God and Contemporary Politics," 1515–21; Dionne, *Why Americans Hate Politics,* 209–24; Diamond, *Roads to Dominion,* 95–106, 161–62; Gottfried, *Conservative Movement,* 102–3; Wilbur Edel, *Defenders of the Faith: Religion and Politics from the Pilgrim Fathers to Ronald Reagan,* 124–29, 135–37; Federici, *Challenge of Populism,* 74–75; Richard V. Pierard and Robert D. Linder, *Civil Religion and the Presidency,* 263–64. For political aspects of conservative Christianity, see Robert Wuthnow, *The Restructuring of American Religion: Society and Faith since World War II;* Leo P. Ribuffo, *The Old Christian Right: The Protestant Far Right from the Great Depression to the Cold War;* Martin E. Marty and R. Scott Appleby, *The Glory and the Power: The Fundamentalist Challenge to the Modern World;* Robert C. Liebman and Robert Wuthnow, eds., *The New Christian Right: Mobilization and Legitimation;* Richard J. Neuhaus and Michael Cromartie, eds., *Piety and Politics: Evangelicals and Fundamentalists Confront the World;* Michael Lienesch, *Redeeming America: Piety and Politics in the New Christian Right;* and Mayer, *Changing American Mind,* 30–34.

42. Himmelstein, *To the Right,* 120–24; Dionne, *Why Americans Hate Politics,* 233–36; Hixson, *Search for American Right Wing,* 258–62, 265; Jorstad, *Holding Fast/Pressing On,* 54; Hunter, *Culture Wars,* 296. See also Sara Diamond, *Spiritual Warfare: The Politics of the Christian Right,* and Patrick Allitt, *Catholic Intellectuals and Conservative Politics in America, 1950–1985.*

43. First quotation in Reagan to Mary E. Rogers, 23 January 1980, RR Correspondence 1980 folder, Ronald Reagan Subject Collection, Hoover Institution; second quotation in Pierard and Linder, *Civil Religion,* 262–63, 267–72; third quotation in Jorstad, *Holding Fast/Pressing On,* 59; Moen, *Christian Right and Congress,* 51; Richard V. Pierard, "Reagan and the Evangelicals: The Making of a Love Affair," 1183–84; Doug Wead and Bill Wead, *Reagan: In Pursuit of the Presidency, 1980,* 166–67, 172–73, 183.

44. Diamond, *Roads to Dominion,* 309; Himmelstein, *To the Right,* 129–51, 161–65; Hixson, *Search for American Right Wing,* 179–82; Berman, *America's Right Turn,* 3, 25–26, 40–42, 45–46, 68–71; Siegel, *Troubled Journey,* 268–69. For a study of PACs, see Larry J. Sabato, *PAC Power: Inside the World of Political Action Committees.*

45. Quotation in von Damm, *Sincerely, Ronald Reagan,* 88, 211–12; Kazin, *Populist Persuasion,* 262; Himmelstein, *To the Right,* 123; Dunn and Woodard, *American Conservatism,* 14–16; Donald J. Devine, *Reagan's Terrible Swift Sword: Reforming and Controlling the Federal Bureaucracy,* 15. For an evaluation of Reagan's brand of conservatism, see Sidney Blumenthal, *The Rise of the Counter-Establishment: From Conservative Ideology to Political Power.*

46. Quotation in von Damm, *Sincerely, Ronald Reagan,* 94, 96–97; Kazin, *Populist Persuasion,* 261–63; Edsall and Edsall, *Chain Reaction,* 138–39; Brennan, *Turning Right,* 134; Dionne, *Why Americans Hate Politics,* 231–32; John Sears interview, 26 August 1977, Reichley papers.

Chapter 4: Governing California, 1967–1974

1. Quotation in Edwards, *Early Reagan,* 488. For books that concentrate on Reagan's California years, see George H. Smith, *Who Is Ronald Reagan?;* Bill Boyarsky, *Ronald*

Reagan: His Life and Rise to the Presidency; Lee Edwards, *Ronald Reagan: A Political Biography;* Gary G. Hamilton and Nicole Woolsey Biggart, *Governor Reagan, Governor Brown: A Sociology of Executive Power;* and Gladwin Hill, *Dancing Bear: An Inside Look at California Politics.*

2. Quotation in Kotkin and Grabowicz, *California, Inc.,* 50–52; Reagan, *An American Life,* 144–45; William French Smith, oral history interview.

3. Quotation in William E. Roberts, oral history interview; Stuart K. Spencer, oral history interview; Reagan, *An American Life,* 146–48; William Bagley, oral history interview. The politically astute Nixon quickly realized that Reagan was a new entrant into California politics and began to offer advice; see unsigned, unaddressed note, "Answers for Ronnie Reagan," 8 January 1965, PPS 501.1.1–41, Reagan folder, Nixon papers.

4. First quotation in Cannon, *Ronnie and Jesse,* 196–97; second quotation in Edwards, *Early Reagan,* 489; third quotation in Kotkin and Grabowicz, *California, Inc.,* 53; Spencer, oral history interview; Nofziger, *Nofziger,* 37, 45–46; Robert T. Monagan, oral history interview; Ronald Reagan, oral history interview.

5. Nofziger, *Nofziger,* 35–36; Franklyn C. Nofziger, oral history interview; Roberts, oral history interview; Spencer, oral history interview; Cannon, *President Reagan,* 42–43; Cannon, *Ronnie and Jesse,* 82.

6. First quotation in Reagan, *An American Life,* 149–50; second quotation in Nixon to Reagan, 30 April 1965, PPS 501.1.4; third quotation in Reagan to Nixon, 7 May 1965, PPS 501.1.5, Reagan folder, Nixon papers; Nofziger, oral history interview; Roberts, oral history interview; Reagan, oral history interview; Nofziger, *Nofziger,* 50–51; Walker, oral history interview; Parkinson, oral history interview; George Christopher, oral history interview.

7. First and second quotations in Cannon, *Reagan,* 115; third quotation in Nofziger, *Nofziger,* 38–42, 45, 83–85.

8. Cannon, *Reagan,* 118; Cannon, *Ronnie and Jesse,* 77–78; John J. Miller, oral history interview; Caspar W. Weinberger, oral history interview.

9. Quotation in Edmund G. Brown, *Reagan and Reality: The Two Californias,* 13; Cannon, *President Reagan,* 43–45; Ed Cray, "California: The Politics of Confusion," 8; Reagan, oral history interview; Reagan, *An American Life,* 150–52; Kotkin and Grabowicz, *California, Inc.,* 55–56; Joe Califano to Lyndon Johnson, 10 June 1966, Reagan folder, WHCF Name File, Lyndon B. Johnson papers, Lyndon B. Johnson Library; Stephen E. Ambrose, *Nixon: The Triumph of a Politician, 1962–1972,* 83.

10. Quotations in Reagan to John A. McCone, 3 October 1961, PPS 501.1.12.2, Reagan folder, Nixon Library; Hill, *Dancing Bear,* 243–44; Joseph Lewis, *What Makes Reagan Run? A Political Profile,* 86–87.

11. Quotation in John A. McCone, Memorandum for the Record, 14 October 1966, PPS 501.1.12.1; see also Reagan to McCone, 10 October 1966, PPS 501.1.13.2, and [McCone] memorandum entitled "Discussions with Senator Kuchel," 18 October 1966, PPS 501.1.15, Reagan folder, Nixon papers.

12. Quotation in Reagan, *An American Life,* 150; Joe Califano to Lyndon Johnson, 10 June 1966, Frederick G. Dutton to Bill D. Moyers, 10 June 1966, Reagan folder, WHCF Name File, Johnson papers.

13. First and second quotations in Dutton to Moyers, 10 June 1966, Reagan folder, WHCF Name File, Johnson papers; third quotation in Cannon, *Ronnie and Jesse,* 79–80.

14. Quotation in Nofziger, *Nofziger,* 222; Ritter and Henry, *Ronald Reagan,* 39–41; Edmund G. Brown, oral history interview, Lyndon B. Johnson Library; Wills, *Reagan's America,* 312. See also Pat Brown's books on his experience with Reagan, Brown, *Reagan and Reality,* and Edmund G. Brown and Bill Brown, *Reagan: The Political Chameleon.*

15. Quotation in Reagan, oral history interview; Cannon, *Reagan,* 118; Cannon, *Ronnie and Jesse,* 80–82, 259–62; Spencer, oral history interview; pamphlet, California Democratic State Central Committee, *Ronald Reagan: Extremist Collaborator, An Expose,* September 1966; Parkinson, oral history interview.

16. First quotation in Dutton to Moyers, 10 June 1966, Reagan folder, WHCF Name File, Johnson papers; second quotation in Louis E. Lomax, "Homosexual Scandal Hits Reagan's Administration," 4/5 November 1967, Reagan folder, Pearson papers; Cannon, *Ronnie and Jesse,* 82–84; Brown, oral history interview, Johnson Library; Reagan, *An American Life,* 152–54; Reagan, oral history interview; Spencer, oral history interview; Charles H. Shreve to John W. Gardner, 7 December 1966, Reagan folder, Office Files of Marvin Watson, Johnson papers.

17. Quotation in Reagan and Novak, *My Turn,* 132; Cannon, *Reagan,* 115–17.

18. First quotation in Cannon, *Ronnie and Jesse,* 130–31; second quotation in Cannon, *Reagan,* 122; third quotation in Ronald Reagan, *Ronald Reagan Talks to America,* 19–28.

19. First quotation in Nofziger, oral history interview; second quotation in Cannon, *Ronnie and Jesse,* 131; third quotation in von Damm, *Sincerely, Ronald Reagan,* 73; fourth quotation in Reagan, *An American Life,* 155–56, 166; Hamilton and Biggart, *Governor Reagan, Governor Brown,* 29; Spencer M. Williams, oral history interview; Vernon L. Sturgeon, oral history interview; Cannon, *President Reagan,* 47–48.

20. Quotation in Kotkin and Grabowicz, *California, Inc.,* 69; Nofziger, *Nofziger,* 57; Cannon, *Reagan,* 121; Cannon, *Ronnie and Jesse,* 135–37; Robert T. Monagan interview (1980), Bill Boyarsky papers, Hoover Institution; Sturgeon, oral history interview.

21. Cannon, *Ronnie and Jesse,* 131–33; Cannon, *Reagan,* 120–21; Kenneth F. Hall, oral history interview; Alex C. Sherriffs, oral history interview; Paul R. Haerle, oral history interview; Edwin Meese interview (1980), George Steffes interview (1980), Monagan interview, Boyarsky papers; Roger Magyar, oral history interview; Deaver and Herskowitz, *Behind the Scenes,* 38–39, 68, 196; Nofziger, *Nofziger,* 161.

22. Cannon, *President Reagan,* 504–5; Cannon, *Reagan,* 141; Cannon, *Ronnie and Jesse,* 139, 159, 164; Reagan and Novak, *My Turn,* 38–39; Reagan, oral history interview; Reagan, transcript of press conference, 2 February 1967, GP: Press Unit, Reagan gubernatorial papers.

23. Deaver and Herskowitz, *Behind the Scenes,* 39, 118; Reagan, *An American Life,* 124, 184; Reagan and Hyams, *On the Outside,* 10; Cannon, *President Reagan,* 505; Cannon, *Reagan,* 146.

24. First quotation in Kathy Randall Davis, *But What's He Really Like?* 14; second quotation in Sherriffs, oral history interview; Reagan, *An American Life,* 160–61; Edwin Meese, *With Reagan: The Inside Story,* 34; Peter Hannaford, *The Reagans: A Political Portrait,* 33–34; Allen F. Breed, oral history interview; Hall, oral history interview; Walker, oral history interview; Meese interview, Boyarsky papers; Peter Hannaford, oral history interview; Reagan, oral history interview.

25. First quotation in Reagan, transcript of press conference, 14 March 1967, GP: Press Unit, Reagan gubernatorial papers; second quotation in Steffes interview, Boyarsky papers; Virna M. Canson, oral history interview; Boyarsky, *Ronald Reagan,* 106.

26. Quotations in Cannon, *Reagan,* 124–25; Boyarsky, *Ronald Reagan,* 106–7; Steffes interview, Boyarsky papers; Hamilton and Biggart, *Governor Reagan, Governor Brown,* 47, 197–99.

27. Bagley, oral history interview; Cannon, *Ronnie and Jesse,* 174–77; Cannon, *Reagan,* 139–41, 168; Reagan, *An American Life,* 160, 170–71, 176; Haerle, oral history interview; Monagan, oral history interview; Hall, oral history interview; A. Ruric Todd, oral history interview; James R. Mills, oral history interview; Meese interview, Monagan interview, Boyarsky papers; Herb Michelson, "Ed Meese: Old-Fashioned, Self-Effacing Reagan Aide," *Sacramento Bee,* 10 August 1980.

28. Quotation in Cannon, *Ronnie and Jesse,* 133–35, 142–48; Cannon, *Reagan,* 122–24; Reagan, *An American Life,* 157–58.

29. Cannon, *Reagan,* 121–22, 154–57; Cannon, *Ronnie and Jesse,* 148–53; Boyarsky, *Ronald Reagan,* 119–20.

30. Quotation from transcript of *Face the Nation,* 18 October 1970, Miscellaneous Speeches and Scripts folder (see also Reagan, transcript of press conference, 17 January 1967,

Press Conference folder, Press Unit, Reagan gubernatorial papers); Smith, *Law and Justice,* 240–41; Reagan, *An American Life,* 180–81.

31. First quotation in Cannon, *President Reagan,* 140; second quotation in Reagan, *An American Life,* 179; Cannon, *Ronnie and Jesse,* 228–31; see also W. J. Rorabaugh, *Berkeley at War: The 1960s.*

32. Sherriffs, oral history interview; Cannon, *Ronnie and Jesse,* 231–34; Fawn M. Brodie, "Ronald Reagan Plays Surgeon," 14; Clark Kerr, oral history interview, Lyndon Johnson Library; Boyarsky, *Ronald Reagan,* 144–45.

33. Quotation in Cannon, *Reagan,* 151–54; Cannon, *Ronnie and Jesse,* 235–41, 249–57, 319; Reagan, *An American Life,* 181–82; Meese interview, Boyarsky papers.

34. Quotation in Nofziger, *Nofziger,* 74–81; Cannon, *Ronnie and Jesse,* 182–86; Cannon, *Reagan,* 132–38; Hamilton and Biggart, *Governor Reagan, Governor Brown,* 186–87; Rus Walton, oral history interview; Reagan, transcript of press conference at Yale University, 4 December 1967, Miscellaneous Speeches and Scripts folder, Reagan gubernatorial papers; Drew Pearson, handwritten notes, undated, Special for Bell-McClure Syndicate (31 October 1967), Reagan folder, Pearson papers.

35. Quotations in Ray Zeman, "Reagan Angrily Denies Report Two Homosexuals Were on Staff," *Los Angeles Times,* 1 November 1967; Cannon, *Ronnie and Jesse,* 186–88; Nofziger, *Nofziger,* 81–82; Nofziger, oral history interview; Reagan, transcripts of press conferences, 31 October, 14 November, 28 November 1967, Press Conference folder, Press Unit, Reagan gubernatorial papers; Pearson to Reagan, 14 November 1967, Melvin M. Belli to Pearson, 30 November 1967, Fred Panzer to Marvin Watson et al., 1 November 1967, Panzer to Watson, 17 November 1967, Reagan folder, Louis E. Lomax, "New Element in Reagan Scandal," 2 November 1967, Lomax, "Homosexual Scandal Hits Reagan's Administration," 4/5 November 1967, Reagan folder, Pearson papers.

36. Quotation in Nofziger, *Nofziger,* 61; von Damm, *Sincerely, Ronald Reagan,* 100–102; Reagan, *An American Life,* 163–64, 174–75; Cannon, *Reagan,* 126–32; Cannon, *Ronnie and Jesse,* 179–82; Sturgeon, oral history interview; transcript of Reagan press conference, 2 April 1968, PPS Campaign 1968 Research File, PPS 500.105.1–8, Reagan folder, Nixon papers; Canson, oral history interview; Reagan, oral history interview; Carolyn Cooper Heine, oral history interview; Anita M. Miller, oral history interview. See also Ronald Reagan, *Abortion and the Conscience of the Nation,* and Edmund Morris, "In Memoriam: Christina Reagan."

37. Quotation in Richard M. Nixon, *RN: The Memoirs of Richard Nixon,* 285–86; Theodore H. White, *The Making of the President, 1968,* 35; Nofziger, *Nofziger,* 65–66, 68–70; Cannon, *Reagan,* 157–59; Cannon, *Ronnie and Jesse,* 263–66; Haerle, oral history interview; Lewis Chester, Godfrey Hodgson, and Bruce Page, *An American Melodrama: The Presidential Campaign of 1968,* 200–209; Ambrose, *Nixon,* 118; Reagan to Hedley Donovan, 6 July 1967, PPS 501.1.1–41, Nixon to Reagan, 4 August 1967, PPS 501.133.1, Reagan to Nixon, 16 August 1967, PPS 501.1.1–41, Reagan folder, Nixon papers. See also Lewis L. Gould, *1968: The Election That Changed America.* For a collection of speeches that served as a campaign document, see Ronald Reagan, *The Creative Society: Some Comments on Problems Facing America.*

38. The Vice President [Hubert Humphrey], Memorandum for the Files, 23 August 1967, Reagan folder, Office Files of Marvin Watson, Johnson papers.

39. Quotation in Patrick Buchanan to Nixon with Nixon's handwritten note to Ray Price (July 1968), PPS 500.105.24.1; the speech they commented on was Reagan, "Excerpts from Speech by Governor Ronald Reagan," 4 July 1968, PPS 500.105.24.2, Campaign 1968 Research folder, notes with heading: RMW [Rose Mary Woods] call Sandy Quinn (June 1966), PPS 501.1.1.8, Pat Hillings to Nixon et al., 3 April 1968, PPS 501.1.42–81, Reagan folder, Nixon papers; Cannon, *Reagan,* 161–64; Reagan, *An American Life,* 176–77; Nofziger, *Nofziger,* 71–73; Nixon, *RN,* 287, 302–4; William French Smith, oral history interview; Ambrose, *Nixon,* 119–20.

40. First quotation in Billy Wickens to RMW [Rose Mary Woods], 2 October 1967, PPS

501.1.1–41, Reagan folder, Nixon papers; second quotation in White, *Making of the President, 1968,* 236; Hubert Humphrey, memorandum for the files, 23 August 1967, Reagan folder, Office Files of Marvin Watson, Johnson papers; Ambrose, *Nixon,* 153. See also RMW [Rose Mary Woods], memorandum for the files, 20 May 1968, PPS 501.1.72, Pat Hilling to Nixon et al., 26 May 1968, PPS 501.1.73, Reagan folder, Nixon papers.

41. Quotation in White, *Making of the President, 1968,* 137–38, 240–41; Nixon, *RN,* 305, 309; Nadine Cohodas, *Strom Thurmond and the Politics of Southern Change,* 396–400; Chester, Hodgson, and Page, *American Melodrama,* 438, 474.

42. First quotation in Nixon, *RN,* 311; second quotation in Reagan, *An American Life,* 178; White, *Making of the President, 1968,* 246–47.

43. Quotation in Cannon, *Reagan,* 187; Reagan, *An American Life,* 186–87; Deaver and Herskowitz, *Behind the Scenes,* 65–66; H. R. Haldeman, *The Haldeman Diaries: Inside the Nixon White House,* 447–48; Reagan, transcript of Telephone Address by Governor Ronald Reagan, 5 September 1971, Reagan, transcript of Remarks by Governor Ronald Reagan, Western Winner's Roundup, 22 June 1974, Gov. Ronald Reagan Speeches: One Time Only folder, transcript, Reagan, *Meet the Press,* 12 September 1971, transcript, *Meet the Press,* 20 January 1974, Miscellaneous Speeches and Scripts folder, Press Unit, Reagan gubernatorial papers; Mary E. Stuckey, *Getting into the Game: The Pre-Presidential Rhetoric of Ronald Reagan,* 31–32; von Damm, *Sincerely, Ronald Reagan,* 73–81; James Cannon, *Time and Chance: Gerald Ford's Appointment with History,* 417–20; Lou Cannon, "The Reagan Years," 365.

44. First quotation in Robert Scheer, "The Reagan Question," Final Chapter: Transition folder, Boyarsky papers; second quotation in Deaver and Herskowitz, *Behind the Scenes,* 44–45; third quotation in Ritter and Henry, *Ronald Reagan,* 46, 52; Stuckey, *Getting into the Game,* 32–34; Tom Goff, "Looking Back: His Bark Has Exceeded His Bite," Final Chapter: Transition folder, Boyarsky papers; Kotkin and Grabowicz, *California, Inc.,* 69–70.

45. Quotation in Cannon, *Reagan,* 166–67, 169–75; Haerle, oral history interview; Ritter and Henry, *Ronald Reagan,* 44.

46. Meese interview, Boyarsky papers; Cannon, *President Reagan,* 50; Cannon, *Reagan,* 184–85, 189–90; Boyarsky, *Ronald Reagan,* 159–65. Reagan also suffered defeats; see Garin Burbank, "Governor Reagan's Only Defeat: The Proposition 1 Campaign in 1973," 360–73, and Hall, oral history interview.

47. Norman B. Livermore to Darrell Trent, 22 October 1980, Chapter 11 folder, Boyarsky papers; Cannon, *Ronnie and Jesse,* 141, 213–27.

48. Quotation in Cannon, *Reagan,* 166, 176–77; Boyarsky, *Ronald Reagan,* 125–39; Anthony Beilenson and Larry Agran, "The Welfare Reform Act of 1971," 474–502; Reagan, *An American Life,* 188–89; Meese interview, Boyarsky papers; Cannon, "Reagan Years," 364–65; Ronald A. Zumbrun, Raymond M. Momboisse, and John H. Findley, "Welfare Reform: California Meets the Challenge," 741–42. For Reagan's opposition to Nixon's national welfare reform plan, see James Jenkins, oral history interview, and von Damm, *Sincerely, Ronald Reagan,* 49–54.

49. Quotations in Zumbrun, Momboisse, and Findley, "Welfare Reform," 740–48; Cannon, *Reagan,* 177–79; Ronald Zumbrun interview (1980), Boyarsky papers.

50. Quotation in David Gergen to Edwin Harper, 3 January 1983, ID: 102930, WHORM: Subject File: FG, Reagan presidential papers; Reagan, *An American Life,* 189–90; Cannon, *Reagan,* 179–81; Michelson, "Ed Meese," *Sacramento Bee,* 10 August 1980.

51. Quotation in Gergen to Harper, 3 January 1983, ID: 102930, WHORM: Subject File: FG, Reagan presidential papers; Zumbrun, Momboisse, and Findley, "Welfare Reform," 748; Cannon, *Reagan,* 181–82; Zumbrun interview, Boyarsky papers.

52. Zumbrun, Momboisse, and Findley, "Welfare Reform," 748–49, 781–82; Cannon, *Reagan,* 182–84; Reagan, *An American Life,* 190; Miller, oral history interview; Cannon, "Reagan Years," 365; Boyarsky, *Ronald Reagan,* 131; Reagan to Gerald R. Ford, 20 December 1974, Welfare Reform folder, Richard Cheney files, Gerald R. Ford papers, Gerald R.

Ford Library; Carl Ingram, "Brown Credits Reagan for Help Braking Welfare," *Sacramento Union,* 11 August 1975; Julie Thompson, "Is Reagan Taking Too Much Credit for 'Slaying' the Welfare Monster?" Poor II folder, Boyarsky papers.

53. Hannaford, oral history interview; Nofziger, *Nofziger,* 163; Wills, *Reagan's America,* 327–28; Cannon, *Reagan,* 192–93.

54. Cannon, *Reagan,* 196–97; Nofziger, *Nofziger,* 164–66; Stuckey, *Getting into the Game,* 68; for examples of his radio commentaries, see RR Radio Scripts folder, Reagan Subject Collection.

55. Cannon, *Reagan,* 193–94; Riccards, *Ferocious Engine of Democracy,* 360–61; Elizabeth Drew, *American Journal: The Events of 1976,* 48, 54–57; Ronald Reagan interview, 24 July 1976, van der Linden papers; Richard Schweiker interview, 17 January 1978, Ronald Reagan interview, 4 January 1978, Philip Crane interview, 30 January 1978, Reichley papers.

56. First quotation in Cannon, *Time and Chance,* 405–6; second quotation in Jerry H. Jones to Don Rumsfeld and Dick Cheney, 26 September 1975, Reagan folder, Jerry Jones Files, Ford papers; third quotation in Robert T. Hartmann, *Palace Politics: An Inside Account of the Ford Years,* 334–36; Drew, *American Journal,* 55–56; John J. Casserly, *The Ford White House: The Diary of a Speechwriter,* 261; Ron Nessen, *It Sure Looks Different from the Inside,* 195–96.

57. Cannon, *Reagan,* 201–9, 211; Hannaford, *The Reagans,* 70–75; Nofziger, *Nofziger,* 171–77; Nessen, *It Sure Looks Different,* 199–201; Jules Witcover, *Marathon: The Pursuit of the Presidency, 1972–1976,* 375–84; James T. Lynn to Ford, 4 November 1975, Reagan folder, Richard Cheney Files, Ford papers; Gerald Ford interview, 27 August 1979, Reichley papers.

58. Cannon, *Reagan,* 211–14; Reagan, *An American Life,* 201–2; Drew, *American Journal,* 238–39; Wayne Valis, memorandum for the record, 10 March 1976, Subject File: Reagan folder, Jerry Jones Files, Ford papers.

59. First quotation in Cannon, *Reagan,* 214–18; second and third quotations in Jesse Helms interview, April 1976, van der Linden papers; Nofziger, *Nofziger,* 178–80; Wills, *Reagan's America,* 328–31; Hannaford, *The Reagans,* 107; Witcover, *Marathon,* 402–3; Drew, *American Journal,* 237; John R. Greene, *The Presidency of Gerald R. Ford,* 164–66; Paul Laxalt interview (1980), van der Linden papers; Ford interview, Reichley papers.

60. Drew, *American Journal,* 175–76, 179–81, 234–37, 239–40, 354–56; Reagan and Novak, *My Turn,* 189–91; Cannon, *Reagan,* 219–20; Nessen, *It Sure Looks Different,* 206–12; Cannon, *Time and Chance,* 406, interviews with Donald Rumsfeld, 23 January 1978, Brent Scowcroft, 1 December 1977, William Scranton, 30 June 1978, Elliot Richardson, 9 January 1978, Gerald Ford, 8 March 1978, Reichley papers.

61. Drew, *American Journal,* 209, Cannon, *Reagan,* 220–23, Ronald Reagan interview, 24 July 1976, van der Linden papers; Foster [Channock] to Dick [Cheney], 25 June 1976, Rob Quartel and Ralph Stanley to Rogers Morton, 21 June 1976, Ford Electability Memo folder, Foster Channock Files, Ford papers.

62. Reagan interview, Laxalt interview, Richard Schweiker interview, 12 May 1980, van der Linden papers; Reagan and Novak, *My Turn,* 192–95; Reagan interview, Reichley papers; Richard Bergholz and George Skelton, "How Reagan Made Choice of Schweiker," Final Chapter: Transition folder, Boyarsky papers; Reagan to Holmes Alexander, 15 January 1980, RR Correspondence 1980 folder, Reagan Subject Collection; Greene, *Presidency of Gerald Ford,* 164.

63. Reagan to Alexander, 15 January 1980, RR Correspondence 1980 folder, Reagan Subject Collection; Schweiker interview, van der Linden papers; Schweiker interview, Reichley papers.

64. First quotation in Drew, *American Journal,* 334, 342–43; second quotation in Philip Crane interview, August 1976, van der Linden papers; third quotation in Schweiker interview, van der Linden papers; Reagan to Sanford C. Bernstein, 28 May 1980, Reagan to Holmes Alexander, 15 January 1980, RR Correspondence 1980 folder, Reagan Subject Collection;

Jim Connor to Dick Cheney, 26 July 1976, Jack Marsh to Ford, 26 July 1976, Political Affairs: Reagan folder, Presidential Handwriting File, Ford papers; interviews with Lyn Nofziger, 5 January 1978, Drew Lewis, 4 December 1980, John Sears, 26 August 1977, Reichley papers.

65. Nofziger, *Nofziger,* 198; Drew, *American Journal,* 343, 345–46.

66. Anderson, *Revolution,* 63–72.

67. Quotations in Cannon, *Reagan,* 225–26.

68. First quotation in Nixon to Reagan, 20 August 1976, second quotation in Reagan to Nixon, 27 August 1976, Reagan folder, Postpresidential file, Nixon papers.

Chapter 5: Changing the National Agenda, 1981

1. Quotation in Elizabeth Drew, *Portrait of an Election: The 1980 Presidential Campaign,* 24, 206–7; Edsall and Edsall, *Chain Reaction,* 140–41, 143–44, 256–57; Tom Evans interview (1980), van der Linden papers; Thomas Ferguson and Joel Rogers, "The Reagan Victory: Corporate Coalitions in the 1980 Campaign," 3–64; see also Aram Bakshian, *The Candidates, 1980.*

2. First quotation in Reagan and Novak, *My Turn,* 205; second quotation in Cannon, *Reagan,* 237–39; third quotation in Reagan, *An American Life,* 209; Deaver and Herskowitz, *Behind the Scenes,* 86–87; Nofziger, *Nofziger,* 234–37.

3. Reagan and Novak, *My Turn,* 205–6; Cannon, *Reagan,* 240.

4. Wead and Wead, *Reagan,* 201–19.

5. Lou Cannon and William Peterson, "GOP," 123; Philip Crane interview, 29 May 1980, van der Linden papers.

6. Quotation in Cannon and Peterson, "GOP," 124, 138; Reagan to John Reagan McCrary, 13 February 1980, Reagan to Mr. and Mrs. John P. Callahan, 19 March 1980, Reagan to Mrs. F. M. Akers, 9 January 1980, RR Correspondence 1980 folder, Reagan Subject Collection; Cannon, *Reagan,* 246–48; Richard Ben Cramer, *What It Takes: The Way to the White House,* 790.

7. Reagan, *An American Life,* 211; Reagan and Novak, *My Turn,* 204; Reagan to John Reagan McCrary, 13 February 1980, RR Correspondence 1980 folder, Reagan Subject Collection; Cannon, *Reagan,* 249–54; Robert Shogan, *The Riddle of Power: Presidential Leadership from Truman to Bush,* 257–58; Fitzhugh Green, *George Bush: An Intimate Portrait,* 179–80.

8. First quotation in Cannon, *President Reagan,* 68 note; second quotation in Cannon, *Reagan,* 253; Reagan, *An American Life,* 211–13; Cannon and Peterson, "GOP," 139–42.

9. First quotation in Meese, *With Reagan,* 4–7, 10–13; second quotation in Reagan and Novak, *My Turn,* 206–7; Reagan, *An American Life,* 213–14; Cannon, *President Reagan,* 66–68; Cannon, *Reagan,* 254–58; Charles Black interview, 16 May 1980, van der Linden papers; Reagan to Ruth V. Johnson, 3 January 1980, Reagan to Mrs. F. M. Akers, 9 January 1980, Reagan to Polly Nelson Hippler, 14 February 1980, RR Correspondence 1980 folder, Reagan Subject Collection.

10. Reagan to Mr. and Mrs. John P. Callahan, 19 March 1980, RR Correspondence 1980 folder, Reagan Subject Collection; Cannon, *President Reagan,* 68; Reagan, *An American Life,* 214.

11. Mark Bisnow, *Diary of a Dark Horse: The 1980 Anderson Presidential Campaign,* 158–59; Reagan to Mr. and Mrs. John P. Callahan, 19 March 1980, RR Correspondence 1980 folder, Reagan Subject Collection; Cannon and Peterson, "GOP," 125; Cannon, *Reagan,* 258–59; George Bush and Victor Gold, *Looking Forward,* 3–4; James A. Baker and Thomas M. Defrank, *The Politics of Diplomacy: Revolution, War, and Peace, 1989–1992,* 20–21; Green, *George Bush,* 174–79.

12. Gerald R. Ford, "Voters Won't Pick Our Next President—The House Will," 27; Cannon, *Reagan,* 262; Hannaford, *The Reagans,* 259, 268–78.

13. First quotation in David M. Alpern et al., "How the Ford Deal Collapsed," 20–26; second quotation in Ford, "Voters Won't Pick Our Next President," 27; third quotation in Reagan to William Loeb, 30 July 1980, RR Correspondence 1980 folder, Reagan Subject Collection; Reagan, *An American Life,* 215–16; Meese, *With Reagan,* 43–44; Larry Speakes and Robert Pack, *Speaking Out: The Reagan Presidency from Inside the White House,* 58; Drew, *Portrait of an Election,* 212–13.

14. Quotation in Reagan to Blanche Seaver, 1 August 1980, RR Correspondence 1980 folder, Reagan Subject Collection; Cannon, *Reagan,* 262–67.

15. Reagan, "Acceptance Speech by Governor Ronald Reagan," 17 July 1980, Reagan Subject Collection.

16. Quotation in Drew, *Portrait of an Election,* 388–92; Austin Ranney, "The Carter Administration," 28–36; Joseph White and Aaron Wildavsky, *The Deficit and the Public Interest: The Search for Responsible Budgeting in the 1980s,* 56; Jimmy Carter, *Keeping Faith: Memoirs of a President,* 543. As usual with Reagan opponents Carter struggled to find issues that worked; see Campaign, 1980 Reagan Book Part I and II, Staff Offices Counsel: Cutler, Al McDonald to Hamilton Jordan et al., 10 October 1980, Staff Offices Press: Powell, Jimmy Carter papers, Jimmy Carter Library.

17. First quotation in Cannon, *Reagan,* 269–74; second quotation in Mollie Dickenson, *Thumbs Up: The Life and Courageous Comeback of White House Press Secretary Jim Brady,* 410–17; Drew, *Portrait of an Election,* 262–63; Cannon, *President Reagan,* 68–69; Pierard and Linder, *Civil Religion,* 264–65.

18. First quotation in Drew, *Portrait of an Election,* 357–58, 365; second quotation in Reagan and Novak, *My Turn,* 217; Meese, *With Reagan,* 46–47; Cannon, *Reagan,* 274–79; Robert C. Wood, *Whatever Possessed the President? Academic Experts and Presidential Policy, 1960–1988,* 141–43; Anderson, *Revolution,* 167–68.

19. Reagan, *An American Life,* 217–18; Meese, *With Reagan,* 45–46; Steven M. Gillon, *The Democrats' Dilemma: Walter F. Mondale and the Liberal Legacy,* 293–95; Sundquist, *Dynamics of the Party System,* 424; Edsall and Edsall, *Chain Reaction,* 200–202; White and Wildavsky, *The Deficit,* 20–21.

20. Quotations in Jimmy Carter, *Public Papers of the President: Jimmy Carter, 1980–81,* 2477–78, 2496, 2501; Drew, *Portrait of an Election,* 322, 324–25.

21. Cannon, *Reagan,* 279, 295–98; Drew, *Portrait of an Election,* 337, 339–41, 344.

22. Mayer, *Changing American Mind,* 1–3; Richard Harwood, ed., *The Pursuit of the Presidency, 1980,* 341; Dionne, *Why Americans Hate Politics,* 138–39; White and Wildavsky, *The Deficit,* 67–69

23. Quotation in Cannon, *President Reagan,* 11–18; Thomas J. Weko, *The Politicizing Presidency: The White House Personnel Office, 1948–1994,* 90; Meese, *With Reagan,* 57–61; Carl M. Brauer, *Presidential Transitions: Eisenhower through Reagan,* 221; White and Wildavsky, *The Deficit,* 63; Barrett, *Gambling with History,* 83–84.

24. Anderson, *Revolution,* 199–200; Strobe Talbott, *Deadly Gambits: The Reagan Administration and the Stalemate in Nuclear Arms Control,* 16; Weko, *Politicizing Presidency,* 90–91; James Baker interview, 15 December 1980, Reichley papers.

25. Meese, *With Reagan,* 78–81; Baker interview, Reichley papers; Anderson, *Revolution,* 202; Cannon, *President Reagan,* 184–85; Ralph Bledsoe, "Policy Management in the Reagan Administration," July 1988, ID: 609984, WHORM: Subject File: FG, Reagan presidential papers; Press Releases, 14 November 1980, 17 December 1980, Reagan-Bush Transition file, Annelise Anderson papers, Hoover Institution.

26. Meese, *With Reagan,* 101–3.

27. Quotation in Mark Hertsgaard, *On Bended Knee: The Press and the Reagan Presidency,* 12, 23; von Damm, *At Reagan's Side,* 198; Cannon, *President Reagan,* 53–54, 66, 71–72, 111–13; Cannon, *Reagan,* 383–84; Barrett, *Gambling with History,* 77, 375–76; Thomas S. Langston, *Ideologues and Presidents: From the New Deal to the Reagan Revolution,* 10–11; Speakes and Pack, *Speaking Out,* 70; Devine, *Reagan's Terrible Swift Sword,*

31–32; Anderson, *Revolution,* 239–40; Noonan, *What I Saw,* 121–22; Deaver and Herskowitz, *Behind the Scenes,* 131, 145, 195; Reagan and Novak, *My Turn,* 238.

28. First quotation in Haig, *Caveat,* 11–12; second quotation in Michael Schaller, *Reckoning with Reagan: America and Its President in the 1980s,* 48; Cannon, *President Reagan,* 78–80, 82–84.

29. Quotation in Persico, *Casey,* 202–3; Barrett, *Gambling with History,* 67; von Damm, *At Reagan's Side,* 135–37; Cannon, *President Reagan,* 83.

30. Cannon, *President Reagan,* 82–85; Barrett, *Gambling with History,* 67; Anderson, *Revolution,* 246–47; Elizabeth Drew, *Politics and Money: The New Road to Corruption,* 120–22.

31. Cannon, *President Reagan,* 85–86.

32. Quotation in von Damm, *At Reagan's Side,* 150; Barrett, *Gambling with History,* 70–72; Anderson, *Revolution,* 232–33; Terrel H. Bell, *The Thirteenth Man: A Reagan Cabinet Memoir,* 16–18.

33. Quotations in Reagan, *Public Papers, 1981,* 1–4; Reagan, *An American Life,* 225–26; Ronald Reagan to Heads of Executive Departments and Agencies, 20 January 1981, ID: 5ca, WHORM: Subject: FG, Reagan presidential papers.

34. Reagan, *Public Papers, 1981,* 109; William A. Niskanen, *Reaganomics: An Insider's Account of the Policies and the People,* 15–16; Paul C. Roberts, *The Supply-Side Revolution: An Insider's Account of Policymaking in Washington,* 69; Anthony S. Campagna, *The Economy in the Reagan Years: The Economic Consequences of the Reagan Administrations,* 3–13, 26–29; Michael J. Boskin, *Reagan and the Economy: The Successes, Failures, and Unfinished Agenda,* 11–25; Benjamin M. Friedman, *Day of Reckoning: The Consequences of American Economic Policy under Reagan and After,* 21–24; see also Wallace C. Peterson, *Silent Depression: The Fate of the American Dream.*

35. Campagna, *Economy in the Reagan Years,* 25–26, 28; Niskanen, *Reaganomics,* 16–18, 20–23; Boskin, *Reagan and the Economy,* 5, 31–41; White and Wildavsky, *The Deficit,* 20–24; Michael A. Bernstein, "Understanding American Economic Decline: The Contours of the Late-Twentieth-Century Experience," 25–26; Margaret Weir, *Politics and Jobs: The Boundaries of Employment Policy in the United States,* 161–62; William F. Ford, "Conference Purpose and Overview," 5; Stephen Entin, undated, untitled memorandum on supply-side theory, attached to Entin to Annelise Anderson, 27 August 1980, Reagan-Bush Transition files, Anderson papers.

36. Entin, undated, untitled memorandum on supply-side theory, attached to Entin to Anderson, 27 August 1980, Reagan-Bush Transition files, Anderson papers; White and Wildavsky, *The Deficit,* 24–27; Robert L. Heilbroner, "The Demand for Supply-Side," 80–87; Bernstein, "Understanding American Economic Decline," 26–27; William Greider, *The Education of David Stockman and Other Americans,* 97–102; Arthur B. Laffer, "Introduction," xv–xvi; Anderson, *Revolution,* 141; Richard W. Rahn, "Supply-Side Economics: The U.S. Experience," 44–50; Robert E. Keleher and William P. Orzechowski, "Supply-Side Fiscal Policy: An Historical Analysis of a Rejuvenated Idea," 121–34, 140–51; see also Bruce R. Bartlett, *Reaganomics: Supply Side Economics in Action,* and Jude Wanniski, *The Way the World Works.*

37. First quotation in Langston, *Ideologues and Presidents,* 145–47; second quotation in David A. Stockman, *The Triumph of Politics: How the Reagan Revolution Failed,* 10; Arthur B. Laffer, "Government Exactions and Revenue Deficiencies," 201; Anderson, *Revolution,* 141–62; Wills, *Reagan's America,* 364–66; Roberts, *Supply-Side Revolution,* 27–29, 87; John Greenya and Anne Urban, *The Real David Stockman,* 97; Owen Ullmann, *Stockman: The Man, the Myth, the Future,* 167–69; Murray Weidenbaum, *Rendezvous with Reality: The American Economy after Reagan,* 19, 288 note 21; Jack Kemp interview, 12 June 1980, van der Linden papers; Meese, *With Reagan,* 121–26; Cannon, *Reagan,* 236, 323; John Sears interview, 12 January 1981, Reichley papers. See also Amos Kiewe and Davis W. Houck, *A Shining City on a Hill: Ronald Reagan's Economic Rhetoric, 1951–1989.*

38. First quotation in Barrett, *Gambling with History,* 138; second quotation in Stockman, *Triumph of Politics,* 39; Cannon, *President Reagan,* 236–38.

39. Quotation in Stockman, *Triumph of Politics,* 8–9, 68, 75–76; White and Wildavsky, *The Deficit,* 82–83; Ullmann, *Stockman,* 14–15, 17, 19, 190–91; Anderson, *Revolution,* 236.

40. Stockman, *Triumph of Politics,* 65–68, 71–75, 81–85; Cannon, *President Reagan,* 106–8; James Baker interview, 15 December 1980, Reichley papers; Niskanen, *Reaganomics,* 5; Donald T. Regan, *For the Record: From Wall Street to Washington,* 152–56.

41. Stockman, *Triumph of Politics,* 85–89; Niskanen, *Reaganomics,* 285–87; Cannon, *President Reagan,* 109–10, 238–39; Regan, *For the Record,* 191; White and Wildavsky, *The Deficit,* 79–81; Meese, *With Reagan,* 22.

42. Stockman, *Triumph of Politics,* 89–92, 102–5, 109–22.

43. Ibid., 92–99; White and Wildavsky, *The Deficit,* 98–101; Greenya and Urban, *Real David Stockman,* 73.

44. Quotation in Stockman, *Triumph of Politics,* 122–31; White and Wildavsky, *The Deficit,* 110–11.

45. Reagan, *Public Papers, 1981,* 109 17, 133.

46. Quotation in Tip O'Neill and William Novak, *Man of the House: The Life and Political Memoirs of Speaker Tip O'Neill,* 332; Reagan, *An American Life,* 233.

47. White and Wildavsky, *The Deficit,* 91–93, 113–18; Dickenson, *Thumbs Up,* 40–68; see also Jack Hinckley and Jo Ann Hinckley, *Breaking Points.*

48. Quotations in Reagan, *An American Life,* 259–62; Reagan and Novak, *My Turn,* 10, 18; Gilbert, *Mortal Presidency,* 187–88; see also Herbert L. Abrams, *"The President Has Been Shot": Confusion, Disability, and the Twenty-Fifth Amendment in the Aftermath of the Attempted Assassination of Ronald Reagan.*

49. Deaver and Herskowitz, *Behind the Scenes,* 23, 27–28; Robert H. Ferrell, *Ill-Advised: Presidential Health and Public Trust,* 157–59; von Damm, *At Reagan's Side,* 195; Meese, *With Reagan,* 78; Cannon, *President Reagan,* 155–56.

50. Reagan, *Public Papers, 1981,* 391–94; Cannon, *President Reagan,* 113–15; Joseph C. Spear, *Presidents and the Press: The Nixon Legacy,* 20–21; O'Neill and Novak, *Man of the House,* 345–46.

51. Quotation in Meese, *With Reagan,* 130; Stockman, *Triumph of Politics,* 142–47, 150–54, 169; White and Wildavsky, *The Deficit,* 121–22; for an example of Reagan's personal political activity, see Reagan telephone call to Senator Lloyd Bentsen, 5 February 1981, ID: 000107ss, WHORM: Subject: PR, Reagan presidential papers. See also Richard F. Fenno, *The Emergence of a Senate Leader: Pete Domenici and the Reagan Budget.*

52. Quotation in Reagan, *An American Life,* 284–86; White and Wildavsky, *The Deficit,* 123–25, 127–32; Stockman, *Triumph of Politics,* 168–77; Reagan telephone calls, 27 April 1981, ID: 019070ss, 22 April 1981, ID: 019070ss, 23 April 1981, ID: 017131ss, WHORM: Subject: PR, Reagan presidential papers (Reagan's notations often summarized the conversations).

53. Quotation in Ullmann, *Stockman,* 232–33; White and Wildavsky, *The Deficit,* 137–38, 145–84; Stockman, *Triumph of Politics,* 194–228.

54. Quotation in Reagan, *An American Life,* 234–35; Reagan, *Public Papers, 1981,* 710; Donald T. Regan to Reagan, 21 March 1981, ID: 171ca, WHORM: Subject: FG, Reagan presidential papers; David Vogel, *Fluctuating Fortunes: The Political Power of Business in America,* 242–45.

55. Quotation in Greider, *Education of David Stockman,* 49–50; Donald T. Regan to Reagan, 21 March 1981, ID: 171ca, WHORM: Subject: FG, Reagan presidential papers.

56. Meese, *With Reagan,* 130–32; Stockman, *Triumph of Politics,* 236–37; White and Wildavsky, *The Deficit,* 158–66.

57. Quotations in White and Wildavsky, *The Deficit,* 168–79; Ullmann, *Stockman,* 236; Reagan, *Public Papers, 1981,* 664–68; Robert J. Spitzer, *President and Congress: Executive Hegemony at the Crossroads of American Government,* 63; Stockman, *Triumph of Politics,* 257–68.

58. Reagan, *An American Life,* 288.

59. Reagan, *Public Papers, 1981,* 706; White and Wildavsky, *The Deficit,* 154–55.

60. Congressional Quarterly, *Congressional Quarterly Almanac, 1981,* 91, 93–95.

Chapter 6: Managing Big Government, 1981–1985

1. Niskanen, *Reaganomics,* 71–72; Anderson, *Revolution,* 243; Lester M. Salamon and Michael S. Lund, "Governance in the Reagan Era: An Overview," 17–18.

2. Sterling Kernek, "Reagan's Foreign Policy Leadership," 20; Abrams, "Reagan's Leadership," 96; Samuel Kernell and Samuel L. Popkin, *Chief of Staff: Twenty-five Years of Managing the Presidency,* 82; Persico, *Casey,* 181; Wills, *Reagan's America,* 298, 343; Cannon, *President Reagan,* 143; Reagan and Novak, *My Turn,* 111–13; Nancy Reagan interview, 4 October 1980, van der Linden papers; Jack Wrather, oral history interview.

3. Cannon, *President Reagan,* 497; Reagan, *An American Life,* 283; Schaller, *Reckoning with Reagan,* 44; Devine, *Reagan's Terrible Swift Sword,* 84.

4. Quotation in Reagan to Robert E. Poli, 20 October 1980, ID: 047510, WHORM: Subject: PE; unsigned memorandum, "Decision Memorandum: Strategy RE: PATCO Situation," 9 December 1980, Reagan-Bush Transition file, Anderson papers; Barrett, *Gambling with History,* 204.

5. Unsigned memorandum, "Decision Memorandum: Strategy RE: PATCO Situation," 9 December 1980; unsigned undated memorandum, "Significant Labor Contract Expirations," Reagan-Bush Transition file, Anderson papers; Niskanen, *Reaganomics,* 191–93; Reagan, *An American Life,* 282–83.

6. Reagan, *Public Papers, 1981,* 689–90.

7. Ibid., 687–89, 697, 707; unsigned memorandum, "Senior Staff Meeting Action Items," 6 August 1981, ID: 061294, WHORM: Subject: FG.

8. Reagan to Dorothy Walton (October 1981), ID: 046553, WHORM: Subject: BE, Reagan to Dale Evans and Roy Rogers, 19 October 1981, ID: 043972, Richard B. Wirthlin to Richard Richards, 3 November 1981, ID: 052714, Wirthlin to Richards, 27 November 1981, ID: 052714, Drew Lewis to Reagan, 9 December 1981, ID: 044165, press briefing by Drew Lewis, 9 December 1981, ADDIS, Reagan to Director of the Office of Personnel Management, 9 December 1981, ADDIS, Reagan to June Browning, 11 December 1981, ID: 052405, Fred F. Fielding to James A. Baker, 15 June 1983, ID: 143006, WHORM: Subject: PE, Reagan presidential papers.

9. Quotation in Anderson, *Revolution,* 283–84; Mayer, *Changing American Mind,* 247–55; Caspar W. Weinberger, *Fighting for Peace: Seven Critical Years in the Pentagon,* 34–35, 39–41; Robert H. Michel to Republican Colleagues, 26 February 1982, ID: 063105sc, WHORM: Subject: FG, Reagan presidential papers; Meese, *With Reagan,* 174–76; John G. Tower, *Consequences: A Personal and Political Memoir,* 236–37; Daniel Wirls, *Buildup: The Politics of Defense in the Reagan Era,* 17–25, 27–28; Charles R. Morris, *Iron Destinies, Lost Opportunities: The Arms Race between the U.S.A. and the U.S.S.R., 1945–1987,* 396–97; see also Tom Gervasi, *The Myth of Soviet Military Supremacy.*

10. Quotation in Anderson, *Revolution,* 335–36; Weidenbaum, *Rendezvous with Reality,* 18; White and Wildavsky, *The Deficit,* 108–10; Weinberger, *Fighting for Peace,* 47–49; Hertsgaard, *On Bended Knee,* 343–44; Stockman, *Triumph of Politics,* 105–9; Morris, *Iron Destinies, Lost Opportunities,* 373–74; Meese, *With Reagan,* 176–77; Wirls, *Buildup,* 36; Mayer, *Changing American Mind,* 255–57.

11. Wirls, *Buildup,* 35; William J. Crowe and David Chanoff, *The Line of Fire: From Washington to the Gulf, the Politics and Battles of the New Military,* 241 note; Morris, *Iron Destinies, Lost Opportunities,* 374–77, 381–83; Meese, *With Reagan,* 179–80; Powell and Persico, *My American Journey,* 258–59; John F. Lehman, *Command of the Seas,* 116–21, 128–29, 153–54. See also Andy Pasztor, *When the Pentagon Was for Sale: Inside America's Biggest Defense Scandal.*

12. See Fred I. Greenstein, *The Hidden-Hand Presidency: Eisenhower as Leader;* Fred I. Greenstein, Address, "Presidential Historians and Biographers Assess the Reagan Presidency," Hofstra Conference; Cannon, *President Reagan,* 88, 94–95; Abrams, "Reagan's Leadership," 98, 116–17.

13. Quotations in Anderson, *Revolution,* 241, 284–85, 288; Meg Greenfield, "How Does Reagan Decide?" 80; Meese, *With Reagan,* 21; Nancy Reynolds interview, 4 October 1980, van der Linden papers; Breed, oral history interview; George P. Shultz, *Turmoil and Triumph: My Years as Secretary of State,* 559; Cannon, *President Reagan,* 34, 508; Barrett, *Gambling with History,* 6; Robert Scheer, "The Reagan Question," Final Chapter Transition folder, Boyarsky papers; Lou Cannon, "Reagan at the Crossroads Again: 1986," 135; Richard S. Williamson, *Reagan's Federalism: His Efforts to Decentralize Government,* 6–7.

14. First quotation in Anderson, *Revolution,* 289–91; second quotation in Regan, *For the Record,* 187–88, 267; Hertsgaard, *On Bended Knee,* 26; Constantine C. Menges, *Inside the National Security Council: The True Story of the Making and Unmaking of Reagan's Foreign Policy,* 386; Cannon, *President Reagan,* 34–35, 181–82; Barrett, *Gambling with History,* 22–23, 489 note 1; Stockman, *Triumph of Politics,* 76.

15. First quotation in Noonan, *What I Saw,* 166; second quotation in Roosevelt, *Keeper of the Gate,* 188–89; Niskanen, *Reaganomics,* 284; Wood, *Whatever Possessed the President,* 140; von Damm, *At Reagan's Side,* 188; Cannon, *President Reagan,* 54–55, 304; Woodward, *Veil,* 403–4.

16. First quotation in Smith, *Law and Justice,* 11; second quotation in Woodward, *Veil,* 24; third quotation in Cannon, *President Reagan,* 714; fourth quotation in Persico, *Casey,* 175.

17. First quotation in Nofziger, *Nofziger,* 46; second quotation in Noonan, *What I Saw,* 152, 166–67; Roosevelt, *Keeper of the Gate,* 190; Cannon, *President Reagan,* 133–34, 137–41, 364; Bell, *Thirteenth Man,* 31; Regan, *For the Record,* 250; Max M. Kampelman, *Entering New Worlds: The Memoirs of a Private Man in Public Life,* 144, 254; Schaller, *Reckoning with Reagan,* 56–57.

18. First quotation in Noonan, *What I Saw,* 151; second quotation in O'Neill and Novak, *Man of the House,* 360; third quotation in Philip Crane interview, 29 May 1980, van der Linden papers; Boyarsky, *Ronald Reagan,* 15; Persico, *Casey,* 305–6; Robert C. McFarlane and Zofia Smardz, *Special Trust,* 106; Cannon, *President Reagan,* 130, 132–33, 364; Jim Wright, *Worth It All: My War for Peace,* 148.

19. Hertsgaard, *On Bended Knee,* 203; Edmund Morris, "Official Biographer Puzzled by Reagan Persona," 4; Cannon, *President Reagan,* 217–18; Shultz, *Turmoil and Triumph,* 1133.

20. Quotation in Cannon, *President Reagan,* 56–57, 96–97, 151–52, 361–62; Donald T. Regan, "The Reagan Presidency: Atop the Second Tier," 53; von Damm, *At Reagan's Side,* 320; for Reagan's schedules and weekly briefing book, see WHORM: Subject: FG, Reagan presidential papers.

21. First quotation in Persico, *Casey,* 306; second quotation in Deaver and Herskowitz, *Behind the Scenes,* 13; Shogan, *Riddle of Power,* 244–45; Reagan, *An American Life,* 249–50; Cannon, *President Reagan,* 56, 139, 144–47, 528; Schaller, *Reckoning with Reagan,* 3; Woodward, *Veil,* 404; Reagan to Dorothy Walton (October 1981), ID: 046553, WHORM: Subject: BE, Reagan presidential papers. For examples of Reagan's schedule, see Nancy Hodapp to Craig Fuller, 17 June 1981, ID: 053619, Richard Darman and Craig Fuller to Reagan, 29 January 1982, ID: 076335sc, "The President's Summary Schedule," 14 June 1982, ID: 083856sc, "Office Cabinet Affairs: Action Tracking Worksheet," 14 December 1982, ID: 077653, WHORM: Subject: FG, "Daily Diary of President Ronald Reagan," 28 September 1983, no ID number, President's Daily Diary, WH Staff Members Office file, Reagan presidential papers.

22. Morton Kondracke, "Cabinet Boardroom," 13; Wills, *Reagan's America,* 319–21; Nofziger, *Nofziger,* 47; Hertsgaard, *On Bended Knee,* 5.

23. Meese, *With Reagan,* 74–77; Anderson, *Revolution,* 224–31; Meese to Members of

Cabinet, 13 February 1981, ID: 51ca, Fuller to Meese, 23 February 1981, ID: 51ca, Meese to Members of Cabinet, 26 February 1981, ID: 51ca, Reagan to Members of Cabinet, 11 March 1981, 128ca, Ralph C. Bledsoe, "Policy Management in the Reagan Administration," July 1988, ID: 609984, WHORM: Subject: FG, Reagan presidential papers; John P. Burke, *The Institutional Presidency*, 140–41, 144–51; James G. Benze, *Presidential Power and Management Techniques: The Carter and Reagan Administrations in Historical Perspective*, 77–78, 84; Chester A. Newland, "Executive Office Policy Apparatus: Enforcing the Reagan Agenda," 153–56; Kondracke, "Cabinet Boardroom," 12–13.

24. First quotation in Gerald S. Strober and Deborah H. Strober, *Nixon: An Oral History of His Presidency*, 476; second quotation in Haig, *Caveat*, 85; third and fourth quotations in Regan, *For the Record*, 142; Anderson, *Revolution*, 281, 284, 291–92; Craig A. Rimmerman, *Presidency by Plebiscite: The Reagan-Bush Era in Institutional Perspective*, 78; William Greider, "Republicans," 173–74; Noonan, *What I Saw*, 65, 167–68; Nofziger, *Nofziger*, 47–48.

25. Quotation in Reagan to Murray W. Ratzlaff, 14 December 1983, Ratzlaff to Reagan, 24 October 1983, ID: 191892, WHORM: Subject: FG, Reagan presidential papers.

26. First quotation in Cannon, *President Reagan*, 32; second quotation in Smith, *Law and Justice*, 243–44; Noonan, *What I Saw*, 153; Reagan, *First Father, First Daughter*, 402; von Damm, *At Reagan's Side*, 60–61.

27. Quotation in Cannon, *President Reagan*, 206; Deaver and Herskowitz, *Behind the Scenes*, 104.

28. Haerle, oral history interview; Noonan, *What I Saw*, 150–51; Nofziger, oral history interview. Maureen Reagan cried when asked what her father was like and said she did not know him any differently from the public's perception of him; Peter Goldman and Tony Fuller, *The Quest for the Presidency 1984*, 27.

29. First quotation in Cannon, *President Reagan*, 133, 172, 435; second quotation in Nofziger, *Nofziger*, 220; third quotation in Mayer and McManus, *Landslide*, 170; Noonan, *What I Saw*, 170; Deaver and Herskowitz, *Behind the Scenes*, 41; von Damm, *At Reagan's Side*, 224, 319; Meese, *With Reagan*, 25–26.

30. Quotation in Noonan, *What I Saw*, 168–69; Roosevelt, *Keeper of the Gate*, 188; Smith, *Law and Justice*, 87; Persico, *Casey*, 485; Don Oberdorfer, *The Turn: From the Cold War to a New Era, the United States and the Soviet Union, 1983–1990*, 100; David Gergen to Reagan, 26 February 1982, ID: 063105sc, WHORM: Subject: FG, Reagan presidential papers.

31. Quotation in Shultz, *Turmoil and Triumph*, 826–27; Noonan, *What I Saw*, 110; Bell, *Thirteenth Man*, 64–65; Anderson, *Revolution*, 88–90, 238; Devine, *Reagan's Terrible Swift Sword*, 30; for an example of senior staff activity, see "Senior Staff Meeting Action Items," 24 March 1983, ID: 131585, WHORM: Subject: FG, Reagan presidential papers.

32. Speakes and Pack, *Speaking Out*, 69–71; Haig, *Caveat*, 83; Deaver and Herskowitz, *Behind the Scenes*, 126–28, 175; Niskanen, *Reaganomics*, 300; Anderson, *Revolution*, 216–19, 241–42; Devine, *Reagan's Terrible Swift Sword*, 16, 18; Regan, *For the Record*, 289; Roosevelt, *Keeper of the Gate*, 223.

33. Cannon, *President Reagan*, 187–89; Haig, *Caveat*, 85.

34. Quotation in Shultz, *Turmoil and Triumph*, 305, 308; Cannon, *President Reagan*, 156–57, 189–93; Barrett, *Gambling with History*, 233–35; Deaver and Herskowitz, *Behind the Scenes*, 129; von Damm, *At Reagan's Side*, 290–91; Reagan and Novak, *My Turn*, 242–43.

35. Reagan, *An American Life*, 448.

36. David Hoffman and Lou Cannon, "The Reagan Cabinet," 18 July 1982, ID: 088853, WHORM: Subject: FG, Reagan presidential papers; von Damm, *At Reagan's Side*, 236–37; Niskanen, *Reaganomics*, 298–99; Regan, *For the Record*, 190–91; Anderson, *Revolution*, 231; Speakes and Pack, *Speaking Out*, 82.

37. Quotation in Cannon, *President Reagan*, 193–98; Bell, *Thirteenth Man*, 66; Haig, *Caveat*, 91–92, 141, 306–7; Barrett, *Gambling with History*, 85–88, 219–22, 224–29; Weinberger, *Fighting for Peace*, 29; Reagan, *An American Life*, 254–56, 361; Meese, *With Reagan*, 65; Speakes and Pack, *Speaking Out*, 77; McFarlane and Smardz, *Special Trust*,

177–81. For a study of Haig's early career, see Roger Morris, *Haig: The General's Progress*.

38. Quotation in Reagan, *An American Life*, 360–62; Haig, *Caveat*, 310–15; McFarlane and Smardz, *Special Trust*, 199–201; Cannon, *President Reagan*, 198–205.

39. Cannon, *President Reagan*, 134; Roosevelt, *Keeper of the Gate*, 211, 218–19; Shultz, *Turmoil and Triumph*, 4–10. For Shultz's meetings with Reagan, see Ellen M. Jones to Frederick J. Ryan, 3 February 1987, ID: 483990, WHORM: Subject: FG, Reagan presidential papers. Colin Powell believed that it was Shultz who put the substance in Reagan's foreign policy vision; Powell and Persico, *My American Journey*, 368.

40. Quotation in Crowe and Chanoff, *Line of Fire*, 127, 221; Shultz, *Turmoil and Triumph*, 144, 968; McFarlane and Smardz, *Special Trust*, 325.

41. Quotation in Oberdorfer, *The Turn*, 98–99; McFarlane and Smardz, *Special Trust*, 286–87; Abrams, "Reagan's Leadership," 114–15; Crowe and Chanoff, *Line of Fire*, 127; Paul H. Nitze, "Reagan and the Realities of Foreign Policy," 39; Woodward, *Veil*, 254; Reagan, *An American Life*, 511.

42. First quotation in James G. Watt and Doug Wead, *The Courage of a Conservative*, 29; second quotation in Cannon, *Reagan*, 359; third quotation in R. McGreggor Cawley, *Federal Land, Western Anger: The Sagebrush Rebellion and Environmental Politics*, ix–x, 9, 11, 25–31, 85, 129–34; fourth quotation in Leilani Watt and Al Janssen, *Caught in the Conflict: My Life with James Watt*, 42–44; C. Brant Short, *Ronald Reagan and the Public Lands: America's Conservation Debate, 1979–1984*, 12–13, 24–25, 50, 56; Ron Arnold, *At the Eye of the Storm: James Watt and the Environmentalists*, 3, 10, 80; Susan Power Bratton, "The Ecotheology of James Watt," 229–30; Cannon, *Reagan*, 358; James G. Watt, Address, "The Cabinet Assesses the Presidency," Hofstra Conference.

43. First quotation in Walter A. Rosenbaum, *Environmental Politics and Policy*, 4–5, 27–28; second quotation in Reagan to Court McLeod, 7 January 1980 folder, RR Correspondence 1980, Reagan Subject Collection; Samuel P. Hays, *Beauty, Health, and Permanence: Environmental Politics in the United States, 1955–1985*, 491–92; Cannon, *Reagan*, 349–53, 369; Cannon, *President Reagan*, 526–31, 836; Jerry Adler et al., "James Watt's Land Rush," 22–23, 29; Short, *Reagan and Public Lands*, 5–9.

44. First quotation in Short, *Reagan and Public Lands*, 51; second and third quotations in Arnold, *Eye of the Storm*, 93, 198; Adler et al., "James Watt's Land Rush," 23–27; Paul J. Culhane, "Sagebrush Rebels in Office: Jim Watt's Land and Water Politics," 296.

45. Quotation in "U.S. Coastal Waters on Auction Block," 6; Robert F. Durant, *The Administrative Presidency Revisited: Public Lands, the BLM, and the Reagan Revolution*, 52–54; Cawley, *Federal Land, Western Anger*, 116–26; Short, *Reagan and Public Lands*, 58, 63–64; George C. Coggins and Doris K. Nagel, " 'Nothing Beside Remains': The Legal Legacy of James G. Watt's Tenure as Secretary of the Interior on Federal Land Law and Policy," 477, 494–97, 522; Rosenbaum, *Environmental Politics and Policy*, 260–64, 283–86; John D. Leshy, "Natural Resource Policy," 25; Culhane, "Sagebrush Rebels in Office," 304; Arnold, *Eye of the Storm*, 135, 160; Fred J. Cook, "Watt Releases the Sea," 104; Eliot Marshall, "For Sale: A Billion Acres of Outer Continental Shelf," 524–25.

46. Quotation in Watt and Wead, *Courage of a Conservative*, 203–4; R. McGreggor Cawley, "James Watt and the Environmentalists: A Clash of Ideologies," 244–50; Adler et al., "James Watt's Land Rush," 23–24.

47. Quotation in Anne Burford and John Greenya, *Are You Tough Enough?* x, 6–7, 20–23, 83–84, 175–86, 281–82; Rosenbaum, *Environmental Politics and Policy*, 97; Cannon, *President Reagan*, 532–34; James N. Miller, "What Really Happened at EPA," 72–78.

48. First quotation in "Notebook," *The New Republic*, 21 February 1983, 7; second and third quotations in Watt and Janssen, *Caught in the Conflict*, 89, 135–37, 148–50, 161–80; Short, *Reagan and Public Lands*, 71–78; Cannon, *President Reagan*, 428–29.

49. Durant, *Administrative Presidency Revisited*, 51; Cawley, *Federal Land, Western Anger*, 12, 150–55, 162; Rosenbaum, *Environmental Politics and Policy*, 5, 25, 286–87; Short, *Reagan and Public Lands*, 38–39, 78–80; Culhane, "Sagebrush Rebels in Office," 294;

Coggins and Nagel, " 'Nothing Beside Remains,' " 476–77, 546, 548–49; Devine, *Reagan's Terrible Swift Sword,* 50–52; Hays, *Beauty, Health, and Permanence,* 525–26.

50. Quotations in Reagan and Novak, *My Turn,* ix, 50; Reagan, *An American Life,* 166–67; Deaver and Herskowitz, *Behind the Scenes,* 105–8; Cannon, *Reagan,* 503; Roosevelt, *Keeper of the Gate,* 200–204.

51. Reagan and Novak, *My Turn,* 22–33, 57; Peter Hay, *All the Presidents' Ladies: Anecdotes of the Women behind the Men in the White House,* 15; Reagan, *An American Life,* 243–44; Marylin Bender and Monsieur Marc, *Nouveau Is Better Than No Riche at All,* 83–90.

52. Quotation in Kelley, *Nancy Reagan,* 192; Reagan and Novak, *My Turn,* 34–37.

53. Reagan and Novak, *My Turn,* 39–43; Betty Boyd Caroli, *First Ladies,* 276–77, 306; Paul F. Boller, *Presidential Wives,* 461, 464; Reagan, *An American Life,* 693–97.

54. Reagan, *An American Life,* 564–66; Reagan, *First Father, First Daughter,* 283–91; Joan Quigley, *"What Does Joan Say?" My Seven Years as White House Astrologer to Nancy and Ronald Reagan,* 12; Davis, *Way I See It,* 11, 105; Regan, *For the Record,* 3–5; Reagan and Novak, *My Turn,* 44–52, 148–49; Wills, *Reagan's America,* 196.

55. First quotation in Reagan, *An American Life,* 287; second and third quotations in Reagan and Novak, *My Turn,* vii–viii, 60–61, 64–65, 109, 184; Cannon, *President Reagan,* 507; Wills, *Reagan's America,* 192–93; von Damm, *At Reagan's Side,* 228–29; James G. Benze, "Nancy Reagan: China Doll or Dragon Lady?" 777–90.

56. Quotation in Cannon, *President Reagan,* 427; Persico, *Casey,* 178–79; Deaver and Herskowitz, *Behind the Scenes,* 39; Reagan and Novak, *My Turn,* 60; Kelley, *Nancy Reagan,* 484, 552; von Damm, *At Reagan's Side,* 72, 307–8.

57. Deaver and Herskowitz, *Behind the Scenes,* 39, 111, 120; Reagan and Novak, *My Turn,* 63–64; Cannon, *President Reagan,* 507–9.

Chapter 7: Facing Defeats, Winning Victories, 1982–1989

1. Weidenbaum, *Rendezvous with Reality,* 14–15; Campagna, *Economy in the Reagan Years,* 31–32; Charles O. Jones, "A New President, A Different Congress, A Maturing Agenda," 277, 280; Alice Rivlin, "The Deficit Dilemma," 135–36; Boskin, *Reagan and the Economy,* 121–23.

2. First quotation in Howard H. Baker, "Baker Recounts His Days as Reagan's Chief of Staff," 2; second quotation in Barrett, *Gambling with History,* 170–74; other quotations in Stockman, *Triumph of Politics,* 269–76, 316–17; White and Wildavsky, *The Deficit,* 183, 185–86.

3. White and Wildavsky, *The Deficit,* 331–32; Langston, *Ideologues and Presidents,* 158–61.

4. Quotation in White and Wildavsky, *The Deficit,* 196–97; Stockman, *Triumph of Politics,* 342–47; Reagan, *Public Papers, 1981,* 1021–22.

5. First quotation in Greider, *Education of David Stockman,* 49–50; second quotation in Barrett, *Gambling with History,* 187; Stockman, *Triumph of Politics,* 1–8, 80–81; Cannon, *President Reagan,* 260–63; Meese, *With Reagan,* 140–41; Reagan, *An American Life,* 314; Ullmann, *Stockman,* 266.

6. Quotations in Reagan, *An American Life,* 315–16; Barrett, *Gambling with History,* 181–86; Meese, *With Reagan,* 142–43; Stockman, *Triumph of Politics,* 358–60; White and Wildavsky, *The Deficit,* 220–24; Roberts, *Supply-Side Revolution,* 214–18, 252–53; David Gergen to Reagan, 11 December 1981, ID: 052476sc, Memorandum, "Press Update—Domestic Issues" 12 February 1982, ID: 062035sc, Memorandum, "Sampling of Initial Senate Reaction to Budget" 12 February 1982, ID: 062035sc, David Gergen to Reagan, 26 February 1982, ID: 063105sc, WHORM: Subject: FG, Reagan presidential papers.

7. First quotation in White and Wildavsky, *The Deficit,* 235–48; other quotations in Reagan, *An American Life,* 317–19; Regan, *For the Record,* 175–85; Reagan, *Public Papers, 1982,* 532–35; see also Reagan telephone calls that contain brief summaries of the conversa-

tions, ID: 065122ss, ID: 080998ss, ID: 065129ss, ID: 065197ss, WHORM: Subject: PR, Reagan presidential papers.

8. Meese, *With Reagan,* 146–47; Nofziger, *Nofziger,* 312–16; Reagan, *An American Life,* 321–22; Reagan to Robert Dole, 2 June 1982, ID: 081971, WHORM: Subject: FI, Reagan telephone call to Jesse Helms, 11 August 1982, ID: 081313ss, WHORM: Subject: PR, Reagan presidential papers; White and Wildavsky, *The Deficit,* 217–18, 249–58; Vogel, *Fluctuating Fortunes,* 252–55.

9. Reagan, *An American Life,* 323.

10. Cannon, *President Reagan,* 232–34, 266–68, 274–75; Boskin, *Reagan and the Economy,* 89–90, 96–105; White and Wildavsky, *The Deficit,* 269, 348; Campagna, *Economy in the Reagan Years,* 90; Niskanen, *Reaganomics,* 155–89; Patric H. Hendershott and Joe Peek, "Interest Rates in the Reagan Years," 161; Bill Alexander et al. to Reagan, 21 April 1983, FG143 folder, WHORM: Subject: FG, Reagan presidential papers. See also William R. Neikirk, *Volcker: Portrait of the Money Man.*

11. Reagan, *Public Papers, 1981,* 1157, *Public Papers, 1983,* 560–62; White and Wildavsky, *The Deficit,* 193, 310–12, 317–26; Cannon, *President Reagan,* 252.

12. Richard A. Harris and Sidney M. Milkis, *The Politics of Regulatory Change: A Tale of Two Agencies,* 8, 97–101, 103–7, 111–13; Charles Noble, *Liberalism at Work: The Rise and Fall of OSHA,* 115–16; Reagan, *Public Papers, 1981,* 63–64, 104–8, *Public Papers, 1985,* 10–12; James C. Miller, *Fix the U.S. Budget! Urgings of an "Abominable No-Man,"* 2–5; David Stockman to Economic Policy Coordinating Committee, 29 December 1980, Reagan-Bush Transition, Anderson papers; Campagna, *Economy in the Reagan Years,* 97–100; V. Kerry Smith, "Environmental Policy Making under Executive Order 12291: An Introduction," 4–37. For studies of Reagan and regulation, see Martha Derthick and Paul J. Quirk, *The Politics of Deregulation;* Roger E. Meiners and Bruce Yandle, eds., *Regulation and the Reagan Era: Politics, Bureaucracy, and the Public Interest;* George C. Eads and Michael Fix, eds., *The Reagan Regulatory Strategy: An Assessment;* Michael Pertschuk, *Revolt against Regulation: The Rise and Pause of the Consumer Movement.*

13. Williamson, *Reagan's Federalism,* 100–33; Philip J. Simon, *Reagan in the Workplace: Unraveling the Health and Safety Net,* i–ii; Vogel, *Fluctuating Fortunes,* 269; Peter J. Boettke, "The Reagan Regulatory Regime: Reality vs. Rhetoric," 117–22; Harris and Milkis, *Politics of Regulatory Change,* 110–11, 113–14, 124; Miller, *Fix the U.S. Budget,* 6–8; Noble, *Liberalism at Work,* 195–96; Salamon and Lund, "Governance in the Reagan Era," 17–18; Cannon, *President Reagan,* 823–24; Kenneth D. Boyer, "The Reagan Regulatory Regime: Comment," 124–27; Campagna, *Economy in the Reagan Years,* 100–104; Jim Miller to Reagan, 3 April 1987, ID: 464686ss, WHORM: Subject: FG, Reagan presidential papers. See also Herbert Burkholz, *The FDA Follies.*

14. First quotation in Reagan, *Public Papers, 1982,* 1331–32; second quotation in Stephen Pizzo, Mary Fricker, and Paul Muolo, *Inside Job: The Looting of America's Savings and Loans,* 1–4, 7, 442–47, 486–87; L. William Seidman, *Full Faith and Credit: The Great S&L Debacle and Other Washington Sagas,* 83–84, 177–81; Kathleen Day, *S&L Hell: The People and the Politics behind the $1 Trillion Savings and Loan Scandal,* 9, 20, 34, 135–36; "Study: S&L Bailout Debacle Price Tag Put at $481 Billion," *La Crosse Tribune,* 13 June 1996; Michael M. Thomas, "The Greatest American Shambles," 30; Steven K. Wilmsen, *Silverado: Neil Bush and the Savings and Loan Scandal,* 36–49, 53–55; Lou Cannon, "A Journalist's Perspective," 56–57; James R. Adams, *The Big Fix: Inside the S&L Scandal,* 197–98, 200–203, 235–39; Cannon, *President Reagan,* 827–28. See also R. Dan Brumbaugh, *Thrifts under Siege: Restoring Order to American Banking;* Edward J. Kane, *The S&L Insurance Mess: How Did It Happen?;* and Lawrence J. White, *The S&L Debacle: Public Policy Lessons for Bank and Thrift Regulation.*

15. Reagan, *Public Papers, 1983,* 362–64.

16. Quotation in Scheer, *With Enough Shovels,* 199–201; Wirls, *Buildup,* 134–36; Weinberger, *Fighting for Peace,* 291–97; Donald R. Baucom, *The Origins of SDI,* 3–14,

20–24, 27–50, 54–71, 87, 89–90; Janne E. Nolan, *Guardians of the Arsenal: The Politics of Nuclear Strategy,* 11–13; James Chace and Caleb Carr, *America Invulnerable: The Quest for Absolute Security from 1812 to Star Wars,* 12, 315, 317; Rebecca S. Bjork, *The Strategic Defense Initiative: Symbolic Containment of the Nuclear Threat,* 1, 18, 61–63, 65–66; F. H. Knelman, *Reagan, God, and the Bomb: From Myth to Policy in the Nuclear Arms Race,* 6–7; Crowe and Chanoff, *Line of Fire,* 301. See also Union of Concerned Scientists, *The Fallacy of Star Wars;* E. P. Thompson, ed., *Star Wars;* Angelo Codevilla, *While Others Build: The Commonsense Approach to the Strategic Defense Initiative;* Frederick Donovan and James E. Goodby, *Changing the Rules: President Ronald Reagan's Strategic Defense Initiative (SDI) Decision;* Louisa S. Hulett, *From Cold Wars to Star Wars: Debates Over Defense and Detente;* and David Z. Robinson, *The Strategic Defense Initiative: Its Effect on the Economy and Arms Control.*

17. First quotation in Anderson, *Revolution,* xxxiii; second quotation in Reagan, *An American Life,* 547, 549–50; third quotation in Cannon, *President Reagan,* 323; George A. Keyworth, SIDO oral history interview, Reagan Library.

18. Quotations in Baucom, *Origins of SDI,* 171–81, 184–92; Cannon, *President Reagan,* 163–71, 323–28; Weinberger, *Fighting for Peace,* 298–304; Nolan, *Guardians of the Arsenal,* 164–65.

19. Quotations in Reagan, *Public Papers, 1983,* 437–43.

20. Quotation in Shultz, *Turmoil and Triumph,* 255–56, 260, 264; Nolan, *Guardians of the Arsenal,* 8, 13, 17–18; Michael R. Beschloss and Strobe Talbott, *At the Highest Levels: The Inside Story of the End of the Cold War,* 114; William J. Broad, *Teller's War: The Top-Secret Story behind the Star Wars Deception,* 133.

21. Quotation in Margaret Thatcher, *The Downing Street Years,* 463.

22. Quotations in Reagan, *An American Life,* 280–82, 288–91.

23. Quotations in Reagan, *Public Papers, 1983,* 1221, 1223–30, 1249; Oberdorfer, *The Turn,* 51–53, 56–57, 59; Reagan to Meldrim Thomson (3 October 1983), ID: 174036, WHORM: Subject: FG, Reagan presidential papers; Christopher Simpson, *National Security Directives of the Reagan and Bush Administrations: The Declassified History of U.S. Political and Military Policy, 1981–1991,* 240. See also Alvin A. Snyder, *Warriors of Disinformation: American Propaganda, Soviet Lies, and the Winning of the Cold War,* 43–72; Seymour M. Hersh, *"The Target Is Destroyed": What Really Happened to Flight 007 and What America Knew About It;* Alexander Dallin, *Black Box: KAL 007 and the Superpowers.*

24. Quotation in Reagan, *An American Life,* 466; Cannon, *President Reagan,* 389; Shultz, *Turmoil and Triumph,* 43–44; David M. Kennedy, *The Reagan Administration and Lebanon,* 1; Weinberger, *Fighting for Peace,* 136–42.

25. Shultz, *Turmoil and Triumph,* 43–44.

26. Weinberger, *Fighting for Peace,* 433–45.

27. Quotation in Cannon, *President Reagan,* 405–6; Weinberger, *Fighting for Peace,* 142–45, 159–60.

28. Shultz, *Turmoil and Triumph,* 76–83; Kennedy, *Reagan Administration and Lebanon,* 2–4.

29. Quotation in Shultz, *Turmoil and Triumph,* 85–99, 429–44; Reagan, *Public Papers, 1982,* 1093–97; Cannon, *President Reagan,* 406–7.

30. Quotation in Shultz, *Turmoil and Triumph,* 100–111; Kennedy, *Reagan Administration and Lebanon,* 6; Cannon, *President Reagan,* 407–9; Reagan, *Public Papers, 1982,* 1187–89.

31. Thatcher, *Downing Street Years,* 327; Weinberger, *Fighting for Peace,* 155–56, 160–61; Cannon, *President Reagan,* 409–416.

32. Quotation in Reagan to Meldrim Thomson (3 October 1983), ID: 174036, WHORM: Subject: FG, Reagan presidential papers; Weinberger, *Fighting for Peace,* 156–59; McFarlane and Smardz, *Special Trust,* 237–54; Cannon, *President Reagan,* 418–22, 436–57.

33. William R. Nylen, *U.S.-Grenada Relations, 1979–1983: American Foreign Policy towards a "Backyard" Revolution,* 1–8, 12, 15–39; Weinberger, *Fighting for Peace,* 101–25; Shultz, *Turmoil and Triumph,* 343; Reagan, *Public Papers, 1983,* 440; Thatcher, *Downing*

Street Years, 329–32; statements by Reagan and Eugenia Charles, 25 October 1983, ID: 162123ca, Phil Peters to Jim Courter, 15 January 1986, ID: 393507, WHORM: Subject: FG, John Tower to Senate Committee on Armed Services, 9 November 1983, ID: 177165, WHORM: Subject: CO, Reagan presidential papers. See also Jorge Heine, ed., *A Revolution Aborted: The Lessons of Grenada.*

34. Quotation in Cannon, *Reagan,* 315; Mayer, *Changing American Mind,* 29–30; David Gergen to Reagan with attachment, 29 January 1982, ID: 076335sc, WHORM: Subject: FG, Reagan presidential papers.

35. First quotation in Cannon, *Reagan,* 316; second quotation in Billy Graham to Reagan, 17 January 1989, ID: 70004, WHORM: Subject: FG, Reagan presidential papers; Diamond, *Roads to Dominion,* 228; Moen, *Christian Right and Congress,* 51–54, 162; Pierard and Linder, *Civil Religion,* 281; Edel, *Defenders of the Faith,* 128; Jorstad, *Holding Fast/Pressing On,* 62; Dionne, *Why Americans Hate Politics,* 236–37; Cannon, *President Reagan,* 813–19; Falwell, *Strength for the Journey,* 380; C. Everett Koop, *Koop: The Memoirs of America's Family Doctor,* 194–224, 228–30, 267–73; Reagan to William F. Buckley (1 June 1982), ID: 082596, WHORM: Subject: FG, Reagan presidential papers.

36. Quotation in Barrett, *Gambling with History,* 61–62; Connie Paige, *The Right to Lifers: Who They Are, How They Operate, Where They Get Their Money,* 226; Richard Viguerie to Reagan, 2 August 1982, ID: 081373ss, Reagan to Meldrim Thomson (3 October 1983), ID: 174036, Mickey Edwards to William P. Clark, 23 February 1983, ID: 134798, Reagan to Clymer Wright (18 May 1982), ID: 079222, WHORM: Subject: FG, Reagan presidential papers.

37. Green, *George Bush,* 185–86, 189; Bush and Gold, *Looking Forward,* 224–28; Cramer, *What It Takes,* 13–15.

38. Quotation in Steven A. Shull, *A Kinder, Gentler Racism? The Reagan-Bush Civil Rights Legacy,* 3–4, 40, 184; Edward G. Carmines and James A. Stimson, *Issue Evolution: Race and the Transformation of American Politics,* 54; Gary Orfield and Carole Ashkinaze, *The Closing Door: Conservative Policy and Black Opportunity,* xiii–xvii, 1, 13, 205–8; Kenneth O'Reilly, *Nixon's Piano: Presidents and Racial Politics from Washington to Clinton,* 366–67; Rieder, "Rise of the 'Silent Majority,' " 244.

39. Quotation in Reagan to Meldrim Thomson (3 October 1983), ID: 174036, WHORM: Subject: FG, Reagan presidential papers; Carmines and Stimson, *Issue Evolution,* 114; Speakes and Pack, *Speaking Out,* 69–70; Cannon, *President Reagan,* 519–25; Reagan, *Public Papers, 1983,* 1487–88.

40. Norman C. Amaker, *Civil Rights and the Reagan Administration,* xxvii, 34–42, 59–65, 79–97, 103–11, 120–30, 157–60, 169–80; Shull, *Kinder Gentler Racism,* 114–17, 151–52, 183–84, 188–89; Orfield and Ashkinaze, *Closing Door,* 209–10; Chester E. Finn, " 'Affirmative Action' under Reagan," 17–26; Smith, *Law and Justice,* 89–94; O'Reilly, *Nixon's Piano,* 363–64; Robert R. Detlefsen, *Civil Rights under Reagan,* 2–13, 60–61; Edsall and Edsall, *Chain Reaction,* 187–90; Moen, *Christian Right and Congress,* 27–28; Charles Fried, *Order and Law: Arguing the Reagan Revolution, A Firsthand Account,* 40–42.

41. Susan M. Hartmann, *From Margin to Mainstream: American Women and Politics since 1960,* 155–57; Tanya Melich, *The Republican War against Women: An Insider's Report from behind the Lines,* 149, 159, 161; Nancy E. McGlen and Meredith Reid Sarkees, *Women in Foreign Policy: The Insiders,* 189–91; Goldman and Fuller, *Quest for the Presidency,* 22.

42. First quotation in Barrett, *Gambling with History,* 4; second quotation in Melich, *Republican War against Women,* 165; third and fourth quotations in Nofziger, *Nofziger,* 245–46; fifth quotation in Noonan, *What I Saw,* 56; sixth quotation in von Damm, *At Reagan's Side,* 266.

43. First quotation in Barrett, *Gambling with History,* 12–13; second quotation in John L. Napier to Dick Cheney, 14 December 1981, ID: 056123, WHORM: Subject: FG, Reagan presidential papers; Noonan, *What I Saw,* 123; White and Wildavsky, *The Deficit,* 297–300. For many articles giving midterm evaluations of the Reagan administration, see ID:

124139, WHORM: Subject: FG, Reagan presidential papers. See also Paul Pierson, *Disman-tling the Welfare State? Reagan, Thatcher, and the Politics of Retrenchment;* Raymond J. Struyk, Neil Mayer, and John A. Tuccillo, *Federal Housing Policy at President Reagan's Midterm;* John P. Zais, Raymond J. Struyk, and Thomas Thibodeau, *Housing Assistance for Older Americans;* John C. Weicher, ed., *Maintaining the Safety Net: Income Redistribution Programs in the Reagan Administration.*

44. Quotation in Ullmann, *Stockman,* 220–21; Campagna, *Economy in the Reagan Years,* 90; Michael B. Katz, *In the Shadow of the Poorhouse: A Social History of Welfare in America,* 278–83, 285–86, 288; report, "Fairness Issues: A Briefing Book," 1 June 1982, ID: 077309cs, WHORM: Subject: FG, Reagan presidential papers.

45. First quotation in Reagan, *Public Papers, 1984,* 109–10; second quotation in Goldman and Fuller, *Quest for the Presidency,* 366; Cannon, *President Reagan,* 510–11, 514–15; J. Leonard Reinsch, *Getting Elected: From Radio and Roosevelt to Television and Reagan,* 295; see also Austin Ranney, ed., *The American Elections of 1984.*

46. Quotations in Germond and Witcover, *Wake Us When It's Over,* 330, 337–39, 468–69; Cannon, *President Reagan,* 501; Goldman and Fuller, *Quest for the Presidency,* 27, 262–63.

47. Albert R. Hunt, "The Campaign and the Issues," 129, 133–35; Gillon, *Democrats' Dilemma,* 366–70, 374, 379; Edsall and Edsall, *Chain Reaction,* 202–14; Melich, *Republican War against Women,* 176–79; Germond and Witcover, *Wake Us When It's Over,* 336.

48. First quotation in Elizabeth Drew, *Campaign Journal: The Political Events of 1983–1984,* 560–64; second quotation in White and Wildavsky, *The Deficit,* 412, 419–21, 425–26; third quotation in Reagan, *Public Papers, 1984,* 1131; Cannon, *President Reagan,* 510–11; Germond and Witcover, *Wake Us When It's Over,* 409–10, 413; Gillon, *Democrats' Di-lemma,* 361.

49. Quotation in Harold W. Stanley, "The 1984 Presidential Election in the South: Race and Realignment," 309; Edsall and Edsall, *Chain Reaction,* 202; Hertsgaard, *On Bended Knee,* 250–51; Berman, *America's Right Turn,* 93–94; Cannon, *President Reagan,* 511–14.

50. First quotation in Cannon, *President Reagan,* 538–46; second quotation in Reagan and Novak, *My Turn,* 266; Mondale quotations in Germond and Witcover, *Wake Us When It's Over,* 510; Gillon, *Democrats' Dilemma,* 382–83; Goldman and Fuller, *Quest for the Presi-dency,* 317–20; debate transcript in Reagan, *Public Papers, 1984,* 1440–62.

51. Goldman and Fuller, *Quest for the Presidency,* 28–29, 322; Hertsgaard, *On Bended Knee,* 245–46; Hunt, "Campaign and the Issues," 152–53; Germond and Witcover, *Wake Us When It's Over,* 2, 514; Rich Jaroslovsky and James M. Perry, "New Question in Race: Is Oldest U.S. President Now Showing His Age?" *Wall Street Journal,* 9 October 1984.

52. Goldman and Fuller, *Quest for the Presidency,* 320–21, 323–25, 336–39, 341; Can-non, *President Reagan,* 547–51.

53. First quotation in Reagan, *Public Papers, 1984,* 1589–1608; second quotation in Reagan, *An American Life,* 328–29; William A. Henry, *Visions of America: How We Saw the 1984 Election,* 255; Germond and Witcover, *Wake Us When It's Over,* 4–11; Gillon, *Democrats' Dilemma,* 386; Geraldine A. Ferraro, *Ferraro: My Story,* 279–80; Goldman and Fuller, *Quest for the Presidency,* 343; Reinsch, *Getting Elected,* 289–90.

54. Paul R. Abramson, John H. Aldrich, and David W. Rohde, *Change and Continuity in the 1984 Elections,* 103–5, 135–40; Cannon, *President Reagan,* 493–94; Ferraro, *Ferraro,* 310–13; Stanley, "The 1984 Presidential Election," 303, 305; Vogel, *Fluctuating Fortunes,* 273; Melich, *Republican War against Women,* 179–80.

55. Cannon, *President Reagan,* 551–52, 554–61, 564–65, 567–71; Reagan and Novak, *My Turn,* 312–14; Noonan, *What I Saw,* 201, 204–13; Reagan, *An American Life,* 488; Regan, *For the Record,* 218–29; Debora Silverman, *Selling Culture: Bloomingdale's, Diana Vree-land, and the New Aristocracy of Taste in Reagan's America,* 156–57.

56. Reagan, *Public Papers, 1984,* 89–90; Regan, *For the Record,* 193–95, 201–3; Patrick Buchanan to Reagan, 6 September 1985, ID: 275995sc, WHORM: Subject: FG, Reagan

presidential papers. See also Jeffrey H. Birnbaum and Alan S. Murray, *Showdown at Gucci Gulch: Lawmakers, Lobbyists, and the Unlikely Triumph of Tax Reform;* Joel Slemrod, ed., *Do Taxes Matter? The Impact of the Tax Reform Act of 1986;* and C. Eugene Steuerle, *The Tax Decade: How Taxes Came to Dominate the Public Agenda.*

57. Regan, *For the Record,* 214–17, 283–86; Reagan, *Public Papers, 1985,* 678–82, *Public Papers, 1986,* 1414–16; White and Wildavsky, *The Deficit,* 470–72, 476–95, 502–4; Joseph J. Minarik, *Making America's Budget Policy: From the 1980s to the 1990s,* xii; Vogel, *Fluctuating Fortunes,* 279–82; Henry J. Aaron, "The Impossible Dream Comes True," 10; Thomas F. Gibson to Donald Regan, 18 December 1985, Taxes-3 folder, Patrick Buchanan Files, Reagan presidential papers.

58. Dionne, *Why Americans Hate Politics,* 298–99; Berman, *America's Right Turn,* 131–32; Mayer and McManus, *Landslide,* 4–7.

59. Quotations in Marilyn W. Thompson, *Feeding the Beast: How Wedtech Became the Most Corrupt Little Company in America,* 64–65, 151–52, 289–90, 298–99, 301; James Traub, *Too Good to Be True: The Outlandish Story of Wedtech,* xiv, 75; Cannon, "Journalist's Perspective," 58; Ben Bradlee, *A Good Life: Newspapering and Other Adventures,* 409; Suzanne Garment, *Scandal: The Crisis of Mistrust in American Politics,* 286–87; Nathan Miller, *Stealing from America: A History of Corruption from Jamestown to Reagan,* 344; Cannon, *President Reagan,* 17, 794–802; Fried, *Order and Law,* 47–48; Ethan Bronner, *Battle for Justice: How the Bork Nomination Shook America,* 34.

60. Quotation in Noonan, *What I Saw,* 244–49; James A. McClure to Patrick J. Buchanan, 31 July 1985, ID: 358840, Beau Boulter to Patrick J. Buchanan, 6 January 1986, ID: 381658, Phil Peters to Jim Courter, 15 January 1986, ID: 393507, Lamar Alexander to Howard Baker, 30 March 1987, ID: 505240, Gary Bauer to Tom Griscom, 19 November 1987, ID: 547487, Richard Wirthlin to Howard Baker, 9 December 1987, ID: 540188, Reagan to William W. Peaslee (18 April 1988), ID: 561134, WHORM: Subject: FG, Lyn Nofziger to Reagan, 3 November 1987, ID: 604143, WHORM: Subject: PR, Reagan presidential papers.

61. Robert H. Bork, *The Tempting of America: The Political Seduction of the Law,* 268, 345; Bronner, *Battle for Justice,* 17, 32, 35, 199–200, 214, 309, 311–12, 347–49; Patrick B. McGuigan and Dawn M. Weyrich, *Ninth Justice: The Fight for Bork,* 224; Thomas C. Griscom to Reagan, 16 October 1987, ID: 492925ss, WHORM: Subject: FG, Reagan presidential papers.

62. Quotation in Smith, *Law and Justice,* xv–xvi, 58–61, 72–73; Bronner, *Battle for Justice,* 38; Herman Schwartz, *Packing the Courts: The Conservative Campaign to Rewrite the Constitution,* xii–xiii, 5–6, 9, 60–62, 86–88; Fried, *Order and Law,* 14–18; T. Kenneth Cribb to Reagan, 26 June 1987, ID: 474566cc, Cribb to Reagan, 13 May 1988, ID: 562270ss, Cribb to Reagan, 4 June 1988, ID: 562488ss, WHORM: Subject: FG, Reagan presidential papers. See also Christopher E. Smith, *Justice Antonin Scalia and the Supreme Court's Conservative Moment;* Sue Davis, *Justice Rehnquist and the Constitution;* and David G. Savage, *Turning Right: The Making of the Rehnquist Supreme Court.*

63. Schwartz, *Packing the Courts,* 63; Cannon, *Reagan,* 315–16; Melich, *Republican War against Women,* 156; Savage, *Turning Right,* 5; Paige, *Right to Lifers,* 222–24; Reagan to Al D'Amato, 15 September 1981, ID: 033433, WHORM: Subject: FG, Reagan presidential papers.

64. Savage, *Turning Right,* 425; Schaller, *Reckoning with Reagan,* 81; Cannon, *President Reagan,* 802–4, 813; Smith, *Law and Justice,* 58; Schwartz, *Packing the Courts,* 3–5, 58–60, 66, 68–73; Bronner, *Battle for Justice,* 47; T. Kenneth Cribb to Reagan, 4 June 1988, ID: 562458ss, WHORM: Subject: FG, Reagan presidential papers.

Chapter 8: Engaging the Soviets, 1981–1985

1. First quotation in Kernek, "Reagan's Foreign Policy Leadership," 5; second quotation in Marlin Fitzwater, *Call the Briefing! Bush and Reagan, Sam and Helen: A Decade with*

Presidents and the Press, 138; Anatoly Dobrynin, *In Confidence: Moscow's Ambassador to America's Six Cold War Presidents, 1962–1986,* 594; Powell and Persico, *My American Journey,* 359; Robert M. Gates, *From the Shadows: The Ultimate Insider's Story of Five Presidents and How They Won the Cold War,* 194; Regan, *For the Record,* 294. For critical accounts of Reagan's foreign policy, see Jeff McMahan, *Reagan and the World: Imperial Policy in the New Cold War;* Holly Sklar, *Reagan, Trilateralism, and the Neoliberals: Containment and Intervention in the 1980s.* For a succinct account of Reagan's policy, see Warren I. Cohen, *America in the Age of Soviet Power, 1945–1991.*

2. Cannon, *President Reagan,* 306–7.

3. First quotation in Woodward, *Veil,* 254; second quotation in Cannon, *President Reagan,* 462, 465–66; other quotations in Pierre E. Trudeau, *Memoirs,* 329, 332.

4. First, second, and third quotations in Reagan, *An American Life,* 551, 588–89; fourth and fifth quotations in Dobrynin, *In Confidence,* 594; White House News Summary, 26 August 1985, Soviet Union folder, Donald Fortier file, Reagan presidential papers.

5. First quotation in Baker and Defrank, *Politics of Diplomacy,* 26–27; second quotation in Powell and Persico, *My American Journey,* 334.

6. Gates, *From the Shadows,* 278, 280–82; Cannon, *President Reagan,* 307–9; Pat M. Holt, *Secret Intelligence and Public Policy: A Dilemma of Democracy,* 197; Shultz, *Turmoil and Triumph,* 311–18, 725–26.

7. First quotation in McFarlane and Smardz, *Special Trust,* 323–24; second quotation in Powell and Persico, *My American Journey,* 314–15; Cannon, *President Reagan,* 301–2, 308–10, 405; Weinberger, *Fighting for Peace,* 331–32; Keith L. Shimko, *Images and Arms Control: Perceptions of the Soviet Union in the Reagan Administration,* 66–71, 74–77; Menges, *Inside the National Security Council,* 94, 129.

8. Cannon, *President Reagan,* 292, 340–41; McGlen and Sarkees, *Women in Foreign Policy,* 259–60; John Prados, *Keepers of the Keys: A History of the National Security Council from Truman to Bush,* 496; Talbott, *Deadly Gambits,* 11; Nitze, "Reagan and the Realities," 38–39; McFarlane and Smardz, *Special Trust,* 254–56, 326–30; Caspar W. Weinberger, "Reagan and International Arms Agreements," 45; Michael A. Ledeen, *Perilous Statecraft: An Insider's Account of the Iran-Contra Affair,* 148; Mayer and McManus, *Landslide,* 52–53, 60; Kampelman, *Entering New Worlds,* 310; Powell and Persico, *My American Journey,* 308–9, 366; Robert Timberg, *The Nightingale's Song,* 371–73; Shultz, *Turmoil and Triumph,* 902–4, 907–8, 990–91, 1080–81.

9. Quotation in Powell and Persico, *My American Journey,* 375; Sidney Blumenthal, *Pledging Allegiance: The Last Campaign of the Cold War,* 5. See also Patrick Glynn, *Closing Pandora's Box: Arms Races, Arms Control, and the History of the Cold War;* William G. Hyland, *The Cold War Is Over;* and Richard Smoke, *National Security and the Nuclear Dilemma: An Introduction to the American Experience in the Cold War.*

10. Quotation in Henry Kissinger, *Diplomacy,* 802; Dobrynin, *In Confidence,* 477; Dana H. Allin, *Cold War Illusions: America, Europe, and Soviet Power, 1969–1989,* xi; McFarlane and Smardz, *Special Trust,* 235; Gates, *From the Shadows,* 535–40; John Lewis Gaddis, *The United States and the End of the Cold War: Implications, Reconsiderations, Provocations,* 130–32; Oberdorfer, *The Turn,* 435–39; David Remnick, "Getting Russia Right," 20–21. See also Jeane J. Kirkpatrick, *The Withering Away of the Totalitarian State and Other Surprises.*

11. First quotation in Reagan, *Public Papers, 1982,* 744–47; second quotation in Peter Schweizer, *Victory: The Reagan Administration's Secret Strategy That Hastened the Collapse of the Soviet Union,* xiii; third quotation in Gates, *From the Shadows,* 194; Kissinger, *Diplomacy,* 784; Allin, *Cold War Illusions,* 177.

12. Quotation in Robert C. McFarlane to Reagan, 3 June 1988, ID: 573582, WHORM: Subject: PR, Reagan presidential papers; Gates, *From the Shadows,* 194–95; Schweizer, *Victory,* xi–xiii; Jack F. Matlock, *Autopsy on an Empire: The American Ambassador's Account of the Collapse of the Soviet Union,* 670; Jay Winik, *On The Brink: The Dramatic, Behind-the-Scenes Saga of the Reagan Era and the Men and Women Who Won the Cold War,*

311–13; Jerry Hough, *Russia and the West: Gorbachev and the Politics of Reform,* 213–14.

13. Quotation in Ronald Reagan Center for Public Affairs, *The Cold War: Ten Years Later,* 35; see also Steve Crawshaw, *Goodbye to the USSR: The Collapse of Soviet Power.*

14. First and fourth quotations in Allin, *Cold War Illusions,* 173–79; second quotation in Robert G. Kaiser, *Why Gorbachev Happened: His Triumphs and His Failure,* 15–17, 115–16, 121–22; third quotation in Martin Walker, *The Cold War: A History,* 232–41; Dobrynin, *In Confidence,* 611–12; Hough, *Russia and the West,* 118–19, 234; Wirls, *Buildup,* 224–25; Richard Crockatt, *The Fifty Years War: The United States and the Soviet Union in World Politics, 1941–1991,* 356–60, 365–66; Nitze, "Reagan and the Realities," 24–25; Matlock, *Autopsy on an Empire,* 69, 86–91, 149, 668–70.

15. First quotation in Gates, *From the Shadows,* 263–66; second quotation in Schweizer, *Victory,* 133–36, 138; Drew, *Portrait of an Election,* 118–19; Cannon, *President Reagan,* 297–98; Reagan, *An American Life,* 548, 551–52; Reagan, *Public Papers, 1981,* 194–95; Wirls, *Buildup,* 224; Haig, *Caveat,* 27–30; Thatcher, *Downing Street Years,* 324–25, 465–67; Dobrynin, *In Confidence,* 611; Baucom, *Origins of SDI,* 197–98; Dusko Doder and Louis Branson, *Gorbachev: Heretic in the Kremlin,* 109–10, 252; Blumenthal, *Pledging Allegiance,* 42; Gaddis, *End of the Cold War,* 43, 225 note 83; Coral Bell, *The Reagan Paradox: American Foreign Policy in the 1980s,* 34; Nitze, "Reagan and the Realities," 32–33; Kissinger, *Diplomacy,* 778; Walker, *Cold War,* 274; McFarlane and Smardz, *Special Trust,* 235.

16. Quotations in Schweizer, *Victory,* xvi, 76–77, 123–26; Simpson, *National Security Directives,* 63–64, 80–81.

17. Quotation in Schweizer, *Victory,* 130–33; Simpson, *National Security Directives,* 227–28, 255–63; McFarlane and Smardz, *Special Trust,* 219–22.

18. First quotation in Reagan, *Public Papers, 1982,* 581–85, *Public Papers, 1985,* 135; second quotation in Kissinger, *Diplomacy,* 773; Gaddis, *End of the Cold War,* 249; Winik, *On the Brink,* 457–58; Jeane J. Kirkpatrick, *The Reagan Doctrine and U.S. Foreign Policy,* 1, 5–14; Holt, *Secret Intelligence,* 155; Cannon, *President Reagan,* 368–72; Walker, *Cold War,* 287–88. See also Mark P. Lagon, *The Reagan Doctrine: Sources of American Conduct in the Cold War's Last Chapter.*

19. First quotation in Haig, *Caveat,* 238–41; second quotation in Vyacheslav M. Molotov and Felix Chuev, *Molotov Remembers: Inside Kremlin Politics,* 54; third quotation in Schweizer, *Victory,* 67–70, 75–76, 225; Reagan, *An American Life,* 302–6; Reagan, *Public Papers, 1981,* 1209; Dobrynin, *In Confidence,* 500; Gates, *From the Shadows,* 226–36; David Gergen to Reagan, 18 December 1981, ID: 053331, WHORM: Subject: FG, Reagan presidential papers. See also Arthur R. Rachwald, *In Search of Poland: The Superpowers' Response to Solidarity, 1980–1989.*

20. First quotation in Reagan, *An American Life,* 237–38, 316, second and third quotations in Schweizer, *Victory,* 20–21, 102–6; Herbert E. Meyer to William Casey, 21 June 1984, Soviet Union folder, Donald Fortier file, Reagan presidential papers.

21. Quotations in Schweizer, *Victory,* 24–32, 81–82, 202–5, 219–20, 236–37, 242–43; Walker, *Cold War,* 328–29.

22. Quotation in Schweizer, *Victory,* 205–8, 212–15, 229–32, 267–73; Winik, *On the Brink,* 416; Gates, *From the Shadows,* 249–52, 256–57; Gaddis, *End of the Cold War,* 123–24; Reagan to Mary E. Rogers, 23 January 1980, RR Correspondence 1980 folder, Reagan Subject Collection; Persico, *Casey,* 225–26.

23. First quotation in David Callahan, *Dangerous Capabilities: Paul Nitze and the Cold War,* 417; other quotations in Dobrynin, *In Confidence,* 530; Shimko, *Images and Arms Control,* 102–10, 113–15, 120.

24. First quotation in Dobrynin, *In Confidence,* 606; other quotations in Reagan, *An American Life,* 256–58, 550, 586.

25. Quotation in Reagan, *An American Life,* 567; Shimko, *Images and Arms Control,* 105, 118, 235, 240–41; Matlock, *Autopsy on an Empire,* 77; Reagan to Meldrim Thomson (3 October 1983), ID: 174036, WHORM: Subject: FG, Reagan presidential papers; Anderson, *Revolution,* 73–74; Crockatt, *Fifty Years War,* 364–65.

26. First quotation in Reagan, *Public Papers, 1981,* 57; other quotations in Dobrynin, *In Confidence,* 484–86; Haig, *Caveat,* 101–5.

27. Quotation in Reagan, *An American Life,* 269–73; Deaver and Herskowitz, *Behind the Scenes,* 262–63.

28. Dobrynin, *In Confidence,* 481, 491–93.

29. Quotation in Shultz, *Turmoil and Triumph,* 119, 122–26, 159–60; Shimko, *Images and Arms Control,* 85–97, 100.

30. Dobrynin, *In Confidence,* 513; Gates, *From the Shadows,* 189–90; Oberdorfer, *The Turn,* 63; Walker, *Cold War,* 272–74, 280–83; Crockatt, *Fifty Years War,* 310–12.

31. Quotation in Shultz, *Turmoil and Triumph,* 162–63, 168; Oberdorfer, *The Turn,* 34–35.

32. Dobrynin, *In Confidence,* 498; Shultz, *Turmoil and Triumph,* 164–65; Oberdorfer, *The Turn,* 16–17.

33. Quotations in Dobrynin, *In Confidence,* 517–21, 529–30; Oberdorfer, *The Turn,* 17–21; Shultz, *Turmoil and Triumph,* 167–71; Cannon, *President Reagan,* 311–13; Reagan, *An American Life,* 572–73.

34. Shultz, *Turmoil and Triumph,* 165–67, 265–84; Oberdorfer, *The Turn,* 35–36; Reagan, *An American Life,* 572.

35. Quotations in Reagan, *Public Papers, 1983,* 363–64; Reagan, *An American Life,* 576–81; Oberdorfer, *The Turn,* 23–25, 37–39; Reagan to Andropov, 11 July 1983, Presidential Correspondence, USSR Chairman Yuri Andropov folder, Head of State file, Reagan presidential papers.

36. Quotation in Dobrynin, *In Confidence,* 536, 539; Cannon, *President Reagan,* 742–43; Reagan, *An American Life,* 582–85; Shultz, *Turmoil and Triumph,* 361–66; Gates, *From the Shadows,* 267–68; Walker, *Cold War,* 275 note.

37. Quotation in Shultz, *Turmoil and Triumph,* 346–47, 358–60, 373–75, 463–65, 510; Winik, *On the Brink,* 293–95, 380; Shimko, *Images and Arms Control,* 149–50; Jeffrey Herf, *War by Other Means: Soviet Power, West German Resistance, and the Battle of the Euromissiles,* 228–29.

38. Quotations in Dobrynin, *In Confidence,* 478–79, 481–82, 495, 522–23, 540–41, 544, 550–51; Walker, *Cold War,* 274–77; Gates, *From the Shadows,* 270–73; Oberdorfer, *The Turn,* 64–68; Molotov and Chuev, *Molotov Remembers,* 52; John W. Parker, *From Brezhnev to Chernenko, 1978 to 1985,* vol. 1 of *Kremlin in Transition,* 65; Strobe Talbott, *The Russians and Reagan,* 119–27.

39. Quotation in Shultz, *Turmoil and Triumph,* 466; Matlock, *Autopsy on an Empire,* 77; McFarlane and Smardz, *Special Trust,* 295; Michael Mandelbaum and Strobe Talbott, *Reagan and Gorbachev,* 40.

40. Quotation in Reagan, *Public Papers, 1984,* 40–43; Dobrynin, *In Confidence,* 544–46; Matlock, *Autopsy on an Empire,* 84–86; Jack Matlock to Robert McFarlane, 12 January 1984, McFarlane Press Briefing, 16 January 1984, SP833 (Soviet/U.S. Relations, WH, 1–16–84) folder, Reagan presidential papers; Oberdorfer, *The Turn,* 69–74.

41. Quotations in Reagan, *An American Life,* 589; Dobrynin, *In Confidence,* 546–47.

42. Quotations in Dobrynin, *In Confidence,* 548–51; Reagan, *An American Life,* 595–602; Doder and Branson, *Gorbachev,* 111–12; Oberdorfer, *The Turn,* 79; Chernenko, "Text of Chernenko Speech to Election Meeting," 2 March 1984, ID: 8401819, Jack F. Matlock file, Barney Oldfield to Reagan, 6 July 1984, Yuri Arbatov to Barney Oldfield, 30 April 1984, ID: 216557ss, WHORM: Subject: FG, Reagan presidential papers.

43. First quotation in Reagan, *An American Life,* 602–4; other quotations in Andrei Gromyko, *Memories,* 304–8; Shultz, *Turmoil and Triumph,* 483–90.

44. First two quotations in Reagan, *An American Life,* 605–6; third quotation in Winik, *On the Brink,* 321; Shultz, *Turmoil and Triumph,* 490–500; McFarlane and Smardz, *Special Trust,* 292.

45. First and third quotations in Reagan, *An American Life,* 611–15; second quotation in Dobrynin, *In Confidence,* 567.

46. First quotation in Gates, *From the Shadows,* 377, 382; second quotation in Powell and

Persico, *My American Journey*, 392; Mandelbaum and Talbott, *Reagan and Gorbachev*, 68–73; Matlock, *Autopsy on an Empire*, 52, 66–67; Hough, *Russia and the West*, 209; A. W. Marshall to Don Fortier, 19 April 1985, Soviet Union folder, Donald Fortier file, Reagan presidential papers. See also Archie Brown, *The Gorbachev Factor*.

47. Quotation in Schweizer, *Victory*, 238–39; Dobrynin, *In Confidence*, 479; Richard N. Lebow and Janice G. Stein, *We All Lost the Cold War*, 373–75; Walker, *Cold War*, 290–91; Matlock, *Autopsy on an Empire*, 121–23.

48. Shimko, *Images and Arms Control*, 133, 140–44; Winik, *On the Brink*, 36–37, 43, 120–21, 123, 144, 156–57. See also Richard Perle's novel dealing with these issues, *Hard Line*.

49. Talbott, *Deadly Gambits*, 6–7; William B. Vogele, *Stepping Back: Nuclear Arms Control and the End of the Cold War*, 106–7; Shimko, *Images and Arms Control*, 127–28, 150–54, 171–76; Paul H. Nitze, *From Hiroshima to Glasnost: At the Center of Decision*, 367–69; Reagan, *An American Life*, 293–97, 550–51; Kernek, "Reagan's Foreign Policy Leadership," 6; Reagan, *Public Papers, 1981*, 1064–65; Cannon, *President Reagan*, 302–4; Winik, *On the Brink*, 164–78. See also John Lofland, *Polite Protesters: The American Peace Movement of the 1980s;* and Sam Marullo and John Lofland, eds., *Peace Action in the Eighties*.

50. Quotation in Shultz, *Turmoil and Triumph*, 351, 354–57, 371–73, 500–502, 510–14; Reagan, *Public Papers, 1983*, 267, 473–74; Shimko, *Images and Arms Control*, 157–61; Vogele, *Stepping Back*, 109–11; Kampelman, *Entering New Worlds*, 294–97.

51. Reagan, *An American Life*, 624–31; Shultz, *Turmoil and Triumph*, 586–89; Kaiser, *Why Gorbachev Happened*, 116–18; Mahley and Linhard to McFarlane, "Intelligence Analysis of Gorbachev's SS-20 Statements in Paris," 3 October 1985, also see unsigned, untitled memorandum, 3 September 1985, ID: 8591020, Executive Secretariat of NSC folder, WH Staff Members and Office file, Reagan presidential papers.

52. Quotation in Reagan, *An American Life*, 11–14, 624, 628, 631–32, 634, 637.

53. Dobrynin, *In Confidence*, 580–81.

54. First quotation in Dobrynin, *In Confidence*, 588; second quotation in Ronald Reagan Center for Public Affairs, *Cold War*, 102; third quotation in Reagan, *An American Life*, 15, 634–35; Cannon, *President Reagan*, 750–51.

55. First and third quotations in Reagan, *An American Life*, 12–13, 15; second quotation in Oberdorfer, *The Turn*, 143–44; Dobrynin, *In Confidence*, 589.

56. First quotation in Shultz, *Turmoil and Triumph*, 601–2; second quotation in Oberdorfer, *The Turn*, 145–47; third quotation in Reagan, *An American Life*, 631, 635–37; Ronald Reagan Center for Public Affairs, *Cold War*, 72.

57. Quotations in Oberdorfer, *The Turn*, 748–50; Dobrynin, *In Confidence*, 590–91; Reagan, *An American Life*, 639–40; Shultz, *Turmoil and Triumph*, 605–6.

58. First quotation in Kaiser, *Why Gorbachev Happened*, 120; other quotations in Ronald Reagan Center for Public Affairs, *Cold War*, 19–20, 40, 66, 85; Dobrynin, *In Confidence*, 564; Oberdorfer, *The Turn*, 154; Schweizer, *Victory*, 246; Blumenthal, *Pledging Allegiance*, 42.

59. Quotations in Kaiser, *Why Gorbachev Happened*, 119; Dobrynin, *In Confidence*, 595–96.

Chapter 9: Coping with Scandal, Exiting with Honor, 1985–1989

1. First and second quotations in Reagan, *Public Papers, 1985*, 228–29, 537; third quotation in McFarlane and Smardz, *Special Trust*, 68; Ben Bradlee, *Guts and Glory: The Rise and Fall of Oliver North*, 551; Harold H. Koh, "Why the President (Almost) Always Wins in Foreign Affairs: Lessons of the Iran-Contra Affair," 1288, 1290, 1294–96, 1319; Kenneth E. Sharpe, "The Post-Vietnam Formula under Siege: The Imperial Presidency and Central America," 552, 569; Richard Secord and Jay Wurts, *Honored and Betrayed: Irangate*,

Covert Affairs, and the Secret War in Laos, 270–71; Cannon, *President Reagan,* 593–94; Theodore Draper, *A Very Thin Line: The Iran-Contra Affairs,* 33–35. See also Peter Kornbluh, *Nicaragua, the Price of Intervention: Reagan's Wars against the Sandinistas;* Jonathan Marshall, Peter D. Scott, and Jane Hunter, *The Iran-Contra Connection: Secret Teams and Covert Operations in the Reagan Era;* Ann Wroe, *Lives, Lies, and the Iran-Contra Affair;* and Charles-Philippe David, Nancy A. Carrol, and Zachary A. Selden, *Foreign Policy Failure in the White House: Reappraising the Fall of the Shah and the Iran-Contra Affair.* For important documents, see Peter Kornbluh and Malcolm Byrne, eds., *The Iran-Contra Scandal: The Declassified History;* and Tom Blanton, ed., *White House E-mail: The Top Secret Computer Messages the Reagan/Bush White House Tried to Destroy.*

2. Draper, *Very Thin Line,* 5–11, 13–14, 563, 576, 580–98; U.S., Senate and House Select Committees, *Report of the Congressional Committees Investigating the Iran-Contra Affair,* 100th Cong., 1st sess., 1987, S. Rept. 100-216, H. Rept. 100-443, 4, 11; Carnes Lord, *The Presidency and the Management of National Security,* 3.

3. First quotation in U.S., Senate and House Select Committees, *Report,* 21; second quotation in U.S., Lawrence E. Walsh, *Final Report of the Independent Counsel for Iran/Contra Matters,* 1:445.

4. First quotation in Shultz, *Turmoil and Triumph,* 285–87; second quotation in Reagan to Meldrim Thomson (3 October 1983), ID: 174036, WHORM: Subject: FG, Reagan presidential papers; Reagan, *An American Life,* 239–40; Meese, *With Reagan,* 220–27, 229–30; Howard J. Wiarda, *American Foreign Policy toward Latin America in the Eighties and Nineties: Issues and Controversies from Reagan to Bush,* 17–20, 23–24; Thomas Carothers, *In the Name of Democracy: U.S. Policy toward Latin America in the Reagan Years,* 118–32, 145, 249–57, 260–61. See also Howard J. Wiarda, ed., *Rift and Revolution: The Central American Imbroglio;* Saul Landau, *The Guerrilla Wars of Central America: Nicaragua, El Salvador, and Guatemala;* Kevin J. Middlebrook and Carlos Rico, eds., *The United States and Latin America in the 1980s: Contending Perspectives on a Decade of Crisis.*

5. Cannon, *President Reagan,* 343–44, 360; Woodward, *Veil,* 116, 121; Meese, *With Reagan,* 230–31; Carothers, *In the Name of Democracy,* 78–80, 82–90; Cynthia J. Arnson, *Crossroads: Congress, the President, and Central America, 1976–1993,* 274–75, 277; Wiarda, *American Foreign Policy,* 23–32. See also Sam Dillon, *Commandos: The CIA and Nicaragua's Contra Rebels;* and Roy Gutman, *Banana Diplomacy: The Making of American Policy in Nicaragua, 1981–1987.*

6. First quotation in U.S., Senate and House Select Committees, *Hearings,* McFarlane testimony (100-2), 270; second quotation in, U.S., President's Special Review Board, *Report of the President's Special Review Board,* III-21 (hereinafter cited as U.S. Tower Board Report); Cannon, *President Reagan,* 360.

7. First quotation in Abrams, "Reagan's Leadership," 102–3; second quotation in Cannon, *President Reagan,* 353–58, 373–74; Reagan, *An American Life,* 476–77; U.S., Senate and House Select Committees, *Report,* 31–32; Meese, *With Reagan,* 232–33; Draper, *Very Thin Line,* 15–17, 27; Michael McClintock, *Instruments of Statecraft: U.S. Guerrilla Warfare, Counterinsurgency, and Counterterrorism, 1940–1990,* 329–448; Simpson, *National Security Directives,* 18, 53–54.

8. Edwin Timbers, "Legal and Institutional Aspects of the Iran-Contra Affair," 32–33; U.S., Senate and House Select Committees, *Report,* 32–33; Reagan, *An American Life,* 477; Draper, *Very Thin Line,* 17–19.

9. First quotation in Timberg, *Nightingale's Song,* 16, 289–90, 353–55, 415; second quotation in Persico, *Casey,* 388–89; third quotation in Robert Parry, *Fooling America: How Washington Insiders Twist the Truth and Manufacture the Conventional Wisdom,* 249; Deaver and Herskowitz, *Behind the Scenes,* 258; Noonan, *What I Saw,* 235–37; Ledeen, *Perilous Statecraft,* 78–81; Draper, *Very Thin Line,* 30–31, 116, 565–67; Jeffrey Toobin, *Opening Arguments: A Young Lawyer's First Case, United States v. Oliver North,* 353; Menges, *Inside the National Security Council,* 191–97; Baker, "Baker Recounts," 2; Howard H. Baker, "The

Reagan White House," 11; Reagan, *An American Life,* 486; Bradlee, *Guts and Glory,* 182; Regan, *For the Record,* 25. See also U.S. News & World Report, *The Story of Lieutenant Colonel Oliver North,* which contains transcripts of his testimony.

10. Draper, *Very Thin Line,* 61–73, 75–78, 80–82, 84–85; U.S., Senate and House Select Committees, *Report,* 4, 37–40; McFarlane and Smardz, *Special Trust,* 68; Reagan, *An American Life,* 484–87; Cannon, *President Reagan,* 384–86.

11. First quotation in Draper, *Very Thin Line,* 23–25, 32, 35–40; second quotation in U.S., Senate and House Select Committees, *Report,* 40–45, *Hearings,* Poindexter testimony (100-8), 53, North testimony (100-7, part 1), 205; U.S., Tower Board Report, C2; John K. Singlaub and Malcolm McConnell, *Hazardous Duty: An American Soldier in the Twentieth Century,* 464; Winik, *On the Brink,* 419; U.S., Walsh, *Final Report,* 1:204.

12. Quotation in U.S., Walsh, *Final Report,* 1:6; McFarlane and Smardz, *Special Trust,* 83–85; Draper, *Very Thin Line,* 116–19.

13. Quotations in Reagan, *Public Papers, 1986,* 352–56.

14. First quotation in Mayer and McManus, *Landslide,* 274; second quotation in Reagan, *Public Papers, 1986,* 1343–44; Draper, *Very Thin Line,* 352–59, 361–63.

15. First quotation in William S. Cohen and George J. Mitchell, *Men of Zeal: A Candid Inside Story of the Iran-Contra Hearings,* 1; second quotation in Reagan, *Public Papers, 1985,* 886; Cannon, *President Reagan,* 599–601; Draper, *Very Thin Line,* 120–21; U.S., Tower Board Report, III-2–3, IV-8.

16. Quotations in Timberg, *Nightingale's Song,* 291–92, 296, 366–67, 424–26, 428; Cannon, *President Reagan,* 594–98; Draper, *Very Thin Line,* 28–30; U.S., Tower Board Report, IV-11.

17. Draper, *Very Thin Line,* 120–22, 155–56; U.S., Tower Board Report, III-2–4.

18. Quotation in Draper, *Very Thin Line,* 122–27, 173, 264; Ledeen, *Perilous Statecraft,* 104–16; Oliver L. North and William Novak, *Under Fire: An American Story,* 22–23; Persico, *Casey,* 452; Cannon, *President Reagan,* 603; U.S., Tower Board Report, B1, B3; for the Israeli role, see Shimon Peres, *Battling for Peace: A Memoir,* 210–18.

19. Quotation in Shultz, *Turmoil and Triumph,* 793; Draper, *Very Thin Line,* 136–41; Gates, *From the Shadows,* 398; Ledeen, *Perilous Statecraft,* 100–103; Cannon, *President Reagan,* 602.

20. First quotation in Shultz, *Turmoil and Triumph,* 793–94; second quotation in U.S., Walsh, *Final Report,* 2:673–74; Weinberger, *Fighting for Peace,* 362–67; Draper, *Very Thin Line,* 148–51; U.S., Tower Board Report, B9–10.

21. Quotations in Gates, *From the Shadows,* 399–400, Weinberger, *Fighting for Peace,* 353, 373–74; Powell and Persico, *My American Journey,* 307–8, 310; Shultz, *Turmoil and Triumph,* 784; McFarlane and Smardz, *Special Trust,* 44; Reagan, *An American Life,* 523; U.S., Tower Board Report, IV-11.

22. Quotation in U.S., Senate and House Select Committees, *Report,* Appendix B, 15:63; U.S., Tower Board Report, III-4, III-11; Draper, *Very Thin Line,* 250 note; Reagan, *An American Life,* 489–90, 492; Meese, *With Reagan,* 209–12, 250–52; McFarlane and Smardz, *Special Trust,* 22–23; Cannon, *President Reagan,* 603–8, 611, 639; Don Lawson, *America Held Hostage: The Iran Hostage Crisis and the Iran-Contra Affair,* 96; Mayer and McManus, *Landslide,* 90–108; Secord and Wurts, *Honored and Betrayed,* 230, 232–33; Max Friedersdorf to Paul Simon, 24 June 1985, ID: 304143, WHORM: Subject: CO, Reagan presidential papers. See also Gavin Hewitt, *Terry Waite and Ollie North: The Untold Story of the Kidnapping—and the Release.*

23. Quotation in U.S., Tower Board Report, B15–16, III-5–6; McFarlane and Smardz, *Special Trust,* 17–31; Meese, *With Reagan,* 252–53; Reagan, *An American Life,* 501–2, 504–5; Regan, *For the Record,* 19–21; U.S., Senate and House Select Committees, *Hearings,* McFarlane testimony (100-2), 46, 68, Appendix 22, 573–76; U.S., Walsh, *Final Report,* 1:466; Shultz, *Turmoil and Triumph,* 794–95; Cannon, *President Reagan,* 601–2, 611–14; Draper, *Very Thin Line,* 156–60.

24. Quotation in McFarlane and Smardz, *Special Trust,* 30–32; Reagan, *An American Life,* 505–7; U.S., Tower Board Report, III-6, IV-12; Cannon, *President Reagan,* 615; Draper, *Very Thin Line,* 160–64; Persico, *Casey,* 569.

25. First quotation in U.S., Tower Board Report, III-6–8, B19–23; second quotation in Weinberger, *Fighting for Peace,* 367–71; other quotations in McFarlane and Smardz, *Special Trust,* 32–35; U.S., Senate and House Select Committees, *Report,* 163; Cannon, *President Reagan,* 615–16; Shultz, *Turmoil and Triumph,* 796; Draper, *Very Thin Line,* 164–69.

26. U.S., Tower Board Report, III-7–8, B19–20; U.S., Walsh, *Final Report,* 1:80; McFarlane and Smardz, *Special Trust,* 40; Shultz, *Turmoil and Triumph,* 796–97; Meese, *With Reagan,* 253; Cannon, *President Reagan,* 616–18; Draper, *Very Thin Line,* 169–72.

27. First quotation in Draper, *Very Thin Line,* 175–77, 182; other quotations in U.S., Walsh, *Final Report,* 1:91, 466, 2:681–84; U.S., Senate and House Select Committees, *Hearings,* McFarlane testimony (100-2), 51; Cannon, *President Reagan,* 619–20.

28. First quotation in U.S., Senate and House Select Committees, *Hearings,* North testimony (100-7, part 1) 51–53; second quotation in Draper, *Very Thin Line,* 181–201, 563; third quotation in U.S., Senate and House Select Committees, *Report,* 181; fourth quotation in McFarlane and Smardz, *Special Trust,* 42–43; *Hearings,* Shultz testimony (100-9), 28–29; U.S., Tower Board Report, IV-6; Meese, *With Reagan,* 253–54; Regan, *For the Record,* 319–22; Shultz, *Turmoil and Triumph,* 797–98; Cannon, *President Reagan,* 620–23.

29. Deaver and Herskowitz, *Behind the Scenes,* 259; McFarlane and Smardz, *Special Trust,* 105; U.S., Tower Board Report, IV-11; Draper, *Very Thin Line,* 217–21; Mayer and McManus, *Landslide,* 176.

30. First quotation in U.S., Senate and House Select Committees, *Report,* Appendix B, 17:126–27; second quotation in *Hearings,* Don Regan testimony (100–10), 14; third quotation in *Hearings,* Shultz testimony (100-9), 523; fourth quotation in *Hearings,* Weinberger testimony (100-10), 140–41; fifth quotation in Cannon, *President Reagan,* 631; Draper, *Very Thin Line,* 224–29; Shultz, *Turmoil and Triumph,* 798–800; Reagan, *An American Life,* 512–13; McFarlane and Smardz, *Special Trust,* 46–47; U.S., Walsh, *Final Report,* 2:686–87; U.S., Tower Board Report, III-10–11, B42–45; Cannon, *President Reagan,* 629–31. See also Senate and House Select Committees, *Hearings,* McFarlane testimony (100-2), 56, 59; Poindexter testimony (100-8), 23–25; Shultz testimony (100-9), 31–32; Weinberger testimony (100-10), 139–40; and Regan testimony (100-10), 46–47.

31. First quotation in Reagan, *An American Life,* 510, 513; second and third quotations in McFarlane and Smardz, *Special Trust,* 47–51; fourth quotation in U.S., Tower Board Report, III-11, B49–52; fifth quotation in Casey to John McMahon, 10 December 1985, U.S., *Hearings* (100-11), 890; U.S., Walsh, *Final Report,* 1:467; Cannon, *President Reagan,* 631–34; Draper, *Very Thin Line,* 229–38; Theodore Draper, "Iran-Contra: The Mystery Solved," 53.

32. Quotation in Shultz, *Turmoil and Triumph,* 803–4; U.S., Walsh, *Final Report,* 1:209, 364, 2:693; Meese, *With Reagan,* 255–56; Anderson, *Revolution,* 343–46; Draper, "Iran-Contra," 56; Draper, *Very Thin Line,* 246–49; Reagan, *An American Life,* 516–17; Cannon, *President Reagan,* 634, 636; U.S., Tower Board Report, B61–65, B70–71; U.S., Senate and House Select Committees, *Report,* Appendix B, 18:24–27, *Hearings,* Weinberger testimony (100-10), 143.

33. Quotation in Cannon, *President Reagan,* 637–38; Draper, *Very Thin Line,* 239–43, 249–63; U.S., Walsh, *Final Report,* 1:467; Cannon, *President Reagan,* 635–36.

34. Quotation in U.S., Tower Board Report, III-13–14, B77, B80, B82–83, B95; Draper, *Very Thin Line,* 279–89, 293–302.

35. Quotation in U.S., Walsh, *Final Report,* 1:97; Draper, *Very Thin Line,* 311–27, 455–56; Reagan, *An American Life,* 520–21; McFarlane and Smardz, *Special Trust,* 53–65; North and Novak, *Under Fire,* 59–60; Cannon, *President Reagan,* 646–52.

36. Quotation in Reagan, *An American Life,* 522–23, 526–27; Draper, *Very Thin Line,* 455.

37. U.S., Tower Board Report, B168–70, C10; Draper, *Very Thin Line,* 435–46, 448–49,

457–59; Reagan, *An American Life,* 522; Mayer and McManus, *Landslide,* 244–45; Winik, *On the Brink,* 551–52; Cannon, *President Reagan,* 675–77.

38. Quotation in Buchanan to Reagan, 5 December 1986, ID: 486496, WHORM: Subject: FG, Reagan presidential papers; Speakes and Pack, *Speaking Out,* 287; Regan, *For the Record,* 48–50; Cannon, *President Reagan,* 677–79, 685–92; Bradlee, *Guts and Glory,* 549–50; Mari Maseng Will, "Speech Writing for President Reagan," 93–94; Parry, *Fooling America,* 288–94; Hertsgaard, *On Bended Knee,* 329–30.

39. First quotation in Mayer and McManus, *Landslide,* 30; other quotations in Cramer, *What It Takes,* 116–17; Regan, *For the Record,* 32–33; Cannon, "Journalist's Perspective," 64–65.

40. Quotations in Shultz, *Turmoil and Triumph,* 827–29; U.S., Senate and House Select Committees, *Hearings,* Shultz testimony (100-9), 541.

41. Reagan, *Public Papers, 1986,* 1567–75; Cramer, *What It Takes,* 118; Ledeen, *Perilous Statecraft,* 9; Regan, *For the Record,* 35–36; Draper, *Very Thin Line,* 482–84.

42. First quotation in Shultz, *Turmoil and Triumph,* 830–33; second quotation in U.S., Walsh, *Final Report,* 1:482, 508–9, 516; Draper, "Iran-Contra," 54, 58; Theodore Draper, "The Iran-Contra Secrets," 44.

43. Quotation in U.S., Senate and House Select Committees, *Report,* 305; Meese, *With Reagan,* 243, 245, 294–98; U.S., Walsh, *Final Report,* 1:xviii; Cannon, *President Reagan,* 692–95; Reagan, *An American Life,* 529–30; Draper, *Very Thin Line,* 496–501.

44. Meese, *With Reagan,* 242–44, 289–92, 298–99; Draper, *Very Thin Line,* 504–34; Cannon, *President Reagan,* 695–700; Cohen and Mitchell, *Men of Zeal,* 69; U.S., Walsh, *Final Report,* 1:200; U.S., Senate and House Select Committees, *Hearings,* Meese testimony (100-9), 1411; Persico, *Casey,* 557, 664–65.

45. First quotation in Reagan and Novak, *My Turn,* 317–18; second quotation in Meese, *With Reagan,* 245, 300–301; Regan, *For the Record,* 37–42; Mayer and McManus, *Landslide,* 347.

46. Quotation in Parry, *Fooling America,* 284; Reagan, *Public Papers, 1986,* 1587; Mayer and McManus, *Landslide,* 344; Draper, *Very Thin Line,* 541–49; U.S., Senate and House Select Committees, North testimony (100-7, part I), 246.

47. First quotation in Shultz, *Turmoil and Triumph,* 857, 863; other quotations in Regan, *For the Record,* 56–59, 88–98, 366–74; Reagan and Novak, *My Turn,* 313–17, 319–22, 324–31; Reagan, *Public Papers, 1986,* 1588; Reagan, *An American Life,* 536–38; Speakes and Pack, *Speaking Out,* 287; Fitzwater, *Call the Briefing,* 118, 171; Bradlee, *Guts and Glory,* 6–7; Draper, *Very Thin Line,* 552; U.S., Walsh, *Final Report,* 1:522; Cannon, *President Reagan,* 704–7, 719–27, 730–32.

48. Cannon, *President Reagan,* 732–33; Fitzwater, *Call the Briefing,* 74, 90, 118; Speakes and Pack, *Speaking Out,* 295; Reagan, *An American Life,* 538; Baker, "Reagan White House," 6–7; Noonan, *What I Saw,* 206; Powell and Persico, *My American Journey,* 393.

49. Shultz, *Turmoil and Triumph,* 838–53, 990; Powell and Persico, *My American Journey,* 331, 334; Cannon, *President Reagan,* 732; Nitze, *From Hiroshima to Glasnost,* 439–40.

50. First quotation in Cannon, *President Reagan,* 708–10, 714; second, fifth, and sixth quotations in Tower, *Consequences,* 281–86; third and fourth quotations in U.S., Walsh, *Final Report,* 1:520–23; seventh quotation in Regan, *For the Record,* 80–83; U.S., Tower Board Report, IV-9.

51. Quotation in Tower, *Consequences,* 287–89; U.S., Tower Board Report, I-3, I-1, III-1, III-24, IV-1, IV-3, IV-5, IV-9–11, V-4–6.

52. Quotations in Reagan, *Public Papers, 1987,* 208–11; Noonan, *What I Saw,* 182–83; Will, "Speech Writing," 95; Powell and Persico, *My American Journey,* 336–37; Shultz, *Turmoil and Triumph,* 877–78; Fitzwater, *Call the Briefing,* 109–22.

53. U.S., Senate and House Select Committees, *Report,* xv–xvi, 3, 20–22, 277, 437; Cohen and Mitchell, *Men of Zeal,* 200–203; Shultz, *Turmoil and Triumph,* 909; Koh, "Why the President (Almost) Always Wins," 1258–59, 1277; Timberg, *Nightingale's Song,* 436;

Timothy M. Cole, "Congressional Investigation of American Foreign Policy: Iran-Contra in Perspective," 42; Frank Donatelli to Reagan, 17 July 1987, Thomas Griscom to Reagan, 17 July 1987, ID: 497456ss, WHORM: Subject: FG, Reagan presidential papers.

54. Quotations in U.S., Walsh, *Final Report*, 1:xiv–xvii, 119, 445; Lawson, *America Held Hostage*, 81–90, 103–4; Robert L. Jackson and Ronald J. Ostrow, "Report: Presidents Part of Iran-contra Deception," *St. Paul Pioneer Press*, 19 January 1994. See also Elliott Abrams, *Undue Process: A Story of How Political Differences Are Turned into Crimes*.

55. Quotation in Timberg, *Nightingale's Song*, 447–48; Meese, *With Reagan*, 288–89; North and Novak, *Under Fire*, 7; U.S., Tower Board Report, III-19–21; U.S., Walsh, *Final Report*, 1:xv, 446; Cannon, *President Reagan*, 590, 703–6; Draper, *Very Thin Line*, 272–77, 571; U.S., Senate and House Select Committees, *Report*, 225, 271–73; *Hearings*, Poindexter testimony (100-8), 89, and (100-11), 37, 40; North testimony (100-7, part I), 109, 245.

56. Baker, "Reagan White House," 10–12; Baker, "Baker Recounts," 2; Reagan, *Public Papers, 1987*, 739–45; Reagan, *An American Life*, 540; Miller, *Fix the U.S. Budget*, 51 note 2; Will, "Speech Writing," 95, 102–3; Tom Griscom, "Core Ideas of the Reagan Presidency," 29–30; Fitzwater, *Call the Briefing*, 123–26; Dennis Thomas to Donald Regan, 16 January 1987, ID: 484685, Fredrick Ryan to Howard Baker, 5 March 1987, ID: 464563, Kenneth Cribb to Baker, 7 April 1987, with "Talking Points for Cabinet Meeting," both ID: 447270ss, Nancy Risque to Baker, 22 April 1987, Kenneth Cribb to Baker, 22 April 1987, both ID: 447463cs, Cribb to Reagan, with attachment, "The President's Strategic Plan," 8 July 1987, ID: 516417, Reagan to George Murphy (3 December 1987), ID: 531138, WHORM: Subject: FG, Reagan presidential papers.

57. Quotation in Shultz, *Turmoil and Triumph*, 699–703, 706–7; Reagan, *An American Life*, 650–59; Matlock, *Autopsy on an Empire*, 93–94; Oberdorfer, *The Turn*, 156–57; Winik, *On the Brink*, 412.

58. Quotation in Oberdorfer, *The Turn*, 158–61; Crockatt, *Fifty Years War*, 360–61; Gates, *From the Shadows*, 380–81; Kissinger, *Diplomacy*, 789; Walker, *Cold War*, 291–92.

59. Quotation in Shultz, *Turmoil and Triumph*, 757, 776; Mikhail Gorbachev, *At the Summit*, 65; Doder and Branson, *Gorbachev*, 157, 159–60; Dobrynin, *In Confidence*, 620–21; Gates, *From the Shadows*, 407–8; Oberdorfer, *The Turn*, 186.

60. First quotation in Winik, *On the Brink*, 504–5; second and third quotations in Reagan, *An American Life*, 675–76, 679; fourth quotation in Kissinger, *Diplomacy*, 783; fifth quotation in Shultz, *Turmoil and Triumph*, 753–54, 757–70, 772–74; Dobrynin, *In Confidence*, 620–22; Nitze, *From Hiroshima to Glasnost*, 427–37; Matlock, *Autopsy on an Empire*, 96–97; Fitzwater, *Call the Briefing*, 138; Oberdorfer, *The Turn*, 209, 444–47; Callahan, *Dangerous Capabilities*, 473; Doder and Branson, *Gorbachev*, 153–54; Mayer and McManus, *Landslide*, 282; Lebow and Stein, *We All Lost the Cold War*, 519–20.

61. First quotation in Thatcher, *Downing Street Years*, 471–73; second quotation in Geoffrey Smith, *Reagan and Thatcher*, 214, 243; third quotation in Mayer and McManus, *Landslide*, 283; Shultz, *Turmoil and Triumph*, 777–78; Beschloss and Talbott, *At the Highest Levels*, 8; Oberdorfer, *The Turn*, 207–8, 329; David Goldfischer, *The Best Defense: Policy Alternatives for U.S. Nuclear Security from the 1950s to the 1990s*, 243, 244 note 52; Crowe and Chanoff, *Line of Fire*, 213, 266–69; Paul H. Nitze, "Reagan as Foreign Policy Strategist," 149–50; attachments to President's Weekly Update, 17 October 1986, ID: 439945ss, WHORM: Subject: FG, Reagan presidential papers.

62. First quotation in Gorbachev, *At the Summit*, 11–12; second quotation in Shultz, *Turmoil and Triumph*, 775–77; third quotation in Reagan, *An American Life*, 683–84; Thatcher, *Downing Street Years*, 470–71; Walker, *Cold War*, 294–95; Max M. Kampelman, "Serving Reagan as Negotiator," 82–83; Oberdorfer, *The Turn*, 209; Goldfischer, *Best Defense*, 225.

63. First quotation in Shultz, *Turmoil and Triumph*, 886–89, 925; second quotation in Dobrynin, *In Confidence*, 610, 622–26; Gail Sheehy, *The Man Who Changed the World: The Lives of Mikhail S. Gorbachev*, 199, 202; Gorbachev, *At the Summit*, 13–14; Blumenthal,

Pledging Allegiance, 44–47; Cannon, *President Reagan,* 771–73; Reagan, *An American Life,* 683–86; Doder and Branson, *Gorbachev,* 161–65, 208–12, 284.

64. Gaddis, *End of the Cold War,* 152–53; Reagan, *Public Papers, 1987,* 634–37; Reagan, *An American Life,* 680–83.

65. Quotation in Powell and Persico, *My American Journey,* 361–63; Fitzwater, *Call the Briefing,* 148; Cannon, *President Reagan,* 774–77; Sheehy, *Man Who Changed the World,* 206; Crockatt, *Fifty Years War,* 361–62; Vogele, *Stepping Back,* 89; Oberdorfer, *The Turn,* 262–63, 266–67. For provisions of the INF Treaty, see Reagan, *Public Papers, 1987,* 1456–87.

66. Quotation in Reagan, *An American Life,* 698–703; Gorbachev, *At the Summit,* 203; Shultz, *Turmoil and Triumph,* 1082–86; Cannon, *President Reagan,* 780–81; Blumenthal, *Pledging Allegiance,* 320; Matlock, *Autopsy on an Empire,* 148–49; Thomas Griscom to Reagan, 8 January 1988, Frank Donatelli to Reagan, 9 January 1988, ID: 538766ss, WHORM: Subject: FG, Reagan presidential papers.

67. Doder and Branson, *Gorbachev,* 319; Kaiser, *Why Gorbachev Happened,* 227; Shultz, *Turmoil and Triumph,* 1094–1105; Reagan, *An American Life,* 705–10, 713–14; Matlock, *Autopsy on an Empire,* 124; Reagan, *Public Papers, 1988,* 488–93, 674–77, 681–92; Oberdorfer, *The Turn,* 23, 284–86, 293; Cannon, *President Reagan,* 781–88; Frank Donatelli to Reagan, 9 January 1988, ID: 538766ss, WHORM: Subject: FG, Reagan presidential papers. See also Joseph G. Whelan, *The Moscow Summit, 1988: Reagan and Gorbachev in Negotiation.*

68. First quotation in Walker, *Cold War,* 308–9; second quotation in Shultz, *Turmoil and Triumph,* 1106–8, 1131; Reagan, *An American Life,* 719–20; Doder and Branson, *Gorbachev,* 356–58; Crockatt, *Fifty Years War,* 363.

Chapter 10: Evaluating Reagan

1. Regan, *For the Record,* 295; Rimmerman, *Presidency by Plebiscite,* 45; Anderson, *Revolution,* xxvii–xxviii; Schaller, *Reckoning with Reagan,* 66; Larry Berman, "Looking Back on the Reagan Presidency," 3; Frank J. Donatelli to Reagan, 2 October 1987, ID: 531893sc, Mari Maseng to Reagan, 14 October 1988, ID: 588694cn, Maseng to Reagan, 11 November 1988, ID: 606560ss, WHORM: Subject File: FG, Reagan presidential papers.

2. First quotation in Reagan to William A. Rusher (17 January 1989), ID: 700001, WHORM: Subject File: FG, Reagan presidential papers; other quotations in Reagan, *An American Life,* 722.

3. Reagan, *An American Life,* 724.

4. Andrew Rosenthal, "Citizen Reagan Won't Be a Retiree," *New York Times,* 2 January 1989.

5. Reagan, *An American Life,* 499–501; Gilbert, *Mortal Presidency,* 176, 199–206; see also Abrams, *President Has Been Shot.*

6. Quotation in Davis, *Angels Don't Die,* 123–24; Morris, "This Living Hand," 66.

7. Quotation in Laurence I. Barrett, "Alzheimer's and the Reagans: An Inside Report on How They're Coping," 23–26; "Nancy Makes a Sad Choice," *Newsweek,* 2 September 1996, 6; Morris, "This Living Hand," 68–69; T. Burton Smith, "The President's Health," 212–13. See also Barry Reisberg, *Alzheimer's Disease: The Standard Reference.*

8. Michael Wines, "Reagan Friends Reflect on the Fading of a Giant," *New York Times,* 7 November 1994; Steven Miles, "Was Reagan Unfit for Office," article given to the author by Dr. Steven Miles; Lawrence K. Altman, "Reagan and Alzheimer's: Following Path His Mother Traveled," *New York Times,* 8 November 1994; U.S., Transcript of Deposition of Ronald W. Reagan, *United States v. John M. Poindexter,* 16 February 1990, United States District Court, District of Columbia; North and Novak, *Under Fire,* 14; Toobin, *Opening Arguments,* 352; Cannon, *President Reagan,* 135–36, 359–60, 467–68; Fitzwater, *Call the Briefing,* 120.

9. Quotation in Ledeen, *Perilous Statecraft,* 8–10, 75–76; Miles, "Was Reagan Unfit for

Office"; Drew, *Campaign Journal,* 573–74; Kelley, *Nancy Reagan,* 417–19, 449–50; Smith, "President's Health," 208–9; Gates, *From the Shadows,* 573; Fred Barnes, "The Reagan Presidency: Moments," 100–101; Mayer and McManus, *Landslide,* ix–xi, 52.

10. Edward N. Wright, "Reagan and Defense," 177–80; Shultz, *Turmoil and Triumph,* 1052–62, 1064–79; Abrams, "Reagan's Leadership," 97–98, 100–101.

11. Quotation in Morris, "Official Biographer Puzzled," 3. Among the many books assessing the Reagan administration, see Wilbur Edel, *The Reagan Presidency: An Actor's Finest Performance;* Richard O. Curry, ed., *Freedom at Risk: Secrecy, Censorship, and Repression in the 1980s;* Richard O. Curry, *An Uncertain Future: Thought Control and Repression during The Reagan-Bush Era;* John L. Palmer, ed., *Perspectives on the Reagan Years;* Lloyd deMause, *Reagan's America;* John L. Palmer and Isabel V. Sawhill, eds., *The Reagan Record: An Assessment of America's Changing Domestic Priorities;* Robert Dallek, *Ronald Reagan: The Politics of Symbolism;* Ronnie Dugger, *On Reagan: The Man and His Presidency;* Helga Haftendorn and Jakob Schissler, eds., *The Reagan Administration: A Reconstruction of American Strength?;* Tinsley E. Yarbrough, *The Reagan Administration and Human Rights;* Kenneth L. Adelman, *The Great Universal Embrace: Arms Summitry, a Skeptic's Account;* Joseph Hogan, ed., *The Reagan Years: The Record in Presidential Leadership;* Larry Berman, ed., *Looking Back on the Reagan Presidency;* Haynes Johnson, *Sleepwalking through History: America in the Reagan Years;* Bob Schieffer and Gary P. Gates, *The Acting President;* Dilys Hill, Raymond Moore, and Phil Williams, *The Reagan Presidency: An Incomplete Revolution?;* Paul Boyer, ed., *Reagan as President: Contemporary Views of the Man, His Politics, and His Policies;* Alan Gartner, Colin Greer, and Frank Riessman, *What Reagan Is Doing to Us;* John D. Lees and Michael Turner, *Reagan's First Four Years: A New Beginning?;* Paul Duke, ed., *Beyond Reagan: The Politics of Upheaval;* Hodding Carter, *The Reagan Years;* Richard A. Brody, *Assessing the President: The Media, Elite Opinion, and Public Support;* Archibald Gillies et al., *Post-Reagan America;* George E. Peterson and Carol W. Lewis, eds., *Reagan and the Cities;* Stanley J. Marks, *A Year in the Lives of the Damned! Reagan, Reaganism, 1986;* Robert A. Shanley, *Presidential Influence and Environmental Policy;* Donald J. Savoie, *Thatcher Reagan Mulroney: In Search of a New Bureaucracy;* David Mervin, *Ronald Reagan and the American Presidency.*

12. Berman, "Looking Back," 5; Steve Fraser and Gary Gerstle, eds., *The Rise and Fall of the New Deal Order, 1930–1980,* ix; George F. Will, "Is Clinton to the Right of Dole?" *La Crosse Tribune,* 12 September 1996; Richard Darman, *Who's In Control? Polar Politics and the Sensible Center,* 10, 29, 178–80; Larry M. Schwab, *The Illusion of a Conservative Reagan Revolution,* 1–7; Everett Carll Ladd, "The Reagan Phenomenon and Public Attitudes toward Government," 222–38; Doug Bandow, *The Politics of Plunder: Misgovernment in Washington,* 95; Linda Bennett and Stephen Bennett, *Living with Leviathan: Americans Coming to Terms with Big Government,* xii–xiii. See also Rowland Evans and Robert Novak, *The Reagan Revolution.*

13. David Frum, *Dead Right,* 3, 6, 11, 32–36, 38–39, 41–47, 49–50; Goldberg, *Barry Goldwater,* 314–15; Nofziger, *Nofziger,* 265–66; Bandow, *Politics of Plunder,* 97–99; Jorstad, *Holding Fast/Pressing On,* 60–74.

14. Richard E. Neustadt, "Looking Back: Meanings and Puzzles," 319–20; Robert K. Murray and Tim H. Blessing, *Greatness in the White House: Rating the Presidents, from George Washington through Ronald Reagan,* 81–89, 164 note 12.

15. Jones, "A New President," 286; Dobrynin, *In Confidence,* 581; Blumenthal, *Pledging Allegiance,* 84–85; Goldwater and Casserly, *Goldwater,* 388, 391; Garry Wills, "It's His Party," 30; Berman, *America's Right Turn,* 4, 123, 166–68; Dionne, *Why Americans Hate Politics,* 319–20; Mervin, *Ronald Reagan,* 208.

16. Quotation in Wills, "It's His Party," 30, 33, 36, 52, 55, 57; Theda Skocpol, *Boomerang: Clinton's Health Security Effort and the Turn against Government in U.S. Politics,* 173–78; Alan Brinkley, "Reagan's Revenge: As Invented by Howard Jarvis," 37.

17. Quotation in Williamson, *Reagan's Federalism,* 50–51. For studies of Reagan as a

communicator, see Robert E. Denton, *The Primetime Presidency of Ronald Reagan: The Era of the Television Presidency;* Michael Weiler and W. Barnett Pearce, *Reagan and Public Discourse in America;* Paul D. Erickson, *Reagan Speaks: The Making of an American Myth.*

18. Quotation in Kevin Phillips, *Arrogant Capital: Washington, Wall Street, and the Frustration of American Politics,* 65; Reagan, *An American Life,* 246–47; Stephen Vaughn, "The Moral Inheritance of a President: Reagan and the Dixon Disciples of Christ," 109–27; Edwards, *Early Reagan,* 105–6; Wills, *Reagan's America,* 1–4, 93–94, 371, 375; Ritter and Henry, *Ronald Reagan,* 4, 11–15, 26–28, 38–39, 53, 62–63, 84–85; Mary E. Stuckey, *Playing the Game: The Presidential Rhetoric of Ronald Reagan,* 3–4, 61; Mary E. Stuckey, *Getting into the Game: The Pre-Presidential Rhetoric of Ronald Reagan,* 7; Mona Harrington, *The Dream of Deliverance in American Politics,* 16–17.

19. First quotation in Noonan, *What I Saw,* 57; second quotation in Reagan, *Public Papers, 1983,* 1522; Reagan draft, "Address to the Nation," 27 October 1983, folder: "SP818 181858," Reagan presidential papers; Reagan, *An American Life,* 246; Griscom, "Core Ideas," 38; Barrett, *Gambling with History,* 33.

20. First quotation in Henry, *Visions of America,* 5–6, 9; second quotation in Berman, "Looking Back," 4, 9; Ritter and Henry, *Ronald Reagan,* 100; Cannon, *President Reagan,* 116–17, 124–25; John K. White, *The New Politics of Old Values,* 3–5, 22, 123–24, 130, 132–44; Meese, *With Reagan,* 10, 331; Noonan, *What I Saw,* 68–71, 185; Erickson, *Reagan Speaks,* 2–5; Ritter and Henry, *Ronald Reagan,* 11.

21. Quotation in Speakes and Pack, *Speaking Out,* 121, 136; Spear, *Presidents and the Press,* 10; Regan, *For the Record,* 251; Hertsgaard, *On Bended Knee,* 23, 47–48, 106–7; Ritter and Henry, *Ronald Reagan,* 97; Rimmerman, *Presidency by Plebiscite,* 56; Cannon, *President Reagan,* 157–59; Marlin Fitzwater to Howard Baker et al., 11 February 1988, ID: 563043, WHORM: Subject File: FG, Reagan presidential papers.

22. First quotation in Spear, *Presidents and the Press,* 8; second and third quotations in Schaller, *Reckoning with Reagan,* 53, 55, 136; Hertsgaard, *On Bended Knee,* 3–6, 33, 42, 47, 54–55, 65–70, 99–101.

23. Quotation in Robert Hughes, *Culture of Complaint: The Fraying of America,* 41; Barnes, "Reagan Presidency," 109–10; Jeffrey C. Goldfarb, *The Cynical Society: The Culture of Politics and the Politics of Culture in American Life,* 9; Greider, *Education of David Stockman,* 73–78; Stuckey, *Playing the Game,* 52–54.

24. Quotation in Niskanen, *Reaganomics,* 320, Cannon, *President Reagan,* 20; Thomas C. Griscom, 15 April 1988, ID: 554923ss, WHORM: Subject File: FG, Reagan presidential papers, Anandi P. Sahu and Ronald L. Tracy, eds., *The Economic Legacy of the Reagan Years: Euphoria or Chaos?* 3, 16–17; Bernstein, "Understanding American Economic Decline," 27–28; Laurence H. Meyer, Joel L. Prakken, and Chris P. Varvares, "Two Revolutions in Economic Policy: Growth-Oriented Macro Policy in the Kennedy and Reagan Administrations," 67–68, 70–71; Charles K. Wilber and Kenneth P. Jameson, *Beyond Reaganomics: A Further Inquiry into the Poverty of Economics,* x, 4–7, 58–64, 96–102; Michael K. Evans, *The Truth about Supply-Side Economics,* 9–12; Friedman, *Day of Reckoning,* 4–6; Berman, *America's Right Turn,* 124–26; Richard B. McKenzie, *What Went Right in the 1980s,* 26–32. For evaluations of Reaganomics, see Martin Feldstein, ed., *American Economic Policy in the 1980s;* Jerry Hagstrom, *Beyond Reagan: The New Landscape of American Politics;* Gregory B. Mills and John L. Palmer, eds., *Federal Budget Policy in the 1980s;* Charles F. Stone and Isabel V. Sawhill, *Economic Policy in the Reagan Years;* John L. Palmer and Isabel V. Sawhill, eds., *The Reagan Experiment: An Examination of Economic and Social Policies under the Reagan Administration;* Frank Ackerman, *Reaganomics: Rhetoric vs. Reality;* Robert Lekachman, *Greed Is Not Enough: Reaganomics;* Lawrence Lindsey, *The Growth Experiment: How the New Tax Policy Is Transforming the U.S. Economy;* Alan Peacock, ed., *Reaganomics and After;* Edwin S. Rubenstein, *The Right Data;* Phillip Cagan, ed., *Essays in Contemporary Economic Problems, 1986: The Impact of the Reagan Program;* Charles R. Hulten and Isabel V. Sawhill, eds., *The Legacy of Reaganomics: Prospects for Long-term*

Growth; Daniel Bell and Lester Thurow, *The Deficits: How Big? How Long? How Dangerous?;* Alfred L. Malabre, *Beyond Our Means: How Reckless Borrowing Now Threatens to Overwhelm Us;* Robert L. Heilbroner and Peter Bernstein, *The Debt and the Deficit: False Alarms/Real Possibilities.*

25. Reagan, *An American Life,* 333–34; Campagna, *Economy in the Reagan Years,* 76–79, 106–9, 115–16, 118, 132; Cannon, *President Reagan,* 275–77; Thomas G. Moore, "The Reagan Economic Performance," 106–10; Schaller, *Reckoning with Reagan,* 78; Darman, *Who's In Control?* 72–73.

26. White and Wildavsky, *The Deficit,* 332–44, 352, 530, 532, 564–65.

27. Quotation in Reagan, *An American Life,* 316; Langston, *Ideologues and Presidents,* 156–57; Campagna, *Economy in the Reagan Years,* 69, 82, 125, 127–30, 164–65.

28. Kevin Phillips, *The Politics of Rich and Poor: Wealth and the American Electorate in the Reagan Aftermath,* xviii, 13, 17, 24–25, 28, 54–59, 76, 82–88, 165, 181, 204, 241–42, 248–49, 251; Minarik, *Making America's Budget Policy,* xii–xiii; Berman, *America's Right Turn,* 147–49; Robert B. Reich, *The Work of Nations: Preparing Ourselves for Twenty-first-Century Capitalism,* 197; Campagna, *Economy in the Reagan Years,* 196–98, 200; McKenzie, *What Went Right,* 82–90, 94–97, 268–70; Wilber and Jameson, *Beyond Reaganomics,* 110–18; Cannon, *President Reagan,* 24–25.

29. Raymond Wolters, *Right Turn: William Bradford Reynolds, the Reagan Administration and Black Civil Rights,* 1–2, 5; Campagna, *Economy in the Reagan Years,* 184–95; Berman, *America's Right Turn,* 97–100; Vogel, *Fluctuating Fortunes,* 283; Patricia C. Sexton, *The War on Labor and the Left: Understanding America's Unique Conservatism,* 13, 16–17, 222; Edsall and Edsall, *Chain Reaction,* 193–94.

30. Quotation in Powell and Persico, *My American Journey,* 334; Walter Williams, *Mismanaging America: The Rise of the Anti-Analytic Presidency,* ix; Schieffer and Gates, *Acting President,* 90; Noonan, *What I Saw,* 165; Woodward, *Veil,* 335–36; Mayer and McManus, *Landslide,* 27; Speakes and Pack, *Speaking Out,* 67; Meese, *With Reagan,* 23; Regan, *For the Record,* 268.

31. First quotation in Baker, "Baker Recounts," 1; second quotation in Nitze, "Reagan and the Realities," 22–23; Berman, "Looking Back," 7; Barrett, *Gambling with History,* 9; Anderson, *Revolution,* xxvi; Cannon, *President Reagan,* 833; Darman, *Who's In Control?* 40, 120–23.

32. First quotation in Williamson, *Reagan's Federalism,* 2–5, 14–15, 64–70, 76–78, 93, 134–41, 193–202; second quotation in Mayer and McManus, *Landslide,* 90–94; third quotation in Phil Peters to Jim Courter, 15 January 1986, ID: 393507, WHORM: Subject File: FG, Reagan presidential papers; George E. Peterson et al., *The Reagan Block Grants: What Have We Learned?* 28–29; Peterson and Lewis, *Reagan and the Cities,* 1. See also David C. Martin and John Walcott, *Best Laid Plans: The Inside Story of America's War against Terrorism.*

33. Quotation in Reagan, *An American Life,* 240–42, 253–56, 273–74, 355–56; Baker and Defrank, *Politics of Diplomacy,* 606; Cannon, *President Reagan,* 468–69, 832–33; William Brock, "The Reagan Presidency: Leadership Revisited," 109–11; Campagna, *Economy in the Reagan Years,* 152–53; Alan V. Deardorff, "Trade Policy of the Reagan Years," 187; Clyde V. Prestowitz, *Trading Places: How We Allowed Japan to Take the Lead,* 16–18, 194–95, 206, 230–33, 252–53.

34. First quotation in Winik, *On the Brink,* 516; second quotation in Wills, "It's His Party," 37, 52. See also a collection of essays, Owen Harries, ed., "The Strange Death of Soviet Communism: An Autopsy," *The National Interest,* spring 1993.

35. Quotation in Kissinger, *Diplomacy,* 767–71; Regan, *For the Record,* 294–95; Reagan, *An American Life,* 268.

36. Cannon, *President Reagan,* 280–81; Crockatt, *Fifty Years War,* 305–6; Reagan, *An American Life,* 265–67; Meese, *With Reagan,* 168–70; Richard G. Powers, *Not Without Honor: The History of American Anticommunism,* 391–420; Wills, "It's His Party," 37.

37. First quotation in Anderson, *Revolution,* xxxi–xxxv; second quotation in Thatcher,

Downing Street Years, 258; Reagan, *Public Papers, 1982,* 742–48; Blumenthal, *Pledging Allegiance,* 40; Dobrynin, *In Confidence,* 477; Wills, "It's His Party," 36; Crockatt, *Fifty Years War,* 363–64.

38. Quotations in Mikhail Gorbachev, *Memoirs,* 165, 401–3; Brown, *Gorbachev Factor,* 226–28, 230–31; see also Valery Boldin, *Ten Years That Shook the World: The Gorbachev Era as Witnessed by His Chief of Staff.*

39. First quotation in Brown, *Gorbachev Factor,* 230, 237–38; second quotation in John le Carré, *The Secret Pilgrim,* 12; third quotation in George Bush, *Public Papers of the Presidents of the United States: George Bush, 1990,* 130; Kissinger, *Diplomacy,* 802–3; Walker, *Cold War,* 297–98, 300–301, 340; Charles H. Fairbanks, "Introduction," 5–6.

Bibliography

Books and Articles

Aaron, Henry J. "The Impossible Dream Comes True." In *Tax Reform and the U.S. Economy,* ed. Joseph A. Pechman, 10–25. Washington, D.C.: Brookings Institution, 1987.

Abrams, Elliott. "Reagan's Leadership: Mystery Man or Ideological Guide?" In Thompson, ed., *Foreign Policy,* 95–120.

———. *Undue Process. A Story of How Political Differences Are Turned into Crimes.* New York: Free Press, 1993.

Abrams, Herbert L. *"The President Has Been Shot": Confusion, Disability, and the Twenty-fifth Amendment in the Aftermath of the Attempted Assassination of Ronald Reagan.* New York: W. W. Norton, 1992.

Abramson, Paul R., John H. Aldrich, and David W. Rohde. *Change and Continuity in the 1984 Elections.* Washington, D.C.: CQ Press, 1986.

Ackerman, Frank. *Reaganomics: Rhetoric vs. Reality.* Boston: South End Press, 1982.

Adams, James R. *The Big Fix: Inside the S&L Scandal.* New York: John Wiley and Sons, 1990.

Adelman, Kenneth L. *The Great Universal Embrace: Arms Summitry, A Skeptic's Account.* New York: Simon and Schuster, 1989.

Adler, Jerry, et al. "James Watt's Land Rush." *Newsweek,* 29 June 1981, 22–24, 29–30, 32.

Allin, Dana H. *Cold War Illusions: America, Europe, and Soviet Power, 1969–1989.* New York: St. Martin's Press, 1994.

Allitt, Patrick. *Catholic Intellectuals and Conservative Politics in America, 1950–1985.* Ithaca, N.Y.: Cornell University Press, 1993.

Allyson, June, and Frances Spatz Leighton. *June Allyson.* New York: G. P. Putnam's Sons, 1982.

Alpern, David M., et al. "How the Ford Deal Collapsed." *Newsweek,* 28 July 1980, 20–26.

Amaker, Norman C. *Civil Rights and the Reagan Administration.* Washington, D.C.: Urban Institute Press, 1988.

Ambrose, Stephen E. *Nixon: The Triumph of a Politician, 1962–1972.* New York: Simon and Schuster, 1989.

Anderson, Martin. *Revolution: The Reagan Legacy.* Stanford, Calif.: Hoover Institution Press, 1990.

Arnold, Ron. *At the Eye of the Storm: James Watt and the Environmentalists.* Chicago: Regnery Gateway, 1982.

Arnson, Cynthia J. *Crossroads: Congress, the President, and Central America, 1976–1993.* 2d ed. University Park: Pennsylvania State University Press, 1993.

Baker, Howard H. "Baker Recounts His Days as Reagan's Chief of Staff." *Miller Center Report* 6 (winter 1990): 1–2.

———. "The Reagan White House." In Thompson, ed., *Leadership, Part II,* 3–20.

Baker, James A., and Thomas M. Defrank. *The Politics of Diplomacy: Revolution, War, and Peace, 1989–1992.* New York: G. P. Putnam's Sons, 1995.

Bakshian, Aram. *The Candidates, 1980.* New Rochelle, N.Y.: Arlington House, 1980.

Bandow, Doug. *The Politics of Plunder: Misgovernment in Washington.* New Brunswick, N.J.: Transaction Publishers, 1990.

Barnes, Fred. "The Reagan Presidency: Moments." In Thompson, ed., *Leadership,* 93–119.

Barrett, Laurence I. "Alzheimer's and the Reagans: An Inside Report on How They're Coping." *New Choices,* July/August 1996, 23–26.

———. *Gambling with History: Ronald Reagan in the White House.* Garden City, N.Y.: Doubleday, 1983.

Bartlett, Bruce R. *Reaganomics: Supply Side Economics in Action.* Westport, Conn.: Arlington House, 1981.

Baucom, Donald R. *The Origins of SDI, 1944–1983.* Lawrence: University Press of Kansas, 1992.

Behlmer, Rudy, ed. *Inside Warner Bros, 1935–1951.* New York: Viking, 1985.

Beilenson, Anthony, and Larry Agran. "The Welfare Reform Act of 1971." *Pacific Law Journal* 3 (July 1972): 475–502.

Bell, Coral. *The Reagan Paradox: American Foreign Policy in the 1980s.* New Brunswick, N.J.: Rutgers University Press, 1989.

Bell, Daniel, and Lester Thurow. *The Deficits: How Big? How Long? How Dangerous?* New York: New York University Press, 1985.

Bell, Terrel H. *The Thirteenth Man: A Reagan Cabinet Memoir.* New York: Free Press, 1988.

Bender, Marylin, and Monsieur Marc. *Nouveau Is Better Than No Riche at All.* New York: G. P. Putnam's Sons, 1983.

Bennett, Linda, and Stephen Bennett. *Living with Leviathan: Americans Coming to Terms with Big Government.* Lawrence: University Press of Kansas, 1990.

Bentley, Eric, ed. *Thirty Years of Treason: Excerpts from Hearings before the House Committee on Un-American Activities, 1938–1968.* New York: Viking, 1971.

Benze, James G. "Nancy Reagan: China Doll or Dragon Lady?" *Presidential Studies Quarterly* 20 (fall 1990): 777–90.

———. *Presidential Power and Management Techniques: The Carter and Reagan Administrations in Historical Perspective.* Westport, Conn.: Greenwood Press, 1987.

Berman, Larry. "Looking Back on the Reagan Presidency." In Berman, ed., *Looking Back*, 3–17.

———, ed. *Looking Back on the Reagan Presidency.* Baltimore: Johns Hopkins University Press, 1990.

Berman, William C. *America's Right Turn: From Nixon to Bush.* Baltimore: Johns Hopkins University Press, 1994.

Bernstein, Michael A. "Understanding American Economic Decline: The Contours of the Late-Twentieth-Century Experience." In *Understanding American Economic Decline,* ed. Michael A. Bernstein and David E. Adler, 3–33. New York: Cambridge University Press, 1994.

Beschloss, Michael R., and Strobe Talbott. *At the Highest Levels: The Inside Story of the End of the Cold War.* Boston: Little, Brown, 1993.

Birnbaum, Jeffrey H., and Alan S. Murray. *Showdown at Gucci Gulch: Lawmakers, Lobbyists, and the Unlikely Triumph of Tax Reform.* New York: Random House, 1987.

Bisnow, Mark. *Diary of a Dark Horse: The 1980 Anderson Presidential Campaign.* Carbondale: Southern Illinois University Press, 1983.

Bjork, Rebecca S. *The Strategic Defense Initiative: Symbolic Containment of the Nuclear Threat.* Albany: State University of New York Press, 1992.

Blanton, Tom, ed. *White House E-mail: The Top Secret Computer Messages the Reagan/Bush White House Tried to Destroy.* New York: New Press, 1995.

Blumenthal, Sidney. *Pledging Allegiance: The Last Campaign of the Cold War.* New York: HarperCollins, 1990.

———. *The Rise of the Counter-Establishment: From Conservative Ideology to Political Power.* New York: Times Books, 1986.

Boettke, Peter J. "The Reagan Regulatory Regime: Reality vs. Rhetoric." In Sahu and Tracy, eds., *Economic Legacy,* 117–23.

Boldin, Valery. *Ten Years That Shook the World: The Gorbachev Era as Witnessed by His Chief of Staff.* New York: Basic Books, 1994.

Boller, Paul F. *Presidential Wives.* New York: Oxford University Press, 1988.

Bork, Robert H. *The Tempting of America: The Political Seduction of the Law.* New York: Free Press, 1990.

Boskin, Michael J. *Reagan and the Economy: The Successes, Failures, and Unfinished Agenda.* San Francisco: ICS Press, 1987.

Boyarsky, Bill. *Ronald Reagan: His Life and Rise to the Presidency.* New York: Random House, 1981.

Boyer, Kenneth D. "The Reagan Regulatory Regime: Comment." In Sahu and Tracy, eds., *Economic Legacy,* 124–27.

Boyer, Paul, ed. *Reagan as President: Contemporary Views of the Man, His Politics, and His Policies.* Chicago: Ivan R. Dee, 1990.

Bradlee, Ben. *A Good Life: Newspapering and Other Adventures.* New York: Simon and Schuster, 1995.

———. *Guts and Glory: The Rise and Fall of Oliver North.* New York: Donald I. Fine, 1988.

Bratton, Susan Power. "The Ecotheology of James Watt." *Environmental Ethics* 5 (fall 1983): 225–36.

Brauer, Carl M. *Presidential Transitions: Eisenhower through Reagan.* New York: Oxford University Press, 1986.

Brennan, Mary C. *Turning Right in the Sixties: The Conservative Capture of the GOP.* Chapel Hill: University of North Carolina Press, 1995.

Brinkley, Alan. "The Problem of American Conservatism." *American Historical Review* 99 (April 1994): 409–29.

————. "Reagan's Revenge: As Invented by Howard Jarvis." *New York Times Magazine,* 19 June 1994, 36–37.

Broad, William J. *Teller's War: The Top-Secret Story behind the Star Wars Deception.* New York: Simon and Schuster, 1992.

Brock, William. "The Reagan Presidency: Leadership Revisited." In Thompson, ed., *Leadership, Part II,* 107–19.

Brodie, Fawn M. "Ronald Reagan Plays Surgeon." *The Reporter,* 6 April 1967, 11–16.

Brody, Richard A. *Assessing the President: The Media, Elite Opinion, and Public Support.* Stanford, Calif.: Stanford University Press, 1991.

Bronner, Ethan. *Battle for Justice: How the Bork Nomination Shook America.* New York: W. W. Norton, 1989.

Brown, Archie. *The Gorbachev Factor.* New York: Oxford University Press, 1996.

Brown, Edmund G. *Reagan and Reality: The Two Californias.* New York: Praeger, 1970.

Brown, Edmund G., and Bill Brown. *Reagan: The Political Chameleon.* New York: Praeger, 1976.

Brownstein, Ronald. *The Power and the Glitter: The Hollywood-Washington Connection.* New York: Pantheon, 1990.

Bruce, Steve. *The Rise and Fall of the New Christian Right: Conservative Protestant Politics in America, 1978–1988.* Oxford: Clarendon Press, 1988.

Brumbaugh, R. Dan. *Thrifts under Siege: Restoring Order to American Banking.* New York: Ballinger, 1988.

Buchanan, Patrick J. *Right from the Beginning.* Boston: Little, Brown, 1988.

Burbank, Garin. "Governor Reagan's Only Defeat: The Proposition 1 Campaign in 1973." *California History* 72 (winter 1993–94): 360–73.

Burford, Anne, and John Greenya. *Are You Tough Enough?* New York: McGraw-Hill, 1986.

Burke, John P. *The Institutional Presidency.* Baltimore: Johns Hopkins University Press, 1992.

Burkholz, Herbert. *The FDA Follies.* New York: Basic Books, 1994.

Bush, George. *Public Papers of the Presidents of the United States: George Bush, 1990.* Washington, D.C.: GPO, 1991.

Bush, George, and Victor Gold. *Looking Forward.* New York: Bantam, 1988.

Cagan, Phillip, ed. *Essays in Contemporary Economic Problems, 1986: The Impact of the Reagan Program.* Washington, D.C.: American Enterprise Institute, 1986.

Callahan, David. *Dangerous Capabilities: Paul Nitze and the Cold War.* New York: HarperCollins, 1990.

Campagna, Anthony S. *The Economy in the Reagan Years: The Economic Consequences of the Reagan Administrations.* Westport, Conn.: Greenwood Press, 1994.

Cannon, James. *Time and Chance: Gerald Ford's Appointment with History.* New York: HarperCollins, 1994.

Cannon, Lou. "A Journalist's Perspective." In Thompson, ed., *Leadership, Part II,* 53–65.

————. *President Reagan: The Role of a Lifetime.* New York: Simon and Schuster, 1991.

————. *Reagan.* New York: G. P. Putnam's Sons, 1982.

————. "Reagan at the Crossroads Again: 1986." In Thompson, ed., *Leadership,* 121–38.

————. "The Reagan Years." *California Journal,* November 1974, 360–66.

————. *Ronnie and Jesse: A Political Odyssey.* Garden City, N.Y.: Doubleday, 1969.

Cannon, Lou, and William Peterson. "GOP." In Harwood, ed., *Pursuit of the Presidency,* 121–55.

Carmines, Edward G., and James A. Stimson. *Issue Evolution: Race and the Transformation of American Politics.* Princeton: Princeton University Press, 1989.

Caroli, Betty Boyd. *First Ladies.* New York: Oxford University Press, 1987.

Carothers, Thomas. *In the Name of Democracy: U.S. Policy toward Latin America in the Reagan Years.* Berkeley and Los Angeles: University of California Press, 1993.

Carter, Dan T. *The Politics of Rage: George Wallace, the Origins of the New Conservatism, and the Transformation of American Politics.* New York: Simon and Schuster, 1995.

Carter, Hodding. *The Reagan Years.* New York: George Braziller, 1988.

Carter, Jimmy. *Keeping Faith: Memoirs of a President.* New York: Bantam, 1982.

———. *Public Papers of the Presidents of the United States: Jimmy Carter, 1980–81.* Washington, D.C.: GPO, 1982.

Casserly, John J. *The Ford White House: The Diary of a Speechwriter.* Boulder: Colorado Associated University Press, 1977.

Cawley, R. McGreggor. *Federal Land, Western Anger: The Sagebrush Rebellion and Environmental Politics.* Lawrence: University Press of Kansas, 1993.

———. "James Watt and the Environmentalists: A Clash of Ideologies." *Policy Studies Journal* 14 (December 1985): 244–54.

Ceplair, Larry, and Steven Englund. *The Inquisition in Hollywood: Politics in the Film Community, 1930–1960.* Garden City, N.Y.: Anchor Press/Doubleday, 1980.

Chace, James, and Caleb Carr. *America Invulnerable: The Quest for Absolute Security from 1812 to Star Wars.* New York: Summit, 1988.

Chester, Lewis, Godfrey Hodgson, and Bruce Page. *An American Melodrama: The Presidential Campaign of 1968.* New York: Viking, 1969.

Codevilla, Angelo. *While Others Build: The Commonsense Approach to the Strategic Defense Initiative.* New York: Free Press, 1988.

Coggins, George C., and Doris K. Nagel. " 'Nothing Beside Remains': The Legal Legacy of James G. Watt's Tenure as Secretary of the Interior on Federal Land Law and Policy." *Environmental Affairs* 17 (spring 1990): 473–550.

Cohen, Warren I. *America in the Age of Soviet Power, 1945–1991.* Cambridge: Cambridge University Press, 1993.

Cohen, William S., and George J. Mitchell. *Men of Zeal: A Candid Inside Story of the Iran-Contra Hearings.* New York: Viking, 1988.

Cohodas, Nadine. *Strom Thurmond and the Politics of Southern Change.* New York: Simon and Schuster, 1993.

Cole, Timothy M. "Congressional Investigation of American Foreign Policy: Iran-Contra in Perspective." *Congress and the Presidency* 21 (spring 1994): 29–48.

Congressional Quarterly. *Congressional Quarterly Almanac, 1981.* Washington, D.C.: Congressional Quarterly, 1982.

Cook, Fred J. "Watt Releases the Sea." *Nation,* 8–15 August 1981, 104–6.

Cramer, Richard Ben. *What It Takes: The Way to the White House.* New York: Random House, 1992.

Crawshaw, Steve. *Goodbye to the USSR: The Collapse of Soviet Power.* London: Bloomsbury, 1992.

Cray, Ed. "California: The Politics of Confusion." *Frontier,* May 1966, 5–9.

Crockatt, Richard. *The Fifty Years War: The United States and the Soviet Union in World Politics, 1941–1991.* New York: Routledge, 1995.

Crowe, William J., and David Chanoff. *The Line of Fire: From Washington to the Gulf, the Politics and Battles of the New Military.* New York: Simon and Schuster, 1993.

Culhane, Paul J. "Sagebrush Rebels in Office: Jim Watt's Land and Water Politics." In *Environmental Policy in the 1980s: Reagan's New Agenda,* ed. Norman J. Vig and Michael E. Kraft, 293–317. Washington, D.C.: CQ Press, 1984.

Curry, Richard O. *An Uncertain Future: Thought Control and Repression during the Reagan-Bush Era.* Los Angeles: First Amendment Foundation, 1992.

————, ed. *Freedom at Risk: Secrecy, Censorship, and Repression in the 1980s.* Philadelphia: Temple University Press, 1988.

Dallek, Robert. *Ronald Reagan: The Politics of Symbolism.* Cambridge: Harvard University Press, 1984.

Dallin, Alexander. *Black Box: KAL 007 and the Superpowers.* Berkeley and Los Angeles: University of California Press, 1985.

Darman, Richard. *Who's In Control? Polar Politics and the Sensible Center.* New York: Simon and Schuster, 1996.

David, Charles-Philippe, Nancy A. Carrol, and Zachary A. Selden. *Foreign Policy Failure in the White House: Reappraising the Fall of the Shah and the Iran-Contra Affair.* Lanham, Md.: University Press of America, 1993.

Davis, Kathy Randall. *But What's He Really Like?* Menlo Park, Calif.: Pacific Coast Publishers, 1970.

Davis, Loyal E. *A Surgeon's Odyssey.* Garden City, N.Y.: Doubleday, 1973.

Davis, Patti. *Angels Don't Die: My Father's Gift of Faith.* New York: HarperCollins, 1995.

————. *The Way I See It: An Autobiography.* New York: G. P. Putnam's Sons, 1992.

Davis, Patti, and Maureen S. Foster. *Home Front.* New York: Crown Publishers, 1986.

Davis, Sue. *Justice Rehnquist and the Constitution.* Princeton: Princeton University Press, 1989.

Day, Kathleen. *S&L Hell: The People and the Politics behind the $1 Trillion Savings and Loan Scandal.* New York: W. W. Norton, 1993.

Deardorff, Alan V. "Trade Policy of the Reagan Years." In Sahu and Tracy, eds., *Economic Legacy,* 187–203.

Deaver, Michael K., and Mickey Herskowitz. *Behind the Scenes.* New York: William Morrow, 1987.

deMause, Lloyd. *Reagan's America.* New York: Creative Roots, 1984.

Denton, Robert E. *The Primetime Presidency of Ronald Reagan: The Era of the Television Presidency.* New York: Praeger, 1988.

Derthick, Martha, and Paul J. Quirk. *The Politics of Deregulation.* Washington, D.C.: Brookings Institution, 1985.

Detlefsen, Robert R. *Civil Rights under Reagan.* San Francisco: ICS Press, 1991.

Devine, Donald J. *Reagan's Terrible Swift Sword: Reforming and Controlling the Federal Bureaucracy.* Ottawa, Ill.: Jameson Books, 1991.

Diamond, Sara. *Roads to Dominion: Right-Wing Movements and Political Power in the United States.* New York: Guilford Press, 1995.

————. *Spiritual Warfare: The Politics of the Christian Right.* Boston: South End Press, 1989.

Dickenson, Mollie. *Thumbs Up: The Life and Courageous Comeback of White House Press Secretary Jim Brady.* New York: William Morrow, 1987.

Dillon, Sam. *Commandos: The CIA and Nicaragua's Contra Rebels.* New York: Henry Holt, 1991.

Dionne, E. J. *Why Americans Hate Politics.* New York: Simon and Schuster, 1991.

Dobrynin, Anatoly. *In Confidence: Moscow's Ambassador to America's Six Cold War Presidents, 1962–1986.* New York: Times Books, 1995.

Doder, Dusko, and Louise Branson. *Gorbachev: Heretic in the Kremlin.* New York: Viking, 1990.

Donovan, Frederick, and James E. Goodby. *Changing the Rules: President Ronald Reagan's Strategic Defense Initiative (SDI) Decision.* Washington, D.C.: Pew Case Studies Center, 1988.

Douglas, Helen Gahagan. *A Full Life*. Garden City, N.Y.: Doubleday, 1982.

Draper, Theodore. "Iran-Contra: The Mystery Solved." *The New York Review of Books,* 10 June 1993, 53–54, 56–59.

———. "The Iran-Contra Secrets." *New York Review of Books,* 27 May 1993, 43–48.

———. *A Very Thin Line: The Iran-Contra Affairs*. New York: Hill and Wang, 1991.

Drew, Elizabeth. *American Journal: The Events of 1976*. New York: Random House, 1977.

———. *Campaign Journal: The Political Events of 1983–1984*. New York: Macmillan, 1985.

———. *Politics and Money: The New Road to Corruption*. New York: Macmillan, 1983.

———. *Portrait of an Election: The 1980 Presidential Campaign*. New York: Simon and Schuster, 1981.

Dugger, Ronnie. *On Reagan: The Man and His Presidency*. New York: McGraw-Hill, 1983.

Duke, Paul, ed. *Beyond Reagan: The Politics of Upheaval*. New York: Warner Books, 1986.

Dunn, Charles W., and J. David Woodard. *American Conservatism from Burke to Bush: An Introduction*. Lanham, Md.: Madison Books, 1991.

Durant, Robert F. *The Administrative Presidency Revisited: Public Lands, the BLM, and the Reagan Revolution*. Albany: State University of New York Press, 1992.

Eads, George C., and Michael Fix, eds. *The Reagan Regulatory Strategy: An Assessment*. Washington, D.C.: Urban Institute Press, 1984.

Edel, Wilbur. *Defenders of the Faith: Religion and Politics from the Pilgrim Fathers to Ronald Reagan*. New York: Praeger, 1987.

———. *The Reagan Presidency: An Actor's Finest Performance*. New York: Hippocrene Books, 1992.

Edsall, Thomas B., and Mary D. Edsall. *Chain Reaction: The Impact of Race, Rights, and Taxes on American Politics*. New York: W. W. Norton, 1991.

Edwards, Anne. *Early Reagan*. New York: William Morrow, 1987.

Edwards, Lee. *Ronald Reagan: A Political Biography*. Rev. ed. Houston: Nordland Publishing International, 1980.

Erickson, Paul D. *Reagan Speaks: The Making of an American Myth*. New York: New York University Press, 1985.

Evans, Michael K. *The Truth about Supply-Side Economics*. New York: Basic Books, 1983.

Evans, Rowland, and Robert Novak. *The Reagan Revolution*. New York: E. P. Dutton, 1981.

Fairbanks, Charles H. "Introduction." *The National Interest* 31 (spring 1983): 5–8.

Falwell, Jerry. *Strength for the Journey: An Autobiography*. New York: Simon and Schuster, 1987.

Federici, Michael P. *The Challenge of Populism: The Rise of Right-Wing Democratism in Postwar America*. Westport, Conn.: Praeger, 1991.

Feldstein, Martin, ed. *American Economic Policy in the 1980s*. Chicago: University of Chicago Press, 1994.

Fenno, Richard F. *The Emergence of a Senate Leader: Pete Domenici and the Reagan Budget*. Washington, D.C.: CQ Press, 1991.

Ferguson, Thomas, and Joel Rogers. "The Reagan Victory: Corporate Coalitions in the 1980 Campaign." In *The Hidden Election: Politics and Economics in the 1980 Presidential Campaign,* ed. Thomas Ferguson and Joel Rogers, 3–64. New York: Pantheon, 1981.

Ferraro, Geraldine A. *Ferraro: My Story.* New York: Bantam, 1985.

Ferrell, Robert H. *Ill-Advised: Presidential Health and Public Trust.* Columbia: University of Missouri Press, 1992.

Fink, Richard H., ed. *Supply-Side Economics: A Critical Appraisal.* Frederick, Md.: Aletheia Books, 1982.

Finn, Chester E. " 'Affirmative Action' under Reagan." *Commentary,* April 1982, 17–28.

Fitzwater, Marlin. *Call the Briefing! Bush and Reagan, Sam and Helen: A Decade with Presidents and the Press.* New York: Times Books, 1995.

Foner, Eric, and John A. Garraty, eds. *The Reader's Companion to American History.* Boston: Houghton Mifflin, 1991.

Ford, Gerald R. "Voters Won't Pick Our Next President—The House Will." *U.S. News & World Report,* 28 July 1980, 27.

Ford, William F. "Conference Purpose and Overview." In *Supply-Side Economics in the 1980s: Conference Proceedings,* ed. William F. Ford, 5–6. Westport, Conn.: Quorum Books, 1982.

Fraser, Steve, and Gary Gerstle, eds. *The Rise and Fall of the New Deal Order, 1930–1980.* Princeton: Princeton University Press, 1989.

Freedland, Michael. *The Warner Brothers.* New York: St. Martin's Press, 1983.

Fried, Charles. *Order and Law: Arguing the Reagan Revolution, A Firsthand Account.* New York: Simon and Schuster, 1991.

Friedman, Benjamin M. *Day of Reckoning: The Consequences of American Economic Policy under Reagan and After.* New York: Random House, 1988.

Frum, David. *Dead Right.* New York: Basic Books, 1994.

Gaddis, John Lewis. *The United States and the End of the Cold War: Implications, Reconsiderations, Provocations.* New York: Oxford University Press, 1992.

Gardner, Howard. *Frames of Mind: The Theory of Multiple Intelligences.* New York: Basic Books, 1985.

Garment, Suzanne. *Scandal: The Culture of Mistrust in American Politics.* New York: Times Books, 1991.

Garrison, Winfred Ernest. *An American Religious Movement: A Brief History of the Disciples of Christ.* St. Louis: Christian Board of Publication, 1945.

Gartner, Alan, Colin Greer, and Frank Riessman. *What Reagan Is Doing to Us.* New York: Harper and Row, 1982.

Gates, Robert M. *From the Shadows: The Ultimate Insider's Story of Five Presidents and How They Won the Cold War.* New York: Simon and Schuster, 1996.

Gergen, Kenneth J. *The Saturated Self: Dilemmas of Identity in Contemporary Life.* New York: Basic Books, 1991.

Germond, Jack W., and Jules Witcover. *Wake Us When It's Over: Presidential Politics of 1984.* New York: Macmillan, 1985.

Gervasi, Tom. *The Myth of Soviet Military Supremacy.* New York: Harper and Row, 1986.

Gilbert, Robert E. *The Mortal Presidency: Illness and Anguish in the White House.* New York: Basic Books, 1992.

Gillies, Archibald, et al. *Post-Reagan America.* New York: World Policy Institute, 1987.

Gillon, Steven M. *The Democrats' Dilemma: Walter F. Mondale and the Liberal Legacy.* New York: Columbia University Press, 1992.

Glynn, Patrick. *Closing Pandora's Box: Arms Races, Arms Control, and the History of the Cold War.* New York: Basic Books, 1992.

Goldberg, Robert A. *Barry Goldwater.* New Haven: Yale University Press, 1995.

Goldfarb, Jeffrey C. *The Cynical Society: The Culture of Politics and the Politics of Culture in American Life.* Chicago: University of Chicago Press, 1991.

Goldfischer, David. *The Best Defense: Policy Alternatives for U.S. Nuclear Security from the 1950s to the 1990s.* Ithaca, N.Y.: Cornell University Press, 1993.

Goldman, Peter, and Tony Fuller. *The Quest for the Presidency, 1984.* New York: Bantam, 1985.

Goldwater, Barry M., and Jack Casserly. *Goldwater.* New York: Doubleday, 1988.

Gorbachev, Mikhail. *At the Summit.* New York: Richardson, Steirman and Black, 1988.

———. *Memoirs.* New York: Doubleday, 1995.

Gottfried, Paul. *The Conservative Movement.* Rev. ed. New York: Twayne, 1993.

Gould, Lewis L. *1968: The Election That Changed America.* Chicago: Ivan R. Dee, 1993.

Green, David G. *The New Conservatism: The Counter-Revolution in Political, Economic, and Social Thought.* New York: St. Martin's Press, 1987.

Green, Fitzhugh. *George Bush: An Intimate Portrait.* New York: Hippocrene Books, 1989.

Greene, John R. *The Presidency of Gerald R. Ford.* Lawrence: University Press of Kansas, 1995.

Greenfield, Meg. "How Does Reagan Decide?" *Newsweek,* 20 February 1984, 80.

Greenstein, Fred I. *The Hidden-Hand Presidency: Eisenhower as Leader.* New York: Basic Books, 1982.

Greenya, John, and Anne Urban. *The Real David Stockman.* New York: St. Martin's Press, 1986.

Greider, William. *The Education of David Stockman and Other Americans.* New York: E. P. Dutton, 1982.

———. "Republicans." In Harwood, ed., *Pursuit of the Presidency,* 159–178.

Griscom, Tom. "Core Ideas of the Reagan Presidency." In Thompson, ed., *Leadership,* 23–48.

Gromyko, Andrei. *Memories.* London: Hutchinson, 1989.

Gutman, Roy. *Banana Diplomacy: The Making of American Policy in Nicaragua, 1981–1987.* New York: Simon and Schuster, 1988.

Hacker, Andrew. *Two Nations: Black and White, Separate, Hostile, Unequal.* New York: Charles Scribner's Sons, 1992.

Haftendorn, Helga, and Jakob Schissler, eds. *The Reagan Administration: A Reconstruction of American Strength?* New York: Walter de Gruyter, 1988.

Hagstrom, Jerry. *Beyond Reagan: The New Landscape of American Politics.* New York: W. W. Norton, 1988.

Haig, Alexander M. *Caveat: Realism, Reagan, and Foreign Policy.* New York: Macmillan, 1984.

Haldeman, H. R. *The Haldeman Diaries: Inside the Nixon White House.* New York: Berkley Books, 1995.

Hamilton, Gary G., and Nicole Woolsey Biggart. *Governor Reagan, Governor Brown: A Sociology of Executive Power.* New York: Columbia University Press, 1984.

Hannaford, Peter. *The Reagans: A Political Portrait.* New York: Coward-McCann, 1983.

Harrell, David E. *Quest for a Christian America: The Disciples of Christ and American Society to 1866.* Nashville: Disciples of Christ Historical Society, 1966.

Harrington, Mona. *The Dream of Deliverance in American Politics.* New York: Alfred A. Knopf, 1986.

Harries, Owen, ed. "The Strange Death of Soviet Communism: An Autopsy." *The National Interest,* no. 31, spring 1993.

Harris, Richard A., and Sidney M. Milkis. *The Politics of Regulatory Change: A Tale of Two Agencies.* 2d ed. New York: Oxford University Press, 1996.

Hartmann, Robert T. *Palace Politics: An Inside Account of the Ford Years.* New York: McGraw-Hill, 1980.

Hartmann, Susan M. *From Margin to Mainstream: American Women and Politics since 1960.* Philadelphia: Temple University Press, 1989.

Harwood, Richard, ed. *The Pursuit of the Presidency, 1980.* New York: Washington Post/Berkley Books, 1980.

Hay, Peter. *All the Presidents' Ladies: Anecdotes of the Women behind the Men in the White House.* New York: Viking, 1988.

Hays, Samuel P. *Beauty, Health, and Permanence: Environmental Politics in the United States, 1955–1985.* Cambridge: Cambridge University Press, 1987.

Heilbroner, Robert L. "The Demand for Supply-Side." In Fink, ed., *Supply-Side Economics,* 80–92.

Heilbroner, Robert L., and Peter Bernstein. *The Debt and the Deficit: False Alarms/Real Possibilities.* New York: W. W. Norton, 1989.

Heine, Jorge, ed. *A Revolution Aborted: The Lessons of Grenada.* Pittsburgh: University of Pittsburgh Press, 1991.

Hendershott, Patric H., and Joe Peek. "Interest Rates in the Reagan Years." In Sahu and Tracy, *Economic Legacy,* 147–62.

Henry, William A. *Visions of America: How We Saw the 1984 Election.* Boston: Atlantic Monthly Press, 1985.

Herf, Jeffrey. *War by Other Means: Soviet Power, West German Resistance, and the Battle of the Euromissiles.* New York: Free Press, 1991.

Hersh, Seymour M. *"The Target Is Destroyed": What Really Happened to Flight 007 and What America Knew About It.* New York: Vintage, 1987.

Hertsgaard, Mark. *On Bended Knee: The Press and the Reagan Presidency.* New York: Farrar Straus Giroux, 1988.

Hewitt, Gavin. *Terry Waite and Ollie North: The Untold Story of the Kidnapping—and the Release.* Boston: Little, Brown, 1991.

Hill, Dilys, Raymond Moore, and Phil Williams. *The Reagan Presidency: An Incomplete Revolution?* New York: St. Martin's Press, 1990.

Hill, Gladwin. *Dancing Bear: An Inside Look at California Politics.* Cleveland: World Publishing, 1968.

Himmelstein, Jerome L. *To the Right: The Transformation of American Conservatism.* Berkeley and Los Angeles: University of California Press, 1990.

Hinckley, Jack, and Jo Ann Hinckley. *Breaking Points.* Grand Rapids: Zondervan Publishing House, 1985.

Hixson, William B. *Search for the American Right Wing: An Analysis of the Social Science Record, 1955–1987.* Princeton: Princeton University Press, 1992.

Hoeveler, J. David. *Watch on the Right: Conservative Intellectuals in the Reagan Era.* Madison: University of Wisconsin Press, 1991.

Hogan, Joseph, ed. *The Reagan Years: The Record in Presidential Leadership.* Manchester, England: Manchester University Press, 1990.

Holt, Pat M. *Secret Intelligence and Public Policy: A Dilemma of Democracy.* Washington, D.C.: CQ Press, 1995.

Hotchner, A. E. *Doris Day: Her Own Story.* New York: William Morrow, 1976.

Hough, Jerry. *Russia and the West: Gorbachev and the Politics of Reform.* 2d ed. New York: Simon and Schuster, 1990.

Hughes, Robert. *Culture of Complaint: The Fraying of America.* New York: Oxford University Press, 1993.

Hulett, Louisa S. *From Cold Wars to Star Wars: Debates over Defense and Detente.* Lanham, Md.: University Press of America, 1988.

Hulten, Charles R. and Isabel V. Sawhill, eds. *The Legacy of Reaganomics: Prospects for Long-Term Growth.* Washington, D.C.: Urban Institute Press, 1984.

Hunt, Albert R. "The Campaign and the Issues." In *The American Elections of 1984,* ed. Austin Ranney, 129–65. Washington, D.C.: American Enterprise Institute/Duke University Press, 1985.

Hunter, James Davison. *Before the Shooting Begins: Searching for Democracy in America's Culture War.* New York: Free Press, 1994.

———. *Culture Wars: The Struggle to Define America.* New York: Basic Books, 1991.

Hyland, William G. *The Cold War Is Over.* New York: Times Books, 1990.

Johnson, Haynes. *Sleepwalking through History: America in the Reagan Years.* New York: W. W. Norton, 1991.

Jones, Charles O. "A New President, a Different Congress, a Maturing Agenda." In Salamon and Lund, eds., *Reagan Presidency,* 261–87.

Jorstad, Erling. *Holding Fast/Pressing On: Religion in America in the 1980s.* New York: Praeger, 1990.

Kahn, Gordon. *Hollywood on Trial: The Story of the Ten Who Were Indicted.* New York: Boni and Gaer, 1948.

Kaiser, Robert G. *Why Gorbachev Happened: His Triumphs and His Failure.* New York: Simon and Schuster, 1991.

Kampelman, Max M. *Entering New Worlds: The Memoirs of a Private Man in Public Life.* New York: HarperCollins, 1991.

———. "Serving Reagan as Negotiator." In Thompson, ed., *Foreign Policy,* 79–93.

Kane, Edward J. *The S&L Insurance Mess: How Did It Happen?* Washington, D.C.: Urban Institute Press, 1989.

Kanfer, Stefan. *A Journal of the Plague Years.* New York: Atheneum, 1973.

Katz, Michael B. *In the Shadow of the Poorhouse: A Social History of Welfare in America.* New York: Basic Books, 1986.

Kazin, Michael. "The Grass-Roots Right: New Histories of U.S. Conservatism in the Twentieth Century." *American Historical Review* 97 (February 1992): 136–55.

———. *The Populist Persuasion: An American History.* New York: Basic Books, 1995.

Keleher, Robert E., and William P. Orzechowski. "Supply-Side Fiscal Policy: An Historical Analysis of a Rejuvenated Idea." In Fink, ed., *Supply-Side Economics,* 121–59.

Kelley, Kitty. *Nancy Reagan: The Unauthorized Biography.* New York: Simon and Schuster, 1991.

Kennedy, David M. *The Reagan Administration and Lebanon.* Washington, D.C.: Pew Case Studies Center, 1988.

Kernek, Sterling. "Reagan's Foreign Policy Leadership." In Thompson, ed., *Foreign Policy,* 3–20.

Kernell, Samuel, and Samuel L. Popkin. *Chief of Staff: Twenty-five Years of Managing the Presidency.* Berkeley and Los Angeles: University of California Press, 1986.

Kiewe, Amos, and Davis W. Houck. *A Shining City on a Hill: Ronald Reagan's Economic Rhetoric, 1951–1989.* New York: Praeger, 1991.

Kirkpatrick, Jeane J. *The Reagan Doctrine and U.S. Foreign Policy.* Washington, D.C.: Heritage Foundation, 1985.

———. *The Withering Away of the Totalitarian State and Other Surprises.* Washington, D.C.: AEI Press, 1990.

Kissinger, Henry. *Diplomacy.* New York: Simon and Schuster, 1994.

Klehr, Harvey, John Earl Haynes, and Fridrikh Igorevich Firsov. *The Secret World of American Communism.* New Haven: Yale University Press, 1995.

Knelman, F. H. *Reagan, God, and the Bomb: From Myth to Policy in the Nuclear Arms Race.* Buffalo: Prometheus Books, 1985.

Koh, Harold H. "Why the President (Almost) Always Wins in Foreign Affairs: Lessons of the Iran-Contra Affair." *Yale Law Journal* 97 (June 1988): 1255–1342.

Kondracke, Morton. "Cabinet Boardroom." *New Republic,* 7 October 1981, 9, 12–13.

Koop, C. Everett. *Koop: The Memoirs of America's Family Doctor.* New York: Random House, 1991.

Kornbluh, Peter. *Nicaragua, the Price of Intervention: Reagan's Wars against the Sandinistas.* Washington, D.C.: Institute for Policy Studies, 1987.

Kornbluh, Peter, and Malcolm Byrne, eds. *The Iran-Contra Scandal: The Declassified History.* New York: New Press, 1993.

Kotkin, Joel, and Paul Grabowicz. *California, Inc.* New York: Rawson, Wade Publishers, 1982.

Ladd, Everett Carll. "The Reagan Phenomenon and Public Attitudes toward Government." In Salamon and Lund, eds., *Reagan Presidency,* 221–49.

Laffer, Arthur B. "Government Exactions and Revenue Deficiencies." In Fink, ed., *Supply-Side Economics,* 185–203.

———. "Introduction." In *Foundations of Supply-Side Economics: Theory and Evidence,* ed. Victor A. Canto, Douglas H. Joines, and Arthur B. Laffer, xv-xvi. New York: Academic Press, 1983.

Lagon, Mark P. *The Reagan Doctrine: Sources of American Conduct in the Cold War's Last Chapter.* Westport, Conn.: Praeger, 1994.

Landau, Saul. *The Guerrilla Wars of Central America: Nicaragua, El Salvador, and Guatemala.* London: Weidenfeld and Nicolson, 1993.

Langston, Thomas S. *Ideologues and Presidents: From the New Deal to the Reagan Revolution.* Baltimore: Johns Hopkins University Press, 1992.

Lawson, Don. *America Held Hostage: The Iran Hostage Crisis and the Iran-Contra Affair.* New York: Franklin Watts, 1991.

Learner, Laurence. *Make-Believe: The Story of Nancy and Ronald Reagan.* New York: Harper and Row, 1983.

Lebow, Richard N., and Janice G. Stein. *We All Lost the Cold War.* Princeton: Princeton University Press, 1994.

le Carré, John. *The Secret Pilgrim.* New York: Alfred A. Knopf, 1991.

Ledeen, Michael A. *Perilous Statecraft: An Insider's Account of the Iran-Contra Affair.* New York: Charles Scribner's Sons, 1988.

Lees, John D., and Michael Turner. *Reagan's First Four Years: A New Beginning?* Manchester, England: Manchester University Press, 1988.

Lehman, John F. *Command of the Seas.* New York: Charles Scribner's Sons, 1988.

Leighton, Frances S. *The Search for the Real Nancy Reagan.* New York: Macmillan, 1987.

Lekachman, Robert. *Greed Is Not Enough: Reaganomics.* New York: Pantheon, 1982.

LeRoy, Mervyn, and Dick Kleiner. *Mervyn LeRoy: Take One.* New York: Hawthorn Books, 1974.

Lesher, Stephan. *George Wallace: American Populist.* Reading, Mass.: Addison-Wesley, 1994.

Leshy, John D. "Natural Resource Policy." In *Natural Resources and the Environment: The Reagan Approach,* ed. Paul R. Portney, 13–46. Washington, D.C.: Urban Institute Press, 1984.

Lewis, Joseph. *What Makes Reagan Run? A Political Profile.* New York: McGraw-Hill, 1968.

Liebman, Robert C., and Robert Wuthnow, eds. *The New Christian Right: Mobilization and Legitimation.* New York: Aldine Publishing, 1983.

Lienesch, Michael. *Redeeming America: Piety and Politics in the New Christian Right.* Chapel Hill: University of North Carolina Press, 1993.

Lifton, Robert Jay. *The Protean Self: Human Resilience in an Age of Fragmentation.* New York: Basic Books, 1993.

Lindsey, Lawrence. *The Growth Experiment: How the New Tax Policy Is Transforming the U.S. Economy.* New York: Basic Books, 1990.

Lofland, John. *Polite Protesters: The American Peace Movement of the 1980s.* Syracuse, N.Y.: Syracuse University Press, 1993.

Lord, Carnes. *The Presidency and the Management of National Security.* New York: Free Press, 1988.

McClelland, Doug. *Hollywood on Ronald Reagan: Friends and Enemies Discuss Our President, the Actor.* Winchester, Mass.: Faber and Faber, 1983.

McClintock, Michael. *Instruments of Statecraft: U.S. Guerrilla Warfare, Counterinsurgency, and Counterterrorism, 1940–1990.* New York: Pantheon, 1992.

McClure, Arthur F., C. David Rice, and William T. Stewart. *Ronald Reagan: His First Career, A Bibliography of the Movie Years.* Lewiston, N.Y.: Edwin Mellen Press, 1988.

McFarlane, Robert C., and Zofia Smardz. *Special Trust.* New York: Cadell and Davies, 1994.

McGlen, Nancy E., and Meredith Reid Sarkees. *Women in Foreign Policy: The Insiders.* New York: Routledge, 1993.

McGuigan, Patrick B., and Dawn M. Weyrich. *Ninth Justice: The Fight for Bork.* Washington, D.C.: Free Congress Research and Education Foundation, 1990.

McKenzie, Richard B. *What Went Right in the 1980s.* San Francisco, Calif.: Pacific Research Institute for Public Policy, 1994.

McMahan, Jeff. *Reagan and the World: Imperial Policy in the New Cold War.* New York: Monthly Review Press, 1985.

Malabre, Alfred L. *Beyond Our Means: How Reckless Borrowing Now Threatens to Overwhelm Us.* New York: Vintage, 1987.

Mandelbaum, Michael, and Strobe Talbott. *Reagan and Gorbachev.* New York: Vintage, 1987.

Marks, Stanley J. *A Year in the Lives of the Damned! Reagan, Reaganism, 1986.* N.p.: Bureau of International Affairs Publication, 1988.

Marshall, Eliot. "For Sale: A Billion Acres of Outer Continental Shelf." *Science* 213 (31 July 1981): 524–25.

Marshall, Jonathan, Peter D. Scott, and Jane Hunter. *The Iran-Contra Connection: Secret Teams and Covert Operations in the Reagan Era.* Boston: South End Press, 1987.

Martin, David C., and John Walcott. *Best Laid Plans: The Inside Story of America's War against Terrorism.* New York: Simon and Schuster, 1988.

Marty, Martin E., and R. Scott Appleby. *The Glory and the Power: The Fundamentalist Challenge to the Modern World.* Boston: Beacon Press, 1992.

Marullo, Sam, and John Lofland, eds. *Peace Action in the Eighties.* New Brunswick, N.J.: Rutgers University Press, 1990.

Matlock, Jack F. *Autopsy on an Empire: The American Ambassador's Account of the Collapse of the Soviet Union.* New York: Random House, 1995.

May, Lary. "Movie Star Politics: The Screen Actors' Guild, Cultural Conversion, and the Hollywood Red Scare." In *Recasting America: Culture and Politics in the Age of the Cold War,* ed. Lary May, 125–53. Chicago: University of Chicago Press, 1989.

Mayer, Jane, and Doyle McManus. *Landslide: The Unmaking of the President, 1984–1988.* Boston: Houghton Mifflin, 1988.

Mayer, William G. *The Changing American Mind: How and Why American Public Opinion Changed between 1960 and 1988.* Ann Arbor: University of Michigan Press, 1992.

Meese, Edwin. *With Reagan: The Inside Story.* Washington, D.C.: Regnery Gateway, 1992.

Meiners, Roger E., and Bruce Yandle, eds. *Regulation and the Reagan Era: Politics, Bureaucracy, and the Public Interest.* New York: Holmes and Meier, 1989.

Melich, Tanya. *The Republican War against Women: An Insider's Report from behind the Lines.* New York: Bantam, 1996.

Menges, Constantine C. *Inside the National Security Council: The True Story of the Making and Unmaking of Reagan's Foreign Policy.* New York: Simon and Schuster, 1988.

Mervin, David. *Ronald Reagan and the American Presidency.* London: Longman, 1990.

Meyer, Laurence H., Joel L. Prakken, and Chris P. Varvares. "Two Revolutions in Economic Policy: Growth-Oriented Macro Policy in the Kennedy and Reagan Administrations." In Sahu and Tracy, *Economic Legacy,* 67–85.

Middlebrook, Kevin J., and Carlos Rico, eds. *The United States and Latin America in the 1980s: Contending Perspectives on a Decade of Crisis.* Pittsburgh: University of Pittsburgh Press, 1986.

Miller, James C. *Fix the U.S. Budget! Urgings of an "Abominable No-Man."* Stanford, Calif.: Hoover Institution Press, 1994.

Miller, James N. "What Really Happened at EPA." In *Reaganomics: The New Federalism,* ed. Carl Lowe, 72–78. New York: H. W. Wilson, 1984.

Miller, Nathan. *Stealing from America: A History of Corruption from Jamestown to Reagan.* New York: Paragon House, 1992.

Mills, Gregory B., and John L. Palmer, eds. *Federal Budget Policy in the 1980s.* Washington, D.C.: Urban Institute Press, 1984.

Minarik, Joseph J. *Making America's Budget Policy: From the 1980s to the 1990s.* Armonk, N.Y.: M. E. Sharpe, 1990.

Moen, Matthew C. *The Christian Right and Congress.* Tuscaloosa: University of Alabama Press, 1989.

Moldea, Dan E. *Dark Victory: Ronald Reagan, MCA, and the Mob.* New York: Viking, 1986.

Molotov, Vyacheslav M., and Felix Chuev. *Molotov Remembers: Inside Kremlin Politics.* Chicago: Ivan R. Dee, 1993.

Moore, Thomas G. "The Reagan Economic Performance." In Sahu and Tracy, eds., *Economic Legacy,* 107–113.

Morella, Joe, and Edward Z. Epstein. *Jane Wyman: A Biography.* New York: Delacorte Press, 1985.

Morris, Charles R. *Iron Destinies, Lost Opportunities: The Arms Race between the U.S.A. and the U.S.S.R., 1945–1987.* New York: Harper and Row, 1988.

Morris, Edmund. "In Memoriam: Christina Reagan." *American Spectator* 26 (August 1993): 18–19.

———. "Official Biographer Puzzled by Reagan Persona." *Miller Center Report* 6 (winter 1990): 4.

———. "This Living Hand." *New Yorker,* 16 January 1995, 66–69.

Morris, Roger. *Haig: The General's Progress.* Chicago: Playboy Press, 1982.

Murphy, George, and Victor Lasky. *"Say . . . Didn't You Used to Be George Murphy?"* N.p.: Bartholomew House, 1970.

Murray, Robert K., and Tim H. Blessing. *Greatness in the White House: Rating the Presidents, from George Washington through Ronald Reagan.* 2d ed. University Park: Pennsylvania State University Press, 1994.

Nash, George H. *The Conservative Intellectual Movement in America since 1945.* New York: Basic Books, 1976.

Navasky, Victor S. *Naming Names.* New York: Viking, 1980.

Neikirk, William R. *Volcker: Portrait of the Money Man.* New York: Congdon and Weed, 1987.

Nessen, Ron. *It Sure Looks Different from the Inside.* Chicago: Playboy Press, 1978.

Neuhaus, Richard J., and Michael Cromartie, eds. *Piety and Politics: Evangelicals and Fundamentalists Confront the World.* Washington, D.C.: Ethics and Public Policy Center, 1987.

Neustadt, Richard E. "Looking Back: Meanings and Puzzles." In Berman, ed., *Looking Back,* 319–25.

Newland, Chester A. "Executive Office Policy Apparatus: Enforcing the Reagan Agenda." In Salamon and Lund, eds., *Reagan Presidency,* 135–168.

Niskanen, William A. *Reaganomics: An Insider's Account of the Policies and the People.* New York: Oxford University Press, 1988.

Nitze, Paul H. *From Hiroshima to Glasnost: At the Center of Decision.* New York: Grove Weidenfeld, 1989.

———. "Reagan as Foreign Policy Strategist." In Thompson, ed., *Foreign Policy,* 145–57.

———. "Reagan and the Realities of Foreign Policy." In Thompson, ed., *Foreign Policy,* 21–41.

Nixon, Richard M. *RN: The Memoirs of Richard Nixon.* New York: Grosset and Dunlap, 1978.

Noble, Charles. *Liberalism at Work: The Rise and Fall of OSHA.* Philadelphia: Temple University Press, 1986.

Nofziger, Franklyn C. *Nofziger.* Washington, D.C.: Regnery Gateway, 1992.

Nolan, Janne E. *Guardians of the Arsenal: The Politics of Nuclear Strategy.* New York: Basic Books, 1989.

Noonan, Peggy. *What I Saw at the Revolution: A Political Life in the Reagan Era.* New York: Random House, 1990.

North, Oliver L., and William Novak. *Under Fire: An American Story.* New York: HarperCollins, 1991.

"Notebook." *The New Republic,* 21 February 1983, 7.

Nylen, William R. *U.S.-Grenada Relations, 1979–1983: American Foreign Policy towards a "Backyard" Revolution.* Washington, D.C.: Pew Case Studies Center, 1988.

Oberdorfer, Don. *The Turn: From the Cold War to a New Era, the United States and the Soviet Union, 1983–1990.* New York: Poseidon Press, 1991.

O'Brien, Pat. *The Wind at My Back: The Life and Times of Pat O'Brien.* Garden City, N.Y.: Doubleday, 1964.

Ogilvy, David. *Ogilvy on Advertising.* New York: Vintage, 1985.

O'Neill, Tip, and William Novak. *Man of the House: The Life and Political Memoirs of Speaker Tip O'Neill.* New York: Random House, 1987.

O'Reilly, Kenneth. *Nixon's Piano: Presidents and Racial Politics from Washington to Clinton.* New York: Free Press, 1995.

Orfield, Gary, and Carole Ashkinaze. *The Closing Door: Conservative Policy and Black Opportunity.* Chicago: University of Chicago Press, 1991.

Paige, Connie. *The Right to Lifers: Who They Are, How They Operate, Where They Get Their Money.* New York: Summit, 1983.

Palmer, John L., ed. *Perspectives on the Reagan Years.* Washington, D.C.: Urban Institute Press, 1986.

Palmer, John L., and Isabel V. Sawhill, eds. *The Reagan Experiment: An Examination of Economic and Social Policies under the Reagan Administration.* Washington, D.C.: Urban Institute Press, 1982.

————. *The Reagan Record: An Assessment of America's Changing Domestic Priorities.* Cambridge, Mass.: Ballinger, 1984.

Parker, John W. *Kremlin in Transition.* Vol. 1, *From Brezhnev to Chernenko, 1978 to 1985.* Vol. 2, *Gorbachev, 1985 to 1989.* Boston: Unwin Hyman, 1991.

Parry, Robert. *Fooling America: How Washington Insiders Twist the Truth and Manufacture the Conventional Wisdom.* New York: William Morrow, 1992.

Pasztor, Andy. *When the Pentagon Was for Sale: Inside America's Biggest Defense Scandal.* New York: Scribner, 1995.

Peacock, Alan, ed. *Reaganomics and After.* London: Institute of Economic Affairs, 1989.

Pemberton, William E. *Harry S. Truman: Fair Dealer and Cold Warrior.* Boston: Twayne, 1989.

Peres, Shimon. *Battling for Peace: A Memoir.* New York: Random House, 1995.

Perle, Richard. *Hard Line.* New York: Random House, 1992.

Perrella, Robert. *They Call Me the Showbiz Priest.* New York: Trident Press, 1973.

Persico, Joseph E. *Casey: From the OSS to the CIA.* New York: Viking, 1990.

Pertschuk, Michael. *Revolt against Regulation: The Rise and Pause of the Consumer Movement.* Berkeley and Los Angeles: University of California Press, 1982.

Peterson, George E., et al. *The Reagan Block Grants: What Have We Learned?* Washington, D.C.: Urban Institute Press, 1986.

Peterson, George E., and Carol W. Lewis. "Introduction." In *Reagan and the Cities,* ed. George E. Peterson and Carol W. Lewis, 1–10. Washington, D.C.: Urban Institute Press, 1986.

Peterson, Wallace C. *Silent Depression: The Fate of the American Dream.* New York: W. W. Norton, 1994.

Phillips, Kevin. *Arrogant Capital: Washington, Wall Street, and the Frustration of American Politics.* Boston: Little, Brown, 1994.

————. *The Politics of Rich and Poor: Wealth and the American Electorate in the Reagan Aftermath.* New York: Random House, 1990.

Pierard, Richard V. "Reagan and the Evangelicals: The Making of a Love Affair." *Christian Century,* 21–28 December 1983, 1182–85.

Pierard, Richard V., and Robert D. Linder. *Civil Religion and the Presidency.* Grand Rapids: Zondervan Publishing House, 1988.

Pierson, Paul. *Dismantling the Welfare State? Reagan, Thatcher, and the Politics of Retrenchment.* New York: Cambridge University Press, 1994.

Pizzo, Stephen, Mary Fricker, and Paul Muolo. *Inside Job: The Looting of America's Savings and Loans.* New York: McGraw-Hill, 1989.

Powell, Colin L., and Joseph E. Persico. *My American Journey.* New York: Random House, 1995.

Powers, Richard G. *Not Without Honor: The History of American Anticommunism.* New York: Free Press, 1995.

Prados, John. *Keepers of the Keys: A History of the National Security Council from Truman to Bush.* New York: William Morrow, 1991.

Prestowitz, Clyde V. *Trading Places: How We Allowed Japan to Take the Lead.* New York: Basic Books, 1988.

Prindle, David F. *The Politics of Glamour: Ideology and Democracy in the Screen Actors Guild.* Madison: University of Wisconsin Press, 1988.

Quigley, Joan. *"What Does Joan Say?" My Seven Years as White House Astrologer to Nancy and Ronald Reagan.* New York: Carol Publishing Group, 1990.

Rachwald, Arthur R. *In Search of Poland: The Superpowers' Response to Solidarity, 1980–1989.* Stanford, Calif.: Hoover Institution Press, 1990.

Rae, Nicol C. *The Decline and Fall of the Liberal Republicans: From 1952 to the Present.* New York: Oxford University Press, 1989.

Rahn, Richard W. "Supply-Side Economics: The U.S. Experience." In Stubblebine and Willett, eds., *Reaganomics,* 43–57.

Ranney, Austin. "The Carter Administration." In *The American Elections of 1980,* ed. Austin Ranney, 1–36. Washington, D.C.: American Enterprise Institute, 1981.

————, ed. *The American Elections of 1984.* Durham, N.C.: Duke University Press, 1985.

Reagan, Maureen. *First Father, First Daughter: A Memoir.* Boston: Little, Brown, 1989.

Reagan, Michael and Joe Hyams. *On the Outside Looking In.* London: Quartet Books, 1988.

Reagan, Nancy, and William Novak. *My Turn: The Memoirs of Nancy Reagan.* New York: Random House, 1989.

Reagan, Ronald. *Abortion and the Conscience of the Nation.* Nashville: Thomas Nelson, 1984.

————. *An American Life.* New York: Simon and Schuster, 1990.

————. *The Creative Society: Some Comments on Problems Facing America.* New York: Devin-Adair, 1968.

————. "Fascist Ideas Are Still Alive in U.S." *AVC Bulletin,* 15 February 1946, 6.

————. "Motion Pictures and Your Community." *Kiwanis Magazine* 36 (August 1951): 25, 54.

————. *Public Papers of the Presidents of the United States: Ronald Reagan, 1981– 1989.* 8 vols. Washington, D.C.: GPO, 1982–91.

————. "The Role I Liked Best." *Saturday Evening Post,* 1 January 1949, 67.

————. *Ronald Reagan Talks to America.* Old Greenwich, Conn.: Devin Adair, 1983.

————. *A Time for Choosing: The Speeches of Ronald Reagan, 1961–1982.* Chicago: Regnery Gateway, 1983.

Reagan, Ronald, and Gladys Hall. "How to Make Yourself Important." *Photoplay,* August 1942, pages unnumbered.

Reagan, Ronald, and Richard G. Hubler. *Where's the Rest of Me?* New York: Duell, Sloan, and Pearce, 1965.

Regan, Donald T. *For the Record: From Wall Street to Washington.* New York: Harcourt Brace Jovanovich, 1988.

————. "The Reagan Presidency: Atop the Second Tier." In Thompson, ed., *Leadership,* 49–67.

Reich, Robert B. *The Work of Nations: Preparing Ourselves for Twenty-first-Century Capitalism.* New York: Alfred A. Knopf, 1991.

Reinhard, David W. *The Republican Right since 1945.* Lexington: University Press of Kentucky, 1983.

Reinsch, J. Leonard. *Getting Elected: From Radio and Roosevelt to Television and Reagan.* New York: Hippocrene Books, 1988.

Reisberg, Barry, ed. *Alzheimer's Disease: The Standard Reference.* New York: Free Press, 1983.

Remnick, David. "Getting Russia Right." *New York Review of Books,* 22 September 1994, 20–26.

Ribuffo, Leo P. "God and Contemporary Politics." *Journal of American History* 79 (March 1993): 1515–33.

————. *The Old Christian Right: The Protestant Far Right from the Great Depression to the Cold War.* Philadelphia: Temple University Press, 1983.

————. "Why Is There So Much Conservatism in the United States and Why Do So

Few Historians Know Anything About It?" *American Historical Review* 99 (April 1994): 438–49.

Riccards, Michael P. *The Ferocious Engine of Democracy: A History of the American Presidency.* Vol. 2. Lanham, Md.: Madison Books, 1995.

Rieder, Jonathan. "The Rise of the 'Silent Majority.' " In *The Rise and Fall of the New Deal Order, 1930–1980,* ed. Steve Fraser and Gary Gerstle, 243–68. Princeton: Princeton University Press, 1989.

Rimmerman, Craig A. *Presidency by Plebiscite: The Reagan-Bush Era in Institutional Perspective.* Boulder, Colo.: Westview Press, 1993.

Ritter, Kurt, and David Henry. *Ronald Reagan: The Great Communicator.* New York: Greenwood Press, 1992.

Rivlin, Alice. "The Deficit Dilemma." In Stubblebine and Willett, eds., *Reaganomics,* 135–37.

Roberts, Paul C. *The Supply-Side Revolution: An Insider's Account of Policymaking in Washington.* Cambridge: Harvard University Press, 1984.

Robinson, David Z. *The Strategic Defense Initiative: Its Effect on the Economy and Arms Control.* New York: New York University Press, 1987.

Rogin, Michael P. *Ronald Reagan, the Movie: And Other Episodes in Political Demonology.* Berkeley and Los Angeles, Calif.: University of California Press, 1987.

Ronald Reagan Center for Public Affairs, *The Cold War: Ten Years Later.* Simi Valley, Calif.: Ronald Reagan Center for Public Affairs, 1995.

Roosevelt, Selwa "Lucky." *Keeper of the Gate.* New York: Simon and Schuster, 1990.

Rorabaugh, W. J. *Berkeley at War: The 1960s.* New York: Oxford University Press, 1989.

Rosebush, James S. *First Lady, Public Wife: A Behind-the-Scenes History of the Evolving Role of First Ladies in American Political Life.* Lanham, Md.: Madison Books, 1987.

Rosenbaum, Walter A. *Environmental Politics and Policy.* 2d ed. Washington, D.C.: CQ Press, 1991.

Rothenberg, Randall. *The Neoliberals: Creating the New American Politics.* New York: Simon and Schuster, 1984.

Rubenstein, Edwin S. *The Right Data.* New York: National Review, 1994.

Sabato, Larry J. *PAC Power: Inside the World of Political Action Committees.* New York: W. W. Norton, 1984.

Sahu, Anandi P., and Ronald L. Tracy, eds. *The Economic Legacy of the Reagan Years: Euphoria or Chaos?* New York: Praeger, 1991.

Salamon, Lester M., and Michael S. Lund, "Governance in the Reagan Era: An Overview." In Salamon and Lund, eds., *Reagan Presidency,* 1–25.

———, eds. *The Reagan Presidency and the Governing of America.* Washington, D.C.: Urban Institute Press, 1984.

Saloma, John S. *Ominous Politics: The New Conservative Labyrinth.* New York: Hill and Wang, 1984.

Savage, David G. *Turning Right: The Making of the Rehnquist Supreme Court.* New York: John Wiley and Sons, 1992.

Savoie, Donald J. *Thatcher Reagan Mulroney: In Search of a New Bureaucracy.* Pittsburgh: University of Pittsburgh Press, 1994.

Schaller, Michael. *Reckoning with Reagan: America and Its President in the 1980s.* New York: Oxford University Press, 1992.

Schary, Dore, and Charles Palmer. *Case History of a Movie.* New York: Random House, 1950.

Scheer, Robert. *With Enough Shovels: Reagan, Bush, and Nuclear War.* New York: Random House, 1982.

Schieffer, Bob, and Gary P. Gates. *The Acting President*. New York: E. P. Dutton, 1989.

Schwab, Larry M. *The Illusion of a Conservative Reagan Revolution*. New Brunswick, N.J.: Transaction Press, 1991.

Schwartz, Herman. *Packing the Courts: The Conservative Campaign to Rewrite the Constitution*. New York: Charles Scribner's Sons, 1988.

Schwartz, Nancy L., and Sheila Schwartz. *The Hollywood Writers' Wars*. New York: Alfred A. Knopf, 1982.

Schweizer, Peter. *Victory: The Reagan Administration's Secret Strategy That Hastened the Collapse of the Soviet Union*. New York: Atlantic Monthly Press, 1994.

Scobie, Ingrid Winther. *Center Stage: Helen Gahagan Douglas, A Life*. New Brunswick, N.J.: Rutgers University Press, 1995.

Secord, Richard, and Jay Wurts. *Honored and Betrayed: Irangate, Covert Affairs, and the Secret War in Laos*. New York: John Wiley and Sons, 1992.

Seidman, L. William. *Full Faith and Credit: The Great S&L Debacle and Other Washington Sagas*. New York: Times Books, 1993.

Sexton, Patricia C. *The War on Labor and the Left: Understanding America's Unique Conservatism*. Boulder, Colo.: Westview Press, 1991.

Shadegg, Stephen. *What Happened to Goldwater? The Inside Story of the 1964 Republican Campaign*. New York: Holt, Rinehart and Winston, 1965.

Shanley, Robert A. *Presidential Influence and Environmental Policy*. Westport, Conn.: Greenwood Press, 1992.

Sharpe, Kenneth E. "The Post-Vietnam Formula under Siege: The Imperial Presidency and Central America." *Political Science Quarterly* 102 (winter 1987–88): 549–69.

Sheehy, Gail. *The Man Who Changed the World: The Lives of Mikhail S. Gorbachev*. New York: HarperCollins, 1990.

Shimko, Keith L. *Images and Arms Control: Perceptions of the Soviet Union in the Reagan Administration*. Ann Arbor: University of Michigan Press, 1991.

Shogan, Robert. *The Riddle of Power: Presidential Leadership from Truman to Bush*. New York: E. P. Dutton, 1991.

Short, C. Brant. *Ronald Reagan and the Public Lands: America's Conservation Debate, 1979–1984*. College Station: Texas A&M University Press, 1989.

Shull, Steven A. *A Kinder, Gentler Racism? The Reagan-Bush Civil Rights Legacy*. Armonk, N.Y.: M. E. Sharpe, 1993.

Shultz, George P. *Turmoil and Triumph: My Years as Secretary of State*. New York: Charles Scribner's Sons, 1993.

Siegel, Frederick F. "Conservatism." In Foner and Garraty, eds., *Reader's Companion*, 220–23.

———. "Liberalism." In Foner and Garraty, eds., *Reader's Companion*, 653–56.

———. *Troubled Journey: From Pearl Harbor to Ronald Reagan*. New York: Hill and Wang, 1984.

Silverman, Debora. *Selling Culture: Bloomingdale's, Diana Vreeland, and the New Aristocracy of Taste in Reagan's America*. New York: Pantheon, 1986.

Simon, Philip J. *Reagan in the Workplace: Unraveling the Health and Safety Net*. Washington, D.C.: Center for Study of Responsive Law, 1983.

Simpson, Christopher. *National Security Directives of the Reagan and Bush Administrations: The Declassified History of U.S. Political and Military Policy, 1981–1991*. Boulder, Colo.: Westview Press, 1995.

Singlaub, John K., and Malcolm McConnell. *Hazardous Duty: An American Soldier in the Twentieth Century*. New York: Summit, 1991.

Sklar, Holly. *Reagan, Trilateralism, and the Neoliberals: Containment and Intervention in the 1980s*. Boston: South End Press, 1986.

Skocpol, Theda. *Boomerang: Clinton's Health Security Effort and the Turn against Government in U.S. Politics.* New York: W. W. Norton, 1996.

Slemrod, Joel, ed. *Do Taxes Matter? The Impact of the Tax Reform Act of 1986.* Cambridge: MIT Press, 1990.

Smith, Christopher E. *Justice Antonin Scalia and the Supreme Court's Conservative Moment.* Westport, Conn.: Praeger, 1993.

Smith, Geoffrey. *Reagan and Thatcher.* New York: W. W. Norton, 1991.

Smith, George H. *Who Is Ronald Reagan?* New York: Pyramid Books, 1968.

Smith, T. Burton. "The President's Health." In Thompson, ed., *Leadership, Part II,* 197–221.

Smith, V. Kerry. "Environmental Policy Making under Executive Order 12291: An Introduction." In *Environmental Policy under Reagan's Executive Order: The Role of Benefit-Cost Analysis,* ed. V. Kerry Smith, 3–40. Chapel Hill: University of North Carolina Press, 1984.

Smith, William French. *Law and Justice in the Reagan Administration: The Memoirs of an Attorney General.* Stanford, Calif.: Hoover Institution Press, 1991.

Smoke, Richard. *National Security and the Nuclear Dilemma: An Introduction to the American Experience in the Cold War.* 3d ed. New York: McGraw-Hill, 1993.

Snyder, Alvin A. *Warriors of Disinformation: American Propaganda, Soviet Lies, and the Winning of the Cold War, an Insider's Account.* New York: Arcade Publishing, 1995.

Speakes, Larry, and Robert Pack. *Speaking Out: The Reagan Presidency from Inside the White House.* New York: Charles Scribner's Sons, 1988.

Spear, Joseph C. *Presidents and the Press: The Nixon Legacy.* Cambridge: MIT Press, 1984.

Spitzer, Robert J. *President and Congress: Executive Hegemony at the Crossroads of American Government.* Philadelphia: Temple University Press, 1993.

Stanley, Harold W. "The 1984 Presidential Election in the South: Race and Realignment." In *The 1984 Presidential Election in the South: Patterns of Southern Party Politics,* ed. Robert P. Steed, Laurence W. Moreland, and Tod A. Baker, 303–35. New York: Praeger, 1985.

Steele, Shelby. "How Liberals Lost Their Virtue over Race." *Newsweek,* 9 January 1995, 41–42.

Steinfels, Peter. *The Neoconservatives: The Men Who Are Changing America's Politics.* New York: Simon and Schuster, 1979.

Steuerle, C. Eugene. *The Tax Decade: How Taxes Came to Dominate the Public Agenda.* Washington, D.C.: Urban Institute Press, 1992.

Stockman, David A. *The Triumph of Politics: How the Reagan Revolution Failed.* New York: Harper and Row, 1986.

Stone, Charles F., and Isabel V. Sawhill. *Economic Policy in the Reagan Years.* Washington, D.C.: Urban Institute Press, 1984.

Strober, Gerald S., and Deborah H. Strober. *Nixon: An Oral History of His Presidency.* New York: HarperCollins, 1994.

Struyk, Raymond J., Neil Mayer, and John A. Tuccillo. *Federal Housing Policy at President Reagan's Midterm.* Washington, D.C.: Urban Institute Press, 1983.

Stubblebine, W. Craig, and Thomas D. Willett, eds. *Reaganomics: A Midterm Report.* San Francisco: ICS Press, 1983.

Stuckey, Mary E. *Getting into the Game: The Pre-Presidential Rhetoric of Ronald Reagan.* New York: Praeger, 1989.

———. *Playing the Game: The Presidential Rhetoric of Ronald Reagan.* New York: Praeger, 1990.

Sundquist, James L. *Dynamics of the Party System: Alignment and Realignment of Political Parties in the United States.* Rev. ed. Washington, D.C.: Brookings Institution, 1983.

Talbott, Strobe. *Deadly Gambits: The Reagan Administration and the Stalemate in Nuclear Arms Control.* New York: Alfred A. Knopf, 1984.

————. *The Russians and Reagan.* New York: Vintage, 1984.

Thatcher, Margaret. *The Downing Street Years.* New York: HarperCollins, 1993.

Thomas, Michael M. "The Greatest American Shambles." *New York Review of Books,* 31 January 1991, 30–35.

Thomas, Tony. *The Films of Ronald Reagan.* Secaucus, N.J.: Citadel Press, 1980.

Thompson, E. P., ed. *Star Wars.* New York: Pantheon, 1985.

Thompson, Kenneth W., ed. *Foreign Policy in the Reagan Presidency: Nine Intimate Perspectives.* Lanham, Md.: University Press of America, 1993.

————, ed. *Leadership in the Reagan Presidency: Seven Intimate Perspectives.* Lanham, Md.: Madison Books, 1992.

————, ed. *Leadership in the Reagan Presidency, Part II: Eleven Intimate Perspectives.* Lanham, Md.: University Press of America, 1993.

Thompson, Marilyn W. *Feeding the Beast: How Wedtech Became the Most Corrupt Little Company in America.* New York: Charles Scribner's Sons, 1990.

Thorne, Melvin J. *American Conservative Thought since World War II: The Core Ideas.* Westport, Conn.: Greenwood Press, 1990.

Timberg, Robert. *The Nightingale's Song.* New York: Simon and Schuster, 1995.

Timbers, Edwin. "Legal and Institutional Aspects of the Iran-Contra Affair." *Presidential Studies Quarterly* 20 (winter 1990): 31–41.

Toobin, Jeffrey. *Opening Arguments: A Young Lawyer's First Case, United States v. Oliver North.* New York: Viking, 1991.

Tower, John G. *Consequences: A Personal and Political Memoir.* Boston: Little, Brown, 1991.

Traub, James. *Too Good to Be True: The Outlandish Story of Wedtech.* New York: Doubleday, 1990.

Trudeau, Pierre E. *Memoirs.* Toronto: McClelland and Stewart, 1993.

Twain, Mark. *Adventures of Huckleberry Finn.* New York: Random House, 1996.

Ullmann, Owen. *Stockman: The Man, the Myth, the Future.* New York: Donald I. Fine, 1986.

Union of Concerned Scientists. *The Fallacy of Star Wars.* New York: Vintage, 1984.

U.S., President's Special Review Board [Tower Board]. *Report of the President's Special Review Board.* Washington, D.C.: GPO, 1987.

U.S., Senate and House Select Committees, *Hearings,* 100th Congress, 1st sess. Washington, D.C.: GPO, 1988.

————. *Report of the Congressional Committees Investigating the Iran-Contra Affair.* 100th Congress, 1st sess. S. Rept. 100-216, H. Rept. 100-433. Washington, D.C.: GPO, 1987.

U.S., Transcript of Deposition of Ronald W. Reagan, *United States v. John M. Poindexter,* 16 February 1990, United States District Court, District of Columbia.

U.S., Walsh, Lawrence E. *Final Report of the Independent Counsel for Iran/Contra Matters.* Vol. 1, *Investigations and Prosecutions.* Vol. 2, *Indictments, Plea Agreements, Interim Reports to the Congress, and Administrative Matters.* Vol. 3, *Comments and Materials Submitted by Individuals and Their Attorneys Responding to Volume I of the Final Report.* Washington, D.C.: GPO, 1993.

"U.S. Coastal Waters on Auction Block." *U.S. News & World Report* 2 August 1982, 6.

U.S. News & World Report. *The Story of Lieutenant Colonel Oliver North.* Washington, D.C.: U.S. News & World Report, 1987.

van der Linden, Frank. *The Real Reagan: What He Believes, What He Has Accomplished, What We Can Expect from Him.* New York: William Morrow, 1981.

Vaughn, Stephen. "The Moral Inheritance of a President: Reagan and the Dixon Disciples of Christ." *Presidential Studies Quarterly* 25 (winter 1995): 109–27.
————. *Ronald Reagan in Hollywood: Movies and Politics.* Cambridge: Cambridge University Press, 1994.
Vogel, David. *Fluctuating Fortunes: The Political Power of Business in America.* New York: Basic Books, 1989.
Vogele, William B. *Stepping Back: Nuclear Arms Control and the End of the Cold War.* Westport, Conn.: Praeger, 1994.
von Damm, Helene. *At Reagan's Side.* New York: Doubleday, 1989.
————, ed. *Sincerely, Ronald Reagan.* New York: Berkley Books, 1980.
Walker, Martin. *The Cold War: A History.* New York: Henry Holt, 1993.
Wanniski, Jude. *The Way the World Works.* Morristown, N.J.: Polyconomics, 1989.
Watt, James G., and Doug Wead. *The Courage of a Conservative.* New York: Simon and Schuster, 1985.
Watt, Leilani, and Al Janssen. *Caught in the Conflict: My Life with James Watt.* Eugene, Ore.: Harvest House Publishers, 1984.
Wead, Doug, and Bill Wead. *Reagan: In Pursuit of the Presidency, 1980.* Plainfield, N.J.: Haven Books, 1980.
Weicher, John C., ed. *Maintaining the Safety Net: Income Redistribution Programs in the Reagan Administration.* Washington, D.C.: American Enterprise Institute, 1984.
Weidenbaum, Murray. *Rendezvous with Reality: The American Economy after Reagan.* New York: Basic Books, 1988.
Weiler, Michael, and W. Barnett Pearce. *Reagan and Public Discourse in America.* Tuscaloosa: University of Alabama Press, 1992.
Weinberger, Caspar W. *Fighting for Peace: Seven Critical Years in the Pentagon.* New York: Warner Books, 1990.
————. "Reagan and International Arms Agreements." In Thompson, ed., *Foreign Policy,* 43–55.
Weir, Margaret. *Politics and Jobs: The Boundaries of Employment Policy in the United States.* Princeton: Princeton University Press, 1992.
Weko, Thomas J. *The Politicizing Presidency: The White House Personnel Office, 1948–1994.* Lawrence: University Press of Kansas, 1995.
Whelan, Joseph G. *The Moscow Summit, 1988: Reagan and Gorbachev in Negotiation.* Boulder, Colo.: Westview Press, 1990.
Whitaker, Robert W. *The New Right Papers.* New York: St. Martin's Press, 1982.
White, John K. *The New Politics of Old Values.* Hanover, Mass.: University Press of New England, 1988.
White, Joseph, and Aaron Wildavsky. *The Deficit and the Public Interest: The Search for Responsible Budgeting in the 1980s.* Berkeley and Los Angeles, Calif.: University of California Press, 1989.
White, Lawrence J. *The S&L Debacle: Public Policy Lessons for Bank and Thrift Regulation.* New York: Oxford University Press, 1991.
White, Patricia M. *The Invincible Irish: Ronald Wilson Reagan, Irish Ancestry, and Immigration to America.* Santa Barbara, Calif.: Portola Press, 1981.
White, Theodore H. *The Making of the President 1968.* New York: Atheneum, 1969.
White, Timothy R. "Hollywood's Attempt at Appropriating Television: The Case of Paramount Pictures." In *Hollywood in the Age of Television,* ed. Tino Balio, 145–63. Boston: Unwin Hyman, 1990.
Wiarda, Howard J. *American Foreign Policy toward Latin America in the Eighties and Nineties: Issues and Controversies from Reagan to Bush.* New York: New York University Press, 1992.

————, ed. *Rift and Revolution: The Central American Imbroglio.* Washington, D.C.: American Enterprise Institute, 1984.

Wilber, Charles K., and Kenneth P. Jameson. *Beyond Reaganomics: A Further Inquiry into the Poverty of Economics.* Notre Dame, Ind.: University of Notre Dame Press, 1990.

Will, Mari Maseng. "Speech Writing for President Reagan." In Thompson, *Leadership, Part II,* 87–105.

Williams, Walter. *Mismanaging America: The Rise of the Anti-Analytic Presidency.* Lawrence: University Press of Kansas, 1990.

Williamson, Richard S. *Reagan's Federalism: His Efforts to Decentralize Government.* Lanham, Md.: University Press of America, 1990.

Wills, Garry. "It's His Party." *New York Times Magazine,* 11 August 1996, 30–37, 52, 55, 57–59.

————. *Reagan's America: Innocents at Home.* Garden City, N.Y.: Doubleday, 1987.

Wilmsen, Steven K. *Silverado: Neil Bush and the Savings and Loan Scandal.* Washington, D.C.: National Press Books, 1991.

Winik, Jay. *On the Brink: The Dramatic, Behind-the-Scenes Saga of the Reagan Era and the Men and Women Who Won the Cold War.* New York: Simon and Schuster, 1996.

Wirls, Daniel. *Buildup: The Politics of Defense in the Reagan Era.* Ithaca, N.Y.: Cornell University Press, 1992.

Witcover, Jules. *Marathon: The Pursuit of the Presidency, 1972–1976.* New York: Viking, 1977.

Wolters, Raymond. *Right Turn: William Bradford Reynolds, the Reagan Administration, and Black Civil Rights.* New Brunswick, N.J.: Transaction Publishers, 1996.

Wood, Robert C. *Whatever Possessed the President? Academic Experts and Presidential Policy, 1960–1988.* Amherst, Mass.: University of Massachusetts Press, 1993.

Woodward, Bob. *Veil: The Secret Wars of the CIA, 1981–1987.* New York: Simon and Schuster, 1987.

Wright, Edward N. "Reagan and Defense." In Thompson, ed., *Leadership, Part II,* 175–96.

Wright, Jim. *Worth It All: My War for Peace.* Washington, D.C.: Brassey's, 1993.

Wroe, Ann. *Lives, Lies, and the Iran-Contra Affair.* London: I. B. Tauris, 1991.

Wuthnow, Robert. *The Restructuring of American Religion: Society and Faith since World War II.* Princeton: Princeton University Press, 1988.

Wymbs, Norman E. *A Place to Go Back To: Ronald Reagan in Dixon, Illinois.* New York: Vantage Press, 1987.

Yarbrough, Tinsley E., ed. *The Reagan Administration and Human Rights.* New York: Praeger, 1985.

Zais, James P., Raymond J. Struyk, and Thomas Thibodeau. *Housing Assistance for Older Americans: The Reagan Prescription.* Washington, D.C.: Urban Institute Press, 1982.

Zumbrun, Ronald A., Raymond M. Momboisse, and John H. Findley. "Welfare Reform: California Meets the Challenge." *Pacific Law Journal,* 4 (July 1973): 739–85.

Manuscript Collections

Anderson, Annelise G. Hoover Institution, Stanford University, Stanford, California.

Boyarsky, Bill. Hoover Institution, Stanford University, Stanford, California.

Burns, Arthur F. Gerald R. Ford Library, Ann Arbor, Michigan.

Carter, Jimmy. Jimmy Carter Library, Atlanta, Georgia.

Finn, Chester E. Hoover Institution, Stanford University, Stanford, California.
Ford, Gerald R. Gerald R. Ford Library, Ann Arbor, Michigan.
Johnson, Lyndon B. Lyndon Baines Johnson Library, Austin, Texas.
Nixon, Richard M. Prepresidential Papers, National Archives, Pacific Southwest Region, Laguna Niguel, California.
————. Richard Nixon Library, Yorba Linda, California.
Pearson, Drew. Lyndon Baines Johnson Library, Austin, Texas.
Reagan, Ronald. Hoover Institution, Stanford University, Stanford, California.
————. Ronald Reagan Library, Simi Valley, California.
————. Subject Collection. Hoover Institution, Stanford University, Stanford, California.
Reichley, A. James. Gerald R. Ford Library, Ann Arbor, Michigan.
Teeter, Robert M. Gerald R. Ford Library, Ann Arbor, Michigan.
van der Linden, Frank. Hoover Institution, Stanford University, Stanford, California.

Oral History Interviews

Interviews conducted by the Bancroft Library, University of California, Berkeley: William Bagley (1982), Paul Beck (1984), Allen F. Breed (1982), Virna M. Canson (1984), Robert Carleson (1983), George Christopher (1977, 1978), Paul R. Haerle (1982), Kenneth F. Hall (1982), Peter Hannaford (1982), Carolyn Cooper Heine (1984), James Jenkins (1983), Roger Magyar (1984), Anita M. Miller (1984), John J. Miller (1982), James R. Mills (1980, 1981), Robert T. Monagan (1981), Franklyn C. Nofziger (1978), Gaylord B. Parkinson (1978), Ronald Reagan (1979), William E. Roberts (1979), Alex C. Sherriffs (1981, 1982), William French Smith (1988), Stuart K. Spencer (1979), Vernon L. Sturgeon (1982), A. Ruric Todd (1981), Robert Walker (1982, 1983), Rus Walton (1983), Caspar W. Weinberger (1978, 1979), Spencer M. Williams (1982), Jack Wrather (1982).
Interviews conducted by the Lyndon Baines Johnson Library: Edmund G. Brown (1969, 1970), Clark Kerr (1985).
Interviews conducted by the Strategic Defense Initiative Organization: George A. Keyworth (1987).

Speeches

Greenstein, Fred I. "Presidential Historians and Biographers Assess the Reagan Presidency." Ronald Reagan Conference, 22–24 April 1993, Hofstra University, Hempstead, New York.
Morris, Edmund. "Ronald Reagan as Metaphor." Ronald Reagan Conference, 22–24 April 1993, Hofstra University, Hempstead, New York.
Reagan, Ronald. "America the Beautiful." Printed in *Echoes from the Woods,* William Woods College, Fulton, Missouri, June 1952.
————. "Encroaching Control." 28 July 1961. Copy in Drew Pearson papers, Lyndon Baines Johnson Library, Austin, Texas.
————. "A Time for Choosing." 27 October 1964. Videotape by Edmonds Associates Inc., 1989.
————. "Acceptance Speech by Governor Ronald Reagan." 17 July 1980. Copy in Ronald Reagan Subject Collection, Hoover Institution, Stanford University, Stanford, California.
Watt, James G. "The Cabinet Assesses the Presidency." Ronald Reagan Conference, 22–24 April 1993, Hofstra University, Hempstead, New York.

Index

William E. Pemberton received his Ph.D. from the University of Missouri in 1974 and is currently a professor of history at the University of Wisconsin at La Crosse. His previous publications include *Bureaucratic Politics: Executive Reorganization during the Truman Administration, Harry S. Truman: Fair Dealer and Cold Warrior,* and *George Bush.*